APPROPRIATING BLACKNESS

E. Patrick Johnson

APPROPRIATING BLACKNESS

Performance and the Politics of Authenticity

Duke University Press Durham and London

2003

© 2003 Duke University Press

All rights reserved

Printed in the United States of

America on acid-free paper ⊗

Designed by C. H. Westmoreland

Typeset in Scala with Univers

display by Tseng Information

Systems, Inc.

Library of Congress Cataloging-

in-Publication Data appear on the

last printed page of this book.

Excerpt from "kevin the faggot"

in chapter 3 used with the

permission of Marvin K. White.

For Jake McHaney,

Ray "Boot" McHaney, Mary Lee Jones, and

Johnny "Shaw" McHaney

CONTENTS

ACKNOWLEDGMENTS

On July 20, 1996, my hometown of Hickory, N.C., celebrated "Dr. E. Patrick Johnson Day." I was given this honor because, to the town's knowledge, I am the first African American born in Hickory to earn a Ph.D. The celebration was initiated by a number of black leaders, namely city councilwoman and family friend Z. Ann Hoyle, who wanted to send a message not only to the whites of this small town in the foothills of western North Carolina, but also to the younger black children in the community aspiring to make something of their lives. The two running themes of that day, both of which were printed on the program and the cake, were "From Zero to Hero" and "They Said It Couldn't Be Done." While I was a little perplexed by the former (I've never thought of myself as ever being a "zero"!), the latter spoke to this black community's indictment of the institutionalized racism that for many years kept the educational system in Hickory separate and unequal. Held in the neighborhood where I grew up and in the gymnasium of the old black high school—Ridgeview High—the ceremony, while *for* me and in my honor, ultimately was not *about* me, for this community had come together to commemorate its fortitude, its undying determination to persevere in the midst of adversity. Indeed, the black folk of Ridgeview were thumbing their noses at *them*—the white folk of Hickory—that said "it couldn't be done." That is, produce children who would make not only the black community of Hickory proud, but all of its citizens. This book, therefore, is in no small part indebted to the folks of Ridgeview who knew not only that it could be done, but also that it *would* be done.

Acknowledgments

In the same way that a community raises a black child, books are never written alone and are never, therefore, one's own, even though the author is ultimately the one praised or criticized for what is contained between the two covers. The writing of this volume is no exception, and it would never have become a book project had it not been for the suggestion of Lyn Di Iorio to combine what looked like, at the time, six disparate essays. I thank her for giving me the "through line."

At Louisiana State University, I would like to thank Ruth Laurion Bowman, my dissertation adviser. Her gentle but consistent direction improved my writing and thinking threefold. Michael Bowman, Jill Brody, Femi Euba, Joyce Jackson, Dana Nelson, Robin Roberts, and Emily Toth were wonderful teachers and always pushed me to take the next step. Finally, thanks to Clovier Torry for all of her support behind the scenes.

A whole host of colleagues and friends at Amherst College and in the Five Colleges consortium supported me during what was one of the most difficult times in my professional career. I would be remiss not to mention them here: David Blight, Horace Boyer, Hermenia Gardner, Ruth Bass Green, Rick Griffiths, Margaret Hunt, Maurice Levesque, Barry O'Connell, Andy Parker, Dale Peterson, Caryl Phillips, Susan Raymond-Fic, Ron Rossbottom, Andrea B. Rushing, Karen Sanchez-Eppler, Kim Townsend, and Lucas Wilson. Many thanks especially to my former colleagues, Michèle Barale and Judy Frank, who read drafts of various chapters and provided invaluable feedback and support. Thanks too, to Lorna Peterson, Director of Five Colleges, Inc., whose friendship and support I will cherish always. Jenny Spencer and all of the participants in the Five Colleges performance studies seminar confirmed that performance studies is a balm in the valley! Judith Espinola and Susan Little and Dale and Lorna Peterson provided love, laughter, and wonderful meals when I needed them the most. My partners in crime, Darien McFadden, Torin Moore, and John McMillan, are dear and near to my heart and have always been unwavering in their support of all of my endeavors. My godmother, Dean Onawumi Jean Moss, deserves thanks for being my biggest fan, my rock in a weary land as well as my lily in the valley. The tenacity, wit, and intellectual curiosity of my former Amherst students, especially Cassie Abodeely, Karine Faden, Rasheema Graham, Shana Harry, Adam Hulbig, Leah Lortie, Michael Oliver,

Acknowledgments

Joe Ravenell, Karima Ravenell, Ramesh Thiyagaragan, Chris Tsang, and Tatsu Yamato, constantly reminded me what engaged pedagogy is all about.

At the University of North Carolina, where my college career began, I am indebted to a number of mentors and friends. D. Soyini Madison took me under her wing early on and helped me fly on my own. I honor her as a mentor, friend, and brilliant scholar. Trudier Harris-Lopez has always been a staunch supporter and friend and taught me never to settle for second best. Della Pollock taught me what it means to be a committed scholar and teacher. Her work continues to inspire me. Beverly Whitaker Long saw potential in me when I was just a cherub and nurtured that potential through graduate school. I am indebted to her for honing my skills as a performer of literature. Mae Henderson's careful reading of chapter drafts pushed my thinking well beyond the veil. Her friendship and brilliance continues to sustain me. Bill Balthrop and other faculty of the Department of Communication Studies created a hospitable environment during my return as postdoctoral fellow to the department. My thinking was also nourished by the late-night drinks, dinners, and formal and informal conversations with Carolina Minority Postdoctoral fellows, namely Natasha Barnes, Crystal Byndloss, Keith Clark, Jerma Jackson, Kirby Moss, Kim Nettles, Jaslean LaTaillade, Karla Slocum, and Karolyn Tyson.

My newfound Chicago "family" propelled me over the final hump to complete this project. My colleagues in Northwestern's Department of Performance Studies, Margaret Thompson Drewal, Paul Edwards, Frank Galati, Carol Simpson Stern, and Mary Zimmerman, all welcomed me to the department and to Northwestern with open arms. No words will express the indebtedness I feel toward my friend and colleague Dwight Conquergood. His work transformed the field and therefore my life. He looms large among these pages. Alan Shefsky manages always to quell a crisis in the nick of time. I want to acknowledge his many interventions in that regard in the preparation of this book. The conversations over coffee, lunch, and dinner with Kevin Bell, Martha Biondi, Tracy Davis, Jillana Enteen, Bob Gooding-Williams, Jay Grossman, Richard Iton, Susan Manning, Jeff Masten, Tessie Liu, Fran Paden, Mary Patillo, Sandra Richards, Helen Thompson, Dorothy Wang, and Alex Wehiliye helped me flesh out ideas. Discussions with participants in the 2001–2002 Post-Millennium Gender Studies seminar, especially with Cora Kaplan, encouraged me to complicate further the relationship between race, gender, and performance. I also benefited from feedback on earlier drafts of chapters from colleagues at other institutions in Chicago, especially Darrell Moore at Depaul University; Chris Castiglia at Loyola University; Mark Canuel, Sharon Holland, and Beth Richie at the University of Illinois, Chicago; Chris Reed at Lake Forest College; and George Chauncey, Cathy Cohen, Jackie Goldsby, Ron Gregg, and Jackie Stuart at the University of Chicago. Jennifer DeVere Brody, Dwight A. McBride, and Lisa Merrill have been monumental in their support of this project. Their praise was delivered as deliberately, gingerly, and as evenly as their critique. I can only aspire to their brilliance.

Colleagues and friends around the country have all in their own way been a comfort and inspiration during the writing of this book. They include Bryant Keith Alexander, Ian Barrett, Myron Beasley, Kent Ross Brooks, Cheryl Clarke, Robert Corber, Sharon Croft, Roderick Ferguson, Luchina Fisher, Craig Gingrich-Philbrook, Jonny Gray, Judith Hamera, Judith Halberstam, Phil Harper, Dan Heaton, Stacie Hewett, D. Nebi Hilliard, Sian Hunter, Kristin Langellier, Lisa Lowe, Genna Rae McNeil, Valerie Moore, José Esteban Muñoz, Dana Nelson, Charles Nero, Chandan Reddy, David Román, Charles H. Rowell, Tracy Stephenson, and John Williams. Joni Jones in particular keeps me grounded by reminding me what's really important. I'm proud to be her "brotha docta." Cedric Brown, my "brister," helped me "push this book on through."

My Australian family, the Café of the Gate of Salvation, the Honeybees, the Glory Bound Groove Train, the Band of Angels, and all the other groups I have worked with made my research in Australia more like a family reunion than work. I have such great admiration and respect for Tony Backhouse. His generosity made my research that much easier. Judy Backhouse, Rhonda Black, Rosie Johnstone, Lauren Martin, Grant Odgers, Sue Piper, and Nicki Solomon opened up their homes, provided transportation around Australia, arranged workshops and radio appearances, and accommodated my needs in ways that I hope one day to repay. I especially want to thank my dear friend Houston Spencer for introducing me to Australian gospel and then letting nature take its course.

My siblings and their spouses—Gilbert, Pamela, Larry and Patricia, Thomas and Mary, Adrian and Paula, and Gregory—while unclear about exactly what I was working on, were unwavering in their support. I am proud to be a part of the Johnson family. My mother, Sarah M. Johnson, is truly a gift from God. The best compliment anyone can give me is to say that I am my mother's child. I know, however, that she is far more gracious, much more courageous, and far smarter than I will ever be. I thank her for her sacrifices, her prayers, her love, but most of all for her friendship. My grandmother, Mary Adams, is the cornerstone of this book. Her faith, courage, and wisdom made my life possible. Her legacy has made my life easier.

Ken Wissoker, editor-in-chief at Duke University Press, is one of the most generous people I know. He was always invested in making this not just a good book but a great book. I thank him for his candor and careful guidance. I would also like to thank the production staff at the press for their insights and diligence in getting this book published.

Finally, but most certainly not least, I would like to thank my partner, Stephen Lewis. I could not ask for a more supportive and giving companion. His friendship, humor, support, and patience kept me on track when I began to falter. I thank him for giving me space to do my work, a shoulder to cry on when I was at my wits' end, and the joy that comes only from knowing that you are loved.

The research for this book enjoyed institutional support from Amherst College through two faculty research grants and the Miner D. Crary Sabbatical Fellowship. The Carolina Minority Postdoctoral Fellowship at the University of North Carolina at Chapel Hill provided two years of resources for focused writing. Northwestern awarded me a University Research Grant to complete research in Australia.

I thank the National Communication Association for permission to use an earlier version of chapter 5 that was published in *Text and Performance Quarterly* (22.2 [2002]: 99–121); it appears here in revised and extended form. A version of chapter 3 appears in William L. Leap and Tom Boellstorff's *Speaking in Queer Tongues: Language, Globalization, and New Articulations of Same-Sex Desire*. I thank the University of Illinois Press for permission to use it here.

APPROPRIATING BLACKNESS

INTRODUCTION

"Blackness" and Authenticity:

What's Performance Got to Do with It?

Have you ever noticed how white always seems to
attract stains? —Crest toothpaste commercial

Color, for anyone who uses it,
or is used by it, is a most complex, calculated
and dangerous phenomenon.
—James Baldwin

From the natural to the jheri curls to shaved
heads; from break dancing to rock; from platform shoes
to Reeboks; from large church congregations to empty
Sunday schools; from Jack and Jill to the Bloods and the
Crips; from Shirley Chisholm and Jesse Jackson to Al
Sharpton and Colin Powell; from Motown to Def Jam
Records; from *Good Times* to the *Jeffersons* to *In Living
Color;* from *Soul Train* to *Yo! MTV Raps*—these
outward manifestations have become signs of
the ways African Americans perceive
their culture, themselves.
—Randall Kenan

how do i get in touch with my blackness?
"blackness where are you?"
—Marvin K. White, "for colored boys"

The fact of blackness is not always self-constituting. Indeed, blackness, like performance, often defies categorization. Richard Schechner's comparison of performance to a sidewinder snake is apropos to blackness: "Wherever this beautiful rattlesnake points, it is not going there."[1] Blackness, too, is slippery—ever beyond the reach of one's grasp. Once you think you have a hold on it, it transforms into something else and travels in another direction. Its elusiveness does not preclude one from trying to fix it, to pin it down, however—for the pursuit of authenticity is inevitably an emotional and moral one.[2] Many times these arbiters of authentic blackness have the economic and/or social clout to secure particular attributes of blackness—for example, dreadlocks, vernacular speech, living in a particular part of town, etc.—as the components of the template from which blackness originates. Often, it is during times of crisis (social, cultural, or political) when the authenticity of older versions of blackness is called into question. These crises set the stage for "acting out" identity politics, occasions when those excluded from the parameters of blackness invent their own.

I suggest here, however, that the mutual constructing/deconstructing, avowing/disavowing, and expanding/delimiting dynamic that occurs in the production of blackness is the very thing that constitutes "black" culture.[3] But how does one theorize these various citations and cultural significations and the politics they engender? What happens when "blackness" is embodied? What are the cultural, social, and political consequences of that embodiment in a racist society? What is at stake when race or blackness is theorized discursively, and the material reality of the "black" subject is occluded? Indeed, what happens in those moments when blackness takes on corporeality? Or, alternatively, how are the stakes changed when a "white" body performs blackness?

The chapters in this book foreground and engage these questions of identity and cultural performance by examining six highly different examples of racial performance. They illuminate the often contradictory, resistive, subversive, and celebratory effects of blackness as they are cited both inside and outside black American culture. Collectively, the subjects in this study all cite, conceal, limit, expand, and give power to the elusive signifier called "blackness."

The title of this book suggests that "blackness" does not belong to any one individual or group. Rather, individuals or groups *appropriate* this complex and nuanced racial signifier in order to circumscribe its boundaries or to exclude other individuals or groups. When blackness is appropriated to the exclusion of others, identity becomes political. Inevitably, when one attempts to lay claim to an intangible trope that manifests in various discursive terrains, identity claims become embattled, or as noted in the quotation above by Baldwin, "color" or "blackness" becomes a "dangerous phenomenon." Because the concept of blackness has no essence, "black authenticity" is overdetermined—contingent on the historical, social, and political terms of its production. Moreover, in the words of Regina Bendix: "the notion of [black] authenticity implies the existence of its opposite, the fake, and this dichotomous construct is at the heart of what makes authenticity problematic."[4] Authenticity, then, is yet another trope manipulated for cultural capital.

That said, I do not wish to place a value judgment on the notion of authenticity, for there are ways in which authenticating discourse enables marginalized people to counter oppressive representations of themselves. The key here is to be cognizant of the arbitrariness of authenticity, the ways in which it carries with it the dangers of foreclosing the possibilities of cultural exchange and understanding. As Henry Louis Gates Jr. reminds us: "No human culture is inaccessible to someone who makes the effort to understand, to learn, to inhabit another world."[5]

When black Americans have employed the rhetoric of black authenticity, the outcome has often been a political agenda that has excluded more voices than it has included.[6] The multiple ways in which we construct blackness within and outside black American culture is contingent on the historical moment in which we live and our ever-shifting subject positions. For example, black Americans, whose vocality, leadership, and rhetoric flourished at the historical moment in which they lived, contested popular constructions of blackness in order to further their own political agendas and occasionally to stake out a space from which to argue for the inclusion of other signs of "blackness."

Indeed, if one were to look at blackness in the context of black American history, one would find that, even in relation to nationalism, the notion of an "authentic" blackness has always been contested:

the discourse of "house niggers" vs. "field niggers"; Sojourner Truth's insistence on a black female subjectivity in relation to the black polity; Booker T. Washington's call for vocational skill over W. E. B. Du Bois's "talented tenth"; Richard Wright's critique of Zora Neale Hurston's focus on the "folk" over the plight of the black *man;* Eldridge Cleaver's caustic attack on James Baldwin's homosexuality as "anti-black" and "anti-male"; urban northerners' condescending attitudes toward rural southerners and vice versa; Malcolm X's militant call for black Americans to fight against the white establishment "by any means necessary" over Martin Luther King Jr.'s reconciliatory "turn the other cheek"; and Jesse Jackson's "Rainbow Coalition" over Louis Farrakhan's "Nation of Islam." All of these examples belong to the long-standing tradition in black American history of certain black Americans critically viewing a definition of blackness that does not validate their social, political, and cultural worldview. As Wahneema Lubiano suggests, "the resonances of [black] authenticity depend on who is doing the evaluating."[7]

White Americans also construct blackness.[8] Of course, the power relations maintained by white hegemony have different material effects for blacks than for whites. When white Americans essentialize blackness, for example, they often do so in ways that maintain "whiteness" as the master trope of purity, supremacy, and entitlement, as a ubiquitous, fixed, unifying signifier that seems invisible.[9] Alternately, the tropes of blackness that whites circulated in the past—Mammy, Sapphire, Jezebel, Jim Crow, Sambo, Zip Coon, pickaninny, and Stepin Fetchit, and now enlarged to include welfare queen, prostitute, rapist, drug addict, prison inmate, etc.—have historically insured physical violence, poverty, institutional racism, and second-class citizenry for blacks.

An even more complicated dynamic occurs when whites *appropriate* blackness. History demonstrates that cultural usurpation has been a common practice of white Americans and their relation to art forms not their own. In many instances, whites exoticize and/or fetishize blackness, what bell hooks calls "eating the other."[10] Thus, when white-identified subjects perform "black" signifiers—normative or otherwise—the effect is always already entangled in the discourse of otherness; the historical weight of white skin privilege necessarily engenders a tense relationship with its Others.

In contemporary society, one of the most palpable examples of the arbitrariness and politics of authenticity is in language use. Particularly among young black American and white American youth, whose cultures overlap in multiple and complicated ways, there exists a crisis of blackness involving language use that remains a permanent schism in identity politics.[11] For example, his inner-city cousins may ridicule the young black professional who lives in the suburbs because, according to them, he talks like a "white" man. In this instance, talking "white" is equivalent to speaking Standard English and talking "black" is equivalent to speaking in the black vernacular. (Race and class are also elided in this instance because many white men do not talk "white" either.) The black American who either chooses not to or simply cannot speak in the (black) vernacular is cast as a traitor to the race—indeed, as "white." On the other hand, the same might be true for white teenagers whose parents chastise them for talking "black" when they speak in the black vernacular. These teenagers may have learned to speak this way from black friends at school or, ironically, from other white friends or from films or television shows that may or may not have been produced by blacks, or from black Hollywood actors whose blackness is implicated in the production/construction of racist stereotypes. "Black" speech parroted in the mouths of white youth, then, cannot be traced to one particular origin. For their part, whites construct linguistic representations of blacks that are grounded in racist stereotypes to maintain the status quo only to then reappropriate these stereotypes to affect a fetishistic "escape" into the Other to transcend the rigidity of their own whiteness, as well as to feed the capitalist gains of commodified blackness.[12] The proliferation of white rap artists such as Vanilla Ice and Eminem, and movies such as *Whiteboyz* are just a few examples. On the other hand, blacks' vernacular performances redound similar results as white appropriations and are also sometimes deployed for monetary gain. As Bendix suggests, "the transformation from felt or experienced authenticity to its textual or material representation harbors a basic paradox. Once a cultural good has been declared authentic, the demand for it rises, and it acquires a market value."[13]

In the instance of both the "white-talking" black and the "black-talking" white, the person's authenticity is called into question by his or her "own" based not solely on phenotype but also on the symbolic relationship between skin color and the performance of culturally inscribed language or dialect that refers back to an "essential" blackness or whiteness. Within racially and politically charged environments in which one's allegiance to "race" is critical to one's in-group status, one's performance of the appropriate "essential" signifiers of one's race is crucial. The white is condemned as a "wigger" ("white nigger") or the more pejorative "nigger lover," and the black is dismissed as an "Oreo" (black on the outside but white in the middle).

And yet human comingling necessarily entails the syncretism whereby cultures assimilate and adopt aspects of each other. Indeed, as "white always seems to attract stains," black similarly seems to absorb light. Given that, is all cross-cultural appropriation an instance of colonization and subjugation? Have not there been instances where the colonized have made use of the colonizer's forms as an act of resistance? Has not the colonizer become more humanized by the presence of the colonized? I suggest that some sites of cross-cultural appropriation provide fertile ground on which to formulate new epistemologies of self and Other.

The trope that I believe facilitates the appropriation of blackness is performance. The term "performance" enjoys currency among various fields and disciplines in the academy. Catapulted into a catch-all for aesthetic, cultural, and social communicative events, interpretive practices, and critical methodologies, performance has become, as Mary Strine, Beverly Long, and Mary Frances HopKins suggest, "bound up in disagreement about what it is." Further, the "disagreement over its essence is itself part of that essence."[14] Indeed, the contested nature of performance may, on the one hand, reveal the seams of rigid disciplinary boundaries while, on the other, delimit the qualities of what constitutes performance in order to describe, interpret, evaluate, and theorize a specific text or sociocultural phenomenon.

Nevertheless, the recent shifts and turns in performance studies provide an encouraging sign that performance is more than a trendy critical trope.[15] Its longevity as a disciplinary practice, along with its recent reconfiguration in other disciplines, suggests that, rather than diminishing as a valuable interpretive strategy, performance continues to offer nuanced methodologies and interpretive frames in which to theorize. That is, performance is dynamic and generative, enabling difficult and controversial stances and poses that ultimately help us better to articulate our objects (and subjects) of inquiry.

My purpose here is to utilize performance to interpret various sites of performed "blackness." In doing so, I wish to demonstrate how performance is useful in studying blackness and vice versa. As an interdisciplinary research practice, then, performance has allowed me to draw on theories from various fields, including folklore, literary and cultural studies, philosophy, anthropology, and performance itself to consider the social, political, and cultural aspects of performance. In turn the sociopolitical and cultural implications of performance inform my analysis of various performance practices found within black American culture. In fact, the performance paradigm illuminates the mirroring that occurs in culture, the tension between stabilizing cultural forces (tradition), and the shifting, ever-evolving aspects of culture that provide sites for social reflection, transformation, and critique. More simply put, I use performance to study black American culture, and I use black American culture as a means of studying performance theory.

In addition to being two contested terms, blackness and performance are two discourses whose histories converge at the site of otherness. It is this particular historical convergence that I find methodologically useful here, for the deployment of these terms in academia is necessarily implicated in the currency of each term as well as in the status of the bodies that have come to be associated with them. Racist constructions of blackness, for example, associate it with denigration, impurity, nature, and the body. Similarly, as Dwight Conquergood notes, performance is also "associated with feelings, emotions, and the body" and "is constructed in opposition to scientific reason and rational thought."[16] In addition to the "antitheatrical prejudice,"[17] the devaluation of performance in Western intellectual traditions simultaneously coincides with the devaluation of black people as subjects of inquiry in the academy and in society as a whole. Black performance (e.g., spirit possession, music, dance, speech, etc.), then, becomes the site at which people and behavior are construed as "spectacles of primitivism" to justify the colonial and racist gaze.[18]

Performance becomes a vehicle through which the Other is seen and not seen, according to Patricia Williams, "depend[ing] upon a dynamic of display that ricochets between hypervisibility and oblivion."[19] The position of the voyeur's "zoom lens" is necessarily predicated on his or her power and privilege. Williams continues: "There is a long tradition of voyeurism as a means of putting culture not just on display but at a condescending distance" (22); thus, the consequences of fetishistic voyeurism are not only the maintenance of the status quo but also the establishment of the sometimes shallow, unself-reflexive appropriation of blackness. This phenomenon takes place among black Americans as well because class, gender, and sexuality also grant authority to various constituents of the "black" community. As I discuss in chapter 2, it is not uncommon for heterosexual black men to appropriate "queer" performances of blackness in order to call into question the authenticity of the black gay subject. Again, the "B(r)Other as Performer" trope, to riff Conquergood's construction, is deployed here in ways that confound queer performance with underdeveloped masculinity and inauthentic blackness.

While the above discussion implies a dialogic relationship between blackness and performance, there is also a dialectic forged between the two. In other words, blackness is not always facilitated by performance. There are ways in which blackness exceeds the performative through what Williams calls in her essay title the "pantomime of race." In other words, blackness does not only reside in the theatrical fantasy of the white imaginary that is then projected onto black bodies, nor is it always consciously acted out; rather, it is also the inexpressible yet undeniable racial experience of black people—the ways in which the "living of blackness" becomes a material way of knowing. In this respect, blackness supercedes or explodes performance in that the modes of representation endemic to performance—the visual and spectacular—are no longer viable registers of racial identification. No longer visible under the colonizer's scopophilic gaze, blackness resides in the liminal space of the psyche where its manifestation is neither solely volitional nor without agency. Indeed, one may experience what Williams calls "a sense of split identity" (27) in a context where one's experience of living blackness (i.e., one's politics, class position, gender, etc.) and the "fantasy of black life as theatrical enterprise" (17) are at odds.

Such examples are chronicled in countless autobiographical narratives where particularly upwardly mobile blacks find themselves in the company of whites who see them as "exceptional" or as a "credit" to their race. These instances usually occur at exclusive "invitation only" white gatherings. The black who has been accepted into the elite circle of whiteness is expected to bracket the blackness that proffered his or her (temporary) invitation to the welcome table of whiteness and in the face of the dissonance he or she feels in relation to the black hands extending the hors d'oeuvre tray. In these instances, Williams suggests, "You need two chairs at the table, one for you one for your blackness."[20] Alternatively, blackness may be deployed as resistance in the face of white colonization.[21] In these instances blackness is not only both pawn and consequence of performance but also an efface-ment of it. The implication of this construction of blackness in rela-tion to performance is not that performance is, as suggested by its naysayers, anti-intellectual, but rather it suggests that performance may not fully account for the ontology of race.

Racial performativity informs the process by which we invest bodies with social meaning.[22] Yet I must reemphasize, following Rinaldo Walcott, that "to read blackness as merely 'playful' is to fall into a will-ful denial of what it means to live 'black.'"[23] Indeed, blackness offers a way to rethink performance theory by forcing it to ground itself in praxis, especially within the context of a white supremacist, patriar-chal, capitalist, homophobic society. Although useful in deconstruct-ing essentialist notions of selfhood, performance must also provide a space for meaningful resistance of oppressive systems.

Ultimately, performance and blackness are distinct discourses with their own agendas, "sidewinders" traveling in their own directions. In this volume, however, I examine the sites where these slippery signifiers both cross paths and diverge, taking advantage of a dia-logical/dialectical relationship that offers a unique perspective from which to understand the maintenance and transformation of identity, difference, and culture more generally.[24]

By capitalizing on the endemic relationship between performance and blackness, I deploy performance in each of the chapters in this book as methodology and disciplinary praxis. In previewing the ways in which this study engages performance as methodology and com-municative event, my goal is to lay the groundwork for my analysis of black cultural performance and the politics of appropriation and authenticity those performances evince.

Because I lived with and among many of the subjects I interviewed for this book in order better to comprehend the meaning of their performances, my presence undoubtedly affected the performances of my informants and vice versa. The multiple identities I performed—black, middle class, southern, gay, male, professor—influenced my ethnographic experience as/of the Other. Therefore, I construe my ethnographic practice as an "impure" process—as a performance. Moreover, rather than fix my informants as static objects, naively claim ideological innocence, or engage in the false positivist "me/them" binary, I foreground my "coauthorship," as it were, of the ethnographic texts produced in this volume, for I was as integral to the performance/text-making process as were my informants. Therefore, in each chapter I mark the ways I am implicated in the performance of blackness in the field, and, because I choose to foreground my role as ethnographer in the field, my effects and affects in relation to the ethnographic Other, I elaborate more fully this "dialogic" practice and the politics implicit in this particular kind of (auto)ethnographic account.

In his study of theater in Shaba, Zaire, Johannes Fabian urges a "performative" anthropology. He contends that ethnographies are "questionable representations" unless they are critical and forthcoming about their process. And he believes that approaching ethnography as performance is one way to engage an exegesis of the ethnographic process. "Performance . . . is not what they do and we observe," he explains, "we are both engaged in it."[25] What Fabian is calling for here is the recognition on behalf of researchers that their entrance into the "field" of the ethnographic Other necessarily implicates them in the performance being witnessed. Both researchers and the researched realize that they are performing for one another, engaged in creating what Clifford Geertz might call a "fragile fiction."[26] To construe ethnographic practice as, in general, a "fiction" and, more specifically, a practice that is "acted out" or performed, is to liberate it from the assumption that the informant is a fixed object and therefore inferior to the ethnographer. Instead, the informant is recognized as a thinking, theorizing, and culture-processing human being. Indeed, as Dwight Conquergood writes, "thinking about ethnographic practice as a disciplinary performance will help displace positivist claims of objectivity by which knowledge of the Other is abstracted from its historical and dialogical conditions."[27]

As a result of my conscious effort to make my ethnographic practice more dialogic, each chapter in this book consists of my own personal experiences, thoughts, and impressions of the Other alongside my interpretation and analysis. In the process I expose my vulnerability as ethnographer as well as my active participation in the making of the ethnographic text—indeed, how I, too, produce, authorize, and even authenticate blackness.

My work here employs performance theory not only to interpret but also to name certain phenomena as "performance"—particularly verbal art/discourse. In the chapter "Nevah Had uh Cross Word," for example, I construe the telling of Mary Rhyne's oral history as performance. Here, I draw on the work of folklorists and black vernacular scholars who characterize verbal art—and by extension, oral histories—as an aesthetic mode of communication, a performance event, and as variable cross-culturally.[28] These theorists' conceptualization of performance directs our attention toward not only what is said but also how something is said—a focus on form and content—in order better to understand the semiotics of performance. This view of performance necessarily takes into account the physical setting in which performances occur, as well as the relationships between performer and audience and performer and self. What frames a performance as performance, then, has as much to do with context as it does with the aesthetics of the event itself. In each context the "rules," conventions, and expectations of the text, setting, performer, and audience vary, and in each context they contribute to our understanding of performance events.

In this volume I examine quotidian expressive forms and practices found in black American culture, and in so doing I examine closely what constitutes performance—specifically the performance of "blackness"—in black American culture. I do so not to suggest a fixed or stable meaning of "blackness." On the contrary, my purpose is to demonstrate its variability inside and outside black culture in order to engage a dialogue about the politics of appropriation and black authenticity. Such an understanding of performance is particularly useful here given the various ways in which "blackness" is signed and embodied. In the chapter "Sounds of Blackness Down Under," for example, I focus on the performance of "blackness" in a context where there is no significant black American population.

In this study I also employ performance as a strategy for understanding literature. The performance of literature enjoys a long history in the academy, owing much of its centrality in literary study to scholars of oral interpretation.[29] By eventually shifting their focus from text-centered analyses to the text-making process itself, oral interpretation scholars provided the foundational work for what is now called "performance studies."[30] As noted above, performance studies has taken a number of theoretical and methodological turns: the study of literature through performance, has, nonetheless, remained a worthy and sustaining component of performance scholarship. In relation to this study, the performance of literature, specifically black American literature, provides yet another means to discuss the ways in which "blackness" is performed on the stage and through the body.

In my first chapter, "The Pot Is Brewing: Marlon Riggs's *Black Is . . . Black Ain't*, I examine the ways in which the film *Black Is . . . Black Ain't* destabilizes notions of authentic blackness. Riggs frames the film with the image of gumbo and a visual diary of his own declining T-cell count and fight with AIDS (he dies before the completion of the film), and in doing so he suggests that, in addition to demanding an appreciation of otherness by white Americans, black Americans must come to terms with their own differences within black culture. Indeed, Riggs's gumbo metaphor for black culture sutures the gap between those who view race as biological essence and those who view race as a discursive category. The film demonstrates the ways in which black Americans, in their attempt to define what it means to be black, delimit its possibilities, which, at times, may be counterproductive to the flavor of the roux that acts as the base of the gumbo that is "blackness." On the other hand, the film also exposes the social, political, economic, and psychological effects of racism, as well as the role that racism has played in defining blackness. The film takes great care to demonstrate how racism and constructions of blackness are interrelated both within and outside black American communities. I argue that Riggs's rhetorical strategy is first to highlight those signifiers of blackness that build community, such as language, music, food, and religion, and then point out how these, too, are unstable categories on which to rest one's blackness. Ultimately, I think Riggs's film serves as an interventionist text, as a text that incorporates queerness as a legitimate signifier of blackness.

Chapter 2, "Manifest Faggotry: Queering Masculinity in African American Culture," expands on the notion of appropriation within black American culture. Specifically, there I investigate the ways in which five black American heterosexual males—Eldridge Cleaver, Imamu Amiri Baraka (LeRoi Jones), Eddie Murphy, Damon Wayans, and David Alan Grier—appropriate signifiers of queerness to stereotype, demean, and repudiate black gay men as well as attempt to delimit the parameters of authentic black masculinity. I then demonstrate how these men, in the act of repudiation, ironically and unwittingly queer heteronormative black masculinity, securing further the dialectic between heterosexuality and homosexuality. In the end, these black heterosexual performances of masculinity queer not only these performers but also black culture in general.

Chapter 3, "Mother Knows Best: Blackness and Transgressive Domestic Space," is the rejoinder to the previous chapter as it focuses on the ways in which black gay men also queer the black "homeplace/space" with transgressive performances of domesticity. Through a series of interviews with homosexual black men, in this chapter I analyze the vernacular of black gay culture and the instances where it appropriates tropes of black domesticity in order to challenge claims of black authenticity grounded in heteronormativity, to build community, and to parody rigid constructions of gender. The appropriation of heteronormative tropes of domesticity by black gay men, similar to the appropriation of homonormal tropes by black heterosexual men, establishes a link between two discursive terrains—heterosexuality and homosexuality—further calling attention to the dependence of one on the other.

Chapter 4, "'Nevah Had uh Cross Word': Mammy and the Trope of Black Womanhood," examines how my aged black grandmother (re)constructs her life history in/through performance by narrating her days as a live-in domestic in North Carolina in the 1960s, as she consciously and unconsciously represents her blackness through the trope of the "mammy." I elaborate on the ways in which she utilizes performance to intervene in her self-construction, calling attention to how she invents or "makes herself up," recasting the past and her place in it so as to enhance her social status within both the narrated and narrative events.[31] In turn, her self-reinvention permits her to control how I as well as those who read her narrative perceive her, and thus she emerges as an authority figure. There are times, however, when my grandmother clearly disclaims authority in the narrated events and in her telling of them. I emphasize the dual-voiced nature of her discourse and the positioning of herself within it in order to highlight the ways her narrative both legitimates and contests sites, systems, and discourses of authority and control.

The chapter 5, "Sounds of Blackness Down Under: The Café of the Gate Of Salvation," moves beyond the U.S. border to consider how blackness is appropriated and performed in an international context. The Australian gospel choir the Café of the Gate of Salvation is unique because of its cultural composition and religious and nonreligious affiliations. On the basis of interviews with the choir's members and with singers who attended the gospel music workshops I conducted, attendance at rehearsals and performances, and my own participation with the choirs, I interrogate the ways in which blackness is performed vis-à-vis gospel music. Given the racial, cultural, and religious composition of the Café and other Australian choirs, this chapter also addresses the politics of appropriation. According to the choir members, the fact that gospel music arose from an oppressed people is what makes it so "empowering." Indeed, given their own history of colonization and the fact that many of them are the descendants of "convicts," many Australians sing gospel as an expression of empathy with the social conditions of black Americans. This romanticization of black American culture and history, used as a justification for singing gospel, exists uneasily beside the virtual obliteration of Australian Aboriginal culture. Yet it is too simple to dismiss these choirs as cases of cultural appropriation, and in this chapter I explore the complexities of cultural usurpation by focusing on these choirs' actual performance of gospel music and how my role as the "authentic" black singer affected their performances.

In the final chapter, "Performance and/as Pedagogy: Performing Blackness in the Classroom," the issues of the previous chapter are extended in order to address more fully the implications of performing a text's "blackness" and to further discuss the implications of "teaching" blackness. For this chapter I draw on as case studies the classes I have taught in the performance of literature. My course "Performance of African American Literature," for example, has brought into clear focus for students, as well as for me, the politics of representation, identity, appropriation, and appreciation of the Other—the slippage between romanticism, solipsism, and genuine dialogic engagement. I raise the question of authenticity not only at the textual level but also at the level of embodiment—at the level of performance—when nonblack bodies perform "black" texts. The resonance of multiple discourses—including those of racist stereotype—all register in that moment of material embodiment. Further, I discuss the ways in which "teacherly" bodies authorize racialized, gendered, and classed readings of literature. Although fraught with political and social consequences, I contend that the performance of African American literature may offer a site of genuine and honest inter- and intracultural dialogue as we all struggle over the meaning of "blackness."

The chapters in this volume bear the mark of individuality, yet they speak to and across one another in subtle and nuanced ways. I make some of these connections explicitly, while others must be inferred by the reader. Furthermore, the chapters are not meant to account for the innumerable ways in which blackness is appropriated, performed, signed, and authenticated; rather, they are offered as a vehicle through which to engage the continuous dialogue on racial identity in the United States and beyond its borders. Indeed, no study of racial identity and politics can accommodate the protean processes of black signification. While the disparate locations in which blackness is cited here speak to this conundrum, they also mark, in a productive manner I hope, the ubiquitous nature of racial identification, performance, and politics. The variety of critical methodologies I deploy are also in keeping with the diverse sites of inquiry, applying or developing, as other scholars have, theories that facilitate a specific reading of blackness and identity politics. I am thinking here of Kimberly Crenshaw's notion of "intersectionality," Patricia Hill Collins's "standpoint" theory, Cathy Cohen's "coalitional" politics, Dwight McBride's "racial authority," and my own "quare" studies.[32] These scholars and I, each in our own way, have devised theoretical frames to expand narrow definitions of blackness that either exclude women (Crenshaw) or gays and lesbians (McBride), or sexual-identity-based political movements and/or theoretical paradigms that exclude gays and lesbians of color (Cohen and Johnson). The deployment of these and other scholars' work continues through the purposeful diversity of the chapters that follow.

The first three chapters in this volume focus explicitly on black queer sexuality, privileging as a subject of inquiry my own subject position as a black queer scholar. Indeed, while my sexuality is explicitly present throughout these first three chapters, this is not the case in chapters 4 and 5, where sexuality—at least my own—is less the focus. And yet the specter of my queerness lurks in these pages as well; that is, although my sexuality is not privileged as an object of inquiry in Australia or in my grandmother's living room, race and sexuality are always already imbricated in those sites. This is nowhere more apparent than in chapter 4, where the "mammy" trope my grandmother deploys in the telling of her narrative revives the discussion in chapter 3 about the ways in which black gay men appropriate and refigure the term "mother." Moreover, the conspicuous silences about my sexuality in chapter 5 in the context of Australia speak less to an exorcism of (my) sexuality than to the fact that Australian culture is less obsessed than is U.S culture with issues of (homo)sexuality. For sure, the margins of my field notes are filled with my exploits of going "Down Under" but, alas, these tales remain tangential to gospel music performance in the land of Oz. I offer this caveat not as an apology, but rather as a way to frame the methods deployed here and to point out the ways in which blackness is imbricated in multiple identity markers.

This book is an explicit attempt to fully entwine theory and praxis. In so doing, its chapters embrace the myriad intersections of culture and politics by calling attention to the process of *doing* blackness. Performance provides a portal for this process, allowing both maladroit and skilled cultural workers to press blackness into service. Finally, however, the chapters demonstrate the fallibility of the question of authenticity. Blackness, ever residing at the site of indeterminacy, leaves the authenticator wanting, posing yet another question: "Blackness where are you?"

1

THE POT IS BREWING

Marlon Riggs's *Black Is . . . Black Ain't*

There has been a history of excluding other black
folk from community to the detriment of our
overall empowerment. —Marlon Riggs

Throughout the 1980s and early 1990s, black gay poet and filmmaker
Marlon Riggs committed his life to chronicling black American life.
His early works, *Ethnic Notions* (1986) and *Color Adjustment* (1991),
for example, documented the history of the images of blacks in art,
artifacts, television, theater, and film. His most controversial work,
Tongues Untied, however, debuted on the PBS *Point of View* series in
1990, and it chronicles Riggs's personal struggles with coming to
terms with his racial and sexual identities, and with homophobia in
black communities and racism in white communities. In one of the
more poignant moments of *Tongues Untied*, a collage of obituaries of
black gay men who have died of AIDS flashes on the screen while the
sound of a heartbeat thumps in the background. This series of pictures is preceded by Essex Hemphill performing his poem "Now We
Think," which emblematizes the paranoia of contracting HIV/AIDS experienced by gay men: "Now we think / as we fuck / this nut / might
kill us. / There might be / a pin-sized hole / in the condom. / A lethal
leak."[1] Echoing the poem's angst-ridden tone, Riggs announces that
"a time bomb is ticking in my blood." The newspaper clippings of
those who have fallen victim to AIDS appear in succession, appearing

more rapidly as they proceed, over which Riggs narrates: "I listen for my own quiet implosion, but while I wait, older, stronger rhythms resonate within me, sustain my spirit, silencing the clock." The last image of this series of pictures is that of Riggs himself, as if foreshadowing his own death that would come four years later. The "older, stronger rhythms" that "resonate" within him and "sustain his spirit" are represented in the collage of images following the series of obituaries, the first picture being one of Harriet Tubman who, for Riggs, is an emblem of the struggle for black freedom and equality, and who Riggs invokes even more prominently in his film *Black Is . . . Black Ain't.*[2]

In some ways *Black Is . . . Black Ain't* is the sequel to *Tongues Untied* in that although it broadens its scope to examine black identity in all of its contradictions and contingencies, the focus of the film is Riggs's battle with AIDS, which he apparently knew he had contracted when he filmed *Tongues Untied.* Riggs thus stages the fight for his life against AIDS within the broader context of black identity politics. For Riggs, the processes by which we fight deadly diseases such as AIDS and those by which we fight over the embattled status of blackness circumscribe the process by which we come into our humanity. In other words, when we "fix" and confine our identity as monolithic, we inhibit our road both to recovery from the diseases that plague our communities and to discovering our humanity. Taking the "fact" of the diseased and "black" body as givens, Riggs, according to Martin Favor, "refuses to delineate the boundaries of blackness even as [the film's title] invokes the category as truly experienced and, indeed, necessary."[3] Resonating the queer theory critique of identity as ontological, the film also allows for the subject's agency and authority by visually privileging Riggs's AIDS experience narrative. Indeed, the film's documentation of Riggs's declining health, highlighted by the reiteration of his declining T-cell count coupled with his own narration, suggests an identity and a body in the process of "being" and "becoming," of identity as performance and performativity.

Insofar as identity is performed and experienced as real, it constitutes a legitimate way through which subjects maintain control over their lives and their image. But performance does not foreclose the discursive signifiers that undergird the terms of its production. Through my reading of the film, then, I will focus on the dialectic created between performance and performativity, demonstrating why one critical trope necessarily depends on the other in the process of identity formation. *Black Is . . . Black Ain't* demonstrates just how over-determined black identity and authenticity are by elaborating on the ways in which skin color alone is simultaneously an inadequate yet sometimes a socially, culturally, and politically necessary signifier of blackness.

In the first half of this chapter I will elaborate the process by which the film engages performativity to underscore the problematic pursuit of authentic identity claims. Although theories of performativity focus primarily on the performativity of gender, I engage a discussion about the performativity of race. One of the ways in which the film engages this critique is by pointing out how, at the very least, gender, class, sexuality, and region all impact the construction of blackness. Indeed, the title of the film—*Black Is . . . Black Ain't*—itself embodies how race defines, as well as confines, black Americans. The running trope used by Riggs to illuminate the multiplicity of blackness is gumbo, a dish whose ingredients consist of whatever the cook wishes. It has, Riggs remarks, "everything you can imagine in it." This trope also underscores the multiplicity of blackness insofar as gumbo is a dish associated with New Orleans, a city confounded by its mixed raced progeny and the identity politics that mixing creates. The gumbo trope is apropos because, like "blackness," gumbo is a site of possibilities. The film argues that when black Americans attempt to define what it means to be black, they delimit the possibilities of what blackness can be. At times, this process of demarcating blackness may be counterproductive to the flavor of the roux that acts as the base of the gumbo that is "blackness."

But Riggs's film does more than just stir things up. In many ways it reduces the heat of the pot to a simmer, allowing everything in the gumbo to mix and mesh yet maintain a distinct flavor; for after all, chicken is distinct from andouille sausage, rice from peas, bay leaf from thyme, cayenne from paprika. Thus, Riggs's film suggests that black Americans cannot begin to ask the dominant culture to accept their difference as Others nor accept their humanity until black Americans accept the differences that exist among themselves. Riggs's film does the work that Dwight McBride calls for: "[To] create new and more inclusive ways of speaking about race that do not cause even good, thorough thinkers . . . to compromise their/our own critical veracity by participating in the form of race discourse that has been hegemonic for so long."[4] Indeed, as I demonstrate below, Riggs's "critical veracity" is relenting in his critique of race-privileging anti-racist discourse such that gender, sexuality, and class constitute subject positions from which one may "speak" about race oppression.

The second half of this chapter focuses on the black body as a site of performance. Here I provide a rejoinder to racial performativity in order to intervene in what I see as some scholars' eclipsing of corpo-reality and materiality. Specifically, I construe Marlon Riggs's black body in the film as a site of discursivity *and* corporeality that calls attention to the social consequences of "having" AIDS and also "being" black. Rather than succumb to the essentialist/antiessentialist binary, I suggest that the "presence" of Riggs's black diseased body forces viewers of the film to confront not only the social impact of AIDS on the black community but also the impact of inhabiting a black identity in a racist society.

Before moving on to the analysis of *Black Is . . . Black Ain't,* I would like to offer a caveat about the terms of the film's production and how those terms could undermine the reading I am about to perform. As a documentary commissioned and funded by PBS, *Black Is* becomes implicated in the ideological trappings of that venue. In other words, although PBS has aired controversial programs, its reliance on public and federal funding has crippled its ability to make completely autonomous decisions about its programming. Indeed, conservatives such as Jesse Helms were instrumental in cutting funding for the National Endowment of the Arts and the National Endowment for the Humanities as well as PBS because these institutions were funding what the conservatives considered "indecent" art. Riggs's own *Tongues Untied* was caught in the backlash of this conservative wave during the late 1980s and early 1990s, which led some local PBS affiliates to keep the film from being aired. Thus, the fact that PBS partially funded and broadcast *Black Is* seems at odds with the fiscal blackmail under which the station now operates.

One way of reading PBS's support for the documentary, then, might be the fact that it chronicles a black gay man dying of AIDS. Viewed from this angle the film becomes an elegy for Riggs's death. The fact that the film is framed by the beginning scene of the announcement that Riggs dies before its completion and at the end by the "in me-moriam" along with Riggs's narration of his desire that the film's por-trayal of his battle with AIDS helps us all see our humanity, makes the documentary complicitous in constructing a "universal" death nar-rative as opposed to pointing to the specificity of dying from AIDS.[5] Given the lack of support from conservatives in Congress for AIDS re-search, especially during the Reagan and Bush (both father and son) administrations, such a representation would necessarily diminish the specificity and devastating effects of AIDS on the black community, which—in light of the recent surge in the number of black Americans infected with HIV/AIDS, especially black women—cripples further the effectiveness of HIV/AIDS activism and advocacy within and outside black communities.[6]

An even more sinister agenda for allowing the film to air on PBS would rely on the racist logic that those viewing the film would auto-matically associate AIDS with blackness.[7] The emphasis on Riggs's ill-ness and the focus on blackness make the film vulnerable to such a reading. Although these conjectures about the terms of the film's pro-duction may appear paranoid and conspiratorial, because film lives in the realm of the representational and therefore the ideological its meaning and interpretation are contingent on its historical and cul-tural reception.

The possibility of such readings notwithstanding, I offer a counter-reading of *Black Is* through what David Román refers to as "critical generosity." "Critical generosity," Román argues, "is a practice that sets out to intervene in the limited perspectives we currently employ to understand and discuss AIDS theatre and performance by looking beyond conventional forms of analysis."[8] Indeed, my analysis of *Black Is* seeks to push past canonical and conventional forms of analysis in order to locate the manner in which this AIDS filmic performance sig-nifies in ways that disrupt any *singular* reading of AIDS, death, and blackness. In fact, the power of Riggs's film might be in its ability to reveal the various modes of racist/antiracist discourse that circulate within and outside black culture. My reading of the film is similar to that of Teresa de Lauretis's reading of the film *Born in Flames:* "The originality of this film's project is its representation of woman as so-cial subject and a site of differences; differences which are not purely sexual or merely racial, economic, or (sub)cultural, but all of these together and often in conflict with one another. What one takes away after seeing this film is the image of the heterogeneity in the female social subject."[9] As opposed to the female social subject, Riggs specifically represents the heterogeneity of the black gay subject and of blackness in general.

My interest in *Black Is* also stems from its particularity as a filmic performance, as a genre that provides for a historiography of AIDS performance not always possible with other genres of performance. Unlike the difficulty theater historians have in documenting AIDS artistic productions because, in Román's words, "many of the artistic collaborators, producers, theatre staff, and spectators who participated in these productions and performances are also dead and therefore may leave no record of the events,"[10] the celluloid medium provides material documentation of such performances to which performance critics and historians may return. As another kind of "intervention," then, my analysis of *Black Is* is an attempt to keep alive and ever in the forefront the political advocacy of and discourse on HIV/AIDS education and prevention.

An Oreo Is Not Just a Cookie:
Blackness and the Middle Class

Class represents a significant axis and divisiveness within black communities. Despite Stuart Hall's assertion that " 'black' is not the exclusive property of any particular social or any single discourse" and that "it has no necessary class belonging,"[11] there are those who trudge forward carrying the class card they believe guarantees their membership in authentic blackness. As Martin Favor persuasively argues, "authentic" blackness is most often associated with the "folk" or the working-class black.[12] Moreover, art forms such as folklore and the blues that are associated with the black working class are also viewed as more genuinely black.[13] This association of the folk with black authenticity necessarily renders the black middle class as inauthentic and apolitical. Indeed, over the years various black scholars, writers, and activists have located authentic blackness within poor and working-class black communities, suggesting, according to Valerie Smith, that the black working class "is an autonomous space, free of negotiations with hegemony, that contains the pure source of musical and spiritual culture and inspiration. The black middle class, in contrast, is a space of pure compromise and capitulation, from which all autonomy disappears once it encounters hegemonic power."[14]

Much of this sentiment stems from the belief that black economic mobility necessarily breeds assimilationists and race traitors because of interracial mixing. Moreover, there is an assumption that educated blacks are much more likely to disavow their racial "roots" than might their poor and illiterate brothers and sisters. Although this rhetoric is problematic on many counts, one of its more disturbing aspects is that it confounds class and race such that it links racial authenticity with a certain kind of primitivism and anti-intellectualism. Langston Hughes, in his famous treatise "The Negro Artist and the Racial Mountain," for example, portrays the black working class in a Cartesian manner by reifying the body/mind split—body as linked to nature, and mind to the abstract world—and romanticizing black folk culture as the impetus for all black aesthetic and cultural production. In contrast, he images the black middle class and intellectuals as "afraid" of black cultural production:

> [The] *low-down folks,* the so-called common element . . . live on Seventh Street in Washington or State Street in Chicago and they do not particularly care whether they are like white folks or anybody else. Their joy runs, bang! into ecstasy. Their religion soars to a shout. Work maybe a little today, rest a little tomorrow. Play awhile. Sing awhile. O, let's dance! these *common people* are not afraid of spirituals, *as for a long time their more intellectual brethren were,* and jazz is their child. They furnish a wealth of colorful, distinctive material for any artist because they still hold their individuality in the face of American standardizations. And perhaps these common people will give to the world its truly great Negro artist, the one who is not afraid to be himself.[15]

Hughes's persistent references to black working-class people as "common," alongside the implications that they are lazy (e.g., "Work maybe a little today, rest a little tomorrow") undermines his valorization of these same "folk" as the site of racial authenticity. And given that Hughes himself was a product of and lived primarily as the black middle class, he ironically presents the black middle class, by implication, as lacking creativity, individuality, and indeed, authenticity. According to Favor a move such as Hughes's was not uncommon among some black intellectuals who, in an attempt to be "down with the cause," found themselves in an awkward position when they aligned themselves with the "folk" in order to allay their own guilt about being middle class.[16]

A similar rhetoric of racial authenticity founded on class difference also circulated during the 1960s Black Power and Black Arts movements. Members of the so-called black bourgeoisie as depicted in the scholarship and poetry of black nationalists were assimilating sellouts, phenotypically black but politically and ideologically white— "half-white" Oreos. In his poem "Black Bourgeoisie" Imamu Amiri Baraka (LeRoi Jones) describes the black middle class thusly:

> [Black Bourgeoisie,] has a gold tooth, sits long hours
> on a stool thinking about money.
> sees white skin in a secret room
> rummages his sense for sense
> dreams about Lincoln(s)
> conks his daughter's hair
> sends his coon to school
> works very hard
> grins politely in restaurants
> has a good word to say
> never says it
> does not hate ofays
> hates, instead, him self
> him black self[17]

In this poem, Baraka renders the black middle-class male as a self-hating materialist whose politics, given his inclination to mimic "whiteness" (e.g., "conks his daughter's hair" and "grins politely in restaurants"), run counter to the 1960s Black Power movement's struggle against "ofays."[18] And in "Poem for Some Half White College Students," a poem whose title announces Baraka's indictment of educated blacks as being inauthentically black, "half white" black college students are associated with white film stars such as Elizabeth Taylor, Richard Burton, and Steve McQueen in order to illustrate the students' sycophantic relationship to whiteness. Baraka encourages the student to "check yourself,/learn who it is/speaking, when you make some ultrasophisticated point, check yourself,/when you find yourself gesturing like Steve McQueen,/check it out, ask/in your black heart who it is you are, and is that image black or white."[19] According to the logic of the poem, then, an educated middle-class black is more susceptible to the seduction of whiteness because his or her socioeconomic status compromises his or her politics.[20]

Both "Black Bourgeoisie" and "Poem for Some Half White College Students' are emblematic of the discourse about the black middle class as the site of capitulation in the face of racial strife. Enshrouded by the militancy of the Black Power and Black Arts movements, this brand of Black Nationalism forecloses the possibility of middle-class inclusion in antiracist struggle. By founding blackness on a socially constructed monolithic black community, the rhetoric of black authenticity discourse before and after the 1960s confounds ideological allegiance and skin color such that radical political coalitions are forestalled. According to Adolph Reed Jr., 1960s Black Nationalism's "naïve" unself-consciousness actually deflated the political efficacy of the Civil Rights movement, reducing the movement to a "simplistic politics of unity."[21] This "simplistic politics of unity" was undoubtedly forged to foreground at least the "appearance" of a unified black community, but rather than stabilizing blackness it paradoxically "gave way to opportunistic appeal to unity grounded on an unspecifiable 'blackness' and commodified idea of 'soul'" (74).

In *Black Is* Riggs intervenes in this construction of the black middle class as less black by featuring a potpourri of blacks from various backgrounds. Coincidentally, the film's focus on the 1960s belies the rhetoric that positions the black middle class as racially inauthentic by seemingly locating the founding moment of politicized blackness in the 1960s among the educated black middle class. Indeed, those black figures most celebrated in the film—Angela Davis, Barbara Smith, Michele Wallace, and Cornel West—are middle-class members of the baby boomer generation. This is significant given that West has argued that the Civil Rights movement was largely "the activity of the black petite bourgeois . . . upon reaching an anxiety-ridden middle-class status in racist American society."[22]

Riggs undermines the idea that "authentic" blackness belongs to the black working class by prominently displaying interviews with Angela Davis, Michele Wallace, and Barbara Smith. The life-experience narratives that these women relate in the film reveal the bigotry of black radical conservatives who, despite these women's contributions to the struggle, tried to exclude them from the movement because of their education and middle-class status. Indirectly exposing the triteness of Baraka's "half white" poem, in one scene of the film Barbara Smith says, "I was very committed to the Civil Rights movement, but I was constantly getting the message that I was not black enough. You know how they did that in those days? They're probably still doing it. I was not black enough because I was at an elite school. I was not black enough because I spoke fairly Standard English." Angela Davis echoes Smith when she reveals that she felt "ashamed" for having studied outside the United States, the implication being that it was not something "real" black folks did. Davis explains: "There was a time when I felt ashamed almost that I had studied in France and studied in Germany, right? Because we were supposed to be talking about Africa not Europe. And I know that the way I act, and the way I talk, and the way I think reflects all the places that I've been. And I've been a lot of places." In essence, Barbara Smith and Angela Davis deny that their middle-class status and all of the accoutrements accorded that position such as education and use of Standard English compromised their "blackness" or their commitment and contributions to antiracist struggle.

Also growing out of the 1960s problematic focus on prescribing authentic blackness was the equation of "African" garb with "real" blackness. Insofar as "Western" clothing was associated with whiteness and upward mobility, one's choice of clothing implicated membership in a certain class. Not surprisingly, the more African garb one donned, the more authentically black and "down" one became. This emphasis on clothing, however, fetishizes and commodifies an ahistorical representation of a mythic African past, whereby Africa is reduced to a monolithic whole. Again, *Black Is* critiques such narrow-minded, unself-conscious cultural nationalism by allowing its "talking heads" to expose the contradictions of yoking authentic blackness to such cultural practices.

Accordingly, Angela Davis suggests that wearing blue jeans is no less black than wearing kente cloth: "I love kente cloth. I wear kente cloth and have kente cloth in my house, but I don't confuse that with my identity. Because I can wear kente cloth if I want, but I can put on a pair of jeans and I feel just as black as I did when I had the kente cloth on." And in one of his many appearances in the film, poet

Essex Hemphill expresses his concern when cultural pride as manifested through wearing African garb or giving up "the master's name"
becomes fundamentalist dogma that creates a boundary around the
category of blackness. Hemphill says, "Putting on our kentes and
whatever cloths and importing from West Africa—all of that's really
wonderful. . . . Whatever makes your spirit rise then I say, by all
means, nurture it, if that's what it takes for you, if that's the affirmation it takes. But that doesn't then give you the privilege to beat someone else down just because they don't want to change their name or
wear African clothes or stay in the inner city." By explicitly critiqu-
ing the notion of an authentic blackness based on clothing or naming rituals, Davis and Hemphill testify that blackness is not something one necessarily wears on the outside (through black skin or
clothing) but something more ephemeral and processual—a performativity that calls attention to the slippages among biology, culture,
ideology, and politics. Thus, wearing kente or acquiring an African
name is one kind of black performance, but it is a no less authentic
performance of blackness than wearing blue jeans or being named
"John" or "Mary."

Returning again to the idea of "folk" as more authentically black,
I would like to end this discussion of class in *Black Is* by focusing
on how it deconstructs the inner city/suburb binary in relation to authentic blackness. At the outset of the segment of the film quoted
above, Essex Hemphill provides an explanation as to why the inner
city has become associated with "real" blackness: "Perhaps the standard, frightening as it may be, is the inner city for defining what blackness is. That you've got to constantly be up on the changes in the hip
language, the hip black language, the hip black fashions, the hip black
music. You've got to use your ghetto experience as your American
Express Card." In addition to the popular black intellectuals featured
in the film, Riggs interviews several average black Americans from
both the inner city and the suburbs to get their perspective on being
black. In one particularly telling moment in the film, three young
black men who live in Inglewood, California—infamously known as
South Central—provide compelling narratives of poverty, "gang bang-
ing," drug dealing, and ever-impending incarceration. As one of these
young men says to Riggs: "We gotta make a living the best we can. If
that means by selling dope, then I guess that means we have to sell

dope. Ain't nobody rich in the ghetto. If we were rich, we wouldn't be here."

Initially, these young men's sense of themselves and their future is overwhelmingly nihilistic—a black nihilism that Cornel West says is to be "understood . . . not as a philosophic doctrine that there are no rational grounds for legitimate standards or authority; it is far more, the lived experience of coping with a life of horrifying meaninglessness, hopelessness, and (most important) lovelessness. The frightening result is a numbing detachment from others and a self-destructive position toward the world."[23] These young black urban dwellers are a far cry from the "low-down folks" Langston Hughes depicts as the progenitors of Negro artistry in "Racial Mountain." Indeed, they do not experience a joy that "runs, bang! into ecstasy" but rather into despair. The testimonies of these young men featured in the film are in contradistinction to the romanticized folk culture depicted by those who unproblematically image the black working class and inner-city dwellers as somehow inoculated from the devastation of their surroundings, reconstructing the weary, worn propaganda that misery breeds creativity. In fact, these young men cast off the nihilism of their surroundings by at least articulating a desire to "leave the ghetto." One of the young men explains his plan to get out of the ghetto, which, incidentally, entails acquiring an advanced degree in order to ascend the socioeconomic ladder:[24]

> I ain't gonna be out here everyday gang banging, man. After I graduate from high school I'm going somewhere. I ain't gonna be out here everyday. Ain't shit out here but pain. Fuck this shit. . . . Right now, I be going to school everyday. Right now I do not miss school a day, cause I gotta have that education, man. Cause the white man's not gonna let you do shit. A high school diploma ain't nothing no more. You gotta master in something. High school diploma ain't nothing no more, man. You can't even work at McDonald's with a high school diploma. That's why I'm gonna try to be something and when I get up, I'm gonna try to take them up with me. You know what I'm saying? Cause I don't want to leave none of my friends or family in the ghetto.

Far from romanticizing the struggle of his existence, this young man desires a better life in which he is able not only to leave the ghetto and acquire an education and a good-paying job but also come back to the community and help his friends and family. Moreover, his narrative points to the slippage between skin color and politics. The fact of this young man's blackness, then, is not sutured to his status as a poverty-stricken, gang-banging ghettoite. As his class status shifts and becomes more malleable, discursively and materially, so too will his blackness. As Favor suggests: "Those who can bend class and geographic position to their own purposes have the power to shape what 'race' is. By reshaping race, they add to the complexity of the discourse of black identity rather than impoverishing it with 'false' notions."[25] One of those "false" notions is that ghetto life is the site of uncompromised authentic blackness.

Black Is alternately moves from the inner city to the suburbs, an editorial choice that further dismantles the black authenticity hierarchy that privileges the inner city as a more authentically black site. Juxtaposed to the interviews with the inner-city young men, for example, are clips of interviews with black suburbanites who articulate their hyperawareness of the black middle-class/working-class divide in the identity politics pool of authentic blackness. To dramatize this divide the film shows one of the black middle-class men Riggs interviews walking up the steps to his relatively large suburban home in Fort Washington, Maryland. During the interview with this particular man, his defensiveness about being accused of being inauthentically black registers in his allusions to a phallic blackness. He quips: "I'll pull out my blackness and you pull out yours. I have no problem in defending mine. And I think I speak for a lot of people in the African American middle class. You know, again, you can't live in this society and not be black. You know, the society won't let you forget you're black. But you don't want to forget you're black. Being black is not about economics, it's about values." Although wrapped in phallocentric machismo, the "pulling out" metaphor nonetheless accedes that blackness is contingent, malleable, performative. Rightfully, this interviewee also unhinges authentic blackness from a particular class status and aligns it with the process of valuation, which is also contingent on context, history, place, and space.

In another moment in this section of the film, a black middle-class man is interviewed: his narrative is initially heard over and intercut with excerpts from rapper Ice Cube's music video "True to the Game," in which a black "yuppie" is kidnapped and brought back to the "hood" because he has forgotten his roots. What makes this montage interesting is the irony that registers in the juxtaposition of these two competing narratives. The interviewee refuses to apologize for his middle-class status because he is a product of the ghetto: "I'm a born, bred, raised Harlemite. I knew what the hood was before most of these kids were born. And the reality is do you live your life in struggle around trying to prove a point to someone who doesn't really give a damn about your reality or do you determine what's important to you?" This self-proclaimed "Harlemite" realizes the futility in trying to prove one's blackness to those who believe that dwelling in the ghetto is a prerequisite for the "real" black experience. The "ghetto experience" is as much an ideological construct as is the category "blackness," a cultural performance with the discursive trimmings of hegemonic identity. As Stuart Hall reminds us: "There is no escape from the politics of representation, and we cannot wield 'how life really is out there' as a kind of test against which the political rightness or wrongness of a particular cultural strategy or text can be measured."[26]

That is not to say that there is no "real" poverty in the black inner city, but rather only that the representation of that poverty may take many discursive turns such that one might actually live in the ghetto but not necessarily *appear* to. The reverse may also be true as witnessed among rappers who sing about life in the ghetto but who themselves don't actually live there. And even in those instances where a rapper does remain "in the ghetto" his geographic location does no more to secure the authenticity of his blackness than it does to diminish the fact of his wealth.

Ice Cube, however, would have us believe that authentic blackness has everything to do with where one lives. In "True to the Game" he chastises the "Oreo" for "living way out" and "trying to be white or a Jew," and he urges him to "stop being an Uncle Tom, you little sellout/House nigga scum." If the suburbanite refuses to heed Ice Cube's warning, it may result in his "ghetto pass" (read "blackness") being "revoked."[27] All three verses of the song in some way or another encapsulate all of the many contingencies on which class-based authentic blackness is founded, including interracial marriage and friendships, speaking Standard English, wearing a suit and tie, or things as trivial as smiling.

Rather than silencing rhetoric such as that enlisted in Ice Cube's song, Riggs's choice to include it and to juxtapose it with narratives by those whom the song indicts only reinforces the notion that blackness cannot be founded on class status. If anything, the cacophony of voices featured in this section of the film resembles the polyvocality of discourses that comprise blackness. By positioning these voices against one another Riggs corroborates Wahneema Lubiano's (paraphrasing Stuart Hall) suggestion that "there is no law that guarantees a group's ideology is consistent with its economic—or, I would add, its racial—position, nor is there any guarantee that the ideology of a group isn't consistent with its economic or race position."[28] Indeed, *Black Is* reminds us that "middle class" is also an ideological construct as contingently constituted as other social and subject positionalities.[29]

It's a Dick Thang, You Wouldn't Understand: Blackness and Gender

In addition to issues of class and color, Riggs unhinges the link between hegemonic masculinity and authentic blackness. Beginning with his early childhood, Riggs sets the stage for what he sees as the masculinization of blackness, a black masculinity that disables communication between him and his father. Drawing on the "Silence = Death" slogan made popular by ACT UP in order to compel individuals to speak openly about their (homo)sexuality and about AIDS, Riggs chronicles the silence surrounding his sexuality, a silence that excluded him from black masculinity. As pictures from Riggs's childhood appear on the screen, including him in football gear, posing with girlfriends, etc., Riggs narrates: "To be a black man required a code of silence. You didn't express your feelings. You couldn't acknowledge hurt, pain, and rage and anger. And what that engendered was silence. No one talked to each other, because that would have been admitting vulnerability and vulnerability was associated with being feminine." This scene is followed by a performance by Essex Hemphill of his poem "Father, Son, and the Unholy Ghosts," in which the speaker invokes homosexual sex as being the "black hole" that separates black father and son. Although silence as sign of masculinity is a trope that circulates in the broader U.S. cultural context, within raced communities, and especially among black men, silence often sustains a dysfunctional denial of sexual difference and the imperialism of patriarchy, or what Phil Harper calls the "proper affirmation of black male [heterosexual] authority."[30]

As explored earlier with regard to class, Riggs locates much of this black male machismo as stemming from the Black Power movement of the 1960s. As I will discuss in chapter 2 in my examination of writers such as Imamu Amiri Baraka and Eldridge Cleaver, much of the rhetoric of Black Nationalism disavows the black homosexual as antiblack in order to maintain the fiction of a coherent black male heterosexuality and to assuage the specter of the homosexual Other within. In *Black Is* Riggs presents images of the Black Panthers marching in their berets, armed as if marching off to war. These images engender the intentional militaristic rhetoric of the Black Panthers as well as the ways in which blackness and masculinity are conjoined with violence.

These images are intercut with bell hooks explaining why the strategies deployed by some Black Nationalists were misguided because the effect was the deification and resurrection (erection?) of a black phallic economy. She explains: "When we translate the history of black oppression sexually, especially through the writings of George Jackson and Eldridge Cleaver, it's all sexualized into emasculation and castration. So the reclamation of the black race gets translated into 'it's a dick thang.' That's why I'm fond of saying that if the black thang is really a dick thang in disguise, then we are really in serious trouble." Her indictment of Jackson, whose misogyny is propagated in the name of saving the black family and Cleaver—a confessed rapist of both black and white women—substantiates her account of black sexual oppression as articulated in the discourse of some black nationalists. Interestingly enough, both Jackson and Cleaver penned their misogynist and homophobic invectives while incarcerated: the prison serving, evidently, as inspiration for their musings on sex and race.[31] Deeply steeped in the cauldron of black nationalist brew, Jackson's commentary on the "crisis" of the black family locates that crisis within the black woman and her disavowal of "traditional" African familial roles. He is less than coy while "slipping in" the dick thang for the black thang. Jackson writes:

> In the society of our fathers and in the civilized world today, women feel it their obligation to be ever yielding and obedient to their men. Life

is made purposely simple for them because of their nature, and they are happy. When the women outnumber the men in the black societies, the men take as many wives as they can afford, and care for them all equally. . . . In the civilized societies the women do light work, bear children, and lend purpose to the man's existence. They train children in the ways of wisdom that history has shown to be correct. Their job is to train the children in their early life to be men and women, not confused psychotics! This is a big job, to train and propagate the race!! Is this not enough? The rest is left to the men: government administration, the providing of means of subsistence, and defense, or maintenance of life and property against any who would deprive us of it, as the barbarian has and is still attempting to do. The white theory of the "emancipated woman" is a false idea. You will find it, as they are finding it, the factor in the breakdown of the family unit.[32]

Jackson makes clear that the black family will only survive if traditional gender roles within the black domestic space cohere. And, similar to arguments made by other black nationalists about homosexuality being a "white disease" that has infiltrated the black community, Jackson implies that women's liberation also is a "white thang" to be rejected in order to curtail the "breakdown of the family unit." Accordingly, within *Black Is* hooks's invocation of Jackson is apropos in relation to Angela Davis's commentary, which proceeds it. Davis says in the film that "twenty-five years ago there was someone in the organization who argued that the role of women was to wear long African dresses, to organize cocktail parties, and to convince rich men to donate money to the organization. And this particular person came in and actually dismantled the whole structure that we had because he felt that the women had too much power."

The similarities are remarkable between Jackson's division of labor in the black family and the roles that black women in the movement were asked to assume by the man in Davis's narrative. Moreover, Jackson's vision of the black family unit and women's place within it turns precisely at the moment when black women's activism outside the home was at its height—their "work" proffering the race a horn aplenty. Robert Reid-Pharr reveals Jackson's paradox when he writes: "As Jackson expressed his rage, his revolutionary ardor inside increasingly small jail cells, female lawyers pressed his case, female activists kept his name before the public, and a handful of celebrity radicals:

Angela Davis, Betty Shabazz, Kathleen Cleaver, Elaine Brown were left with the mantle of Black radicalism as the men in whose shadow they had once stood either died or ran."[33] Reid-Pharr's portrait of Jackson's sexist vision of black women's roles versus the roles they actually played in the movement is in keeping with Riggs's filmic presentation of Davis. In *Black Is,* Riggs juxtaposes Davis's "radical" celebrity status as captured in a film clip from her arraignment when she was arrested on kidnapping charges during her antiprison protest days, with a clip of her narrative about the misogynist black male leader. As with the concurrent events of Jackson's vision and black women's activism, Riggs's presentation of Davis's black cultural work in the movement resists the black male leader's attempts to diminish Davis's and other women's power.

Black Is also features gay black dancer Bill T. Jones. Regarding the critique of black masculinity, Riggs asks Jones to characterize the "woman inside" him. As Jones describes his inner femininity, he and dancer Andrea E. Woods choreograph a piece that symbolizes what Jones narrates: a black masculinity that embraces and celebrates the feminine as much as it does the masculine. Importantly, Jones resists constructing a feminine/masculine binary; rather, through the fluidity of his dance moves with Woods he suggests a fluidity of gender as well.

Perhaps the most powerful critique of hegemonic black masculinity in the film occurs when Riggs excerpts misogynist speeches by Louis Farrakhan, a Mississippi preacher, and the leader of an "African" village located in St. Helena, South Carolina. As deployed elsewhere in the film to attenuate the fixity and call attention to the process of blackness, hegemonic discourse is countered with opposing constructions. In this instance, bell hooks's personal narrative provides the oppositional frame through which to undermine the historical equation of "real" blackness with black masculinity, a black masculinity defined by power acquired at the expense of black women and homosexuals. In her narrative hooks recalls her mother being abused by her father while her uncles and siblings stood by and did nothing:

> My father used to come home from work humming a tune. And I mean that tune was like a terroristic threat. When we heard that tune hittin' those steps, we knew we had to get ourselves in order. My dad didn't have

The Pot Is Brewing

bell hooks narrating her father's tyranny.

to speak, Honey. He had to hum his tune. He didn't have to come in, say, "Do this. Do that. I'm the ruler here." It was all taking place.

Once I think my father heard that my mother was having an affair with somebody and he came home from work and he got his gun. And I remember my father screaming, "I will kill you." That very night he said, "This is *my* house. I will not have this." And she had to pack her bags. It's like when you're a kid and you think your parents are equal. But when I saw my mother weeping and packing her bags and throwing her shit into suitcases and I thought he has the power to do this. When my uncles came together—the other patriarchs—came together, I expected that there would be some discussion, that they would try to convince my father that you can't do this, you can't throw her out of what is her house as well. But it was like one patriarch had spoken and the other patriarchs had nodded their heads. If the woman has done wrong you gotta punish her. This man is saying he's gonna kill our mama, who takes care of us every day, and we're just going to go up and go to bed and go to sleep? I never forgave my brothers and sisters for a long time for the fact that they actually went upstairs and went to bed and went to sleep. I was like, "No. I can't go upstairs and go to sleep. I have to witness this."

This narrative regarding hooks's mother's spousal abuse is intercut with and undercuts Farrakhan's sexist and misogynist justification of Mike Tyson's sexual advances, which eventually led to his being accused of and convicted for raping Desiree Washington. The narrative also brackets the sexism inherent in the speeches given by the Mississippi preacher ("The head of Man is God and the head of woman is Man") and the African village leader ("In every society there are roles

35

that men and women have to play") where the justification of the sub-jugation of women is based on biblical and African mythology. Musi-cally framing this montage of narratives is rap artist Queen Latifah's performance of "u-n-i-t-y," a song that urges black women to "let black men know you ain't a bitch or a 'ho." Riggs's choice to use Latifah's song to administer this critique is interesting on a number of levels; for example, Latifah's own public persona, as well as her tele-vision and motion picture roles, embody a highly masculinized femi-ninity or, alternatively, what Judith Halberstam might call "female masculinity."[34] Thus Riggs uses Latifah's song and the invocation of her persona in the service of further disrupting hegemonic construc-tions of black masculinity, as well as illuminating the sexism found within the black community.

In general, splicing together competing discourses and images in *Black Is* evinces the lacuna within the logic of black nationalist mi-sogyny, and it does this in three ways. First, the montages denatural-ize masculinity from authentic blackness by exposing the amount of discursive labor required to sustain the pursuit of such an unattain-able ontological linkage between race and gender. Second, the dialogic and dialectical exchange created by the montage renders blackness as a site of contestation rather than congealment. Third, this technique excavates the black misogynist's "real" agenda: that is, reinscribing black masculinity as the site of authentic blackness in the name of lib-erating and protecting the "race"—or, to put it more bluntly, making the *black* thang a *dick* thang.

True Niggers Ain't Faggots:
Blackness and Homosexuality

Wherever there exists sexism and misogyny, homophobia is not far behind. Thus the ravings of George Jackson, Eldridge Cleaver, Imamu Amiri Baraka, Louis Farrakhan, and other racial purists vary only in degrees in their homophobia. If, as George Jackson suggests above, the black woman exists solely for reproducing the race and thus becomes the black man's possession and object of his desire, then the black homosexual represents sexuality run amuck—a perversion that threatens the very essence of black heteronormative masculinity.

Given the constant surveillance by whites of black bodies within the institution of the family, black heterosexual men in particular have a vested interested in disavowing any dissident sexuality in their quarters. Thus, the specter of the black fag haunts the mythic cohesive black heterosexual familial unit. "He" registers what Robert Reid-Pharr refers to as a "black boundarylessness" that must be contained such that the image of the black family, and in particular that of the black heterosexual man, appear "normal" in the eyes of whites. The discursive and physical antihomosexual violence motivated by the fear of the incoherent black subject, according to Reid-Pharr, "operates in the production of black masculinity."[35]

Riggs captures the various manifestations of black homophobia and antihomosexual violence through a variety of ways, including poetry, personal narratives, interviews, music, and quotations. An interview with Essex Hemphill frames this part of the film as Hemphill conjectures why black gay men are excluded from authentic blackness. He states: "This idea that somehow my blackness is diminished because I love men is purely out of that sense that black men have been chatteled, black men have been lynched; black men have been shot, beaten, brutalized by the police, the government every which way, etc. So some people view black homosexuality as the final break in masculinity and don't see the love, don't see the empowerment, don't see the caring, the sharing, don't see the contributions." Hemphill's explanation for black homophobia highlights the conflation of the often-violent feminization, emasculation, and trafficking of black male bodies with black male homosexuality. Thus the "final break in masculinity" assumes a former coherence, a stasis that never existed except as a social construct. Paradoxically, the fact that homosexuality is seen as the "final" break suggests that the direct line to an original template of black masculinity was cut in spite of rather than because of homosexual identification. Nonetheless, the black homosexual becomes the site of displaced anger for the black heterosexual, the scapegoat used to thwart his own feelings of inadequate manhood. The result is a disavowal that locks the homosexual outside the bounds of authentic blackness even when the black homosexual's "caring," "sharing," and "contributions," like that of black women, stand for some of the most radical political efforts in the struggle for racial equality.

In *Black Is* Riggs seeks answers from his black queer "fathers" as to why black gay men are excluded from blackness and rendered invisible in black history. He asks: "Oh dear fathers, tell me what to do. I search for ancestral affirmation to find only this pathos or worse, historical erasure. How much longer can I walk this winding road?" This narration is followed by feature segments on civil rights activist Bayard Rustin, who organized the 1963 march on Washington, and Shirley Clarke's *Portrait of Jason* (1967), a documentary film about a middle-aged black gay man's struggles in growing up gay in a homophobic black community. In a voice-over Riggs narrates: "How long, Jason? How long had they sung about the freedom and the righteousness and the beauty of the black man and ignored you? How long?" By invoking Martin Luther King Jr.'s "I've Been to the Mountain Top" speech given in Memphis, Tennessee—at the end of which King repeats the rhetorical question "How long?" and then answers "Not long"—Riggs calls attention to the homophobia and hypocrisy of black civil rights leaders (including King) who drew on the capabilities and leadership of black homosexuals while at the same time distanced themselves from them. Indeed, some of King's associates convinced him to distance himself from Bayard Rustin because of his homosexuality. Here, again, the period of the 1960s is a central locus of critique in the film because of the ways in which black leadership during that time prioritized a simplistic definition of race that rawly exorcised the femaleness and queerness out of blackness.

Given that the black church was and continues to be the site of political and social activism for black people, it is undoubtedly implicated in the homophobia of the 1960s and the present. Indeed, the opening of *Black Is* with the chantlike call-and-response of black folk preaching references a communal cultural site instantly recognizable to many black Americans: the black church. But just as the black church has been a political and social force in the struggle for the racial freedom of its constituents, it has also, to a large extent, occluded sexual freedom for many of its practitioners, namely gays and lesbians. Typically, the stance taken by the black church is one of "don't ask, don't tell." In other words, gays and lesbians may actively participate in the church as long as they are silent about their homosexuality. This complicity of silence maintains not only the false dichotomy between the spirit and the flesh but also perpetuates the most oppressive and repressive aspects of fundamentalist Christianity.[36] In this context the homosexual's "membership" in the church is contingent on her or his willingness not only to remain silent about his or her sexuality, but also to fully participate in the activities of the church in spite of being denigrated by the rhetoric of the pulpit.[37] In *Black Is,* for example, the pastor of St. John's AME Church in Drew, Mississippi, says to Riggs: "God loves the individual, but God does not love the homosexual part, the sin that is involved. God does not love that, but as a person, God loves the individual." The "hate the sin, not the sinner" and "don't ask, don't tell" discourses that circulate in the black church fail to accommodate the homosexual subject by making one's subjectivity as "Christian" and "black" contingent on sealing off one's sexuality.

Thus, in the opening scenes of *Black Is,* Riggs calls attention to the double standard found within the black church by exemplifying how blackness can "build you up or bring you down," hold you in high esteem or hold you in contempt. Throughout the film, however, Riggs expands the traditional construction of the black church by featuring a black gay and lesbian church service. The two lesbian members of this church who are interviewed testify to how whole they feel within this church that validates their sexuality and spirituality. It is also evident from the clips of the worship service that this gay and lesbian church practices the rituals and many of the tenets of black Christianity. In one scene the pastor is shown delivering his message, admonishing his parishioners to give up pork chops, while in another scene he is shown fervently leading them in singing a traditional devotional service song, "I'm So Glad He Prayed for Me."

Given the black church's typical stance on homosexuality, some might view this avowal of Christianity as an instance of false consciousness. I would argue, however, that the worship service is an instance of queering blackness or creating what Michael Dyson calls a "theology of queerness" insofar as these black gay and lesbian Christians are reclaiming a tradition of which they are clearly a part. Their embrace of Christianity might also be characterized as an instance of "disidentification," whereby queers of color perform within dominant ideologies in order to resist those same hegemonic structures.[38] In the end, the film intervenes in the construction of black homosexuality as antiblack by propagating gay Christianity as a legitimate signifier of blackness.

The Black Body as Performance/Performativity

Riggs's film implicitly employs performativity to suggest that we dismantle hierarchies that privilege particular black positionalities at the expense of others; that we recognize that darker hue does not give us any more cultural capital or claim to blackness than do a dashiki, braids, or a southern accent. Masculinity is no more a signifier of blackness than femininity; heterosexuality is no blacker than gayness; and poverty makes one no more authentically black than a house in the suburbs. Indeed, what Riggs suggests is that we move beyond these categories and these hierarchies that define and confine in order to realize that, depending on where one is from and where one is going, *black is and black ain't.*

While the film critically interrogates cleavages among blacks, it also exposes the social, political, economic, and psychological effects of racism and the role racism has played in defining blackness. By adopting this dual focus rather than exclusively interrogating black performativity, Riggs offers a perspective that compels us to think more complexly about the interplay between discourse and materiality. He calls attention to differences among blacks and between blacks and their "others";[39] he grounds blackness and lived experience; and he calls attention to the consequences of embodied blackness. The montage of footage from the Los Angeles riots and the interviews with young black men who characterize themselves as gang bangers, along with images of blacks being hosed down during the Civil Rights movement, bring into clear focus the material reality of black America and how the black body has historically been the site of violence and trauma. It is these consequential aspects of bodily harm that I believe racial performativity fails to account for. Gender, sexuality, race, and even class are discursive categories that are subject to mediation; nonetheless, they are categories that exist beyond abstraction and function within the realm of the "real." Like Elizabeth Alexander, I believe that "there must be a place for theorizing black bodily experience into the larger discourse of identity politics."[40]

Riggs's AIDS-riddled black body presents an occasion to theorize "black bodily experience" because his body forces us to bear witness to this devastating disease. Although we might concede at the intellec-

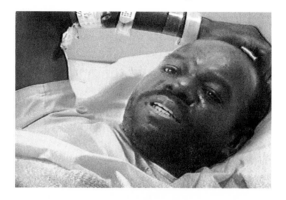

Marlon Riggs, in his hospital bed, in a scene from
Black Is . . . Black Ain't.

tual level that "experience" is not beyond the realm of the discursive, as historian Joan Scott has persuasively argued,[41] we nonetheless cultivate collective narratives to strive toward articulating the very real pain and oppression that black bodies absorb in order to strategize political efficacy. Thus, while we must acknowledge the salience of construing "experience" as discursively mediated, we must also recognize that the the radical destabilization of experience simultaneously limits the ways in which people of color may name their oppression. Dwight McBride writes: "The danger . . . is that since the fundamental way of identifying racism is by narrating its instances, by deauthorizing the witness it could become virtually impossible to ever name 'the beast' at all. This is one reason that I think it is important that African American intellectuals continue to learn new ways of strategizing and essentializing in racialized discourse: because what is at stake is nothing less than the ability to narrate our own stories, witness our own experience."[42]

The value of the "evidence of experience" then, lies in its deployment by those whose livelihood is at stake if it were not available as a tool in the struggle against oppression. Moreover, although *Black Is* functions as a kind of autoethnographic account of Riggs's "experience" of blackness and AIDS, it does not "take as self-evident the identities of those whose experience is being documented and thus naturalize their difference," as Joan Scott warns against.[43] As I explain in detail below, the ethnographic gaze upon Riggs's body documents his experience narrative in such a way that it calls attention to his body/bodily experience as discourse and also grounds and situates that discourse and corporeality within a particular historical context. Accordingly, I do not think that experience as figured in the film necessarily precludes arguing for instances where identity as evinced in experience (however discursively predetermined) can be effectively politically effectuated in a particular context and historical moment.

Nowhere in the film is a black body historicized more pointedly and powerfully than in the scenes where Riggs is featured walking or running through the forest naked or narrating from his hospital bed from which his T-cell count is constantly announced. According to Riggs, these scenes are important because he wants to make the point that not until we expose ourselves to one another will we be able to communicate effectively across our differences. Riggs's intentions notwithstanding, his naked black body serves another function within the context of the film: it is simultaneously in the state of "being" and "becoming." I intend here to disrupt both of these terms by refusing to privilege identity as either solely performance or solely performativity and by demonstrating the dialogic/dialectic relationship of these two tropes housed in and by the body.

Paul Gilroy's theory of diaspora is useful in clarifying the difference between "being" and "becoming." According to Gilroy, "Diaspora accentuates *becoming* rather than *being* and identity conceived diasporically, along these lines, resists reification."[44] Here, Gilroy associates "being" with the transhistorical and transcendental subject and "becoming" with historical situatedness and contingency. In what follows, I supplement Gilroy's use of both terms by suggesting that "being" and "becoming" are sites of performance *and* performativity. I construe "being," for example, as a site of infinite signification *as well as* bodily and material presence. "Being" calls the viewer's attention not only to blackness as *discourse*, but also to embodied blackness in that moment where discourse and flesh conjoin in performance.

In relation to Riggs's body, therefore, I wish to suggest a more nuanced reading of "being." In the first instance, if we look beyond Riggs's intent to "expose" himself to encourage cross-difference communication, we find that his nakedness in the woods functions ideologically in ways that he may not wish. For example, his nakedness may conjure up the racist stereotype of the lurking, bestial, and vir-

Marlon Riggs running through the woods
in *Black Is . . . Black Ain't.*

ile black male threatening the white race that became popular in the
eighteenth- and nineteenth-century American imaginary. His embodied blackness in the woods and in his hospital bed also indicate a
diseased body that is fragile, vulnerable, and a site of trauma, a site
that grounds black discursivity materially in the flesh. This counternarrative is represented through Riggs's voice-over announcing his
declining T-cell count, his desire being to expose his diseased body to
make his blackness and sexuality visible. That very visibility, however,
performs double duty. On the one hand, Riggs's visible black male
body is exposed as fragile and vulnerable, but on the other it also syn-
ecdochically stands in for a larger body of racist discourse on the black
male body in motion. This trope of black bodily kinesthetics is manifest in various forms: in the vernacular-laden expression "Keep this
Nigger-Boy running,"[45] in the fugitive slave, and even in contemporary hypermasculinized images of black athletes.

Racist readings of Riggs's black male body are made possible by
the context in which his body appears: the woods. Within this setting,
blackness becomes problematically teleologically fastened to nature,
reinscribing the black body as bestial and primal, while whiteness becomes fastened, indirectly, to the life of the mind. This imagery works
against Riggs's intentions—namely, running naked in the woods as a
way to work through the tangled and knotty web that is identity. Indeed, those images signify in multiple troubling ways that cannot be
contained by either Riggs's authorial intentions or the viewer's gaze.

As Elizabeth Alexander reminds us: "Black bodies in pain for public consumption have been an American spectacle for centuries. The history moves from public rapes, beatings, and lynchings to the gladiatorial arenas of basketball and boxing. . . . White men have been the stagers and consumers of the historical spectacles I have mentioned, but in one way or another, black people have been looking, too, forging a traumatized collective historical memory which is reinvoked, I believe, at contemporary sites."[46] Riggs's naked body imaged running through the woods thus is implicated in the historical racist spectatorial practices of antiblack violence. Moreover, there is a way in which the representation of his AIDS-infected body is implicated in the ways in which the homophobic gaze already equates the gay body with AIDS. Riggs's foregrounded body, then, may also be read as a "spectacle of contagion" that further disseminates the linkage between AIDS and the homosexual body.[47]

The beauty of "being," however, is that where it crumbles under the weight of deconstruction it reemerges in all its bodily facticity. Although Riggs's body signifies in ways that constrain his agency, his embodied blackness also enlivens a discussion of a "fleshy" nature. Whatever his body signifies, the viewer cannot escape its material presence. Accordingly, Riggs's body as a site of corporeal trauma may incite a "collective historical memory" in the contemporary crisis that AIDS has created in black communities. This spectatorial experience may serve to asseverate not only the traumatic bodily history that black Americans have survived but also the current contagion ravishing black bodies—a contagion, I might add, that is not disconnected from both old and contemporary forms of institutionalized racism.

Riggs's body is also a site of "becoming." He dies before the film is completed and his body thus physically "fades away," but its phantom is reconstituted in our current discourse on AIDS, race, gender, class, and sexuality. His body discursively rematerializes and intervenes in hegemonic formulations of blackness, homosexuality, and the HIV-infected person. As a filmic performance, *Black Is* resurrects Riggs's body such that when the film is screened at universities, shown to health care providers, viewed in black communities, or rebroadcast on PBS where it debuted, the terms and the stakes for how we think about identity and its relation to HIV/AIDS are altered. Indeed, the film becomes part of a body of performances by gay men that serve as what David Román calls "acts of intervention."

In the final scenes of the film and those last recorded before Riggs's death, he recalls dreaming about Harriet Tubman during the peaks of his illness. An unidentified source off screen asks Riggs to recall the dream and describe its significance.

> Riggs: This is when I was feeling really sick in ER. Just her [Harriet Tub-man] coming and standing by me, not saying anything so I had be-come aware of her presence and then just looking into my eyes and then looking into the river in front of us.
> Camera Operator: Where were you?
> Riggs: I don't know. Some dark foresty place with a river running through it and the river running pretty fiercely. And she didn't say anything, she just looked at me and we started walking. Harriet and I walked across the river.
> Camera Operator: What do you think that dream was about?
> Riggs: Overcoming the current crisis. I know there will be more. I know that I'll be laid up in the hospital again. But as long as I have Harriet and *Black Is . . . Black Ain't* to go traveling with, I'm gonna cross that river. If I have work then I'm not going to die. Because work is the living spirit in me—that which wants to connect with other people and pass on something to them that they can use in their own lives and grow from.

I believe that Riggs's dream allegorizes the process of birth. The "dark foresty place" metaphorically images the crowning of a newborn's head in the vaginal opening, while the "fiercely" running river suggests a woman's water breaking. In this case, however, the process of birth is paradoxically and simultaneously the process of death.

In this way, Riggs's dying is similar to Toni Morrison's character Sula, whose deathbed scene also allegorizes a "birth into death." Morrison writes: "It would be here, only here, held by this blind window high above the elm tree, that she might draw her legs up to her chest, close her eyes, put her thumb in her mouth and float over and down, down until she met a rain scent and would know the water was near, and she would curl into its heavy softness and it would envelop her, carry her, and wash her tired flesh always."[48] Sula's rebirthing is sym-bolized by her assuming a fetal position and traveling down the birthing "tunnel." Like Riggs, Sula believes she is dreaming when in actuality she is experiencing a transition into the afterlife: "While in this state of weary anticipation, she noticed that she was not breathing, that her heart had stopped completely. . . . Then she realized, or rather she sensed, that there was not going to be any pain. She was not breathing because she didn't have to. Her body did not need oxygen. She was dead" (149). Once she has crossed over, she realizes and acknowledges her living spirit when she thinks to herself, "Well, I'll be damned . . . it didn't even hurt. Wait'll I tell Nel" (149).

Riggs dreams of a similar journey through water with Harriet Tubman, who serves as a midwife cradling his head at the tunnel's opening—"some dark foresty place"—helping him make the journey across the river. Once on the other side, Riggs, like Sula, lives on and also makes good on his promise to return through his "living spirit" captured in the film. Although we know that Riggs is physically dead when the film opens, he does not realize he will not live to complete the project. He rebukes death in the name of the work that he feels he must do. Indeed, Riggs is still the authorial voice, the auteur, from beyond the living world as he posthumously directs the editorial decisions. Near the end of the film he says, "I hope they keep those clips of me running through the woods." Ultimately, then, the residual traces of Riggs's body become embedded in the ideological battle over identity claims and the discourse surrounding the disproportionate number of AIDS-infected people of color. His becoming, then, belies our being.

Ultimately, *Black Is* performs what its title announces: the simultaneity of bodily presence and absence, being and becoming. Although Riggs offers his own gumbo recipe that stands in for blackness, he does so only to demonstrate that, like blackness, the recipe can be altered, expanded, reduced, diluted. At the same time, Riggs also asks that we not forget that the gumbo (blackness) is contained within a sturdy pot (the body) that has weathered abuse, that has been scorched, scoured, and scraped, a pot/body that is in the process of becoming but nonetheless already *is*.

Black Is . . . Black Ain't provides a space to bear witness to the ways in which blackness is produced, appropriated, politicized, and experienced. I particularly find the gumbo metaphor apropos on this accord because it draws our attention to the discursive constitution of the recipe for blackness and celebrates its improvisational aspects as well as the materiality of the pot. The film accomplishes this by discrediting but not silencing the voices of those whose recipe for blackness leaves out as much as it adds by sieving out many of the ingredients contained inside the pot. Riggs's recipe, however, promises to reduce the spillage, allowing the various and multiple flavors to coexist—those different flavors that make it spicy, hot, unique, and sumptuously "black."

2

MANIFEST FAGGOTRY

Queering Masculinity in African American Culture

No one wants to be called a homosexual.
—Leo Bersani

I'm afraid of gay people. Petrified. I have night-
mares about gay people.—Eddie Murphy

To strike the homosexual, the scapegoat, the sign
of chaos and crisis, is to return the community to
normality, to create boundaries around blackness,
rights that white men are obliged to recognize.
—Robert F. Reid-Pharr

Negro Faggotry is the rage. Black gay men are not.
—Marlon Riggs

As revealed by Marlon Riggs's *Black Is . . . Black Ain't* in chapter 1, black
authenticity has increasingly become linked to masculinity in its most
patriarchal significations. That this particular brand of masculinity
epitomizes the imperialism of heterosexism, sexism, and homophobia, therefore, is not surprising. The ironic and paradoxical manifestations of these oppressions enacted by black heterosexual men, however, might reveal the slippage between the mask of black masculinity
as always already heterosexual and the unacknowledged desire for the
homosexual Other. Accordingly, the ambivalence of sexual desire and
its connectedness to black masculinity, black authenticity, and perfor-

mance is my focus in this chapter. To explain this process, I employ Sigmund Freud's theories of mourning and melancholia and Judith Butler's elaboration of those theories.

In his volume *General Psychological Theories* Freud outlines two ways in which grief is expressed—mourning and melancholia—and adds that the mourning process is a "normal" response to the loss of a love object, whereas melancholia is pathological. He writes: "Mourning is regularly the reaction of the loss of a loved person, or to the loss of some abstraction which has taken the place of one, such as fatherland, liberty, and ideal and so on. As an effect of the same influences, melancholia instead of a state of grief develops in some people, whom we consequently suspect of a morbid pathological disposition."[1] Freud theorizes further that melancholia, as opposed to mourning, manifests in the unconscious as an unacknowledged loss of a love-object and therefore a refusal to grieve this loss. This refusal to grieve becomes part of the formation of the ego through a complex process of loss, denial, and identification. In other words, the melancholic "loses" the love-object and fails to acknowledge the loss, but then "digests" or incorporates the lost love-object into his or her psyche. This process of incorporation and identification is fraught with contention, however, because in the melancholic ego "countless single conflicts in which love and hate wrestle together are fought for the object; the one seeks to detach the libido from the object, the other to uphold this libido-position against assault" (177).

The ambivalence toward the love-object in the melancholic ego is the jumping-off point for Judith Butler's deployment of Freud to theorize heterosexual gender-identity formation. For Butler, the ungrieved love-object of heterosexuality is homosexuality. Thus, homosexuality becomes a site of identification and repudiation for the heterosexual. It is the very avowal and disavowal dynamic in melancholia that Butler sees as the founding scene of heterosexual gender formation. Heterosexual melancholy, then, is "the melancholy by which a masculine gender is formed from the refusal to grieve the masculine as a possibility of love."[2] Performance, specifically drag performance, is one instance in which Butler suggests that heterosexual melancholy is allegorized, for drag "exposes . . . the 'normal' constitution of gender presentation in which the gender performed is in many ways constituted by a set of disavowed attachments or identifications that constitute a different domain of the 'unperformable'" (236). Butler is motivated here by her need to make clear that she is not suggesting that all of the interworkings of gender are displayed through performance, for "the unconscious sets limits to the exteriorization of the psyche . . . [and also] what is exteriorized or performed can be understood only through reference to what is barred from the performance, what cannot or will not be performed."[3] Rather, drag performance enacts an "imitation of an imitation" of gender, in this case feminine gender.

There is, however, a dimension of Freud's theory of melancholia that Butler does not elaborate but that is useful for my purposes here. In Freud, the melancholic's "erotic cathexis of his object . . . undergoes a twofold fate: part of it regresses to identification, but the other part . . . is reduced to the stage of *sadism*."[4] Indeed, the melancholic receives gratification from such sadism directed toward the Other within, sadism that, in part, is due to his ambivalence toward the newly introjected love-object. As Anne Cheng suggests: "The melancholic's relationship to the object is now no longer just love or nostalgia but also profound resentment. The melancholic is not melancholic because he or she has lost something but because he or she has introjected that which he or she now reviles."[5] For reasons I will explain below, the sadistic dimension of heterosexual melancholy may explain the intensity of the homophobia inherent in black heterosexual male performances of black homosexuality.

The foregoing discussion of melancholia serves as both backdrop and context for the implicit psychoanalytic frame throughout the remainder of this chapter. Specifically, I focus on racial, gender, and sexual identification in/through the performance of that process. In this sense I construe performance broadly from literary production, stand-up comedy, and drag. As these modes of representations via performance are disseminated into popular culture, they affect intracultural politics among black Americans. Insofar as, in the words of Phillip Brian Harper, "debates over and claims to 'authentic' African–American identity are largely animated by a profound anxiety about the status specifically of African-American masculinity,"[6] this chapter discusses how and why the anxiety around black masculinity is symptomatic of heterosexual melancholia.

Through a close reading of performances by heterosexual black men such as Imamu Amiri Baraka (LeRoi Jones), Eldridge Cleaver,[7] Eddie Murphy, Damon Wayans, and David Alan Grier—all of whom deploy what Marlon Riggs refers to as "negro faggotry" to demean and disparage and ultimately exclude black gays from authentic blackness[8]—I wish to demonstrate how the black heterosexual male's repudiation of the feminine (read homosexual), according to Butler, "requires the very homosexuality that it condemns, not as its external object, but as its own most treasured source of sustenance."[9] The implications for such theorizing are, first, that black heterosexual men are always already "queered" because they enact (perform) the loss of the one for whom they cannot express desire; second, that despite the imperialism of heteronormativity in black culture it cannot disavow its queer palimpsests; and, finally, that black heteronormative constructions of masculinity as fixed signs of authentic blackness are deconstructed. My analysis here not only examines these black men's complicated personal relationships to homosexuality but, more important, how their performances raise larger questions about performance and authentic blackness.[10]

In all of their performances these men's target of ridicule is the effete black gay man. The representation of effeminate homosexuality as disempowering is at the heart of the politics of hegemonic blackness. For to be ineffectual is the most damaging thing one can be in the fight against oppression. Insofar as ineffectiveness is problematically sutured to femininity and homosexuality within a black cultural politic that privileges race over other categories of oppression, it follows that the subjects accorded these attributes would be marginalized and excluded from the boundaries of blackness. Despite the imperialism of heteronormativity in black culture, however, it cannot disavow the specter of the black fag within. Indeed, in Cheng's words, "the melancholic ego is formed and fortified by a spectral drama, whereby the subject sustains itself through the ghostly emptiness of a lost other."[11] Accordingly, my analysis examines how these black men's performances raise larger questions about racial, sexual, and gender identification.

Notes on a Native (Black) Man:
The Case of Eldridge Cleaver

In his 1968 Black Nationalist cult classic *Soul on Ice,* Eldridge Cleaver verbalizes his badge of honor, the credentials that, in his mind, rightfully position him as the authentic black man: "I'm perfectly aware that I'm in prison, that I'm a Negro, that I've been a rapist, and that I have a Higher Uneducation."[12] Given Cleaver's credentials, who could compete with his black or masculine authenticity? According to this logic, criminality (for good or naught, justified or unjustified), misogyny, sexism, and a general hatred of the white establishment (whom he implicitly indicts for his "uneducation") are the tenets of black masculinity and black authenticity. But it is not Cleaver's self-aggrandizement here, or elsewhere, in which I am interested. Rather, I am invested in a close reading of one particular chapter of *Soul on Ice* in which Cleaver openly expresses his homophobia and directs it toward black gay writer and cultural critic James Baldwin.

In the chapter "Notes of a Native Son," Cleaver begins his missive with a rhetorical performance par excellence, teasing the reader with what appears to be a humble admiration of James Baldwin's work:

> After reading a couple of James Baldwin's books, I began experiencing that continuous delight one feels upon discovering a fascinating, brilliant talent on the scene, a talent capable of penetrating so profoundly into one's own little world that one knows oneself to have been unalterably liberated, liberated from the frustrating grasp of whatever devils happen to possess one. Being a Negro, I have found this to be a rare and infrequent experience, for few of my black brothers and sisters here in America have achieved the power, which James Baldwin calls his revenge, which outlasts kingdoms: the power of doing whatever cats like Baldwin do when combining the alphabet with the volatile elements of his soul. (96)

After another paragraph of orgasmic praise (to which I shall return later), however, the reader soon discovers that the opening of the chapter was merely a ruse, a precursory decoy for what would inevitably become some of the most homophobic rhetoric ever to be written by one black writer about another. Indeed, Cleaver's missive not only undermines the quality of Baldwin's work based on its literary quality but on its "sycophantic love of the whites" as well. Cleaver writes: "There is in James Baldwin's work the most grueling, agonizing, total hatred of the blacks, particularly of himself, and the most shameful, fanatical, fawning, sycophantic love of the whites that one can find in the writings of any black American writer of note in our time" (97). In a moment that is no more over the top because of its hyperbole and drama than its outrageousness, Cleaver links Baldwin's "hatred of the blacks" and of himself to Baldwin's homosexuality. In Cleaver's twisted logic, Baldwin's homosexuality is symptomatic of a sickness (a white man's disease) that forestalls his (authentic) blackness and replaces it with what he terms a "racial death-wish" (101).

The association of homosexuality with disease and whiteness stems from both the racist stigmatization of black sexuality and blacks' response to it.[13] To the extent that homosexuality is equated with effeminacy or the feminine and whiteness with homosexuality, and given Cleaver's own admission of misogyny ("I've been a rapist"), it is not surprising that Cleaver's invective positions James Baldwin and black homosexuals in general as self-hating, effeminate pawns of white men. Cleaver writes:

> The black homosexual, when his twist has a racial nexus, is an extreme embodiment of this contradiction. The white man has deprived him of his masculinity, castrated him in the center of his burning skull, and when he submits to this change, and takes the white man for his lover as well as Big Daddy, he focuses on "whiteness" all the love in his pent up soul and turns the razor edge of hatred against "blackness"—upon himself, what he is, and all those who look like him, remind him of himself. He may even hate the darkness of night.
>
> The racial death-wish is manifested as the driving force in James Baldwin. His hatred of blacks, even as he pleads what he conceives as their cause, makes him the apotheosis of the dilemma in the ethos of the black bourgeoisie who have completely rejected their African heritage, consider the loss irrevocable, and refuse to look again in that direction. (101)

Cleaver makes it clear here that the black homosexual is not only a race traitor, but also a feminized version of a white man. Moreover, and more to the point I want to stress, Cleaver insists that middle-class status and homosexuality are unequivocally antiblack. Therefore, James Baldwin becomes a threat to black people: his homosexual "sickness" establishes him as a "white man in a black body," inauthentically black, as "the white man's most valuable tool in oppressing other blacks" (101).

It is even more interesting to note that Cleaver's definition of homosexuality is almost always couched in interracialist terms. He conflates interracial *homosocial* envy (i.e., the black man wanting what the white man has) with *homosexual* desire, as if to suggest that same-sex desire can only occur within an interracial context. Although some gay theorists have traced a genealogy of black homosexual subjectivity to the scene of sexual domination by white men of black men in slavery,[14] such logic forecloses the possibilities or even the significance of *intra*racial same-sex desire. If "black men loving black men is *the* revolutionary act," as Marlon Riggs has argued,[15] then does black same-race, same-sex desire still figure as a "racial death-wish"? Might Cleaver's silence about this possible coupling signal a denial of his own unspoken desire *for* Baldwin—a desire registered in the seductive language with which he begins the essay?

Let us return to the second paragraph of Cleaver's missive, which, I believe, reflects Cleaver's actual longing for the one for whom he cannot express his love. He writes:

> I, as I imagine many others did and still do, *lusted* for anything that Baldwin had written. It would have been a gas for me to *sit on a pillow beneath the womb of Baldwin's typewriter* and catch each newborn page as it entered this world of ours. I was delighted that Baldwin, *with those great big eyes of his*, which one thought to be fixedly focussed on the macrocosm, could also pierce the microcosm. And although he was so full of sound, he was not a noisy writer like Ralph Ellison. He placed so much of my own experience, which I thought I had understood, into new perspective.[16]

Rather than render an overdetermined "queer" reading of this passage, I think Cleaver's own words (queerly) speak for themselves. Indeed, here Cleaver chooses metaphors that clearly position him as the "sycophant," as he "lusts" after Baldwin's words. Moreover, although he feminizes Baldwin by comparing Baldwin's typewriter to a "womb," Cleaver also feminizes himself by imagining himself "[sitting] on a pillow beneath" that womb to "catch each newborn page as it entered this world of ours." Whether as midwife there to aid with "literary" birth or as homosexual lover feeling "those great big eyes" gaze upon him while he performs the cultural work of fellatio, Cleaver imagines intimate knowledge of Baldwin's inside parts.

Like a repressed homosexual who experiences panic after his first same-sex encounter, Cleaver is self-aware of the homoeroticism evoked in this passage and he immediately tries to assuage its visceral effect by registering reservations about Baldwin's writing after having studied it more intently. Ironically, his reprieve only calls more attention to the fact that there is something *in* Baldwin that Cleaver desires: "Gradually, however, I began to feel uncomfortable about something in Baldwin. I was disturbed upon becoming aware of an aversion in my heart to part of the song he sang. Why this was so, I was unable at first to say. Then I read *Another Country,* and knew why my love for Baldwin's vision had become ambivalent" (97). Cleaver's use of the word "ambivalent" here is telling, for it names explicitly not only his once-purported love for Baldwin's "vision" but also for Baldwin himself, which makes Cleaver's discourse around "self-hatred" all the more ironic. He writes: "Self-hatred takes many forms; sometimes it can be detected by no one, not by the keenest observer, not by the self-hater himself, not by his most intimate friends" (99). Although Cleaver is referring to self-hatred in racial terms, it would not be a far leap to read these words as sexual self-hatred, namely his own. My point here is not to "out" Cleaver as a homosexual; instead, I wish to demonstrate the process by which black masculinity secures its power by repudiating the (homosexual) Other, and how that repudiation ironically conjoins masculine gender identification with (homo)sexual identification. In other words, Cleaver's disavowal of Baldwin and his (homo)sexuality fails to banish the homosexual or call his validity into question as much as it secures its copresence. Homophobic repudiation becomes unspoken homosexual desire.

In less theoretical terms, former Black Panther Party leader Huey P. Newton also describes Cleaver's "hatred" of Baldwin as repressed desire. In a May 1973 interview in *Playboy Magazine,* Newton suggests that Cleaver's attack on Baldwin is motivated by Cleaver's own "shaky sexual identity." Newton candidly shares his reading of Cleaver:

> I think Eldridge is so insecure that he has to assert his masculinity by destroying those he respects. . . . It's a very self-destructive thing; he probably hates himself very much. I think Eldridge has to be understood as

a disturbed personality rather than as a serious political problem. In a book I'm now writing . . . I make a long analysis of his book *Soul on Ice* and his attack on James Baldwin. Baldwin is a homosexual, and Eldridge finds it necessary to make a vicious attack upon him for this reason. [It] has always struck me that a male who goes out of his way to attack another male because of his sexual relations must have a psychological fear that he, too, might not be so masculine.[17]

Although Newton's ontological link of homosexuality with effeminacy is problematic, he aptly calls attention to the fact that Cleaver's motivation for attacking Baldwin stems from an unexpressed anxiety over Cleaver's own masculinity and sexuality. He also theorizes that Cleaver's participation in the Black Panther Party and his obsession with guns was an attempt to "prove" his masculinity and assuage his homosexual desires. Newton states, "I think the gun was a substitute for his penis; he called it his 'rod.' That's what the party meant to him: a masculine kind of demonstration that he needed in order to reinforce his very shaky sexual identity" (84). According to Newton, then, the gun became a phallic symbol through which Cleaver could register his masculinity and, I would add, his blackness.

In perhaps the most provocative section of his interview, Newton shares a story in which he says that Cleaver's attraction to Baldwin was made tangible through a kiss. Newton recalls:

Well, there was something that happened on the occasion when he and I met Baldwin. We met Baldwin shortly after he returned from Turkey, I guess in 1966 or the early part of '67. Eldridge had been invited to a party to meet him, and he asked me to go along. So we went over to San Francisco in his Volkswagen van and we got there first. Soon after, Baldwin arrived. . . . Baldwin just walked over to him and embraced him around the waist. And Eldridge leaned down from his full height and engaged Baldwin in a long, passionate French kiss. They kissed each other on the mouth for a long time. When we left, Eldridge kept saying, "Don't tell anyone." I said all right. And I kept my word—until now.

I didn't understand it at the time, but now I realize that Baldwin, who hadn't written a word in response to Cleaver's attack on him, had finally spoken at that meeting. Using nonverbal communication, he had dramatically exposed Cleaver's internal ambivalence. (84)

Besides being an explosive bit of gossip, Newton's recollection of the events at this party become rich fodder for discussion of Eldridge

Cleaver's anxiety regarding his relationship to James Baldwin, race, gender, and sexuality.[18] Given the chronology of events, it becomes clear why Cleaver felt no guilt about publishing "Notes of a Native Son" prior to his meeting Baldwin in the flesh, as it were. For from the safe distance of his "mourned" Other, Cleaver, in his attempt to secure his own heterosexuality and blackness and, perhaps, to deny his own homosexuality, projected this angst "onto an external self—Baldwin —in order to defend his own threatened ego."[19] Cleaver's disavowal of Baldwin's homosexuality in "Notes of a Native Son," then, is actually symptomatic of Cleaver's guilt about his ungrieved homosexuality. According to Butler, "in opposition to a conception of sexuality which is said to 'express' a gender, gender itself is here understood to be composed of precisely what remains inarticulate in sexuality." She continues: "If we understand gender melancholy in this way, then perhaps we can make sense of the peculiar phenomenon whereby homosexual desire becomes a source of guilt."[20]

Viewed in this light, Cleaver's rhetorical performance in "Notes of a Native Son" actually articulates "what remains inarticulate in [his] sexuality." In other words, rather than suturing his heterosexuality to his masculinity and blackness, he actually unhinges this ontology in his repudiation of Baldwin, only the repudiation is a decoy for what lies elsewhere—deferred (unconsciously?) until sealed, made manifest, with a kiss. Indeed, in *Soul on Ice* Cleaver speaks the love that dare not speak its name in the very act of not speaking. This occurs, however, in the *absence* of his mourned Other—Baldwin, the homosexual. On the other hand, Baldwin's silence, both about Cleaver's attack and during their encounter, functions differently in that his "nonverbal communication," and mere presence, make manifest Cleaver's faggotry—queering not only the event (the actual one and Newton's recollection of it) but Cleaver's masculinity and blackness as well.[21]

Baraka's Hell:
The Changing Same in Imamu Amiri Baraka

As a product of the 1960s Black Arts movement, LeRoi Jones-*cum*-Imamu Amiri Baraka was no less virulently homophobic and sexist than Eldridge Cleaver. Although, according to Phillip Brian Harper,

Baraka "can certainly be seen as the founder of the Black Aesthetic of the 1960s,"[22] the rhetoric of his poetry, fiction, and nonfiction inheres masculinity and heterosexuality to authentic blackness in troubling ways. Again, like Cleaver, Baraka's invectives do not cohere outside the double bluff of gender and sexual masquerade. While Baraka's rhetoric necessitates the founding of blackness on heterosexual masculinity and portrays whiteness as haunted by homosexual effeminacy, his work also reveals how his necessity to eschew homosexuality actually activates the queering of (his own) blackness. In his essay "American Sexual Reference: Black Male," for instance, Baraka espouses the whiteness = effeminacy = homosexuality = antiblackness equation in the first full paragraph: "Most American white men are trained to be fags. For this reason it is no wonder their faces are weak and blank, left without the hurt that reality makes—anytime. That red flush, those silk blue faggot eyes."[23] The training those white men acquire on their road to being "fags," we must assume, stems from their privileged position in the world. What is interesting to note, however, is how Baraka, like Cleaver, in his attempt to secure his black masculinity and heterosexuality, must disavow whiteness. In so doing, however, he recapitulates Butler's gender melancholy theory in racial terms. In other words, Baraka can be a masculine heterosexual black male if and only if he has an effeminate white homosexual Other against which to supplant his subjectivity.[24] It is no wonder, then, that Baraka sees the black homosexual as the penultimate embodiment and site of political capitulation and antiblack sentiment, for "insufficient racial identification," according to Phillip Brian Harper, is "figured specifically in terms of a failed manhood for which homosexuality, as always, was the primary signifier."[25] In "Civil Rights Poem," for instance, Baraka takes then NAACP leader Roy Wilkins to task about his ineffectualness, which is measured, according to Baraka, in terms of Wilkins's "faggot" status:

> Roywilkins is an eternal faggot
> His spirit is a faggot
> his projection
> and image, this is
> to say, that if I ever see roywilkins
> on the sidewalks

imonna
stick half my sandal
up his ass[26]

Although the poem implicitly indicates Baraka's dissatisfaction with Wilkins's leadership, the poem fails, curiously, to state explicitly Baraka's motivation for such a homophobic attack. Harper provides an explanation for such an omission: "So well understood was the identification between inadequacies of manhood and black consciousness in the Black Arts context that this poem needed never render explicit the grounds for its judgment of NAACP leader Roy Wilkins, for the perceived racial-political moderation of both him and his organization clearly bespoke his unforgivable 'faggotry.'"[27]

Interpellating Wilkins as the composite "faggot," however, only breeds suspicion about Baraka's own gender and sexual anxiety. Although the violent homophobic rhetoric of the poem is palpable, therein lies a homoerotic desire, the sodomitical image of "stick[ing] half [his] sandal" up Wilkins's ass. The implied rape evoked by the image palliates this desire, however. "Sticking" a phallic foot up Wilkins's ass implies Baraka will service him forcefully. Thus, the sex, regardless of if it's "homosexual" or not, evinces a dominator/dominated, top/bottom discourse that positions Baraka as the "masculine" dominater/top and Wilkins as the "feminine" dominated/bottom.

In other work by Baraka, the homosexual is less an object of scorn and ridicule and more the site of ambivalent sexual identity for Baraka himself. Ron Simmons persuasively argues that Baraka's pseudoautobiographical novel, *The System of Dante's Hell,* explains Baraka's homophobia in his later work, suggesting that it stems from anxiety regarding his own sexual and gender identity. Simmons writes:

Perhaps it is the homosexual desires Baraka had as an adolescent and young adult that motivate his homophobia. His homosexual desires are not revealed in *The Autobiography of LeRoi Jones.* No, to truly understand the paradox of Baraka's need to denounce faggots while at the same time suppressing his attraction, one must read an autobiographical novel he wrote some twenty years earlier, *The System of Dante's Hell.* It is a story many gay brothers can relate to. After reading it, one's anger toward

Baraka's homophobia is replaced with sympathy. We understand the pain and the fear.[28]

Simmons then provides excerpts from *The System of Dante's Hell* that substantiate his claims. In one particular passage from the novel, the first-person narrator recounts a homosexual encounter with a preacher under the train tracks in Chicago:

> In Chicago I kept making the queer scene. Under the "El" with a preacher. And later, in the rotogravure, his slick (this other, larger, man, like my father) hair, murrays grease probably. He had a grey suit with gold and blue threads and he held my head under the quilt. The first guy . . . spoke to me grinning and I said my name was Stephen Dedalus. . . . One more guy and it was over. On the train, I wrote all this down. A journal now sitting in a tray on top the closet, where I placed it today. The journal says "Am I like *that*?"[29]

Based on close readings of passages such as this, as well as poems from Baraka's poetry collection titled *Black Magic,* Simmons "proves" Baraka's homosexual desires if not his actual homosexuality. For my purposes, however, I am invested less in the "fact" of Baraka's homosexuality per se, as gleaned from his fiction and nonfiction, as I am engaged by his discursive performance of problack rhetoric vis-à-vis black masculinity and heterosexuality and how that performance redoubles to expose the queering of black masculinity. Baraka's putative heterosexuality and (black) masculinity notwithstanding, imbedded within the rhetorical logic of his work is an unspoken queerness that manifests precisely at the moment its silence is supposedly guaranteed. Put slightly differently, Baraka's heterosexual identity subsists through the continual sustenance that his homosexual disavowal provides. This might explain why the reader is not blind to the specter of the queer in Baraka's writing. His writing embodies heterosexual melancholy, the loss of the one for whom he can never have. Ironically, faggotry is made manifest through heterosexual designs of living. Ultimately, this dialectic rescues blackness from the confines of the heterosexual matrix, queering it, as it were, against its will.

Manifest Faggotry

Murphy's Law: Eddie Murphy and the Fag Within

The 1960s Black Nationalist and Black Arts movements provided the cultural backdrop for the establishment of blackness as antigay. Although there was a lull in homophobic discourse in popular culture during the 1970s (primarily due to the activism of lesbians of color who were forcing the white heterosexual women's movement to address its racism and homophobia)[30] the 1980s saw the resurgence of antigay sentiment. The reemergence of much of this misogyny and homophobia was largely the result of the Reagan-led conservatism of the White House, and there was a general backlash against the social and economic strides made by women, witnessed in the plethora of Hollywood films in the late 1980s and early 1990s (e.g., *Fatal Attraction* and *The Hand That Rocks the Cradle*) that demonized the independent, single working woman as "deranged."[31] An uncomplicated return to heterosexual "family values" was the sentiment that automatically marginalized those outside the heteronormative sphere of family, including gays and lesbians and single working women or single parents. In addition, HIV/AIDS had begun to ravish gay communities around the country: black gay men represented 23 percent of the total number of AIDS cases reported in 1991, even though black males "accounted for less than 6 percent of the total U.S. population."[32] Because of the lack of knowledge about the disease, the swiftness with which it killed, and the fact that it was disproportionately affecting gay men, HIV/AIDS fueled the antigay discourse already emerging and it became fodder for the far Right to justify their homophobia and name AIDS a "gay" disease.[33]

Given this cultural landscape, it was only a matter of time that the hegemony of homophobia and heterosexism would become imbricated in the fabric of popular culture. Indeed, the imperialism of heteronormativity was ubiquitous. From television, billboard, and magazine ads to sitcoms and Hollywood films to stand-up comedy routines, the representation of heterosexuality reiterated and performed the cultural logic of the American dream: a household with two parents, two children, a pet, and a white picket fence.[34] Representations of homosexuals only reinforced the myth of heterosexuality as morally superior, and also further delineated the boundaries of blackness.

The popularity of comedian Eddie Murphy in the early 1980s was no doubt fueled by the pervasive antigay, profamily sentiment of that era. Thus, Murphy's audiences were primed not only for the limp-wristed sissies of his films but also for the general homophobia of his stand-up comedy routines, including the irresponsible miseducation about how AIDS is contracted. Only in a society where hatred of the sexual dissident is tolerated and encouraged would such bigotry be commodified and sold as "entertainment."

Although Murphy had made Negro faggotry popular through his parodies of Little Richard on *Saturday Night Live,* it was not until *Delirious,* his 1983 live performance at Constitution Hall in Washington, D.C. (which first aired on Home Box Office), that his homophobia congealed into an insidious heteronormative hegemony. Murphy opens his performance with the words cited in the epigraph at the beginning of this chapter: "I'm afraid of gay people." He then proceeds to articulate the reasons for his "fear," one of which is the fear of catching AIDS. Murphy says, "Girls hang out with them [the gays], and one night they're having fun and they give them a little kiss and they go home with AIDS on their lips."[35] Besides irresponsibly giving false information about how AIDS is contracted, Murphy's comment obscures the agency of presumably "straight" men in contracting HIV/AIDS by placing the origin of the disease with gay men and heterosexual women as the transporters of contagion.[36] As discussed in chapter 1, this particular kind of discursive ploy attributes gayness with sickness and immorality, associations commonly accorded gays and lesbians prior to the HIV/AIDS epidemic. In fact, Murphy's comments echo Cleaver's language about the Negro homosexual's "death-wish," as well as other afrocentrists who proffer homosexuality as a "white disease" that has infiltrated the black community.[37]

Despite an outcry of criticism from parts of the gay community and Murphy's subsequent "apologies" ("I want to apologize to the gay people—I've never really apologized. And to anyone else who's been offended by any kind of things I've done"),[38] Murphy went on to include another homophobic routine in his 1987 film, *Raw.* In *Raw,* Murphy goes beyond espousing homophobic commentary to actually embodying a "gay" person as a vehicle for his denigration of homosexuality. He draws an uproarious laugh from the audience when performing this routine. In the sketch, Murphy draws on the fact that he has "pissed some gay people off" with his comedy and that they are "looking" for him. Murphy apes a mob of effeminate gay men whose "radar" detects his arrival at the airport:[39] "He's here," he says with a lisp. As he's driving down the freeway, Murphy hears a siren and thinks that the police are trailing him. When he looks into his rearview mirror, however, he discovers that rather than a siren on top of the police car it is actually a "faggot" on the roof of the car, making a lasso motion with one arm while holding a megaphone in the other, screaming in a high-pitched voice, "pull ovah, pull ovah."[40]

In this performance Murphy—clad, ironically, in feminizing tight, lavender leather pants that prominently feature the ass he so desperately wants to hide from the faggots in his audience ("Faggots aren't allowed to look at my ass while I'm on stage. That's why I keep moving. You don't know where the faggot section is.")[41]—camps up the performance by embodying this gay persona, pretending to be on top of the police car as the queeny "siren." The punchline of the joke, which, incidentally, perpetuates the myth of the sex-crazed homosexual who wants nothing more than to fuck, comes when the gay cop commands Murphy to "spread 'em," and commences to feel up his crotch and ass.

Based on these and other performances, Eddie Murphy understandably garnered a reputation as homophobic. Despite his justifications ("I poke fun at everybody, 'cause I'm not a racist, I'm not a sexist; I'm just out there"),[42] Murphy's persistent homophobic performances created a tension between him and the gay community, leading him in 1996 to officially apologize for his homophobic routines, some fifteen years after the fact.[43] Moreover, because of the venomous nature of the routines and because of Murphy's seemingly intimate knowledge of gay codes and vernacular and his performer competence as gay characters, rumors began to emerge about Murphy's own sexuality. These rumors suggested that his homophobia was actually a projection of his own repressed homosexuality. Although Murphy's homosexuality was never confirmed and the gossip about his homosexuality diminished when he married and fathered four (now five) children with his wife, Nicole, the rumors resurfaced in May 1997 when he was pulled over by sheriff's deputies in West Hollywood (known, incidentally, as the "gay ghetto" of Los Angeles) after observing a transsexual prostitute get into his car. Subsequently, the transsexual was arrested on an outstanding warrant for prostitution charges, while Murphy was released. According to his spokesperson, "Murphy had trouble sleeping . . . felt restless and decided to drive to a newsstand. After leaving the newsstand, Murphy spotted someone who appeared to be 'having a problem.' The star stopped his vehicle to see if the person was all right. At that time, the individual asked Murphy for a ride, and he agreed."[44]

The irony of these events, particularly given Murphy's "gay cop" skit, is remarkable. Murphy is "hailed" and interpellated in multiple ways in this scenario. First, he is interpellated as the socially constituted subject bound to the law in that moment of hailing by the state—"Hey you!"[45] This representation of such a hailing is common in narratives of black male experience regarding police harassment and the inability to "hail" a cab based on gendered racism.[46] Murphy is also constituted as a potential "trick" for the transsexual prostitute, and, finally, he is constructed as "rescuer" to the same transsexual prostitute whom he perceives as "having a problem." These bizarre and intricate machinations demonstrate the complexity of identity claims as experienced, performed, and proclaimed. It is not, however, of interest to me here whether or not, for instance, Eddie Murphy's being "caught" with a transsexual prostitute in lieu of his homophobic comedy routines, marriage to a woman, and status as a father provide "proof" of his repressed homosexuality in the fashion of "thou dost protest too much." I only draw attention to these events to once again demonstrate the coextensive dialectic between black masculinity, heterosexuality, and homosexuality.[47]

Indeed, if Murphy's performances, especially his stand-up comedy routines, are scrutinized further, we discover that the homophobic tirades reveal more about the leakage of black heterosexuality and masculinity than they do about their fixity. Insofar as Murphy's parody of gayness is a kind of drag performance, a hyperbolic effeminacy associated with homosexuality, his attempt to solidify his own masculinity and heterosexuality merely reiterates their malleability. For, contrary to what Murphy's parodies imply (and the purpose he no doubt believes them to serve), gender and sexuality are discursive categories that cohere to no original. Rather, gender parody and, by extension, sexuality is parody "*of* the very notion of an original";[48]

therefore, his parody of the effeminate gay man reveals not the "fact" of masculine heterosexuality or effeminate homosexuality but rather, paradoxically, the incoherence of originary gender and sexual identity formations in general. Although Murphy's parodies do reinstall hegemonic notions of gender and masculinity within the context of heterosexual popular discourse, outside those contexts they signify differently and thus may work against such heteronormative logic, as is the case in gay communities in which the parody is offensive but also manifests as fodder for speculations about Murphy's queerness.[49]

The contexts of Murphy's performances are multiple and complicated because of his status as a popular cultural icon. Heterosexual black audiences receive him very differently than do white heterosexual audiences or do black or white, male or female homosexual audiences, and hence his homophobic discourse reverberates and signifies in dramatically different ways. If volunteerism plays no role in the process of gender performativity and sexual identity, then, Murphy's intentions notwithstanding, his parodic performances of the effete gay man reveal heterosexuality for the sham that it is—a "phantasmatic identification," in the words of Judith Butler.[50] In Murphy's performances, and perhaps in Murphy himself, the image of the black queer emerges in spite of the continual attempts of its murder at the hands of his heterosexual Other.

"Hated It": Faggotry in Living Color

When comedians are challenged on their insensitivity toward a particular group, they most often justify their bigoted comedy by rationalizing that they, like Eddie Murphy, "poke fun at everyone," as if blanket sexism, homophobia, and prejudice is somehow justifiable. The same can be said of the cast of the now defunct but recently syndicated Fox Network comedy *In Living Color*. Produced and directed by Keenan Ivory Wayans, *In Living Color* is a comedy variety show that was successful during its run in the late 1980s and early 1990s. The show's success, according to Herman Gray, stemmed "from its ability to appeal to audiences across a very broad gulf of racial, class, gender, and sexual difference."[51]

Although the show featured a number of parodic gender performances, including the "Wanda, the Ugly Woman" skits in which a very unattractive drag queen played by actor Jamie Fox constantly scared men away because of "her" looks and sexual aggressiveness, the most popular gender and sexuality parody was called "Men On. . . ." In this skit, heterosexual black comedians Damon Wayans and David Alan Grier portray, respectively, Blaine Edwards and Antoine Meriwether, two effeminate men who wear flashy chiffon blouses, tight pants, hair poufs, and feathered slippers. Because they never explicitly state that they are gay, their pseudodrag garb along with their effete mannerisms are meant to signify the "gayness" of the characters. Blaine and Antoine review films, books, and other texts in a manner similar to film critics Gene Siskel and Roger Ebert. However, instead of giving the films a "thumbs up" or "thumbs down," the two invent an appropriate SNAP!, a nonverbal communicative action once popular among black gay men that literally consists of snapping the fingers.[52] In fact, much of this skit's popularity was due to the anticipation by the audience of what the SNAP! for the week would be.

Blaine and Antoine act out "gayness" in a stereotypical fashion and demonstrate random misogyny when they review works by or for women. Indeed, when they feature films in which women star or show products designed for women, they reply in unison, "Hated it." On the other hand, when they review works by men or those that feature a male star, they deliver a favorable review infused with sexual innuendo. It is not surprising that the skit's theme song is "It's Raining Men," a popular song in gay nightclubs. The following is an excerpt from one of the skits:

Blaine: Hi. I'm Blaine Edwards.
Antoine: And I'm Antoine Meriwether.
Together: Welcome to "Men on Film."
Antoine: The show that looks at movies from a male point of view. Tonight we'll be wrapping up the summer films. First up is the box office smash, *Total Recall.*
Blaine: Yes. This is the movie where muscle-bound Arnold Schwarzenegger goes in search of his past. (looks at camera) Just a hint Arnold: Try the closet! (laughs) Next we have *Betsy's Wedding.*
Together: (looking at each other) Hated it!
Antoine: Then there's *Ghost.* You know, Patrick Swayze was the *real* standout in this film. You know, I'd breathe life into his spirit any day—

Manifest Faggotry

Blaine and Antoine promote "Hungry Men Dinners"
as one the sponsors of their show, "Men On . . ."
from *In Living color.*

even if I did have to go through Whoopi Goldberg! (rolling his eyes)
Perish the thought.
Blaine: Yes, indeed. Now we come to *Dick Tracy.*
Antoine: You know, I like the title, but the movie just left me limp.
Blaine: I know what you're saying. This is what I don't get: all the char-
acters fit their names—you know, Flat Head had a flattop, Prune Face
looked just like a little prune, but I never did get a chance to see . . .
Antoine: Ooh. It's gettin' hot in here! Then there's *Pretty Woman.*
Together: Hated it!
Blaine: This one should have been called "A Fish Called Julia."
Antoine: Next, Eddie Murphy was back in *Another 48 Hours.* You know,
I'm sorry. This movie just got off on the wrong track. I feel that they
should have spent more time where the real story is: in the prisons.
I'd like to see more about them old sweaty mens all together in them
tiny little cells with no one to turn to but each other.
Blaine: Ooh. Drop the soap—I'll pick it up! (laughs)
Antoine: Hush! Finally, we have *Die Harder.* What a way to go: ninety
minutes with Mr. Bruce Willis.
Blaine: Oh yes! Don't tempt my tummy with the taste of Nuts-n-Honey.
(laughs) You know the thing I didn't understand was all the violence
in the film, 'cause the title suggested a love story.
Antoine: I second that emotion. I think this one still deserves the new
and improved two snaps up, a twist, and a kiss. (the two perform the

snaps and twist, move their heads toward one another, pause, and look
at the camera)
Together: Not! Can't touch this![53]

This parody stereotypes all gays as "queeny" and promiscuous
in addition to perpetuating the myth that all gay men are woman
haters. Within this context and within this parodic form, however, the
misogyny becomes hyperbolic, further perpetuating the myth that
woman hating and homosexuality are enjoined. In stating his dis-
taste for *In Living Color,* Ron Simmons reiterates how this particular skit imbricates homosexuality and misogyny: "People assume that
gay men don't like women. Whenever 'Men On . . .' critiques a female
work, they say, 'Hated it.' That's a running joke. A country that's
known for females they hate. A book about females they hate. A movie
about females they hate. They had the audacity to call a black woman a
'fish' in a recent segment."[54] There is more than one disavowal at work
here. Beyond the disavowal of homosexuality there is an attempt to
displace the responsibility of all black male misogyny onto gay men.
Given the rabid sexism and misogyny espoused by some of the most
preeminent black heterosexual leaders of the black community, it is
incredible that black heterosexual men would disingenuously project
the responsibility of all misogyny onto black gay men, especially in
light of black homophobia and its relation to the devaluation of femininity. Placed within the larger context of black cultural politics, this
displacement and the skit in general may reflect a general anxiety over
the status of black masculinity spawned by the social and political
gains of black women and homosexuals, as well as a growing body of
theoretical critiques of black male dominance. Herman Gray suggests
that "the sketches may even reaffirm masculine heterosexual power
(and hostility) in relationship to, if not gay men, then growing interro-
gations and critiques of masculinity by black feminists, lesbians, and
gay men."[55]

To "get" the double entendres imbedded in Blaine and Antoine's exchanges one must have knowledge of black gay culture, both as it is
constructed and lived by black gay men themselves and as it is stereo-
typed by heterosexuals. Indeed, this particular skit's success depends
on what I would call an epistemology of misogynistic homophobia.
That is, the skit caters to its audiences' homophobic stereotypes of

black gay men, a homophobia grounded in misogyny. For instance, Blaine's interest in *Dick Tracy* is fueled by the "dick" he hopes to see in the film, furthering homophobic beliefs that black gay men are dick obsessed. Blaine also reviles actress Julia Roberts by calling her a "fish," a derogatory term for a woman that refers to the supposedly "fishy" smell of women's vaginas while menstruating. Thus, the character relies on this misogynistic knowledge to draw a laugh. Blaine's final comment of the skit also relies on the epistemology of homophobia in that it images gay men as lascivious dick suckers who enjoy the taste of and swallowing semen ("Don't tempt my tummy with the taste of Nuts-n-Honey"). Further, Antoine's desire that *Another 48 Hours* focus more on prison, where the "real story is," followed by Blaine's comment about bending over in the prison shower to pick up soap, perpetuates the myth that homosexuality stems from "prison breeding," a myth often espoused by black heterosexual Afrocentrists such as Molefi Asante and contemporary Black Nationalist leaders such as Louis Farrakhan.[56] All of these sexual innuendos, then, rely on a homophobic epistemology in order to get a laugh. In so doing, the skit attempts to further pathologize homosexuality as perverted, abnormal, and antiblack.[57]

Because femininity is always already devalued in patriarchal societies, those associated with the feminine are also viewed as inferior. Given the ways in which effeminacy in men is read as a sign of homosexuality, particularly in the United States, it follows that homosexual men are devalued. As bell hooks suggests: "Much black male homophobia is rooted in the desire to eschew connection with all things deemed 'feminine' and that would, of course, include black gay men."[58] Drawing on this logic, then, Wayans and Grier's performances, like those of Cleaver, Baraka, and Murphy, work to signify black masculinity and heterosexuality as authentic and black homosexuality as trivial, ineffectual, and, indeed, inauthentic. Although Wayans and Grier perform in drag, a potentially subversive critique of essentialist gender identity, their parodic performance must be viewed within the context of compulsory heterosexuality and hegemonic masculinity that depends on the disavowal of homosexuality for its coherence. Through parody, these heterosexual males assume a symbolic distance from femininity and homosexuality but, as Carole Anne Tyler suggests, "when roles are already alienated and unreal, the problem may not be how one holds them at a distance but how one responds to that distance."⁵⁹

These performers' response to that distance is disavowal and re-pudiation. The fact that the performers refuse to kiss at the end of the skit is illustrative of this point. Indeed, the characters stop short of kissing because such an act would subvert the parody, for "real" men in drag don't kiss. The act of moving toward each other "as if" they were to kiss but stopping short provides a homoerotic image by titil-lating the audience but then reminding it that this is "play" through refusing to kiss and saying, "Not! Can't touch this." "This" in this con-text refers to homosexuality vis-à-vis a "homosexual" (same-sex kiss-ing) act. Engaging in such activity would be too risky, for it might call into question the performers' "real" masculinity and sexual orienta-tion. Clearly, Wayans and Grier experience some anxiety about their performance of homosexuality when they refuse to "touch this," thus attempting to regulate their sexuality by "policing and shaming" femi-nine gender.

The same disavowal occurs in another skit in which Blaine is hit over the head, which causes him to lose his memory—especially the fact that he is gay. This particular sketch was a "to be continued . . ." episode to keep viewers on edge to see what would happen to Blaine and Antoine's relationship and their reviews. After the blow to the head, Blaine is repulsed by his drag garb and dresses more "like a man." Moreover, much to Antoine's chagrin, when they review films during this episode Blaine registers desire for women, often com-menting on their breasts. In their review of Madonna's pseudodocu-mentary *Truth or Dare,* for instance, Antoine focuses his attention on one of Madonna's dancers, Olivier, whom he compels to come out of the closet. Blaine responds accordingly: "I didn't look at Olivier very much, but I think Madonna is pretty hot. I could forget truth or dare. I'd like to play spin the bottle. Did you see the way she wrapped her lips around that bottle, Man?" Horrified by Blaine's response to Ma-donna (a response which, ironically, objectifies her), Antoine picks up a brick and hits Blaine over the head in hopes that it will bring back the "gay" Blaine. After the strike fails to "make him gay again," Blaine says to Antoine in a masculine posture: "That's it, man. I'm going to bust your ass. Come on, give me your best shot." Antoine then "punches" Blaine and then looks for a "sign" that he's gay again. Blaine's posture changes, he cups his hands to his mouth and squeals, "Tony?" The two embrace and Blaine proclaims, "I'm free, I'm free," while Antoine calls others to come join in the celebration of the return of "gay" Blaine. The others are clad in leather, short cut-off jeans, and other stereotypical gay garb as they dance to "It's Raining Men."

Like the other "Men On . . ." skits, this one has the potential to subvert essentialist notions of gender and sexual identifications. In fact, this particular sketch calls attention to the fact that gender and sexuality is performative in that one may "switch" back and forth between genders and sexualities with just a bump on the head. The subversive potential is thwarted, however, by the reinstallation of hegemonic heterosexuality. In other words, the representation of heterosexuality and homosexuality remain fastened to essentialist notions of masculinity and femininity. When Blaine "loses" his homosexuality, for instance, he no longer displays signs of femininity. Alternatively, when he "turns" gay again, his femininity also returns.

Germane to this discussion is the fact that masculinity as performed by Blaine is not as spectacular as femininity, which implies that masculinity is the more robust of the genders. In addition, as a "straight" man Blaine registers no interest in things remotely feminine or even homoerotic—clothes, speech, mannerisms, good-looking men—but rather eschews those signifiers in order to establish the seriousness of hegemonic masculinity. What presented itself as an occasion to imagine a broader continuum of stylized black masculinity became instead another instance of black masculine hegemony. Commenting on this vicious cycle of black machismo, Cornel West writes: "Black gay men are often the brunt of talented black comics like Arsenio Hall and Damon Wayans. Yet behind the laughs lurks a black tragedy of major proportions: the refusal of white and black America to entertain seriously new stylistic options for black men caught in the deadly endeavor of rejecting black machismo identities."[60]

Moreover, because of Damon Wayans's iconic status as a "macho" character actor (established in films like *The Last Boy Scout*) his "straight" Blaine only reconsolidates and congeals the heterosexualized masculine persona that circulates in popular culture. Thus, this template of "true" black masculine identity becomes the vehicle through which to measure the "gay" Blaine's inauthentic gender and sexual identity. This process is accomplished because of the cultural authority that Wayans's public persona barters. Indeed, as Herman Gray suggests, "play and performance" of effeminacy "is very much the point, because audiences are also mindful that it is black heterosexual men who perform these roles."[61]

Thus, rather than serve as a critique of essentialist notions of gender and sexual identification, in the context of an already hostile, antigay black culture these parodies discredit gayness as a "legitimate" signifier of blackness. Marlon Riggs argues that the skits perpetuate homophobic discourse about black gays beyond the boundaries of black culture such that Negro faggotry becomes the model through which black homosexuality is understood:

["Men On . . ." offers] an image of queens who function in a way that justifies all of the very traditional beliefs about black gay sexuality and allows a larger public—beyond gay and lesbian people—to box gay people into this category that allows them to deal with them by not really dealing with them. . . . [The show] plays into a notion of black *gay* sexuality held by the black community . . . [that is] now being embraced by the larger dominant community. A notion that black gay men are sissies, ineffectual, ineffective, womanish in a way that signifies inferiority rather than empowerment.[62]

Although the intent and the effect of these skits is one of perpetuating stereotypical representations of black gay men and of reifying hegemonic masculinity and heterosexuality, queering still occurs. Gray suggests, for instance, that most of the skits that appear on *In Living Color* are informed by a politics of ambivalence because of the show's "preoccupation with these themes [race, class, gender, and sexuality] of difference, and the disturbances they produce within but also outside blackness."[63] While the "potential to politicize its disturbances . . . is at the heart of the show's critical possibilities," Gray argues, "the show's disturbance is often ambivalent and, at times, even reactionary" (140). Regarding the "Men On . . ." skit, Gray believes that although it is "a kind of public acknowledgement, contestation, and renegotiation of blackness, especially in terms in which masculinity, sexuality, desire, and identity have been figured in commercial culture," the skit is nonetheless "anchored by the politics of ambivalence, because the particular discursive space within which the contestation of sexuality occurs in the show is still mediated by the privileged position that black heterosexual masculinity enjoys" (142).

Gray's insightful reading of "Men On . . ." predicates the skit's ambivalent politics on the privileged positioning of the black heterosexual performers in a move that suggests that the skit's transgressive possibilities are undermined by the heterosexual authority of the performers. I would like to suggest, however, that the "ambivalence" of the skit, as it were, stems not *only* from the performers' "proclaimed" or "visible" gender and sexuality, but also from the discursive redoubling that occurs within the space of their performance. In other words, in their attempt to stabilize their own masculinity and heterosexuality through the disavowal of homosexuality and effeminacy vis-à-vis "drag" performance, Wayans and Grier's masculinity and heterosexuality is actually queered in the very act of disavowal. For drag performance, as Butler has argued, actually allegorizes the very process by which "the masculine gender is formed from the refusal to grieve the masculine as a possibility of love."[64] When viewed from this perspective, then, Wayans and Grier's black masculine heterosexual "privilege" as a site of stability paradoxically becomes a site of instability.

In sum, "Men On . . ." is an ambivalent discourse insofar as it problematically reduces homosexuality to Negro faggotry at the same time that it calls into question essentialist notions of gender and sexual identification, particularly in the episode where Blaine "loses" his gayness. But the heuristic circle through which this ambivalence obtains is not closed. Gray himself suggests that "whatever one thinks of *In Living Color* and its particular treatment of black gay men, the reading of its cultural politics must not simply stop at or remain within the closed system of the text."[65] Indeed, yet another redoubling occurs beyond the text whereby the drag parody reiterates the logic of loss, the mourning of the sexual Other—a logic that ironically queers the one for whom the love of the homosexual is impossible.

Other paradoxes abound. "Men On . . ." has rightfully been criticized for its "negative" stereotypical representation of black gay men as ineffectual sissies and, by extension, as existing outside the realm of "authentic" masculinity. Of course, part of the skit's appeal is that very representation because for some it solidifies what they already think about black gay men. For others for whom the show is their only exposure to black gay male culture (and this is what many black gay men find potentially dangerous about the skit), this representation is taken as the "truth" of black gay experience. The fact that the authority of this representation resides with self-identified black heterosexual male performers becomes all the more problematic in terms of a privileged group having control over the representation of a marginalized group. The wonderful thing about performance, however, is the space it provides for possibilities and transgressions. Accordingly, the parody of gay men in "Men On . . ." became such a "hit" that the SNAP!, once a discursive practice that circulated exclusively in black gay subculture, emerged in black popular culture among black and white heterosexuals alike.[66] Again, although the intent behind appropriating the SNAP! for most was to poke fun at black gay men, the actual performance of the SNAP! by black heterosexual men is another example of manifest faggotry, and thus the queering of black American culture.

The dialectic formulated through the process of gender and sexual performativity demonstrates the incoherence of black heterosexuality. The cultural performances by Cleaver, Baraka, Murphy, and Wayans and Grier illustrate how blackness is bound up, constipated by the hegemony and imperialism of heteronormative black masculinity. Moreover, their performances exemplify the complex process through which black male heterosexuality conceals its reliance on the black effeminate homosexual for its status. This is not to suggest yet another binary construction of black gender and sexuality; rather, it calls attention to the process through which gender and sexual identity inhere when predicated on the repudiation of its Other. Through the "acting out" or performance of the Other as a register of that repudiation, then, the black heterosexual male performer conjures the specter of the queer Other that suggests not only his disavowal but also, at the very least, his psychic mourning of the same. The "rules" of gender and sexual identification in hegemonic patriarchal society are much too stringent. "Indeed, we are made all the more fragile under the pressure of such rules, and all the more mobile when ambivalence and loss are given a dramatic language in which to do their acting out."[67] Blackness, too, is fragile when subsumed by rules of inclusion; yet, like gender and sexual performativity, its mobility is never fore-stalled once it is set into motion in/through performance, no matter who is in the driver's seat.

3

MOTHER KNOWS BEST

Blackness and Transgressive Domestic Space

> Honey, I am more man than you'll ever be, and
> more woman than you'll ever get!
> —"Lindy," from the film *Car Wash*

> A house is not a home.—Luther Vandross

> this boy on your block
> he the double dutch champ
> he teach the boys to slow dance
> the girls, how to please their men
> they listen
> he keep house better than your wife
> or your mama
> —Marvin K. White, "kevin the faggot"

In this chapter I reverse gears a bit to look at the ways in which gender melancholy might apply to black gay men's performances of heterosexuality. Indeed, homosexual melancholia is also a component of homosexual identity formation. Similar to heterosexuals who repudiate homosexuality as a strategy to consolidate heteronormative masculinity, the tendency among some homosexuals, according to Judith Butler, is "to disavow a constitutive relationship to heterosexuality." She warns, however, "to specify gay and lesbian over and against its ostensible opposite, heterosexuality, that cultural practice culminates paradoxically in a weakening of the very constituency it is meant to unite." Butler further suggests that "not only does such a strategy attribute a false, monolithic status to heterosexuality, but it misses the political opportunity to work the weaknesses in heterosexual subjectivation, and to refute the logic of mutual exclusion by which heterosexism proceeds."[1] Rather than "miss[ing] the political opportunity" to expose the falsity of "static" heterosexual masculinity, black gay men's performance of black heterosexuality reveals the interrelationships between heterosexual and homosexual identity formation. By appropriating heteronormative tropes of domesticity, black gay men challenge the notion of the domestic site as only a heterosexual paradigm, constituting a reconfiguration of the very notion of "family."

Insofar as heterosexual formulations of "home" and "family" are intimately sutured to notions of nationhood and citizenship, the reappropriation of such terms in black gay communities suggests a transgressive deployment that serves to recast the domestic space in a "queer" light. These performances also manifest as instances of spectacles of homosexual melancholy in that they publicly dramatize, through what Butler calls "collective institutions for grieving," the mourning or loss of the heterosexual Other for whom there is no culturally sanctioned space to grieve. Unlike the motivations of black heterosexual men, black gay men's performance of heterosexuality has less to do with the *need* or desire to repudiate the Other as much as it does with an attempt to expand the discourse of the heterosexual Other to include a black gay subjectivity. Black gay men's appropriation and performances of heterosexual tropes work against congealing stable notions of homosexuality and heterosexuality and, indeed, call attention to the "weaknesses in heterosexual subjectivation" as well as, in Butler's words, "refute the logic of mutual exclusion by which heterosexism proceeds" (35).

These vernacular performances also redress the breach committed by black heterosexuals when they exclude black homosexuals from the category of blackness. In so doing, black gay men disrupt the idealization of the nuclear family and the cultural logic of sexual citizenship as lodged in "normative" sexuality. The emergence of black gay vernacular into popular discourse challenges the naturalization of heterosexual sex as "representative" of "normal" sexual citizenship.

Although I argue that the vernacular provides a space to theorize the transgression of black domesticity, I do so cognizant of the pitfalls along the way. In other words, similar to the ways I have discussed the "folk" as ontologically linked to authentic blackness, there is a way in which the vernacular may be caught up in the web of authentic blackness as well, especially given the association of vernacular speech with the working class. Wahneema Lubiano deftly observes that "vernacular language and cultural productions allow the possibility of discursive power disruptions, of cultural resistance, but they do not guarantee it."[2] Fully aware of the vernacular as an impure, inauthentic discourse, my goal in this chapter is not to exempt the vernacular from corruption, as it were. Rather, I argue that because it is a hybrid mixture of tropes that circulate in black and gay communities, black gay vernacular may afford, in strategic moments, opportunities to subvert black heterosexual claims of black authenticity specifically through tropes of domesticity.

The research for this chapter stems from participant observation and personal experience in black gay settings such as informal dinner parties, nightclubs, and church services.[3] I also draw on films such as *Paris Is Burning* and *Living with Pride: Ruth Ellis @ 100,* both of which feature some form of black gay vernacular in the ways I articulate below. The analysis of all of these texts together provides a space to examine in more detail the ways in which black gay men appropriate the heteronormative discourse of domesticity.

"A House Is Not Home":
Deconstructing the American "House"

In his 1981 hit single "A House Is Not a Home" Luther Vandross sensually croons over a full orchestra the words to a song that solidifies the notion of "home," as opposed to "house," as the epitome of the heterosexual American dream:

> A chair is still a chair even when there's no one sitting there
> But a chair is not a house
> And a house is not a home when there's no one there to hold you tight
> And no one there you can kiss goodnight . . .
> I'm not meant to live alone.

Turn this house into a home when I climb the stair and turn the key
Please be there saying that you're still in love with me.[4]

Following the logic of the song, an empty chair is still physically as
well as symbolically a chair, but a "home," on the other hand, is just a
mere "house" unless it is inhabited physically by two loving (heterosexual?) people. While one could persuasively argue that the song
could also apply to homosexuals feeling a desire to "nest," the subtext of the song undergirds the pervasive heteronormative logic that
"homemaking" is the ultimate sign of wholeness. Single persons, for
example, who do not wish to live with another; those who might prefer
polygamy over monogamy; or those who are not themselves heterosexual may only inhabit "houses," because a "house is not a home" if
"there's no one there you can kiss goodnight." The transformation of
a "house" to a "home," then, occurs under heteronormative terms—if
and only if the speaker's significant other is waiting behind the door
to declare her (his?) love.[5]

Vandross's song reveals how deeply the discourse of heteronormativity is embedded in the fabric of American popular culture. This
investment in heteronormativity has everything to do with maintaining the image of the American dream: the stereotypic portrait of the
(white) father, mother, two kids, and a dog outside their "home" with
a white picket fence. That this image has long since been diminished
by the economic realities of late capitalism, the changing "face" of
America, and the end of the cold war, is the very reason why such
images, songs, and discourse are now back in circulation.[6] Although
most Americans are living in "houses," the imperialism of patriarchy
dictates that the happy image of the "home" be maintained.

Having been denied access to the dream or reality of "home" (at
least in the Norman Rockwell sense) black gay men have reconfigured
the discourse of "home" as "house." Simultaneously included and
excluded from its discursive and material reach, "home" has always
been an ambivalent site for black gay men. As such, it may provide
the most fertile ground on which to transgress heteronormativity. Accordingly, Chandan Reddy suggests that queers of color, "with their
history of the home as a contradictory location that is open and hybrid," are primed to refigure "home" as "house" because they "can re-

member the interaction between the 'structure in dominance' and the 'home,' enabling other subjective logic mappings of the 'home.'"[7]

One place where this transgression has occurred is within the space of black gay nightclubs. These nightclubs, like many sites of counter-cultural performance, function as a space where black gay subjectivity is celebrated and affirmed.[8] The vehicle through which this celebration and affirmation occurs is through "house" music. Disavowing the heterosexual mask of songs such as "A House Is Not a Home," house music is unapologetically gay and unmistakably black. The roots of house, according to Anthony Thomas, a former Chicago deejay, stem from the Chicago black gay club scene: "Like the blues and gospel, house is very Chicago. Like rap out of New York and go-go out of D.C., house is evidence of the regionalization of black American music. Like its predecessors, disco and club, house is a scene as well as a music, black as well as gay."[9]

Although Thomas locates Chicago as the scene of origin for house, it enjoys a wider circulation in black gay nightclubs around the country. Indeed, house music is arguably one of the most integral aspects of black gay subculture, and it has become so because it is a musical genre that emerged within the context of the black gay dance clubs, "the only popular institutions of the gay black community that are separate and distinct from the institutions of the straight black majority," (438) as well as white institutions, straight or gay. Therefore, according to Thomas, "gay black dance clubs . . . have staked out a social space where gay black men don't have to deal with the racist door policies at predominately white gay clubs or the homophobia of black straight clubs. Over the past twenty years the soundtrack to this dancing revolution has been provided by disco, club, and now—house music" (438).

Predating the emergence of house music is the concept of the "house party." For example, in Yvonne Welbon's 1999 documentary film *Living with Pride,* Ruth Ellis, a one-hundred-year-old black lesbian, tells the story of how she and her partner, Ceceline "Babe" Franklin, bought a house in Detroit, Michigan, which became a safe haven for black gay, lesbian, bisexual, and transgendered people. Between 1941 and 1971 Ruth and Babe's house functioned as the "gay spot" for black homosexuals who were denied admission to the white gay bars in the city. Their house also functioned as a shelter for those who had been dispossessed by their own families and needed a place to stay until they "got on their feet." According to Ellis, most of the people who frequented their house were black gay men. In fact, she contends that she and Babe helped many of them attend college:

> We paid for it [their house] in seven years. It didn't cost but five thousand dollars. And that's the house where we had all the lesbians and gay people to gather on the weekend. There weren't very many places to go when I first came to Detroit, unless it'd be somebody's home. And then after we bought our home we just opened our home to gay people. Everybody knew where Babe and Ruth were because we had a gay couple who lived downstairs . . . so if we had a party, we'd open up the whole house. Now most of them were college students going to college, trying to finish college. Every Saturday we'd have a little get-together, play the piano, and they would sing. And some of them would play cards and some of them would just sit and talk. And that's the way we'd spend the evenings. It was sort of a haven for the young people who didn't have no place to go. Mostly, it would be men or boys [who] would come in. And we'd let them stay until they'd get on their feet. Sometimes we'd try to help them through school. We tried. It wasn't much because we didn't have much back then.[10]

The sense of compassion and community-building explicit in Ellis's description of the way her house functioned for black gays and lesbians in the 1940s captures the ways in which the term "house" has evolved in the black gay community over time. In general, the notion of the house party derives from the practice of black folks creating their own spaces to socialize because white racism often blocked their entrance into public spaces. These house parties not only functioned as an agent of racial solidarity against racism but also as a communal site where black homosexuals could love and support one another. Similarly, black homosexuals who were ostracized by their heterosexual brothers and sisters adapted the practice as a way to provide a space to escape homophobia and to build their own sense of community.

In Jennie Livingston's 1990 documentary film *Paris Is Burning*, black and Latino men who participate in the drag/vogue balls of Harlem also belong to "houses."[11] In the film, "legendary"[12] drag/vogue ball performer Dorien Corey says that a house is a family: "They're families, for a lot of people don't have families. But this is a new meaning of family. The hippies had families and no one thought nothing about it. It wasn't a question of a man and a woman and children, which we grew up knowing as family. It's a question of a group of human beings in a mutual bond."[13] This definition of "house" dovetails with that of Ruth Ellis insofar as the ball houses serve as a place where black gay men who may be homeless or in need of shelter have a place to go. Banned from both the public spaces of the heterosexual black "home" and the white gay clubs, black gay men and women create private spaces (the nightclub, another gay person's house, a ball house, etc.) to create community. Indeed, according to Phil Hubbard, "private spaces . . . may be the only spaces where [black gay men] feel comfortable expressing their sexuality or adopting dress codes that signify their membership as members of particular sexual communities."[14] Black gays' appropriation of the popular and very public meaning of "house," however, signals a transgression of heteronormative configurations of sexual and, indeed, American citizenship in two important ways. First, reconfiguring "house" subverts "dominant notions of sexual [and American] citizenship [as being] based on the normalization (and encouragement) of the idealized nuclear family."[15] Second, it counters the assumption that houses are only occupied by these same heterosexual nuclear families.

For the drag/vogue ball performers, membership in a house also means being loyal to your "family." Many of the performers in *Paris Is Burning,* for instance, speak with great pride when narrating how they became members of their particular houses, how their house is the grandest, and how the other houses do not compare to their own. This sense of loyalty to one's house by these black sexual dissidents belies the myth of the treacherous, racially disloyal "sissy" and highlights the paradoxes of the representation of the "healthy," stable, morally superior heterosexual household. The fact that 50 percent of heterosexual marriages end in divorce and that most children today are not raised in two-parent households is testament to the dissolution of the American heterosexual idealization of "family." That some of the house members are the dispossessed offspring of these heterosexual homes is even more ironic given that these gay men exhibit toward one another more love and support than they were shown in the homes in which they grew up. In this way, the "house" as configured in these drag/vogue communities becomes the place where they "make themselves from scratch," to borrow Joseph Beam's poignant phrase—a place where they "make do" with the leftovers from a world that has disowned and abused them. These houses become a polyglot space of celebration and affirmation as well as an image of a dream deferred. Essex Hemphill captures the ball houses well when he writes:

> In a country where "membership" and "privileges" translate into white, male heterosexuality . . . *Paris Is Burning* comes to the screen with a dressing room full of articulate butch/femme queens who collectively say, "I am" and are so, so real.
>
> Transsexuals, drag queens, gays and sexual transgressives, gender benders, legendary children, up and coming legendary children, mothers, fathers, elders; surrogate families are constructed from this to replace the ones that may no longer exist as a resource, or that may be too dysfunctional to offer any sense of safety, support, or love. Houses of silk and gabardine are built. Houses of dream and fantasy. Houses that bear the names of their legendary founders or that bear the names of fashion designers such as Chanel or Saint Laurent parade and pose at the balls. Houses rise and fall. Legends come and go. To pose is to reach for power while simultaneously holding real powerlessness at bay.[16]

Hemphill's description of these "houses" as opposed to "homes" suggests that houses are sites of much more than a coming together of those who share a sexual identity. Indeed, houses are also sites of creativity, imagination, performance, and liminality in which identity is affirmed and yet is also still in process. This dialectic of identity creation is an example of what Victor Turner calls "communitas." According to Turner, communitas is not

> a structural reversal, a mirror-imaging of "profane" workaday socioeconomic structure, or a fantasy-rejection of structural "necessities," but the liberation of human capacities of cognition, affect, volition, creativity, etc., from the normative constraints incumbent upon occupying a sequence of social statuses, enacting a multiplicity of social roles, and being acutely conscious of membership in some corporate group such as a family, lineage, clan, tribe, nation, etc., or of affiliation with some pervasive social category such as a class, caste, sex or age division.[17]

The "liberation" from "normative constraints" is what is at the center of the houses. And, as Turner suggests, rather than a rejection of the structural norms of heterosexual "home" or, I would add, of black cul-

Various house members in Jennie Livingston's
Paris Is Burning.

tural rituals, the black gay men engage in "disidentification" by working on and against oppressive forces while at the same time remaining
inside that system.[18] In other words, the black gay house-dwellers create communitas by maintaining the heteronormative structural concept of house while at the same time subverting the hegemonic limitations on "house" by appropriating the heteronormative familial and
domestic connotations of the term in relation to "home."

We Are Family: I Got All My "Sisters" with Me

In her book *Families We Choose,* anthropologist Kath Weston argues
that the heterosexist culture in which we live assumes that there is
a single model of what constitutes a family. "By representing 'the
family' as unitary object," she writes, "these depictions also imply that
everyone participates in identical sorts of kinship relations and sub-
scribes to one universally agreed-upon definition of family."[19] As revealed in *Paris Is Burning,* "family" is a term that is used to name the
"mutual bond" that black gay men feel toward one another. For the

members of the ball houses and for black gay men in general, the concept of "family" is less about biological relationships and more about kinships formed through a sense of communitas. Again, this conception of family has its roots in the black community at large in that black communities have always valued the notion of extended family whereby nonbiological kin are considered to be part of one's kinship circle.

In *One of the Children,* an ethnography of black gay men in Harlem, anthropologist William Hawkeswood reveals that "family" among his informants pertained to "fictive kin" established through social networks of established gay friends. According to Hawkeswood, "close gay members of each individual's social network become his 'family' and are accorded familial titles."[20] Growing up in a small town in western North Carolina I had several "aunts," "uncles," and "cousins" who were not related to me by blood but who either lived in my neighborhood or who were longtime close friends of my biological family. Residential proximity and personal history both contributed to this sense of extended family. In most cases, my "aunts" and "uncles" were also surrogate "mothers" and "fathers" as they were allowed to punish their peers' children if they caught them misbehaving. In almost formulaic ways, many a black person who grew up in this kind of environment will testify that a whipping from one's "aunt" was just a precursor to the whipping one would get when one got home.

As "bi"cultural workers, black gay men incorporate and expand this notion of family within their gay circles. Thus, family has come to signify anyone who is gay whether they are "out" or not. Rather than asking directly whether or not a person is "gay," one might ask if he is "family." The interesting aspect of the notion of "family" in this context is that it is used both as a coded term in the presence of heterosexuals and as part of ordinary gay vernacular in all-gay contexts. One of my informants, "Rob," a native North Carolinian, explained to me why family is used in both contexts:

> You might use "family" in front of straight people, but only say it to another gay person in the room. You know how straight folks take everything so literally anyway. [laughs] Case in point: I remember going home with one of my friends to his family reunion. He introduced me to one of his uncles who was fine as hell. And I was getting this little "tingle ling" [a feeling] from my gaydar when he shook my hand. So, I asked

my friend if his uncle was family and his mama turned around and said, "Yes, he's family. That's Roger's uncle." Me and Roger just fell out because we both knew what I meant! So we use family as a code, but we also use family when it's just gay people. I don't know why, because it's not a code in that context because we don't have to hide, but I guess it's just a way of including someone into the fold. It's like you enjoy the fact that somebody else may be like you.[21]

Homosexual use of the term "family" in heterosexual company functions to purposely disguise the gay vernacular meaning of the term. One of the reasons heterosexuals are unable to read the double meaning of the term (in addition to "tak[ing] everything so literally") is that many heterosexuals view the world from a heteronormative perspective. So while black Americans in general may practice a more inclusive definition of the term "family," that practice does not necessarily include sexual dissidents. Thus, in Rob's anecdote above, Roger's mother's misreading of the meaning of "family" may have had as much to do with the ways in which her heterosexuality limited the possibilities for what the term could mean as it did her ignorance of gay vernacular.

The function of "family" among black gay men draws on black discursive and social practices and incorporates them in ways that simultaneously maintain and subvert their meaning. In other words, "family" is practiced in black gay culture in the same ways as done by black heterosexuals, except that gays use the term to also include other gays. Again, the biculturality of black gays allows for the dual function of certain social practices that discursively manifest in black gay idiom. From this perspective, Rob's comment about using family to "include someone into the fold" dovetails with the way in which family functions in black communities in general. According to Anthony Thomas, this should not be surprising because "unlike their white counterparts, gay black Americans, for the most part, have not redefined themselves—politically or culturally—apart from their majority community. . . . Lesbian and gay Afro-Americans still attend black churches, join black fraternities and sororities, and belong to the NAACP."[22] At the same time, the use of family by black gays is more nuanced and malleable than that of black heterosexuals. Rob explains:

Rob: If I ask somebody if another person is family, I want to know if the other person is gay or not. To me, it just means another person who is like me or gay, and so they're "family." Most of the time if I'm asking the question, it means that I suspect that the other person is gay, but I can't tell for sure—my gaydar may be on the outs. [laughs] So if I'm asking it means I'm not sure, but if I *know* the person's gay, but trying to perpetrate, I'll just say, "Oh chile, he's family."

EPJ: So "family" is sort of a generic term for someone who's gay? Why would you refer to someone as family if they are trying to pass as straight? Why would you want someone in your "family" who doesn't want to be included?

Rob: Because they're included whether they want to be or not. It's like black people who try to act white. No matter how much they try to get away from who they are they still black. And most black folk will still claim them even if they [black people who act white] don't claim their blackness. Black is black like gay is gay. And family is family. We just have to love all of our disillusioned brothers and sisters.

Although Rob's response borders on essentialist views of identity (e.g., "black is black like gay is gay"), the point he makes is clear: those who share a common signifier of difference in relation to the majority culture are family whether they claim to be or not. Thus "disillusioned" (i.e., closeted or self-hating) gays or blacks must be loved and cared for in spite of themselves. This is a more ecumenical practice of family than in heterosexual black families in that often one's homosexuality places one outside the bounds of "blackness," "home," and "family."

Members of the "Family"

There can be no family without family "members." In a traditional family, the father is the head of the household and thus is responsible for taking care of "his" family. While it may be the mother who does all of the actual caregiving for the children and who supervises the daily activities of the family, in a white, heterosexist, patriarchal, phallocentric society, deference is always given to the "Law of the Father."[23]

Historically, the black family has not been afforded the "privilege" of being headed by a male. According to historian Deborah Gray White, "slave traders frequently perceived the slave family as a woman and her children. Thus, when sale destroyed a slave family, wives lost husbands but husbands very often lost wives and children."[24] The conditions of slavery to a larger extent defined the parameters of black family life, including the roles each member could play in her or his familial setting. To the extent that black men were denied agency over their own lives, for good or naught, they were unable to participate in white forms of masculinity, whether it be protecting the wife's honor, keeping the family together, or being allowed to support the family in material ways. This limited access to one's role as provider and protector became the source of a very complicated trajectory for the black family. Namely, black men may have felt emasculated by black women who themselves had no more power than their male counterparts but who, because of racism, could obtain work as domestic workers.[25] In this sense, black women became de facto heads of households. This fact only further pathologized black women as emasculators, particularly after the infamous Moynihan report of 1965.[26] Although an exploration of the complexities of the black family and the ways in which black men and women responded to racism within familial systems is beyond the scope of my project here, suffice it to say that the black family emerged as a nontraditional site in relation to white families and, thus, so did the roles that men and women played within them.

Given the historical backdrop of the black family in the United States, it is not surprising that the term "father" is not an integral part of black gay vernacular. On the one hand, the fact that many black households were/are headed by single mothers may explain why the father figure is not a prevalent trope in black gay vernacular. On the other hand, some of the reasons for this absence may also be due to the fact that black heterosexual men are often as sexist and homophobic as their white counterparts. Indeed, as my reading in chapter 2 of Eldridge Cleaver and Imamu Amiri Baraka makes clear, historically black male leaders have been some of the most outspoken opponents of homosexuality. Given the general machismo found in black communities, femininity in black men is frowned on and homosexuality is considered an affront to black masculinity. Consequently, when a son comes into his homosexuality it is most likely his father who will react most negatively, for in the eyes of many heterosexual men homosexuality and masculinity are incongruous. Perhaps this excerpt from Essex Hemphill's "The Father, Son, and Unholy Ghosts" captures the deadly silence and tension that strangles black father/gay son relationships:

> A black hole, gaseous,
> blisters around its edge,
> swallows our estranged years.
> They will never return
> except as frightening remembrances
> when we are locked in closets
> and cannot breathe or scream.
>
> Communications down
> Angry in alien tongues.
> We use extreme weapons
> to ward off one another.
> Some nights, our opposing reports
> are heard as we dream.
> Silence is the deadliest weapon.
> We both use it.
> Precisely. Often.[27]

The reference in the poem to the "black hole" that stands between the speaker and his father is a metaphor; the father has reduced his son's (homo)sexuality to "a black hole, gaseous/blisters around its edge." The father's answer to Leo Bersani's disturbingly profound question, "Is the rectum a grave?"[28] is a resounding "Yes." Consequently, homosexual sex announces the death toll on the father's prospect of having (biological) grandchildren and the passing down of the family (i.e., the father's) name. Further, it means the loss of a son because of the ways in which AIDS is thought of as a gay disease; and, in some cases, it signals the death of the black community because homosexuals are not "real" men and therefore cannot possibly lead their people.[29]

There are also other possible explanations for why black gay men adopt more tropes of black femininity than black masculinity.[30] One reason might be a general connection to black women as another oppressed minority.[31] Because black gay men and black women are groups that have been on the other end of racial, gender, and sexual oppression there are ways in which their creative responses to such oppression overlap. Origins of particular vernacular terms, phrases, and gestures, for example, are often disputed between the two groups because they are performed within both.[32] Another possible reason, however, may stem from black gay male misogyny. The fact that black gay men choose tropes of black femininity to perform may suggest that black masculinity or masculinity in general is a more stable, fixed construct and therefore is not susceptible to appropriation. On a more personal note, I have witnessed firsthand a general misogyny among black gay men that manifests itself in references to women as "fish" or "cunts" or in a general repulsion of the sight or mention of female genitalia. Gil, a native of the California Bay Area who now lives in New York City, explains black gay men's simultaneous admiration and rejection of black women when he responds to my question as to why very few tropes of black masculinity exist in black gay culture:

> EPJ: Why don't you think there is a counterexpression, "father" or whatever?
>
> Gil: Well, I think part of that is that there has been, perhaps, a cultural convention among many black gay men to do a gender switch in talking about themselves and each other. And I think there are a whole bunch of reasons why that happens. Some of them have to do with [pause] some of them come from different directions. Sometimes they come from polar-opposite directions. So I think the reasons why black gay men will identify themselves and others as women stem, on the one hand, from a recognition of women as less powerful and often times a group, who, like gay men, are [pause] targets of violence, of powerlessness—those kind of realities. But, at the same time, it also stems from, in some respects, a certain abiding misogyny that exists among black gay men. That often happens, I think [pause] when men talk about each other in a way that really signifies of the most stereotypically "least desirable" attributes of women: the cattiness and the simplistic sort of image consciousness, even in some cases the sort of libidinousness that's assumed to exist within black women. Those are some often very negatively understood traits and that's partly what's being treated.[33]

Gil's candidness about what he perceives as the reasons for an absence of black masculine tropes is compelling on a number of different levels. That one group could hold another in high regard while, at the same time, disdain them should come as no surprise given the history of American race relations. The fact that whites held black people in bondage for over three hundred years yet appropriated next to all of their art forms as well as other aspects of their culture is testament to this paradox. Nonetheless, my intention here is to unravel some of these paradoxes as they pertain to black gay men's performance of femininity within the realm of the domestic space.

Mother's Pearls

As opposed to the "father," the mother figure is perhaps the most prevalent familial trope in black gay vernacular and culture. To be hailed as "mother" is to be held in high esteem and regarded with great respect. The house mothers in *Paris Is Burning* serve as a prime example of the respect given to those considered "mother." According to Peppa LeBeija, mother of the House of LeBeija: "When someone has rejection from their mother and father, their family, when they get out in the world they search. They search for someone to fill that void. I know this from experience because I've had kids come to me and latch hold to me like I'm their mother or like I'm their father. They can talk to me and I'm gay and they're gay and that's where a lot of that ball mother business comes in. Because their real parents give them such a hard way to go, they look up to me to fill that void." Willie Ninja, the mother of the House of Ninja, narrates a similar story: "You have to have something to offer in order to lead. The mother usually becomes the mother because she's usually the best one of the group. To be mother of the house you have to have a lot of power. Take a real family, it's the mother that's the hardest worker and the mother gets the most respect." Both Peppa LeBeija and Willie Ninja became "mothers" because they were seen as leaders and "elders" who not only had compassion for those who became their "children" but also were wise about "the life" and what it takes to live life on the margins of society.[34] As if they were biological children, the men in these houses "latch hold" to their mothers for advice, support, and nurturing. Because they "have something to offer" the mothers in turn take care of their flock the same ways in which a female mother would take care of her children. Indeed, as Jackie Goldsby suggests, the "houses" in *Paris Is Burning* are sites where "(wo)men of color raise and nurture each other, not only to provide a measure of protection against the violent dangers facing them as sexual outcasts in Manhattan, but also to groom themselves to become 'legends' at the balls."³⁵

The term "mother" has currency outside the context of the ball/ vogue houses of Harlem, however. As the interviewees in this study attest, "mother" is used in black gay communities around the country. In the following interview with Gil, the term "mother" is used in a general way to address the "elders" of the black gay community:

> EPJ: "Mother." For you what does that signify? What does that term mean for you?
>
> Gil: Well, basically it means a nurturing, loving kind of person. Now, I have a friend, Clarence, who was introduced to me as mother. I understood from the mutual friend who introduced us that he was often referred to as mother and he, in fact, will refer to himself as mother. And in a sense it has a lot to do with his place as a somewhat older gay man. It's a sort of acknowledgment that his experience is something more profoundly varied, perhaps, or more extensive obviously, than mine because he's older. And because the moment that we live in, there have been so many profound changes from year to year in the experiences and the rights of gay people—gay black people—it serves as an acknowledgment of someone who has been, if you will, through the storm and has perhaps survived a lot.

The important thing to note in Gil's commentary about a "mother" being someone who has had "profoundly varied" experiences as a black gay man, is that the position of mother does not necessarily come with chronological age. Indeed, designating someone as "mother" stems from the perception of those who refer to others as mother that the person so called is a mentor, leader, or nurturer. "Kirby" and "Vancouver," from North Carolina and South Carolina, respectively, provided similar definitions of "mother":

> Kirby: Mother is a wise, gay man, a gay man who's number one, very comfortable in being gay and who has been there, done that, has seen the ups and downs, and is the force of stability and reason for gay males who are not necessarily younger, but who are in the infancy of their coming out process. And mothers are funny, they make you laugh and they're venerated, I mean, you've got to love them.³⁶
>
> Vancouver: Usually it's somebody, like myself, who generally gives advice, who generally is, in situations of friendship—close friendship—

is the nurturing one, the one who generally is in the middle. You know, if there's a dispute between friends, they're generally [pause] they understand this friend, they understand the other friend, they try to make situations better. They're the nurturing types. I think that in terms of the gay community, that's what that term closely aligns itself with.

EPJ: And how is one bestowed that title?

Vancouver: Through friendships.

EPJ: Any friendship? Age is probably a factor, right?

Vancouver: I don't think age has anything to do with it as much as, you know, one's disposition. I've met people of all age ranges—young and old—and some have a disposition that [pause] I've seen the old people that just don't have no concept, just go out and do stuff, don't even think about it. And then I know some young people who, you know, think of all the consequences, who have similar "mother" type instincts, but have not reached or gained the title of "mother" yet [pause] it's a respect factor and it's generally an unspoken agreement among a group of folk.[37]

In keeping with Vancouver's definition, to my surprise, two of my friends who live in North Carolina (both of whom are younger than I am but relatively close to my age) revealed to me that the two of them refer to me as "mother." When I asked them why they do so and why they had never called me "mother" to my face, they said that, initially, it was something they did in jest because I was always giving them advice about their love lives. After a while, however, they began to call me "mother" because they realized that they admire how I lead my life as an openly gay man. Because they are still somewhat closeted, they aspired to being as comfortable as I am in my sexuality. Now, whenever they call or e-mail me, the first thing they say is, "Hey, Mother, it's the children."

In each of these instances the use of the term "mother" is an appropriation of the word as signified in heteronormative discourse. Beyond the obvious discursive cross-gender performative of dislodging "mother" as ontologically cemented to the female gender, the transubstantiation of mother as black gay man sutures the familial rupture experienced by black gay men who have been abandoned by their biological mothers. This kind of role-playing is more than an instance of gender performativity because the black gay male performance of "mother" is a resistive act against hegemonic heterosexuality and homophobia, as well as an agent of community building and communitas. It also exemplifies a cross-gendered public mourning and literal loss of the heterosexual m(other).

The term "mother" also enjoys a usage that is beyond the stereotypical reference to someone who is nurturing. These other uses of "mother" most often emerge in black gay discourse. In this realm of usage, a speaker may refer to another black gay man whom he believes is a diva who deserves his respect as "mother," or he may refer to himself as "mother" in the third person. The term "mother" in these contexts calls attention to the admiration of black mothers in the black community. Seen as a kind of "everywoman," black women who mother are admired because of the sheer stamina it takes to take care of a family (and in most cases by herself), work a full-time job, and make sacrifices for the good of her children—and to do all of this with grace. In addition, the black mother is often depicted as being a stern disciplinarian whose mythic status as such is a mainstay in stand-up comedy acts, television shows, and films.[38] Common, formulaic stories circulate among black folk about mothers who need only to give a look to stop a child from misbehaving; who are known to administer corporal punishment with the closest available inanimate object; who have no patience for back talk. In general, the black mother is "fierce" in that she does not suffer fools lightly, works hard but makes it look easy, and is the epitome of grace, style, and flair.

These attributes of black mothers are appropriated and celebrated in black gay discourse. An example of this usage is in a conversation with my Atlanta friend "Kyle," whom I was visiting for the weekend. He and some other friends were planning to go to a drag show, but I had decided not to go with them. We had the following conversation when he returned that evening:

EPJ: Y'all must have had a good time because it's way past your bedtime. Wasn't the show over at 2:00?

Kyle: No, chile. You should have come with us. This was one of the best shows I've seen this year. Those girls WORKED! Oh my God, they were just *too* fierce!

EPJ: Really? What was so great about it?

Kyle: They were just very, very good. But it was this one girl, honey. I think her name was Maxi Cummings or something like that. She gave you DRAMA! Mother came out in this form-fitting red dress with a scoop neck and these stiletto pumps. Her face was beat back into her temples. Her wig was tight. She was giving you Whitney Houston drama!

EPJ: What did she perform?

Kyle: "I Will Always Love You." But the remix version! Honey, when Whitney started holding that note, Mother started twirling like those heels weren't but a thang! Mother twirled and twirled for life![39]

In this context, Kyle's reference to the drag performer as "mother" is complementary of her "dramatic" dress and, more important, her ability to pull off the performance/illusion. A performer's face that is "beat back into her temples" is one where the makeup is applied heavily but also effectively to give the illusion of femaleness. The "tight" wig refers to one that is appropriate for the dress and theme it accompanies. The "twirl" could have been referring to the performer's walk or to her actual twirling—the point is that she was doing it with skill and grace while in stiletto heels. All of these compliments form the status of "mother," based on the attributes outlined above that are associated with black mothers. And although one could argue that taking on the persona of "mother" by black gay men further contributes to the sexist practice of characterizing femininity as spectacular and thereby rendering masculinity discrete, in this instance male-to-female *linguistic* drag performance may also be read as paying homage to particular strains of black gender performance.

"Mother" is also used to refer to one's self as if one were a "real" black mother. By drawing on what a black mother might say after a hard day's work or just before a daunting chore, or by just taking on the black mother persona, black gay men align themselves with the figure of the black mother. As "Brett," a Jamaican-born immigrant to Atlanta said to me, "I feel very comfortable using 'mother.' You might say something like 'Mother's gonna do so and so. Mother *ain't* gonna do so and so.' Like our mothers used to tell us all the time."[40] Or "BJ" from North Carolina, who stated similarly that when a person designates himself as "mother" it "means that they're in charge or they're the boss. Normally your mother has the last say and no matter what you do—especially in black families—when Mom says something, that's it. So, I think they just kind of transpose that [pause] when they say that 'I'm the mother' [they are communicating] that my word is. What I say goes."[41] The following exchange between "Lee," who lives in Washington, D.C., and myself is an example of this usage.[42] The scene is Lee's apartment; he has just come from work.

> Lee: [plopping down on the couch] Whew! I am one tired sister.
> EPJ: Hard day at work?
> Lee: Yes, girl. Mother earned her coins today. She was working so hard at one point she had to sling her pumps off! [pause] She almost had to clock one of them bitches in the head with one. They get on my *last* nerve sometimes!
> EPJ: Well, you can take a little nap. I figure we can meet Tom and James for dinner around 8:00.
> Lee: That's a good idea. Mother does need her rest—cause you know she has to be cute for her future husband, Tom. [laughs][43]

In this exchange it is clear that Lee has transposed onto himself, in the way that BJ suggests above, the figure of the black mother. Not only is his alignment with the black mother a commentary on the hard work a black mother has to do in order to make ends meet (i.e., earning "coins"), but also the frustration that black mothers sometimes feel toward their work. The latter is captured in Lee's reference to himself as "mother" in the third person as wanting to hit one of his co-workers ("bitches") with one of "her" shoes ("pumps"). As mentioned earlier, one of the narratives that circulate in black folklore about black mothers is their propensity to punish misbehaving children with inanimate objects, of which a shoe is perhaps one of the most common. Thus Lee's reference is an appropriation of that trope. Accordingly, Lee's reference to himself as "mother" in this context is both an act of self-aggrandizement and a commentary on black gay men's high regard for black mothers. At the same time it is also a transgression of the very trope of "mother" because of the cross-gender reference and the fact that some of these men's biological mothers do not support them as gay men. In other words, the fact that these men honor even those mothers who have disowned them or who are embarrassed by them speaks to the complexity of black gay familial relations and their reconciliation of their gayness and blackness and their unwillingness to prioritize one over the other. Ultimately, when black gay men perform "mother" they are reclaiming heteronormative constructions of the "motherly," queering them in ways that subvert biological determinism and gender ontology. It also disrobes the sham of the heterosexual family as the morally sanctioned site of nurturing and support.

When a black gay man "becomes" "mother," "she" stakes out her claim to full sexual citizenship.

There also exist other phrases that are associated with those who refer to themselves as "mother." One of the more common phrases that emerged in the research for this study was "clutch the pearls," which is also often spoken in combination with the gesture of "clutching" or grabbing an imaginary pearl necklace. The phrase has a slightly different connotation depending on the context in which it is spoken. In the following, two informants describe some of the uses to me:

> Gil: If we were walking down the street and we saw a beautiful man, one of us might say, "Oh, child, clutch the pearls." In that context it would mean you've seen a breathtaking man.
>
> EPJ: So, what does that action connote? What does that mean?
>
> Gil: For me, it connotes an older woman who goes to church, wears her pearls, and who would never say anything salacious or wanton, but for whom the action, in this particular case, indicates a certain realization or recognition of someone who is really very beautiful and very desirable.
>
> EPJ: So is it a gesture of shock, surprise?
>
> Gil: I guess I would call it in that case a gesture of desire.

> EPJ: What about "clutch the pearls"? What does it mean?
>
> CB: That someone was surprised, someone was taken aback.
>
> EPJ: Where does that come from?
>
> CB: Probably looking at older women, thinking about situations in which older women have been surprised by some sort of news and have literally clutched their pearls or put their hands to their chests and been aghast at something or another.
>
> EPJ: Older women of any race?
>
> CB: Well, I guess I think less about race and more about class at that point, because it seems like a very middle-class action. So rather than slapping you [laughs], they clutch their pearls [grabs his chest and gasps as if surprised], "Oh my" and kind of take a step back.[44]

In both instances, "clutch the pearls" indicates some sense of surprise or shock and, as Gil suggests, the origin of that shock or surprise may be indicative of desire. I wish to examine more closely here the nuances of this phrase in both contexts in relation to "mother" in order to discuss the broader implications of black gay discourse as an agent of sexual citizenship and the transgression of the heteronormative domestic paradigm.

In the earlier discussion of "mother," the term was associated with stereotypical notions of motherhood that stem from "universal" as well as black cultural tropes: nurturer, caregiver, confidant, efficient worker, disciplinarian, no-nonsense parent, etc. In relation to the phrase "clutch the pearls," however, there seems to emerge yet another persona related to "mother": the prim and proper "lady." The examples given by both Gil and CB suggest that this type of mother persona is a hybrid of the black "church" mother and the conservative-minded upper- and middle-class woman. The black church mother persona is a black woman whose propriety does not necessarily stem from her socioeconomic standing but more from her Christian values.[45] Thus, she refrains from saying anything "salacious or wanton" because it would be sinful. Instead, she signals her surprise and dismay at a situation or controls her desire to "slap" her offender by placing her hand over her chest as if "clutching" her pearls.

The significance of "pearls" as a metaphor as opposed to other kinds of jewelry, such as diamonds, is due to the cultural value placed on pearls. Although diamonds are seen as jewelry associated with the rich they are not necessarily associated with the "cultured." Indeed, pearls are often described in terms of the way they are created: oysters in the process of enclosing irritating objects "cultivate" pearls. Thus, the pearl, like the "lady," is created and made out of something less than what it was before. That is why, particularly in southern culture, pearls are given to young women on their sixteenth or eighteenth birthday to mark their "coming out" or coming into womanhood. Pearls are understated, while diamonds are flashy; pearls are associated with the dignified and chaste, while diamonds are associated with the garish and "knowing" woman. A string of pearls, then, is an appropriate metaphor because of its association with not only a certain attitude about one's sexual mores, but also because of its association with a particular class standing. "Dee," a native of New York City, suggested that "pearls" is used in the phrase because pearls are "pure" and refer to "high society": "I think it's a take on the very cultured, sort of Mrs. Howell from *Gilligan's Island,* the very cultured, aristocratic social white, or definitely, lady. . . . I think pearls are a pure gem, a pure stone that somehow is different from diamonds. . . . If you could find a really rare pearl, I think it's worth more in some way, so I think maybe it has to do with social class and maybe women who are on a higher social class would have more pearls than they would diamonds. So, I think maybe it's referencing a high-society lady."[46]

Complementing Dee's suggestion that pearls are "a pure stone" is Gil's revelation of yet another pearl phrase used by black gay men: "casting one's pearls before swine." According to Gil, "Casting your pearls before swine means succumbing to the advances of an unworthy suitor. So, for example, you're giving it up to someone who really shouldn't be getting it [sex] in the first place." In the same way a pearl-wearing "lady" might allow an undeserving man to have his way with her, the black gay "mother" might also "cast her pearls before swine" by sleeping with someone she feels is undeserving. Ultimately, the association of pearls with the "lady" is integral to the ways in which the phrase "clutch the pearls" emblematizes a critique of heteronormative constructions of sexuality.

In Gil's anecdote about the use of "clutch the pearls," for instance, he makes it clear that in the context of his example the expression connotes a gesture of desire. Given that the typical "lady's" desire is policed or sealed off by the conventions of "proper" feminine gender performance, the black gay male appropriation of the lady persona vis-à-vis "clutch the pearls" to outwardly indicate "salacious" or "wanton" desire highlights the fiction of the sexually pure or chaste lady. Gil says that for the "real" lady, the gesture could be a sign that she is "ultimately human and however much she tries to distance herself from the desires of the flesh and the temptations of the flesh, she's still human and she succumbs to those things like any human would." Following Gil's logic, the black gay man's appropriation of the clutching gesture along with the phrase calls attention to the fact that the lady cannot always mask her sexual desire and thus the gesture reveals her vulnerability to the flesh and her human sexual desire.

The phrase and gesture as performed by black gay men serves double duty here. In one sense it undermines the cultural logic of the heteronormative constructions of femininity. The notion of the virtuous woman is a construct meant to maintain patriarchy and its constant surveillance and objectification of women's bodies. To the extent that Christianity encourages disavowing the temptations of the flesh and bourgeoisie heterosexuality encourages female chastity, it makes sense that the church lady and "high-society" lady are those chosen by black gay men to parody. The parody of this particular type of woman is reflected in the double entendre of the phrase itself, for "clutching pearls" also signifies the sexualized act of grabbing someone's "jewels" (testicles). In this light the phrase is both an ironic commentary on the *repression* of female sexual desire and the *expression* of black gay male desire. Arguably, the former use is undergirded by black gay male misogyny, as expressed by Gil earlier.

At the same time, however, it is also a commentary on bourgeois heterosexuality as related to citizenship. If, as Phil Hubbard argues, citizenship refers to "the political and social recognition that is granted to those whose behaviour accords with the moral values underpinning the construction of the nation-state," then homosexual sex necessarily falls outside the conditions of nationhood.[47] As anathema to the procreative, monogamous family unit, black gay men are deemed noncitizens. And although the "lady" is a sexist construct that maintains gender inequality, the heterosexual woman who performs as the lady nonetheless enjoys the "privileges" of citizenship in ways that black gay men do not.[48] Black gay men's vernacular performance of "clutch the pearls" is a polymorphous signifier that simultaneously calls attention to black gay male misogyny, the admiration of women, the myth of the chaste "lady," the hegemony of heteronormative sexuality, and the free play of gender roles in American society.

What about the Children?

One of the most predominate signifiers of heterosexuality is the child. Not only do children signal heterosexual sex but also procreation and the continuation of the name of the father. Indeed, the centrality of the nuclear family as the "normal" or "natural" site of sexual citizenship relies, according to Hubbard, "on the perpetuation of the idea that mothering and fathering are the only appropriate modes of sexual activity, with procreation represented as the ultimate (and emotionally fulfilling) product of the sexual relation."[49] Drag/vogue house mothers Peppa LeBeija, Willie Ninja, and Angie Xtravaganza featured in *Paris Is Burning* know not of this conception of children. Their "children" are neither the product of heterosexual sex nor are they biologically related to their "mother"; and, in yet another transgressive move, they take on the "name of the mother." Hemphill writes:

The houses function as surrogate families for Black and Puerto Rican gay youth who may be homeless, orphaned, or rejected by their families because of their gayness. When joining a house, it is customary for members to adopt the name of the house for their surname to signify that they "belong" to a family.

"Mothers" are usually those who have made legendary names for themselves on the ball circuit. A mother's duties can be numerous, but the primary function is to manage and nurture the illusions of the children because the children are all-important. A mother must ready the children for competition. They have to be fierce enough to snatch trophies and bring prestige and honor to the house.[50]

In the context of the drag/vogue house, "children" are not the progeny of heterosexual procreation but an emblem of the very rejection of it. As outcasts of their biological families, they are "produced" by cross-gendered "mothers" and become the children of houses that celebrate all of who they are.

The use of "children" in the black gay community again undermines a number of assumptions about the status of the familial nation-state. Its deployment in these communities brings a black culturally inflected notion of what constitutes a family by extending membership to like-minded souls. It also draws on the deep and long history of the black church vernacular, which often accords to black people the plight of oppressed groups as described in biblical stories.[51] That oppression is often associated with the power of white supremacy that has denied blacks the status of citizen. In its specific usage in black gay communities the term departs from generic gay vernacular because of its black cultural reference. With regard to heteronormative constructions of the family, the term "children" rejects the normalizing trope of the child as the ontological link to heterosexuality and destabilizes the notion of procreation as the sole model of sexual activity.

There's No Place Like . . .

In his powerful essay "Brother to Brother: Words from the Heart," Joseph Beam captures well the complicated feelings that black gay men feel about "home." Alienated from their biological families because of their sexuality; from the white gay communities because of their race; and from the white heterosexual world because of both, home becomes an ambivalent site for black gay men.[52] Beam writes: "When I speak of home, I mean not only the familial constellation from which I grew, but the entire Black community: the Black press, the Black church, Black academicians, the Black literati, and the Black left. Where is my reflection? I am most often rendered invisible, perceived as a threat to the family, or am tolerated if I am silent and conspicuous. I cannot go home as who I am and that hurts me."[53] Beam's hurt soon turns to anger. Rather than use that anger destructively, however, he desires to cull it in order to rebuild home as a place to which he can return: "Use it [anger] to create a Black gay community in which I can build my home surrounded by institutions that reflect and sustain me. Concurrent with that vision is the necessity to repave the road home, widening it, so I can return with all I have created to the home which is my birthright" (233).

One of the ways that black gay men have culled that anger into a productive rebuilding of home is through black gay vernacular performance. Appropriating and reclaiming presumably heterosexual tropes of nation, citizenship, family, and blackness, black gay men have devised intricate discursive as well as material spaces to proclaim their subjectivity as family members and sexual citizens. Through discourse that draws on the most innovative vernacular practices of black culture and the campy idioms and codes of black gay culture, black men have created "houses" that allow them to go home "as who they are"—not as essential subjects, but as subjects who, according to Chandan Reddy, "negate the demand for identity, embracing collectivities founded precisely on heterogeneity and nonidentity."[54] Indeed, as Jackie Goldsby reminds us regarding the houses formed by black gay men: " 'Home' no longer stands as the unproblematic site of black cultural salvation . . . it is instead, a fount of homophobia that damns difference and sponsors rejection, which, in turn, inspires the rebirth of the 'house.' "[55] Through this "rebirth" of "house," black gay dissidents also refigure "mother" as a complex mix of fierce gender-bending love and protection; perform the hyperbolic "lady" who "clutches her pearls" with an iron fist in a velvet glove; and become "children" who commune with one another on the dance floor, on the streets, or together against homophobia.

While the work of black gay men in the realm of the vernacular to reclaim their subjectivity appears to be merely symbolic, the pervasiveness of these terms in mainstream popular culture is the beginning point of queering hegemonic heterosexuality. Indeed, as black gay uses of these terms and phrases leak across racial, class, and gender borders, they call attention to the by now general acknowledgment that gender and sexuality are unstable categories. The transgression of black gay men into the heteronormalized space of domesticity is reflected in the discursive tactics that they employ to claim their sexual citizenship in a nation that masquerades as homogenous. Butler suggests that "it may be in the *reformulation of kinship,* in particular, the redefining of 'house' and its forms of collectivity, mothering, mopping, reading, and becoming legendary, that the appropriation and redeployment of the categories of dominant culture enable the formation of kinship relations that function quite supportively as oppositional discourse."[56]

"Citizenship" implies loyalty to one's own. Because we inhabit multiple social locations the labor of allegiance to one over the other becomes an impossible burden. Despite the efforts of black cultural conservationists who seek to demarcate blackness as unproblematically heterosexual and masculine, their efforts are inevitably forestalled, blinded by their inability to mourn the black queer within. Enshrouded in gender, sexual, and racial performativity, black heterosexuals and homosexuals exist in the vortex that is the process of identification. Performance allows for that performativity to reveal itself as it materializes the dialectic forged by the bump and grind, as it were, over identity claims. Indeed, the inertia one feels is symptomatic of being, according to Butler, "implicated in that which one opposes, this turning of power against itself to produce alternative modalities of power, to establish a kind of political contestation that is not a 'pure' opposition, a 'transcendence' of contemporary relations of power, but a difficult labor of forging a future from resources inevitably impure" (241). The "fruit" reaped from such "difficult labor" in the vineyard of blackness may provide an "inevitably impure," yet decadently rich, taste of the possibilities that performing blackness provides.

4

"NEVAH HAD UH CROSS WORD"

Mammy and the Trope of Black Womanhood

The mammy image represents the normative
yardstick used to evaluate all Black women's
behavior. — Patricia Hill Collins

The image of mammy is so deeply rooted in
American culture that it can be found in virtually
every form of print and visual media.
— Sue K. Jewell

Unlike the white southern image of mammy,
[the real mammy] is cunning, prone to poisoning her
master, and not at all content with her lot.
— Barbara Christian

"Mother" is a trope that registers in various discursive terrains and is
deployed for various aims. While black gay men sign the titular moni-
ker as a way to subvert heteronormative gender roles and to declare
their legitimacy (authenticity) as sexual citizens, black women's relationship to and deployment of the mother trope is peculiar to their
unique history in the United States. Given that history, particularly regarding the exploitation of labor, black women's "mothering" is linked
to a slave economy that forged a trajectory of black women's bodies
as sites of labor and laboring.[1] Thus "mother" became coterminous
with the more pejorative "mammy," which in the realm of domestic

work became one of the most prevalent tropes of black womanhood. Terms created to subjugate a group of people may, however, be appropriated and redeployed to signify in subversive and transgressive ways. In this chapter I examine such a reappropriation by illuminating the ways in which my grandmother's performance of "mammy" in her oral narrative about her days as a live-in maid avows and disavows that prototypical image. My grandmother's vernacular performance, like that of black gay men, challenges essentialist notions of race and gender identity as well as illustrates the ways in which black authenticity is and is not authorized through performance. Before I take up my grandmother's story, however, I want to survey the literature on the "mammy" in relation to domestic workers.

In response to the proliferation of "Dinahs," "Aunt Jemimas," and "Mrs. Butterworths" that populate fictional texts and the consumer-culture marketplace, literary and cultural theorists often study and discuss the domestic worker in terms of the codes and characteristics of the prototypical "mammy" figure. For instance, in *From Mammies to Militants: Domestics in Black American Literature,* Trudier Harris discusses how African American writers represent the African American domestic worker.[2] In her analysis, Harris theorizes the complex relationship between the black domestic and her white employer, and in doing so she directs attention to the many masks worn by the domestic and to the psychological and physical "warfare" that characterizes the employer/employee relationship.

Another example is Judith Rollins's *Between Women: Domestics and Their Employers,* which analyzes the employer/employee relationship by means of an ethnographic study in which she hires herself out as a domestic.[3] In her discussion of her experiences in the field and in subsequent interviews with other domestics, Rollins foregrounds her study with a historical purview of domestic labor in the United States. Following this discussion, she focuses on the physical, psychological, and emotional hardships of domestic labor. In a fashion similar to that of Harris, Rollins also illuminates the multiple and complicated roles performed by both the domestic and her employer. Both Harris and Rollins offer reasons why domestics both claim and disclaim the mammy prototype.

In addition to Harris and Rollins, Patricia Turner offers a historical perspective on the domestic as an icon in popular culture. In *Ce-*

ramic Uncles and Celluloid Mammies, Turner explains how the mammy figure manifests itself in different forms in consumer culture during specific moments in U.S. history.[4] The state of race relations within these historical sites, Turner argues, determines and is reflective of the mammy's cultural value in the consumer marketplace. Given what my grandmother recounts in her narrative, the domestic-as-mammy perspective is an applicable and helpful point of comparison and contrast. At times, my grandmother's words about her experiences as a domestic appear to uphold the surface characteristics common to the "mammy" figure. At other times, however, her performance of the "mammy" appears more complicated. As Frantz Fanon might observe, it operates in at least two dimensions.[5]

Throughout her social and cultural history, the domestic-as-mammy has been characterized as a childlike, subservient, promiscuous, sassy "handkerchief-head" whose mission in life is to serve her mistress and her mistress's family. According to Turner, the mammy "is happy to make your pancakes and wash your clothes. Her culinary skills are evident in her thick waistline. The mammy figures convey the notion that genuine fulfillment for black women comes not from raising their own children and feeding their own man (black families are rarely featured) but from serving in a white family's kitchen."[6] The mammy figure referenced by Turner is commonly found in the popular-culture marketplace.

The mammy's obliging attitude and behavior are part of a survivalist strategy and are commonly aligned to the "Uncle Tom" and "Stepin Fetchit" strategies used by slaves to appease the master or to vent anger in a nonthreatening way, or even as a way to disguise an ulterior motive such as escape, murder, or some other form of revenge. The "Stepin Fetchit" persona is characterized by his toothy grin, shuffle, and bow-and-scrape behavior in the presence of whites. His female counterpart is the Aunt Jemima figure, who is also characterized by a broad grin and a shuffle and who enjoys cooking for the master. Both personas project the image of the "happy-go-lucky" slave content with the status quo. On the other hand, the "Uncle Tom" mammy draws on her Christian-based belief in a better life in the hereafter. She is less overtly affable in the presence of her master/mistress than the "Stepin Fetchit" prototype, but, as Judith Rollins explains, because she acts out her understanding that things aren't fair in an unaggressive manner (i.e., spiritual rather than material-based redemption), the mistress/employer does not feel threatened. Rollins writes:

> The black who "Uncle Toms" derives pleasure from the performance. This "unaggressive aggressiveness" yields two kinds of psychological rewards: appeasement of guilt and a sense of superiority. If she is a Christian . . . she believes it is sinful to hate; acting meekly, even lovingly, relieves her of the guilt she feels for these "conscious and unconscious feelings of hostility and aggression toward white people." Additionally, this role may make the domestic feel superior in these ways: hers will be the final victory in the hereafter; she is demonstrating that she is spiritually superior to her employer; and she enjoys the success of being about to fool whites.[7]

The domestic who embodies the gospel tradition, then, transforms "passive" tenets of Christian faith—e.g., forgiveness and humility— into active forms of resistance.

Similar to the slaves who sang spirituals such as "Steal Away" to signal an escape to the North as opposed to a longing for Heaven, domestics also engage in behavior that is duplicitous. Thus their deference to their employers' authority is a performance or, as Harris discusses, a form of mask-wearing: "She can bow and scrape and say 'yes'um' until eternity if she separates the circumstances of her existence in the white woman's house from her conception of herself. If she maintains her cultural reference and believes in that reality, then the impositions that are made upon her will have less of a traumatic effect."[8] The success of the domestic's mask-wearing is contingent on her ability to separate her own concept of herself and her work from the image projected on her.

According to Frantz Fanon, colonized people have always used these performances or role-playing strategies: "The black man has two dimensions. One with his fellows, the other with the white man. A Negro behaves differently with a white man and with another Negro. That this self-division is a direct result of colonialist subjugation is beyond question."[9] Fanon further argues that with the mastery of the oppressor's language the oppressed acquires more power and, in the eyes of the oppressor, more humanity. Indeed, "he becomes whiter as he renounces his blackness, his jungle" (18). Within the domestic site, the "language" or cultural standards that are elemental to survival are those that commonly characterize the "mammy," especially an acquiescence toward her employer.

As the domestic's performance becomes more polished, her status within the domestic site increases. Or, in Fanon's terms, as the domestic learns how to play an increasingly more "white-inscribed" role, she acquires more authority, control, and power within the home of the employer. Her performance is, in Michel de Certeau's terms, a "tactic" whereby she "makes do" within the domestic site:

> The space of a tactic is the space of the other. Thus, it must play on and with a terrain imposed on it and organized by the law of a foreign power. It does not have the means *to keep to itself*, at a distance, in a position of withdrawal, foresight, and self-collection; it is a maneuver "within the enemy's field of vision" . . . and within enemy territory. . . . It operates in isolated actions blow by blow. It takes advantage of "opportunities" and depends on them, being without any base where it could stockpile its winnings, build its own position, and plan raids. . . . It must vigilantly make use of the cracks that particular conjunctions open in the surveillance of the proprietary powers. It poaches them. It creates surprises in them. It can be where it is least expected. It is guileful ruse.[10]

Constructed as a "tactic," the domestic's mask-wearing is imposed on and organized by "the law of a foreign power"—that is, by the worldview that her employer values. Accordingly, in practice the use of tactics facilitates "opportunities" to temporarily subvert power relations. Because the domestic appears to be abiding by the language and laws of the labor site, she is permitted, and thereby takes advantage of, more freedom of movement within the site. In short, as she becomes more "white" in appearance her actions are less monitored. These "tactics," then, reveal the performative nature of racial identity—both as experienced and as imagined—by calling attention to ways in which racial authenticity is and is not a matter of skin color.

As Patricia Collins explains, the movement toward and construction of a more "trusting" relationship between the domestic and her employer is frequently satisfying to both parties. On the other hand, because the domestic's economic livelihood is dependent on her employer's needs and satisfaction, her position is always subordinate to that of her employer. She is always an "outsider-within."[11] It is this outsider-within stance, of course, that allows the domestic the opportunity to say and do things that resist, or temporarily subvert, her subordinate position within the household. As de Certeau explains, "power is bound by its very visibility. In contrast, trickery is possible for the weak."[12] Once the domestic learns the necessary "language" and is a trusted subordinate within her employer's home, her visibility decreases, and thus she is able covertly to insert her own language (e.g., black vernacular) and pursue motives that are not necessarily those of her employer (e.g., acquiring material goods and providing for her own family). Like the monkey in the "signifying monkey" tales, the domestic bides her time until she finds an opportunity to dupe her employer.[13]

This ability to play the "white man's game" while maintaining and pursuing one's own "language" or cultural standards and motives is very like the abilities associated with Esu Elegbara, the Yoruba god of fate who resides at the crossroads.[14] In West African and various African American cultures, Esu is the high priest/priestess of trickery and masking. In the tradition of trickster figures, Esu is a duplicitous boundary crosser. He/she can talk out of both sides of his/her mouth because he/she has two of them—one on the male side of the head and the other on the female side of the head. Conceived as an Esu-type, the domestic is often a duplicitous, double-mouthed, bilingual boundary crosser as well. To claim and keep her job, she must learn the language and play the role of the "outsider-within" mammy. To maintain her own self-respect, language, and culture, as well as pursue motives that benefit her own material and spiritual life (i.e., her own family, home, and values), she frequently, consciously, and covertly breaks the rules of the domestic contract. Ella Turner Surry, an informant in John Langston Gwaltney's collection of African American narratives, *Drylongso*, reflects on this double-edged game:

> I think black people are more reasonable than white people. I don't know, maybe the word is not "reasonable," but I think that we are much more clever than they are because we know that we have to play the game. We've always had to live two lives—you know, one for them and one for ourselves. Now, the average white person doesn't know this, but of course, the average black person does. If you sit on any bus coming from the suburbs and hear black people laughing about the fool things they have done at work, you'll know how many of us are playing this game.[15]

As Ella Surry's testimony suggests, being a "clever" trickster who can "play the game" is common among domestics, for they see their role playing as necessary to their survival in the white employer's home.

As with any racist stereotypic image, the mammy trope came to be taken as exemplary of "authentic" black womanhood. In other words, the attributes of the mythic figure became ontologically fastened to the black female bodies onto which they were projected. As I recount below, black women responded to this depiction of self in various and complicated ways. My grandmother, Mary Rhyne,[16] reveals some of the strategies domestics deployed to counter these depictions in her oral narrative about her days as a live-in domestic in the South. Through the act of performing her narrative, she reveals the ways in which the notion of black authenticity is contingent on context, history, and cultural values. Although the "mammy" prototype and the accompanying acquiescing behaviors attributed to her may be viewed as representative of authentic black womanhood in the white racist imaginary, my grandmother's narrative constructs a counterimage. Indeed, in her performance of self she supplants her own black authenticity on terms that correspond to her experiences as an aged black woman in a racist and sexist society.

Before I continue I wish to pause to say a word or two about my methodology. As I noted in the introduction, my goal throughout this book, and in each of the instances where I cite performed blackness, is to effect a performative dialogic ethnographic account. Toward that aim I wish to be ever cognizant of the ways in which my presence in the field affected the people I observe as well as my production of blackness. In this regard, this chapter on my grandmother warrants a more in-depth discussion given our personal relationship and the slipperiness of representing the life narrative of someone to whom I am closely related.

During the ethnographic encounter my role as audience to my grandmother's narrative varied. I listened to her stories as "grandson," as "ethnographer," and as "academic." I related to her and responded to what she said personally and culturally and in light of my academic and professional obligations and goals. My role-playing was, however, more impure than pure. I did not substitute one mask for another. Rather, my role-playing effected what Vincent Crapanzano identifies as a "bifurcated" sense of self.[17] According to Crapanzano, bifurcation is not a schizophrenic condition where one has no control over his or her actions. Instead, bifurcation refers to the conscious balancing act a researcher performs in the ethnographic encounter. This multiple subject position stems from the researcher's need to appear ethical and credible in the eyes of the academy and to be ethically responsible to the culture and the subject studied.

Within the ethnographic site of my grandmother's home, the information was processed in several different ways because of my multiple subject positions. For example, as I listened to and recorded my grandmother's life history, there were many moments of recognition because I either knew the people, places, or events to which she referred or because I had heard the story before. There were times during the interview when I mentally made notations about how what she was saying tied into a particular theory. There were still other times when I felt she was withholding information, and I tried to come up with an explanation for her reluctance. The process of being drawn into the story of a performer while maintaining a critical distance is the challenge of doing fieldwork and is that which makes it dialogic. It requires playing roles—that is, performing—and these roles effect shifting perspectives and shifting meanings, which destabilize "the expert."

In addition to interviewing my grandmother, I spent time getting to know her neighbors at her home at Tate Terrace, a public housing community for seniors in Kings Mountain, North Carolina. I also interviewed my grandmother's former employer, Mrs. Smith (see appendix B). My interactions with the community members and Mrs. Smith functioned to complicate or problematize my grandmother's narrative and my personal, cultural, and academic interpretation of it. My interactions with the residents of Tate Terrace revealed nuances about these people that sometimes contradicted my grandmother's construction of them—for example those whom she termed "pickles" (i.e., crazy) I found to be "sane." Likewise, sometimes my experience concurred with her views—for example, she declared that one neighbor was "homalsexual," and indeed he suggested that he was. Whereas Mary's attitude toward her relationship with Mrs. Smith was ambivalent, Mrs. Smith tended toward a romanticized or idealized depiction of the relationship. In addition, while conducting the interview with Mrs. Smith, I found it difficult to remain silent when hearing her refer to my grandmother as a "mammy." The interview was one moment in the process where my role as an academic/ethnographer transcended, to the point of silence, my role as grandson/black American.

My performance of heterosexuality or, at least my silence about my queerness, also affected the ethnographic encounter and implicated me in my grandmother's sometimes homophobic, sometimes ambivalent, attitude toward members of her community and toward homosexuality in general. For example, there was one resident, David, in whom my grandmother had a particular interest. I soon learned that David was a seventy-four-year-old white man who had to walk with the support of a walker, and who had moved to my grandmother's community from across town. But that was not the most important thing about David. Based on the fact that David "gardens, bakes pies, and keeps a clean house," my grandmother concluded that he was a "homalsexual." She followed with, "but some people can't he'p the way God made 'em." Whether or not her last statement was an opening for me to come out to her is unclear. Nonetheless, I never (and still have not) revealed my sexual orientation to my grandmother, and I have condoned her homophobic remarks about her neighbor, and even let her throw away pies that he made for me during my visit. On the other hand, my grandmother always made me thank him personally for the "gifts" he brought to me, and she asked me to run errands for him when he needed help—thus illustrating once again her ambivalent stance regarding sexuality and the ways in which I was implicated.

Finally, methodologically and otherwise I feel it is important to include in its entirety my grandmother's narrative from my interview with her in 1993 (see appendix A). Although it is positioned at the end of the text, its inclusion contextualizes my discussion of other topics and issues that I formulate throughout the chapter. Further, the inclusion of the narrative is also a political move. My desire is to allow my grandmother to speak for herself in her own words: this is my way of grounding theory in political praxis, of granting agency to the marginalized, and of helping to bring a silent voice from the margin to the center. Finally, including the entire narrative is a practical choice. Unlike traditional texts about which scholarly research is conducted, Mary's narrative is not available in bookstores or university libraries. If it were not included here, the reader would have no way of accessing it. I transcribed Mary's narrative using a performance-centered method in order to represent, as closely as possible, the sound and sense of her voice and gestures.[18] A full explanation of the symbols I use is given in the introduction to appendix A. Further, I have divided the full narrative into episodes; readers who wish to find the complete text of the material I quote in this chapter will find it in the appendix under the episode title.

Mary Rhyne's Labor History: 1955 to 1973

Mary Rhyne was born on February 26, 1914, in York County, South Carolina. The second oldest of five children, she was raised by her paternal grandfather on a small farm outside Gastonia, North Carolina. In 1930, she moved to Kings Mountain, North Carolina, where she met and married "Jim" McHaney. Together, they had five children—two girls and three boys. When she and Jim separated in 1949, Mary moved forty miles north to Hickory, North Carolina, where she moved in with her oldest daughter, Sarah. Shortly thereafter, however, she secured a place of her own in an apartment complex called the Embassy Apartments. She made a living by cleaning homes and by working part-time in a factory. By 1954, all of her children had relocated to Hickory.

Hickory residents Gene and Virginia Smith hired Mary as their domestic in fall 1955. Initially, Mary worked for the Smiths and for Virginia's parents, Mr. and Mrs. Friar, as a day worker. In spring 1956, after the birth of the Smiths's youngest daughter, Carol, Mary quit her job with the Friars and became a live-in domestic for the Smiths. For the next seventeen years (for a total of eighteen years of service) Mary lived with and worked for the Smiths.

Mary's workday included cleaning the Smiths' eight-room house, taking care of their lawn, and preparing all of their meals. She spent most of her day washing and ironing clothes, especially those of the children. She prepared only two meals a day, breakfast and dinner, because the children had lunch at school and the Smiths were at work. On the holidays, especially Thanksgiving and Christmas, the Smiths and their extended relatives helped Mary prepare the meal. During each of these holiday meals Mary was expected to sit at the dinner table and eat with the entire family, which she often did. Although

Mary with her grandfather and siblings: (left to right) DeMaxie,
Ervin, Ernest, Mary, and Taylor Adams, 1929.

the family helped Mary prepare the meal, they did not help her with
the dishes, and thus she washed them by herself without the aid of a
dishwasher.

More than anything else, Mary was the major care provider of the
Smith children. During the weekdays, the Smiths' four children, Eddie, Patti, Jimmy, and Carol, were under Mary's supervision because
their parents spent those days and nights forty-five minutes away in
Shelby, North Carolina, where they owned and managed a hotel. During the week, Mary sent the children off to school, made sure that they
did their homework, and prepared their meals. She also disciplined
them at her discretion. On the weekends, the Smiths went to their
home in Hickory to pick up Mary and the children and take them to
Shelby. On Sunday evenings they were driven back to Hickory. Except
for a few days out of the year (excluding holidays), Mary never had a
day off. On some days, after she completed her chores at the Smiths',
Mary was able to visit with her own family, who lived across town. This
routine continued until 1970 when the Smiths sold their hotel, three
years before Mary left their employ.[19]

Mary's tenure with the Smiths lasted through significant social and

The Smith family: (left to right) Virginia Smith, Carol, Patti,
Gene Smith, Jimmy, and Eddie. (standing, back center)

political events: the Civil Rights movement; the assassinations of John
and Robert Kennedy, Martin Luther King Jr., and Malcolm X; and the
sit-ins, to name a few. These events served as the backdrop of Mary's
employment and marked a tenuous time in American history regarding race relations, particularly in the South. Despite this period of social unrest, Mary maintained an amicable and respectful relationship
with her employers and their children. Indeed, according to Mary,
they "nevah had uh cross word." Although Mr. Smith is now deceased,
Mrs. Smith and her children keep in contact with Mary and speak
fondly of her.[20] On many occasions Mrs. Smith has asked Mary to
join her on trips to visit the Smith children, who live in various cities
on the East Coast. The children, now parents themselves, send Mary
Christmas and birthday cards and presents as well as pictures of their
children.

In May 1973, a week before the youngest child, Carol, was to be
married, Mary left the Smiths' home and never returned. According
to both Mary and Mrs. Smith, Mary went to visit her sick brother in
Washington, D.C. Because his sickness was life threatening, Mary remained in Washington for a period of two weeks. When she returned

from visiting her brother, she decided not to go back to work for the Smiths. Rather than speak with the Smiths herself to inform them of her decision, she called one of the Smiths' neighbors and instructed her to tell the Smiths that she had decided to quit. For three years, between 1973 and 1976, Mary had little contact with her former employers. During those years, she worked in a shirt factory in Kings Mountain. After three years, however, the factory was sold and Mary was laid off. Thus, at the age of sixty-two, she retired, keeping her residence in Kings Mountain. She regained contact with the Smiths, however, and occasionally from 1976 to 1985 she did housework for them when she went to Hickory to visit her family.

Until the early 1990s, Mary continued to work as a domestic a few days a week to supplement her income. However, due to arthritis and failing eyesight, she is no longer able to work. Now, at the age of eighty-nine, Mary collects "whatnots" and enjoys quilting and watching her grandchildren, great-grandchildren, and great-great-grandchildren grow up.

She also enjoys her life at Tate Terrace, although many of her closest friends and neighbors are now deceased. Notably, for the past five years she has been the only African American resident in the community, although in the past there were as many as three African American women and one African American man.

The two rows of apartments that comprise Tate Terrace sit at the bottom of a hill in one of the town's poorer neighborhoods. Each apartment has a small front porch with guardrails and an aluminum-framed screen door. In front of the apartments is a small lawn area dotted with rose bushes and young maple trees. Behind the apartments are four rows of clotheslines that run parallel to a narrow sidewalk. The back porches, which are smaller than the front ones, contain a garbage bin and a conglomeration of different items—chairs, chests, bottles, cans—that the residents have placed there. My grandmother and a few other residents also have planted flowers or tomato plants in front of and behind their apartments.

Before my visit in 1993, the last time I walked along the narrow sidewalk that leads to my grandmother's apartment was in summer 1990. Nonetheless, on this visit I remembered to follow her instructions not to park in Nanna's parking space and to approach her apartment from the back, not the front, so that her nosy neighbors would not "know her business." However, no matter her precautions, my grandmother's neighbors always seemed to know when she had company. Life at Tate Terrace is marked by a set of issues, rituals, and "rules," including parking spaces contested by folks who cannot drive or do not own cars; a preoccupation with each other's lives, especially on occasions when visitors are present; and the constant acts of politesse in face-to-face encounters followed by swearing in the privacy of their own apartments—at least in my grandmother's.

A few people have died since my last visit, while others, as ill as they may be, rebuke death whenever it comes calling. The folks of Tate Terrace know that their lives are drawing to a close, and their aches and pains, multiple bottles of medicine, and forgetfulness serve as constant reminders. Yet, there is something in the way that Ruby smiles at me, or the way Claudine cocks her head when she tells me lies about herself or her neighbors, that suggests to me that life, or living, occupies these people's minds and time more so than death.[21] Perhaps the presence of an outsider offers these people an audience for their performances. Their behavior becomes a "show," as my grandmother says, that is as involving, complicated, and entertaining as performances produced for the stage or in motion pictures.

Living in this community, among these people, is where my grandmother feels most comfortable. Her relationships with her neighbors designate her as special and, to a certain extent, confirm that she is in control of her life. How ironic that my brother called me on the first night of my visit in 1993 to try to convince me to persuade my grandmother to move to Hickory to live with family.[22] It was ironic because on this same night I realized how much my grandmother is needed at Tate Terrace and how much the community is a part of her. In fact, it is, so it seems, centered on her. All of the residents know and respect her. For instance, during my stay a number of residents came to her for advice, others to borrow food items, and one to borrow money. In addition, she mediated disputes between feuding residents. Also, her apartment is located in the center of the community and, therefore, she is audience to most of the dramatic events of the day. Thus, in many ways my grandmother feels more needed by the residents of Tate Terrace than by her own family, who have their own lives and families. Her family does not depend on her as do the folks of Tate Terrace.

When my grandmother visits with her children she lacks the autonomy and self-reliance she has at home. Her children and grandchildren feel the need to protect her because of her age. Although she is not resentful of such attention my grandmother is too independent to be ruled by her children. At Tate Terrace she enjoys her independence and freedom to come and go as she pleases. She enjoys the control she has over her life and, to a certain extent, over the lives of others.

She also enjoyed the autonomy that she experienced working in the Smiths' household. Five days out of the week, my grandmother was left alone and in charge of the Smiths' home and their four children. The autonomy, authority, and control that she experienced during the week at the Smiths seems to have carried over into how she lives her life at Tate Terrace.

On the third day of my visit in 1993 my grandmother told me that she wanted to perform her narrative. The way she communicated this desire suggested that she did not look forward to telling me about her life as a domestic. She would much rather talk about the people of Tate Terrace. Three years earlier I had interviewed her as part of a project for graduate school.[23] At the time she was excited and eager and she could not wait to tell me stories about Claudine and her grandchildren, as well as about her other friends at Tate Terrace. In those stories, my grandmother was always the one who was smarter than everyone else—the trickster. I can only assume that she felt that her stories about being a domestic would cast her in a different light—one in which she was no longer the weaver of tales, the joker duping the gullible. Instead, she might have seen herself as the trickster whose "tricks" were matters of survival rather than "play." Whatever the reasons, my grandmother's attitude toward talking about her years with the Smiths influenced her performance style. It was stiff, reserved, and formal. I found I had to work hard as an interviewer to obtain information. Most of her answers to my questions were short and to the point unless something I asked or she said sparked a fond memory, at which point she would elaborate and tell a more detailed or exclusive story.

Performing Domestic Labor:
"Making Do" and Remaking Blackness

I wish to draw here on Mary Rhyne's narrative to identify how she views, constructs, and performs the role of domestic laborer. I compare and contrast her perspective with that of other fictional and nonfictional texts concerned with the black American female laborer in the United States in the twentieth century. In addition to analyzing the narrated events that Mary recounts, I frequently address how Mary performs her labor history in the "present," in the narrative situation. Whereas in the past events Mary frequently constructs a persona who "makes do" within the site and in light of the rules of her employer's home, it is by means of her present performance that Mary remakes her (or the) identity of the domestic laborer. If for no other reason than that Mary speaks (speaks to and about her experiences as a domestic laborer), performance becomes a site where a typically silent, or silenced, part of our history is given voice.

As articulated by Mary in her narrative, four key characteristics of her domestic labor experience stand out. First, the work was physically demanding and the pay was low. Second, in lieu of sufficient monetary compensation for the work that she performed, nonmonetary forms of "compensation" became part of the employer-employee contract. In addition to receiving material goods (i.e., hand-me-downs), Mary felt that because the Smiths were *"very"* nice people" who treated her with respect, the job was worth keeping. As I discuss below, this exchange of physical labor for "nice" treatment presupposed that Mary would also be "nice" to the Smith family. Based on the experiences that Mary recounts, I interpret the term "nice" to reflect a mutual understanding between her and the Smiths concerning her position within the home and her relationship to the family. In brief, she was an "outsider-within." On one level, she was treated as an adult member of the family and she claimed authority (and responsibilities) accordingly. On another level, however, her "familial" position and authority was constantly qualified by the fact that she was a paid employee and she was black. She was clearly not a member of the family and any claim to authority was in deference to that of her employers.

Third, my grandmother took pride in her work. In her narrative, she explicitly highlights her culinary talents and skills. She implies that her knowledge and experience in raising children is and was superior to that of Mrs. Smith. And she boasts of her honesty. According to Mary, because she was "a l w a y s honest," she "COULD A L W A Y S GET UH JOB." Finally, my grandmother's narrative demonstrates how her experiences as a domestic influence her present life and relationships at Tate Terrace. In particular, she identifies herself as part of what she terms the "*sick* group" and yet also as one of its caretakers.

Before I discuss these four characteristics of domestic labor as articulated by and emphasized in Mary's narrative, I wish to offer one caveat about my analysis of her narrative. Namely, in general terms, a number of contemporary theories concerned with race, gender, age, and class systems enable me to identify and interpret my grandmother and her experiences in terms of her being part of an oppressed and victimized group of people. And, in my analysis, I do at times claim and specifically pursue this perspective. What my grandmother says in her narrative, however, contradicts this perspective. In other words, she does not view herself as oppressed. Or, more specifically, domestic labor was not, for her, oppression. It was a job—work that she did, and did well, in order to support and nurture what was far more important to her and her identity, that is, her own life, home, and family.

In so saying, I do not intend to inscribe my grandmother as "unique" within the domestic labor force nor as an icon of "motherly" sacrifice. Rather, I intend to point out that my grandmother did not, and does not, identify herself and what she values solely in terms of domestic work and a white family and its worldview. Indeed, her refusal to be labeled "oppressed" suggests a detachment from or an indifference toward the labor site that may well be more resistant, or resistant in a different way, than those strategies that grant the "oppressor" the authority she or he assumes or desires.

"Ah Done Ol' an' Broke Down":
The Physical Hardships and Low Pay of Domestic Work

Mary's narrative defines, if nothing else, domestic work as physically and emotionally challenging: hard on the body and on the mind. Her tale relates long days of cooking, cleaning the house, washing and ironing clothes, and tending to the children. She also talks about both the temporary and long-term effects that the labor has had on her body.

At several points in the narrative Mary speaks briefly of her chores. She began her workday by preparing breakfast for the Smiths, followed by washing and ironing clothes, cleaning the eight-room house, and preparing dinner. In addition to these chores, Mary relates that she was responsible for seeing the children off to school and to church. She maintained this routine for over eighteen years.

The amount and kind of work my grandmother was expected to do in the Smiths' home is characteristic of domestic work in general. In addition, the domestic's daily schedule is frequently filled with more work than can be accomplished in a single day by a single laborer. Washing, ironing, and folding a week's laundry for an entire family, preparing meals, taking care of the children, and completing "special" projects such as cleaning the closets or attic suggests an intense schedule. And, as Mrs. Smith acknowledged in her conversation with me, my grandmother appears to have followed such a schedule: "So, she just got in there and she did the cooking and taking care of the kids and I think running day, morning to night."[24]

In Rollins's study of domestic workers, one participant, Julia Henry, states that many women choose to quit rather than meet the demands of the job. She recounts: "It was too much work from the beginning. It was two day's work in one. I was washing clothes, ironing. Then I had to do two bathrooms, three bedrooms, vacuum. I'd be so tired. I'd come home. I couldn't go anywhere except to bed. It really wasn't worth it. I told her [the employer] I couldn't do it all in one day. I finally left."[25] Although, like Julia Henry, Mary disliked housework that was physically taxing, in the episode of her narrative "As Long as Ah Stay Black" she states that she didn't mind housework "if it ain't / lot uh dat ol' / washin' an' ahrnin'." In other words, she did not seem to mind housework if it were not overly taxing, or at least if she were able to do tasks that she enjoyed, such as cooking. Some of her dislike of housework was due to her having to use poor equipment or, in the case of dishwashing, no equipment at all. Rollins confirms in her study that "dilapidated, outdated, or very cheap equipment [forced] the worker to compensate for its ineffectiveness with extra physical effort" (69).

In the episode "Dey Nevah Was Too Much Trouble," grandmother contrasts the pleasure she and the Smiths derived from her culinary skills with her displeasure in having to wash all the dishes by hand. Grandmother says:

> dey l o v e d squash casserole
> Ah'd fix dat
> Ah/was/all/de/time/makin'/som'in'
> yeah dey liked what Ah cooked
> dey loved mah *cookin'* —
> fo' dey got uh dishwasher
> Ah washed dishes everyday__ —
> dey looked
> Mrs. uh
> Mrs.
> Grandmama say
>
> (switches to old, decrepit voice)
>
> "Ah 'clare"
> say
> "one of dese days yuh jus' look out ovah deah"
> say
> "jus' look in dat windah
> she'll be standin' in dat windah
> washin' dishes"__
>
> (smiles)
>
> Ah thought
> not ef dey had uh *dish*washer

While Mrs. Smith's mother, "Mrs. Grandmama," romanticizes the image of Mary "standin' in dat window/washin' dishes," Mary signifies on the woman by stating "Ah thought / not ef dey had uh *dish*washer."

Rather than vocalize to her employers her dislike of washing dishes by hand (a complaint for which she might have been reprimanded), she uses indirection (silence) in the narrated event and verbal Signifyin' in the narrative event. Mary makes it known, then, that while she enjoyed cooking the physical labor of having to cook *and* clean up by hand was not, as "Mrs. Grandmama" would like to configure it, an ideal experience. In other words, in her performance of the past events Mary refuses to adhere to the "Stepin Fetchit" prototype of mammy. She recodes, or clarifies the duplicitous coding of, a happy mammy washing dishes by offering her own contradictory view of the situation.

One aspect of Mary's physical labor that is more difficult for her to recode by means of performance is the long-term effects that the work has had on her body. Mary's hands are burned and scarred from cooking, and she presently experiences severe hip and back pain due to the years that she spent on her feet. In addition, as she explains in the episode "Oh Dey Nice People," the combined effect of living in a "mill house" and working in the Smiths' house is that she now suffers from arthritis in her legs:

an' d e n
an' d e n
Ah got
Ah tol' dat Ah had tuh have uh *house*—
DAT'S/HOW/COME/MY/LEGS/LIKE/DEY/IS
my arthritis
dis is all from de *mill* houses
dese ain't nuthin' but mill floors
dese ol' cement floors
my legs[26]

Mary's "ol' an' broke down" physical condition is not uncommon to domestic workers. Rollins confirms that the older domestics in her study "had various physical ailments associated with their work: lower back problems, varicose veins, and most common, ankle and foot problems."[27]

Until the early 1990s, despite her physical condition, Mary continued to do housework for Mrs. Smith and others. Although she contended that she could not "do uh w h o l e lot of *hard* work" when, as she states, "my hip don't hurt meh so bad," she did accommodate the various requests for light housework. The pay she received supplemented her income and, as I discuss later in the chapter, until Mary was physically unable to do so, there appeared to be an implicit assumption on the part of Mrs. Smith that Mary would always be available, and able, to tend to her home. And, although Mary often said it "ain't worth" it, she regularly chose to fulfill Mrs. Smith's and her other employers' expectations.

One of the most disheartening aspects concerning domestic work is the pay. According to Rollins, between 1960 and 1980 many domestics who worked ten- and twelve-hour days often were paid as little as thirty dollars a week. Live-in domestics, who were essentially at work twenty-four hours a day, were paid even less (72–75). Marva Woods, a live-in domestic in Rollins's study, tells of how she was paid as little as thirty-seven dollars a week:

> I just worked until I got the children to bed. Every Thursday and every other Sunday was off. I got up in the morning, fixed breakfast, got the children ready for school, and carried little John to nursery school. I'd get them all off then start doing my housework: the washing, cleaning up. John would come home about twelve. I'd go and get him and give him his lunch and put him to bed. I would iron or something while he was in bed. When he got up, I'd take him for a walk. Then I'd cook dinner and serve it. After I cleaned up the kitchen and got the children to bed, I was finished. . . . She started me off at thirty-seven dollars a week, then she gave me a raise and I was making fifty-five dollars. (71)

Marva Woods's workday resembles that of Mary's, although Mary did not have fixed days off and, as she states in her account, she was paid only twenty-five dollars a week. Rollins admits that live-in pay is more difficult to measure due to the nonmonetary compensation that the domestic receives, such as meals and a room of her own. Nonetheless, the highest estimates for live-in work that Rollins obtained (from agencies in Boston) were one hundred to one hundred seventy-five dollars a week (74–75).

Mary also never received monetary benefits such as vacation pay or bonuses. In fact, when I asked her if she had ever received a bonus, she found my question ridiculous:

(abruptly)

naw

(looks at me and sneers and begins to laugh)

what?∧∧

(more laughing)

what kind uh BONUS?

(turns her head away from me)

no
no bonus
Ah didn't git no bonus—

Although Mary did not receive monetary bonuses of any kind, she was and is fortunate that the Smiths deducted social security from her pay. Following her retirement Mary's main source of income was her social security check. According to Mary, the woman who followed her in service at the Smiths' home was not so fortunate:

THEY DIDN'T HIRE ANYBODY AFTER YOU?

yeah dey got somebody
dey got somebody tuh work fuh 'em
an' dey didn't
take out de woman's
social security
social security or some'in' or another
an'
Ms. Smith had tuh pay back uh lot uh dat social security
. . . .
so
Ah thank she went tuh go draw huh lil' social security
say

(giggles)

dey hadn't took none out on 'uh
an' see dey got on tuh Mrs. Smith nem

(crosses her legs)

an' dey had tuh pay all dat *back*
had tuh pay dat
had tuh pay it
you know dey s'ppose tuh take out social security on yuh
everywhere you *work*
dey-didn't-take-it-out-on-'uh

The Smiths' actions are, apparently, commonplace. According to Rollins, "In domestic service, non-compliance with Social Security legislation is rampant" (76).[28]

Throughout her telling of the various stories that dealt with the physical aspects and demands of domestic work, Mary supported her verbal account with nonverbal performance. Whether by means of closing her eyes, mixing and stirring "imaginary" ingredients, or pointing to parts of her body, Mary used her body in ways that are discursive, in ways that paint a portrait of her life as a domestic as *she* sees it. Moreover, her incorporation of the body provides the interpreter of her narrative with images—however fleeting—that facilitate a point of entry into the performance and domestic sites of narration.

Most commonly, Mary used repetitive and rhythmic physical movements to communicate the work that she did. On the one hand, her repetition of certain actions served as a metaphor for what she viewed as redundant work. On the other hand, her use of repetition directly denoted, or illustrated, the fact that the work was repetitious. Not only did it effect a repetitive sensation or quality, it was repetitive. For example, in the episode "Dey Didn't Pay Nuthin'" Mary uses nonverbal repetition to augment or accent her repetitive, verbal listing of the chores. Each time she says "an' den Ah'd fix," her hands rise up, and on the word that follows, whether it be "dinnah" or "suppah," her hands fall in a prancing motion. The up-and-down physical movement and accentuation of the words produce a "rhythmic-iconic coding."[29] The motions do not convey word content as much as they convey rhythmic content—that is, the repetitive rhythm of the work.

In her performance, Mary frequently pointed to her body to emphasize a particular verbal point. In other words, she used nonverbal discourse to direct attention to her corporeal body. In "Dey Didn't Pay Nuthin'" Mary relates how she received third-degree burns on her hand from a grease fire in the Smiths's kitchen. She recalls:

dey/put/me/in/de/hospital
dey took ca'uh of d a t
an'
dem s c a r s deah

(points to her left hand and makes a circling motion)

Ah got all dat burned off
a l l dat deah
all dat was cooked/all dat just cooked
so
it took me uh l o n g time tuh get up
so
dey had tuh take ca'uh of all uh dat

By pointing to the scars on her hand, Mary supports the fact that she was burned. Her illustration lends credibility to her verbal account. The scars also mark her body as a historical text, a discursive site where the past experience is retold in and through the present performance. As Carol Stern and Bruce Henderson explain, "the body creates language and participates in its performance simultaneously."[30]

In this case, the body language and its performance produce duplicitous meanings.[31] The scars reference the labor site, her work and its damaging effect. The past labor site permanently claims, marks, and disfigures the body. Simultaneously, Mary's public display of the scars speaks against, or defiles, the domestic site. In Mikhail Bakhtin's terms, her "grotesque" body degrades any reading of the past site (and her body) that would tend toward a "high, spiritual, ideal, abstract" conception of them.[32] Although "the essential principle of grotesque realism is degradation" (17), according to Bakhtin, degradation "is always conceiving" (19). It works to reposition the high and the ideal in "contact with [the] earth as an element that swallows up and gives birth at the same time" (21). As Peter Stallybrass and Allon White remind us: "The grotesque physical body is invoked both defensively and offensively because it is not simply a powerful image but fundamentally constitutive of the categorical sets through which we live and make sense of the world."[33]

In this case, Mary shows her scars to defend her account, as if to say "look what the work did to me." She took the offense in that her physical display criticizes the past event. By means of performance, then, the performer rewrites her body—she assigns it new or additional meanings. The meanings do not idealize the body, however; indeed, it is precisely because the body itself is not idealized that the past (Mary's history as a domestic) cannot be idealized either. Performance permits Mary to show the grotesque body as the "body in the act of becoming." "The grotesque body continually builds and creates another body."[34]

Authorizing Power: "Like One of the Family"

Although Mary never complained to the Smiths about the low pay that she received for the amount of work that she did, she was well aware of the inequity. She was conscious of her hard work as well as her indispensability. In the episode "Ah'd Cut de Grass" when I asked her "What would they have done if you hadn't been there?" she gave the following response:

n o
they wouldn't have *done*
dat's what everybody say__
good Lord
l o r d/Ah say
dey ought tuh have paid me uh thousand dollahs uh week
'cause see Ah stayed—
you/heah/me/say/ah/stayed/deah/an'/took/care
uh/dem/*chaps*
an'
an' dey was down yondah in
in *shelby*
an' wouldn't nobody else
nobody else

(fold her arms)

wouldn't nobody else stay deah an—
day an' night an' take care uh dem chil'ren like *Ah'd* do it
. . . .
Ah did uh w h o l e lot of work fuh dem
dey oughten nevah forget me

(shakes her head)

"Nevah Had uh Cross Word"

DEY OUGHTEN *NEVAH*
'cause Ah s h o' saved dem uh many time
many uh time

In lieu of monetary compensation, Mary expects that "dey oughten nevah forget me . . . DEY OUGHTEN *NEVAH*." And, indeed, in her comments to me, Mrs. Smith clearly has not forgotten Mary (or, as Mrs. Smith refers to her, "Daisy"). Mrs. Smith appears to realize the quality of Mary's service to her when she reflects, "Everybody says, 'Oh we won't have another Daisy. You won't find another Daisy.'" After her retirement, then, it is the fact of being remembered for her years of service that is important to Mary, whereas earlier her employer's "nice" treatment of her appears to compensate for the "hard work."

In what follows, I discuss the various episodes in Mary's narrative that deal with what, as compared to the hard-work/low-pay characteristic, appears to me to be a more subjective component of the domestic contract. In brief, I discuss the unwritten interpersonal contract that Mary continually alludes to in her narrative. I describe what constitutes this contract and how Mary adhered, or did not adhere, to the unstated expectations by consciously and unconsciously donning the mammy mask. Ultimately, the point I wish to communicate is twofold: on the one hand "authentic" blackness is constructed by Mary's white mistress vis-à-vis her construal of what a "real good mammy" should be. Mary performs and obliges that construction in various ways. On the other hand, within her narrative performance, she also performs her own version of "authentic" blackness by drawing on black cultural performance traditions that reposition and ground her authority as a "black" subject.

As described earlier, for twenty-five dollars a week Mrs. Smith expected Mary to prepare meals, clean the eight-room house, and provide care for the four children. For reasons that seem inadequate, Mrs. Smith offered Mary other nonmonetary forms of compensation: her own bedroom, free movement through the house, a place at the dinner table, and gifts and hand-me-downs. When Mrs. Smith cleaned out her closets or garage, Mary usually had first choice of the clothes or items to be given away. She would then bring these goods home to her children and grandchildren. Mary received items such as televisions, armchairs, lamps, coffee tables, and clothes. After her family took what they wanted, Mary shared the leftovers with our neighbors. This practice went on for years and saved my mother and her siblings a considerable amount of money. Moreover, it was a way for Mary to provide for her family. Although she could not always be there for them physically or emotionally, she was materially and financially supportive of her own children.

Mary was also permitted to move about the Smiths' home as she pleased—even when the Smiths were home she had free reign in the house. And, unlike most domestics, she ate in the dining room with her employers. One of her fondest memories is having Christmas dinner with the Smiths, which she describes in the episode "Every Chris'mas." During that memory, she recalls where everyone sat, including herself:

den
everybody had tuh come in the dining room

(spreads her arms to show the size of the table)

round de big family table
everybody be sittin' deah
'round dat table
so
Dr. Niles

(points to each place each person would be around the table)

he'd be right heah at *dis* end
an' Ah'd be right *heah*
Mrs. Smith would be right *deah*
Mr. Smith would be right *deah*
an' de othah chil'ren 'round
everybody sittin' 'round dat table
an' Dr. Niles would
would as'

(closes her eyes)

de blessin'
he would as' one of de sweetes' blessin's__
so
everybody would eat
Chris'mas
an' Ah'd he'p tuh *cook*

In relation to accounts offered in other studies, the image my grandmother paints here is not a common one. For example, traditionally most domestics were allowed only to serve food but never to sit down to eat with their employers. Moreover, many domestics were not permitted to move about the house freely but instead were relegated to the kitchen. Because the kitchen is where most domestics did much of their work, most were expected to remain there even when not on duty. Relegating servants to the kitchen was common; there their employers would be able to exert physical as well as psychological control.[35] Another anomalous "perk" permitted my grandmother but not most other domestics was having a "room of her own," which was located on the same floor as the children's rooms. Unlike my grandmother's situation, most live-in domestics' sleeping arrangements ranged, according to David Katzman, from "a third-story attic filled with worn out family furniture" to a room "with hardly more space than a closet," to no room at all.[36]

In my interview with Mrs. Smith, she offers that, prior to Mary's employ, she (Mrs. Smith) was looking for "a good mammy." "I wants me a real mammy," she said. And because Mary worked for Mrs. Smith for eighteen years, apparently Mary fulfilled Mrs. Smith's requirements. In light of what Mary recounts, Mrs. Smith expected a "real mammy" to do a large amount of work for little pay. To compensate, Mrs. Smith rewarded "Daisy" with material gifts and hand-me-downs, a nice room, free reign of the house, and a seat at the family dinner table. In other words, for Mrs. Smith a "real mammy" is or becomes "one of the family." And this interpersonal "reward" appears to be primary to the contract that Mrs. Smith and Mary "negotiated."

In so saying, I do not intend to inscribe Mrs. Smith as a lone agent. Her personalization of the economic (and political) aspects of domestic work was, and is, common to our mass culture. Regardless of race or gender, people who do housework and/or care for children are not paid well. The "domestication" of domestic work functions to contain the labor in the home site, and thereby its economic operations can be privatized, disassociated from the public marketplace and its regulations. As a result, and throughout our social history, women (and, more recently, men) who work in the home are either not paid or are paid very little. As with the contract agreed upon by Mrs. Smith and Mary, personalized forms of compensation are substituted for equitable pay (e.g., "gifts" from the breadwinner, unmonitored time in the home, and the understanding that tending to children is self-fulfilling in itself).

To the extent that Mrs. Smith constructs authentic blackness as the ability and *willingness* to perform as a "real mammy," however, her authority within her household and within her relationship with my grandmother maintains the racist hierarchy placed on the value of "black" as opposed to "white" bodies and labor reflected in larger society. Regarding the interpersonal contract arranged between the employer and employee, then, benevolence (being nice) compensates for low pay, and it is to be repaid by the expectation that the domestic is to fulfill the "outsider-within," "family/not-family" role as given.

The contradictions inherent in this role were, in the 1960s, apparent on a broader social-cultural level as well. As my grandmother relates in the episode "Ain't Nuthin' but uh Sick Group" that she had to ride in the back of the bus when using public transportation and, yet, it was also commonplace for her to bathe the Smith children. That is, as the Smiths' maid and nanny she entered public places that were otherwise barred to her. The social restrictions on blacks, as compared to blacks-as-servants, were not uncommon in the South—and, I suspect, in other regions of the country as well.[37]

My grandmother appears to have variously adhered to the "mammy" contract I discussed above. At times, her adherence appears genuine. She played the role in goodwill and/or out of pride in doing "GOOD HONES' HARD WORK." Other times she "made do" by covertly finding a way to subvert the contract in order to service her own needs or desires. In other words, she appropriated the "white" construction of the mammy and used it to her own "black" advantage.

In the episode "Dey Nevah Was Too Much Trouble," Mary conforms to the prototypical mammy figure in that she constructs an image of herself as a caretaker who loved tending to her white charges. She insists that the children "nevah was too much trouble," although elsewhere in that episode Jimmy appears to have been quite a handful. The youngest child, Carol, is clearly Mary's favorite and, as the following excerpt suggests, eventually leaving Carol was very difficult:

Ca'uh was uh different story/she was *so* sweet

(closes her eyes)

Jimmy Smith, age five.

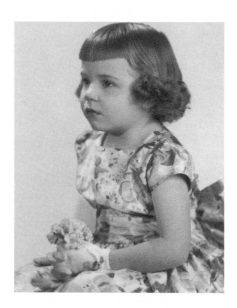

Carol Smith, age three.

Ah jus'
L o r d Ah jus' love dat lil' ol' youngin' tuh death
Ah hated tuh leave—
Ah had tuh cry one day
Ah/jus'/hated/tuh/leave/Ca'uh
Ah jus' had got attached tuh Ca'uh 'cause she was jus' uh sweet lil' ol'
youngin'

Mary's seeming adoration of Carol and her general coddling attitude toward the other children are attitudes not uncommon to domestics, real or fictional. In Toni Morrison's *The Bluest Eye,* for example,
the character Pauline Breedlove dotes on her employer's little girl very
much like Mary fawns over Carol when Carol wears the hat "wit' one of
dem lil' ol' ribbons in it" to church. Morrison writes: "When [Pauline]
bathed the little Fisher girl, it was in a porcelain tub with silvery taps
running infinite quantities of hot, clear water. She dried her in fluffy
white towels and put her in cuddly night clothes. Then she brushed
the yellow hair, enjoying the roll and slip of it between her fingers.
No zinc tub, no buckets of stove-heated water, no flaky, stiff, grayish
towels washed in a kitchen sink, dried in a dusty backyard, no tangled
black puffs of rough wool to comb."[38] Pauline's love and affection for
her employer's child, however, is often to the neglect and ill treatment
of her own children. In doing so, Pauline perpetuates the stereotype
of the overprotective mammy whose primary concern is the welfare of
her white employers' children. As Harris observes, Pauline "becomes
another example of the maid who cannot effect an acceptable compromise between the kind of work she does and the person she is."[39]

Although my grandmother pampered the Smith children but was
unable to spend the amount of time she would have liked with her
own children, she did not to my knowledge physically abuse her children. Rather, to compensate for the lack of time she made sure that
they were provided for in other ways. She used her leverage with the
Smiths to make her children's lives more comfortable, such as when
she accepted the hand-me-downs that her employers gave her. Grandmother's acceptance of the Smiths' leftovers speaks to her need to substantiate her income. To do this, she played the "outsider-within" role
as contracted: she gratefully accepted the "gifts" from her employers.
Then, when with her own family, she would turn her attention to what
to do with what were, in actuality, "leftovers."

Mary, holding Carol Smith, 1959.

In the episode "Oh Dey Nice People" my grandmother explains how she informed the Smiths that if she could not find a house for herself with wood floors, she could not work for them any longer. Her rationale was that the apartment in which she lived had cement floors that hurt her legs. In this case, grandmother's explanation disguised an additional motive. At the time she had two sons who lived in poor housing conditions and were struggling with rent. They needed a better and cheaper place to live. Grandmother was aware that the Smiths owned several houses in the poor black neighborhood where she and my mother lived. Behind my mother's apartment was a small white house with wood floors that the Smiths owned. So, my grandmother prodded the Smiths into renting the house to her, which she then in turn shared with her sons. By means of indirection, then, my grandmother got her wood floors; my uncles, a better place to live; and the Smiths held on to their "Daisy" by helping her out.

Although these gifts may inscribe the dominant/subordinate relationship between the employer and her employee in terms of the gift giving being, in Rollins's words, a "statement to the servant of what kinds of material goods the employer considers appropriate for her,"[40]

The author in front of the house the Smiths
"gave" to Mary.

therein also lies the potential for the recipient to reassign meaning
to the gifts and motive to their acceptance. As de Certeau might observe, domestics "have to get along in a network of already established forces and representations."[41] To survive in their employer's
household, they have to accept the gifts and act grateful. It is part
of the established "performance," to use Rollins's term (194). And
yet, as is the case with most bricoleurs, there is, per de Certeau, "a
pleasure in getting around the rules of constraining space" (18)—
in reshaping the leftovers into something new and for a different
purpose.

Another aspect of "making do" within the constraining space of
the "mammy" contract surfaces in Mary's narrative when she relates
occurrences where she chose to defer, or not to defer, to authority.
As Erving Goffman defines it, deference is ceremonious attitude that
"functions as a symbolic means by which appreciation is regularly
conveyed to the recipient."[42] But between those in an unequal relationship, it is considered "as something a subordinate owes to his
superordinate" (479). The consequence of deferential treatment in
unequal relationships is that the behavior affirms the inequality between the superordinate and the subordinate. White employers, for

example, expect not only good and efficient work but also that their employees appear happy doing it. Deferential behavior appears in various forms, such as linguistic and gestural expressions, spatial relations, task embeddedness, avoidance, and presentational rituals.[43] Linguistic deference and avoidance rituals are often related in that to avoid showing displeasure a domestic will often choose not to speak—for example, Mary contends that she and the Smiths "nevah had uh cross word." "Keeping quiet," however, is a part of the prototype where "mammy" is expected to speak only when spoken to; to be invisible and silent while tending to the needs of her employers.

On the other hand, some domestics, like the fictional character Mildred in Alice Childress's *Like One of the Family,* do not defer to their employers by remaining silent. In the title story, "Like One of the Family," Mildred's employer, Mrs. C, tells a visitor that Mildred is like one of the family. Mildred hears her remark, and after the visitor leaves, Mildred "speaks up" directly to her employer:

> In the first place, you do not *love* me; you may be fond of me, but that is all. . . . In the second place, I am *not* just like one of the family at all! The family eats in the dining room and I eat in the kitchen. Your mama borrows your lace tablecloth for her company and your son entertains his friends in your parlor, your daughter takes her afternoon nap on the living room couch and the puppy sleeps on your satin spread . . . and whenever your husband gets tired of something you are talkin' about he says, "Oh, for Pete's sake, forget it. . . ." So you can see I am not *just* like one of the family.
>
> Now for another thing, I do not *just* adore your little Carol. I think she is a likable child, but she is also fresh and sassy. I know you call it "uninhibited" and that is the way you want your child to be, but *luckily* my mother taught me some inhibitions or else I would smack little Carol once in a while when she's talkin' to you like you're a dog, but as it is I just laugh it off the way you do because she is *your* child and I am not like one of the family.[44]

In this case, Mildred refuses to play the role of the docile mammy who speaks only when spoken to. And yet, Mildred's claim to authority is temporary and sporadic. She finds she cannot discipline the children because the children expect her to defer to Mrs. C and, because Mrs. C rarely disciplines the children, Mildred finds herself in a catch-22 situation. And thus it is that Mildred is able to authorize her own image but not use that image (regardless of her responsibilities) to exert control over others.

Even though my grandmother had some of the privileges denied Mildred, she too recognized the paradox of being granted such privileges in terms of who maintained social and economic power in the relationship. And although it is true that she rarely "had uh cross word" with the Smiths, there were several instances when she did act as if she were like one of the family.

The episode "Y'all Ain't Havin' No Party" is an example of how my grandmother establishes her authority in the past narrated event as well as the narrative site, but it is also an example of the contradictions of her self-representation. Her performance of this particular story both affirms and subverts her own authority as she concedes near the end of the episode that it is the Smiths who actually have the final word when it comes to disciplining their children. But there is also irony in my grandmother's concession in that even though she feels that the Smiths have the ultimate authority in their children's lives, it is actually my grandmother to whom the children respond and for whom they have the most respect.

WELL
dey wanted tuh have uh
party
dis night
Saturday night__—
mother/nem/wa'n't/neah—
dey git so mad at me til dey didn't know what tuh do/wanted tuh have
uh p a r t y
Ah said
"Y'all ain't havin' no party h e a h."
Ah said
"Your mother an' daddy tol' me tuh stay heah an' take ca'uh uh y'all
an' take care of dis house."/an'
Ah said
"I'm gonna *do* it."

(switches to a whiny voice)

"You can go tuhnight."
Ah said
"Ah ain't goin' *no*where!"__

(shakes her head)

Ah said
"Ah ain't goin' nowhere."
Oh dey'd get so mad at me dey didn't know what tuh do/Ah said
"Ah ain't goin' nowhere"/an' Ah said
"An' y'all ain't havin' no *party* in heah *either.*"

(emphatically)

Ah said
"Y'all ain't *havin'* no party."
Dey'd get so mad at me dey'd didn't know what tuh do＿＿.

(15 sec. pause)

(abruptly, in whiny voice)

"Daisy won't let us do *nuthin'* "
"Don't want us tuh do *nuthin'* "
Ah said
"YOU AIN'T GONNA DO IT WHILE *AH'M* HEAH.
wait till your mama an' daddy come home."

As this excerpt demonstrates, Mary both claims and defers her authority in the past narrated event. On the one hand, she claims authority by stating that "YOU AIN'T GONNA DO IT WHILE *AH'M* HEAH." On the other hand, she undermines her authority when she tells them to "wait till your mama an' daddy come home." Thus her claim to authority vacillates between claiming and deferring. Like that of a trickster, Mary's verbal "play" in the past events, in the words of Victor Turner, "makes fun of people, things, ideas, ideologies, institutions, and structures; it is partly a mocker as well as mimic and a tease, arousing hope, desire, or curiosity without always giving satisfaction."[45] Thus Mary fashions herself as a trickster or joker, whose authority is, in Turner's words, "recalcitrant to localization, to placement, to fixation" (168). According to Turner, the "elusive" nature of verbal play is what gives it subversive potential, for verbal plays can "deceive, betray, beguile, delude . . . dupe, hoodwink, bamboozle, and gull" (169). Mary's deliberate gaming in the past event, then, is but one way that she establishes her authority in the present performance event.

Earlier in the episode "Y'all Ain't Havin' No Party" Mary claims and disclaims her authority again in another anecdote. The event she relates concerns Jimmy, the youngest son, who has been out at night riding his motorcycle, apparently in a reckless manner:

so
de police brought Jimmy in
an' heah come Jimmy
an' he started cryin'__

(closes her eyes and shakes her head)

he s t a r t e d c r y i n'__
Ah said
"Jimmy∧"
Ah said
"Now Ah tol' you not to go out uh dis yard."
Ah said
"Now you been WAY OVAH YONDAH ON DE HIGHWAY WIT DAT MOTORBIKE."
Ah said
"Now you know bettah than t h a t."
he was just uh *cryin'*__/he just cried__
so
de police brought 'im on
an' Ah said,
"Your/mothah/an'/fathah/gwoin/git/you/boy"__
dat was tuh scare 'im up

In her performance, Mary recreates the complexity of her position as an authority figure in the family. To establish her authority in the past event, she sits erect and increases her volume when she scolds, "Now you been WAY OVAH YONDAH ON DE HIGHWAY WIT DAT MOTORBIKE." Then, to appeal to Jimmy's sense of right and wrong, she decreases her volume and draws out the last word of the line, "Now you know bettah than t h a t." After she recreates the incident and dialogue, she comments on how "he was just uh *cryin'*/he just cried__," which indicates, to her and to her audience, that her scolding was effective. Nevertheless, Mary undercuts her own authority and reinforces that of the Smiths when she warns Jimmy, "Your/mothah/an'/fathah/gwoin/git/you/boy," after which she evaluates, "dat was tuh scare 'im up." Her commentary indicates that, for her, the Smiths are the final authority. But Mary's actions here are double-edged. Although we can view what she says as deference, we can also view it as a tactic to show that she obeys the rules of authority in the household and thus can dismiss herself as the parental figure. She is not the parent and therefore she refuses to bear the burden of ultimate responsibility by deferring and referring it to the "real" parents.

At the very end of this episode my grandmother's performance style shifts from enthusiasm to despondency. After I ask the question "Did they listen to you pretty well?" my grandmother responds nonverbally with a head nod and then with a faint whisper, "yeah." It is at this point that Mary concedes that the only reason the children listened to her was because "dey mutha' an' dey fatha' *allowed* 'em to." In other words, she feels that if the Smiths had not made sure that the children listened to her then the children would have done as they pleased. She even points out that perhaps the Smiths instructed the children to obey her only until they were of a certain age, for "uh-numbah-uh-yeahs." She mumbles this statement and does not elaborate on its meaning, but the subtext suggests that she lost control of the children at one time or another.

This particular episode reveals the ambiguities inherent in the role Mary was expected to play in caring for the children. In brief, she both was and was not authorized to be the authority figure. The episode also reveals contradictory shifts in the performer's attitude toward the event that she tells. At first, her performance is lively and energetic as she constructs herself as a powerful person to whom the children listen and over whom she asserts control. Near the end of the episode however, she is reserved as she recognizes the limits of her authority within the domestic site.

Mary's ambivalence regarding her authority is also exemplified in the episode "We Just All One Family," in which she recalls a time when a drunken Mr. Smith threatens to leave his wife and children. According to Mary, it is she who takes charge of the situation and persuades Mr. Smith to stay. In so doing, Mary's responses are not in the least pedestrian. In this particular instance, she chooses not to defer to the standard code of conduct regarding authority. Moreover, she appears to remove the "mammy" mask completely. She does not play the mammy's prototypical exterior qualities nor does she appear to have a covert agenda or an ulterior motive. In this case, Mary constructs herself as an authority figure whose agenda seems to be to help the Smith family through a serious crisis. She recalls:

> he came in deah drankin' one time an' said he was gwoin *leave*
> he went in neah an' got de
> *suitcases*
>
> (points to the floor)
>
> an' he was gonna leave/dem little youngins just uh hoopin' an' uh
>   hollerin'
> an' uh screamin' an' uh holdin' de do'
> got on mah nerves so bad/Ah went in neah/Ah tol' 'em
> Ah said
> "Now
> what in de w o r l d do you mean?"
> Ah said
> "Dese lil' chil'ren is jus' hollerin' an'
> an' goin' on heah"
> Ah said
> "PUT DEM SUITCASES DOWN!
> SET DEM SUITCASES BACK DOWN"
> an' de chil'ren/a l l
> *fo'* of 'em
> just whoopin' an' hollerin'
> "*d a d d* y don't leave/*d a d d y* don't leave/*d a d d y* don't leave"
> Ah didn' wanna git in to it/but Ah had tuh git in to it *dat* time
>
> WHAT DID MRS. SMITH SAY?
>
> (emphatically, jerking her head to the right)
>
> NOTHIN'
> just
>
> (begins to giggle)
>
> NOTHIN'
> 'cause see him an' huh had been into it
> she wa'n't doing nu'in' but just *stan'in'* neah
>
> (stiffens her body)
>
> Ah went in neah/Oh Lord Ah was jus'/dis/upset me so bad
> Ah didn't know what tuh do__

The Smiths' home, where Mary worked and lived for eighteen years.
(photo by Sarah M. Johnson)

Ah jus' got all ovah Mr. Smith
he come brought the suitcase in neah an' sat it down
an' dem chil'ren

(makes pulling motion)

dey just *pullin'*
dey was pullin' de suitcase
some at de do'
holdin' de do'
so he couldn't go out de do'

During this family crisis, Mary refuses to play the docile servant
whose membership in the family is qualified by her status. Although
Mary knows that she is expected to stay in her place when she states,
"Ah didn' wanna git in to it," she opts to "break the rules" instead:
"but Ah had tuh git in to it *dat* time." Interference such as this is not
common to domestics nor is it commonly accepted by the superordinate. In this case, however, Mary removes the mammy mask, speaks
up, and moves to action. She becomes the superordinate when she
gets "all ovah Mr. Smith" and demands that he "PUT DEM SUITCASES
DOWN!" And, it is Mrs. Smith who assumes the role of silence and
docility while Mary takes charge. Significant to this case, Mary does
not "trick" within the confining space of the home and its "status quo"

rules of conduct. She temporarily changes the rules to redress the family crisis. In other words, Mary breaks, or breaches, the normative rules of the domestic contract by taking charge—by, in effect, telling her employers how they should behave. In sum, she conceives of and directs the participants in a set of new roles that effects a redressive performance that resolves the conflict and, also, offers reflexive commentary concerning the normative family structure, authority, and Mary's relation to both.

In addition, in the present-tense narrative situation Mary uses performance to redress a personal-as-social conflict that exists between her and the role she played for so many years. By means of ritual storytelling, she claims authority over and against silence. As Richard Schechner suggests, "rituals carry participants across limens, transforming them into different persons."[46] The "different person" Mary becomes is one where she acquires agency over the construction of her own life. In the context of the story about Mr. Smith's leaving, she redresses the social conflict incited by the "mammy" myth by refusing it in the past and by speaking in the present. She thus claims authority over her self-representation in the past and the present.

The artificiality and constructed nature of the performance event provided a safe space for my grandmother to perform this story. Within the narrative site she could reconstruct her life in affirming and empowering ways without fear of retaliation from her employers. Grandmother took advantage of this site, her homeplace, to present herself as a powerful figure in this incident and, thereby, in the eyes of her audience. Indeed, she constructs her own image of "authentic" blackness.

Moreover, my grandmother's performance of her oral history takes the harsh realities of her life as a domestic and the present conditions of her life as an elderly, poor, southern black woman and, despite evidence to the contrary, transforms the world of that life into a discourse where she is treated and she treats herself with respect and dignity. Therefore, her performance serves as an agent of transformation and healing. It is in the performance site, then, where the cognitive dissonance between life as lived and life as imagined is less conflictual. Grandmother's ordinary and marginalized existence as an elderly, poor, black woman became secondary in the narrative event. The paradoxical relationship between memory and "rememory" in performance is what gives oral personal narratives subversive potential.[47] In particular, the narratives of members of marginalized groups have subversive potential, whether marginalized because of race, class, gender, age, sexual identity, or ethnicity.

In most instances, Mary does not defer to the Smiths' authority over the children in terms of disciplining them the way she sees fit. She refuses to let the children have a party in the house and chastises Jimmy at every possible moment. More important, she does not defer authority over the children in the presence of their parents. Even Mrs. Smith notes that "she'd [Mary] tell Jimmy if he didn't stay in that house she was gonna whip his butt." Thus Mary asserted her authority over the children in the presence of the Smiths in the manner of a grandmother, aunt, or other older family member, as is customary in black American communities, and in doing so legitimized her role as a "real" family member. Mary's response to Mr. Smith and her assertion of authority over the children were both instances where she "salvages" her dignity and reclaims her humanity, disputing the confounding of authentic blackness and inferiority.

"Proud Mary": The Valuing of Domestic Work

In the episode "As Long as Ah Stay Black" Mary expresses contempt for factory work. She vows, "as long as Ah stay black/Ah'll nevah have another *production* job." The job to which Mary refers is one that she held in a shirt factory immediately following her employment at the Smiths'. For three years, Mary collected, stacked, and ironed thirty dozen shirts in each eight-hour day. At age sixty-two, Mary was dismissed from her job.

Recalling the difficulty of factory work, my grandmother says that she prefers housework. Although both types of work involve repetition, physical labor, and long hours spent standing, the production job did not allow her as much control over her work. As opposed to domestic work, the factory job places time restrictions on the laborer, monitors how she does her job, and provides no variance in the tasks to be performed. Therefore, despite the hard work, low pay, and complicated relationship with her employers, my grandmother speaks with pride about her domestic work. In general, it was "GOOD HONES'

HARD WORK." And, in particular, her descriptions of her cooking, her housekeeping, and her skills as a care provider for the Smith children illustrate her pride in her work.

On the surface, Mary's pride and interest in taking care of the Smith children, cleaning house, and cooking appear to uphold the mammy prototype. The stereotypical mammy is invincible: she never gets tired of cooking, cleaning, and nurturing. But, unlike the popular mythic figure, this particular woman is not invincible. After years of cooking, cleaning, tending to the children, and managing the kitchen, Mary is tired. In addition to her age, her health is failing. Her muscles ache, her bones are worn out: indeed, she "done ol' an broke down." Mary sadly notes:

(puts her hand on her heart)

when Ah use tuh/Ah/done/done/dat/sorta/cookin'/
Ah/can't/do/now
it jus' done
it jus' done
left meh
Ah done done mah part of it—

More than her "duties" as a domestic, however, Mary seems most proud of the fact that she maintained her integrity while under the Smiths' employ. Indeed, according to Mary, her honesty and trustworthiness is "DE EXACT REASON AH COULD A L W A Y S GET UH JOB." In other words, the fact that Mary did not steal from her employers guaranteed that she could always find domestic employment. The stereotype of the black domestic in the white imaginary is that of one who is dishonest and a thief. Mary's comments concerning this issue suggest that she is and was aware of the preconceptions that many employers hold toward the domestic when she is first hired and, in many cases, throughout her employment. She states:

so
you know
now Ah stayed
as long as Ah s t a y e d at dey
at dat house _ _
long as Ah stayed deah

"Nevah Had uh Cross Word"

Ah nevah
rambled
in dey *stuff*

(opens imaginary drawers)

in dey d r a w s
in dey stuff
Ah didn't know bit mo' dan some of de thangs on de—only
foldin' de chil'ren's *clothes*
but like RAMBLIN' IN EVERYTHANG/SEE
Ah didn't *do* that
Ah didn't do that
Ah nevah did—
when dey come back everythang was jus' like dey *left*/it
Ah didn't *ramble* in dey stuff
Ah'd fol' de chil'ren's c l o t h e s
Ah'd fol' 'em
de chil'ren's clothes

DID SOME PEOPLE DO THAT?

yeah
some people stayin' de house
dey ramble thu' thangs
you know
ramble an'
tamper

(10 sec. pause)

SOME MAIDS TALK ABOUT HOW THEY USED TO STEAL STUFF AND TAKE
THINGS

(cuts me off)

n o
DAT'S DE EXACT REASON AH COULD A L W A Y S GET UH JOB/'CAUSE
peoples k n o w

(spreads her hands)

when Ah went tuh dey house
Ah didn't bother *nuthin'*
everythang was jus' like dey *left* it
Ah didn't bother dey stuff—
an' people s t e a l—/dey/can't/git/no/job

147

yuh *heah* me∧∧
dey/can't/git/no/job
an' peoples ain't wantin' nobody in dey house dat *steal*

(emphatically)

an' Ah don't *blame* 'em

(15 sec. pause)

<small>THEY'D TAKE STUFF?</small>

<small>UH HUH</small>
dey *take* it
Ah jus' nevah did do that
Ah nevah did do that
Ah was always
a l w a y s honest
Ah didn't want nuthin' Ah didn't work fuh
if dey give me some'in' Ah'd take it
if she didn't
if she didn't *give* it Ah didn't *git* it__
Ah nevah *did*
an' Ah nevah *would*
take de chile's stuff—
an' dat's de reason NOW
people's uh
uh *suffer*
wantin' help
but
you know
you can't trust peoples in yuh house like you—
dey'll steal
dey'll steal
shortenin' out uh *biscuit* now
an' people jus' rather
jus' do de bes' dey *can*
dan tuh have somebody in de house *workin'*

Grandmother's responses to my questions exemplify her pride in living her life in terms of values such as honesty, integrity, and Christian beliefs. Indeed, her pride kept her from taking things that she did not work for: "if dey give me some'in' Ah'd take it/if she didn't/if she didn't *give* it Ah didn't *git* it."

Mary recognizes that some white employers assume that, until proven otherwise, all domestics will *"ramble* an' *tamper"* and "steal" when she euphemistically exclaims that "peoples k n o w." Her statement reveals another "clause" in the unwritten agreement between the domestic and her employer. From Mary's point of view, "thou shall not steal" because the employer is watching and will monitor your actions. As is the case with assuming that the domestic wants to be a "part of the family," the assumed "fact" of thievery on the part of the employer functions to legitimize low wages, personalize the service, and perpetuate racist views.

Mary appears to perpetuate these views herself when she comments that she understands why employers will not hire blacks because "dey'll steal/dey'll steal/short'nin' out uh *biscuit* now." Although some domestics do steal, Mary's comments reflect internalized racism because she verbalizes the racist ontology of blackness and dishonesty and deviancy. Similar to the perceptions of many employers, grandmother projects "dishonesty" onto the domestic as if it were an innate quality. She also appears to not recognize (at least in her statements) that if a domestic steals it may be the domestic's way of compensating for low wages—a way to "make do" within the confining space of the highly personalized (i.e., "subjective") domestic contract. On the other hand, another reading of her comments might suggest that her characterization of other domestics serves as a means to distance herself from the image of the stealing mammy, given the fact that she prides herself on not taking her employer's things.

In addition, when Mary observes that "people's uh/uh *suffer*/wantin' help," she is, it appears, conforming to the view that domestics exist to ease the suffering of those more-fragile, less-hearty white women. In other words, Mary perpetuates the black woman-(and/or domestic)-as-mule myth. The mule is to sacrifice a legitimate business contract in order to help out those in need. In light of this perception—this myth of the self-sacrificing mule—the white employer views the economic aspects of the contract as equitable. Mary's comments assume that the social conditions under which we live are such that the white employer and the black domestic's social statuses are equitable. Given the current economic and social status of many black Americans, however, these assumptions are false.

In both historical studies and slave narratives, stealing arises as a strategy used by slaves to compensate for poor living conditions and a lack of food. This practice extended into domestic work. According to historian Lawrence Levine, however, "not only did . . . masters deny [slaves] the fruits of their labors but the whites themselves practiced theft far more serious than that of blacks."[48] And, yet, as Katzman observes, "whites denigrated blacks in part because what a white Southerner might tolerate among whites became reprehensible when practiced by Negroes."[49] Perceived as racially and morally superior to blacks, whites projected onto blacks a stereotypical behavior in which they themselves participated. On the other hand, blacks did steal in order to survive and, as a consequence, they also helped to perpetuate the stealing stereotype. Each instance validates the notion of blackness as co-constructed by whites and by blacks.

When I interviewed Mrs. Smith, my grandmother was present, and at one point she and Mrs. Smith discussed the subject of trust. Mrs. Smith explained that she was at that time afraid to hire a domestic because she did not feel that she could trust them. In turn, my grandmother echoed her sentiments:

EPJ: Did you have anybody to come work for you after [Mary]?

Mrs. Smith: No, cause I couldn't ever trust nobody. That's why I make her [Mary] come up here now. I told somebody the other day. I said I wouldn't have one of those girls down there at the college or one of those guys come over here and work for me cause they might break in . . .

Mary: [interrupting] Ah tell de chil'ren now, Ah say well Lord de reason why peoples can't get jobs anymore is because dey do nothin' but steal, steal, steal. And take things that don't belong tuh 'em.

. . . .

Mrs. Smith: And it was this lady over here—over there—who works at the library at the college. She was over there helping her. She was getting ready to leave and Roxy said, "I just tell you, you never know with people. Trust 'em and everything." Said this lady worked for [unintelligible] and she asked me if I needed some help. She was gonna help me out twice a week. I said, "That's the way I am about Daisy." I said, "I'm not gonna get no one I don't know to come in." And it's just me and I just wait till Daisy comes up here.

In this passage, when Mrs. Smith projects the stereotype of the stealing domestic, my grandmother confirms it. Ultimately, Mary's seemingly accommodationist comments regarding black servitude cannot be pinned down to any one meaning, for as is the case in other places in her narrative, she often speaks out of both sides of her mouth. Like the trickster that she is, she may ventriloquize the speech of the master while simultaneously signifyin' on him or her. In any case, Mrs. Smith uses her fear and distrust of strangers to justify her reclamation of the old domestic contract between her and "Daisy." As I discuss above, personal reasons are used by Mrs. Smith to construct and maintain the contract. The agreement appears to be that Mary should continue to work for Mrs. Smith, otherwise Mrs. Smith will "suffer."[50] The present understanding between Mrs. Smith and Mary is based, then, on a complex interweaving of race and class stereotypes, the personalization of the domestic contract (i.e., economics), Mrs. Smith's trust in Mary, Mary's pride in being trustworthy, and their shared past and current status as senior citizens.

"Homeplace": After Domestic Work

The years Mary spent at the Smith home affect how she interacts with the residents of Tate Terrace. The authority and control she exhibits at certain moments in the domestic site are carried over into her homeplace. At Tate Terrace, Mary constructs herself as a self-determined individual, as an authority figure from whom others seek advice, and as a care provider. Because Tate Terrace, specifically Mary's home, was the storytelling context, it affected the telling of the narrative. It affirmed how she at times claimed authority in the telling of her past domestic experiences because her sense of self-authorization is so strong at Tate Terrace. In the few stories that she relates in her narrative concerning the people of Tate Terrace, grandmother's performance style is lively and energetic. It is clear that she feels more comfortable talking about her Tate Terrace community and lifestyle than her experiences at the Smiths'.

At Tate Terrace, Mary positions herself as a care provider. In the episode "Ain't Nuthin' but uh Sick Group," for instance, Mary says that all of the residents of Tate Terrace are physically disabled and basically helpless, including herself. Yet in the same episode she contends: "Ah check 'em—/not all of 'em but/Ah check on 'em" suggesting that even though she is a member of the "sick group," she still looks after most of the other residents in the community. Similar to the ways in which she took care of the Smith children, she takes care of the residents at Tate Terrace. In "Ain't Nuthin' but uh Sick Group" grandmother relates how all of the people who live in Tate Terrace are unable to care for themselves because they are elderly:

everybody down heah ain't able tuh pull one anothah out de FIRE
dey ain't able tuh do nuthin'__
NANNA
see
she's about dead__
an' Mrs. *Johnson*
she ain't able tuh do nuthin'__
Madeline ain't able tuh do nuthin'__
Mr. *Bullock* ain't able tuh do nuthin'__
Mr. *Littlejohn* ain't able tuh do nuthin'__
an' *Ah'm* not able tuh do nuthin'__

(wrinkles up her nose)

Claudine ain't able tuh do nuthin'__
dat ol' *man* is seventy-fo'
he ain't able tuh do nuthin'__
an'
Glenn an' his wife ain't able tuh do nuthin'__
an' Pauline is sick__
an' *Ruby's* sick__
an' dat othah one on de othah end/she ain't able tuh do nuthin'__

(giggle)

dis heah's uh
uh *sick* group down *heah*
ain't nuthin' but uh
sick group

Mary incorporates repetition and rhythm in her speech to affect the listener's view of the Tate Terrace residents and to encourage the listener's participation in her narration. Her narrative rhythm encouraged my involvement in the narrative event as I leaned forward and listened more intently, following along as she mentally moved from one apartment to the next. Further, the rhythm is enhanced through the emphatic intonation placed on each of the resident's names at the beginning of each poetic line. Mary's message about this community being a "sick group" is highlighted through her utilization of repetition and rhythm so that her statement is persuasive to her audience.

Mary's use of repetition and rhythm reflects the indigenous musical and vernacular traditions of black Americans, including the rap, spiritual, gospel, and blues musical traditions as well as folk preaching. Through storytelling, Mary draws on her cultural and experiential knowledge of these traditions and internally dialogizes them. Accordingly, the repetition found in Mary's narrative functions the same as the repetition in these musical traditions. In the excerpt above it sustains the focus on the central idea that the residents of Tate Terrace "ain't able tuh do nuthin," while at the same time it incorporates subtle shifts in voicing and words as in, "an' Pauline is sick__/an' *Ruby's* sick__," before it returns to the original pattern of "ain't able tuh do nuthin'" near the end of the passage. The use of repetition to focus attention on a central idea within black American musical traditions encourages emotional engagement on the part of the audience as well as intensifies the emotional engagement of the performer. This active participation occurs through a call-and-response dynamic whereby the rhythm created by the repetitive force effects active participation on the part of the audience.

Mary's repetitive and rhythmic speech also resembles that found in folk preaching, where repetition and rhythm are integral to the preacher's performance style. When describing the effect of this performance style, literary and cultural critic Hortense Spillers notes: "The thrust of the sermon is passional, repeating essentially the rhythms of plot, complication, climax, resolution. The sermon is an oral poetry—not simply an exegetical, theological presentation, but a complete expression of a gamut of emotions whose central form is the narrative and whose end is cathartic release. In that regard the sermon is an instrument of a collective catharsis, binding once again the isolated members of community."[51] The notion that the folk sermon is oral poetry, that it evokes catharsis and that it binds members of a community, is reflected in Mary's narrative. The repetition and variations of the phrase "ain't able tuh do nuthin'" create a rhythmic force that draws the listener into the speech by creating suspense as to whom she will refer to next. She uses a fire as the framing meta-phor so that the fire becomes the symbolic image against which the residents of Tate Terrace "ain't able tuh do nuthin'."

Grandmother's goal is to symbolically bind the people of Tate Ter-race into a collective whole. Rather than summarize what the resi-dents cannot achieve if isolated one from the other, at the end of her testimony grandmother binds the community together by emphasiz-ing what they are together: a sick group. She achieves cathartic release by, near the end of the passage, giggling. The giggle is cathartic be-cause it functions to alter and "mend" the effect of helplessness that the preceding imagery has created. By giggling, grandmother mocks or pokes fun at the group, herself, and the imagery that her verbal repetition has created. Her reflexive giggle tells the listener that if the image is accurate she knows about it and, therefore, the listener should feel no pity or sympathy for her and her collective. They may be sick but they are not inept nor are they without humor.

By drawing on these various indigenous oral traditions to narrate her story, Mary affirms a "black" cultural identity. The significance of this cultural identity is that Mary constructs it within the narrative site of Tate Terrace, a predominately white community. Although she is a minority there, she resists being marginalized as such. Rather, she "speaks" her culture as much as it "speaks" her in order to forge a space for herself at Tate Terrace. At the same time, she is able to tran-scend issues of race and form relationships with the other residents who live there. In doing so she inhabits a "liminal" space, betwixt-and-between social and cultural boundaries where, to use Turner's words, she "draws [her] materials from all aspects of [her] experience, both from [her] interior milieu and [her] external environment."[52] This pro-cess speaks to the performativity of racial identity—to the reiterative performances that condition authenticity.

While Mary drew on her own self-affirming cultural identity in many of the events about which she spoke, it is most prevalent in the narrative site—Mary's homeplace. Outside the confines of the domes-tic site and within her homeplace, Mary makes life happen accord-ing to her own cultural codes. It is within her homeplace, then, that Mary constructs herself as a subject rather than as an object, as one who reacts rather than as one who is manipulated. Likewise, I should also note here that Tate Terrace provides the context for Mary to counter the representation of the accommodating mammy as the site of authentic blackness. Inasmuch as authenticity is culturally and socially conditioned, Mary evinces a counter black-authenticating performance that transgresses the popular logic regarding black women and their value. Ultimately, then, Mary appropriates blackness for her own means, utilizing her homeplace as a site of resistance.

The racial and social stratification that defined relationships between slaves and their masters also defines relationships between domestic workers and their employers. In addition to the hard work, domestics also contend with the mammy stereotype associated with black women in general and domestics in particular. Black women respond to this image in complicated ways. In her narrative, my grandmother both defers to and claims authority by at times adhering to the performance of the mammy as represented in the white imaginary—for example, her contention that her employers were "very n i c e people," although "dey didn't pay nuthin'," and the fact that she "nevah did . . . *ramble* an' *tamper*" with her employers' things. On the one hand, my grandmother's confirmation of the mammy myth can be viewed, according to Collins, as an "effective [conduit] for perpetuating racial oppression."[53] On the other hand, my grandmother frequently showed how the "mammy" is a constructed role that can, therefore, be altered to serve motives, needs, and desires other than those of the employer—for example, when she "got all ovah Mr. Smith" to keep him from leaving his family or when she took secondhand items in order to provide for her family. Among other things, she strategized a way to get a better house and goods for her children, and she intervened in family matters when she was expected to stay in her place, countering the racist mammy image with her own subversive performances of blackness. "Such contradictions," says Harris, "are the way things are. The pattern is handed down from slavery and the majority of mistresses and maids are not inclined to alter it. But there have been a few iconoclasts, in art as in life."[54] For her part, Mary can be counted among the iconoclasts. While a "co-conspirator" in the perpetuation of the trope of the mammy as inferior, she nonetheless "co-produces" alternative versions of the mammy that accord her with agency and that offer a productive dialectic to the racist discourses currently circulating in the cultural marketplace.

Coda: Stories Never Told

Perhaps Mary's penultimate "guileful ruse" lies in what she does not say in her narrative. Indeed, her silence about why she left the Smiths' employ may be her most strategic move in subverting her status as a "real mammy." Although Mary remains silent about the subject, Mrs. Smith describes the circumstances under which my grandmother left her employ in the following way:

> Mrs. Smith: And then. Carol . . . she was gettin' married. And your
> mother [my grandmother's daughter]—Jimmy said Sarah had been
> here. And I had to work at the sale that day. Said that your grand-
> mother was going to Washington to see her brother—real bad off. And
> of course I told her all the time that she would have to come down the
> aisle right after me when Carol and Patty got married and sit down
> there with me. Cause she *raised* those kids. So Daisy went up there
> to her brother that was so bad off. She went up there and she didn't
> come home.
> Mary: Didn't I come back?
> Mrs. Smith: NOOOOOOOO. You finally got up the nerve to call Tanya. Told
> Tanya to tell me that you was gonna stay up there, cause he was real
> sick and you weren't coming back.
>   She was with us 18 years.

It is Mrs. Smith's belief, then, that after eighteen years of service my grandmother quit her job in order to take care of her sick brother. It is odd, however, that my grandmother never mentions the story about her sick brother in Washington, D.C. In fact, her only reference to leaving the Smiths is found in her cursory remark: "Ah got ti'ed/an' den Ah left/an moved/back tuh Kings Mountain."

Because my grandmother never mentioned a "sick brother," I went to my mother for more information. At first my mother confirmed Mrs. Smith's story, but after some prodding she offered an alternative version. She told me that instead of going to Washington, D.C., Mary returned home to Kings Mountain. Mother said that it was a culmi-nation of Mary's being tired of housework, being away from her chil-dren, and being away from her siblings that led to Mary's decision to leave the Smiths' employ. She then said that another reason that Mary left the Smiths was because of Carol's wedding. According to mother,

Mary at age eighty-eight in 2002.
(photo by the author)

Mary's fictional trip to Washington, D.C., to visit her "sick" brother occurred a week before Carol, the Smiths' youngest daughter for whom
Mary had such great affection, was to be married. Mrs. Smith wanted
Mary to walk down the aisle and sit with her at the wedding. In other
words, she wanted to make a public display of Mary as the ultimate
possession of mammydom. Although Mrs. Smith aptly contends that
Mary *"raised* those kids," I recognized the irony of Mary's sitting in a
public space as "mother" of the bride, whereas all in attendance would
still see her as "mammy." She had too much pride and dignity to allow
herself to participate in such a spectacle. In this instance, Mary refused to embody the mammy prototype in favor of, according to her
standards, a more "authentic" performance of black womanhood, and
she quit the job altogether.

Like the able-minded trickster, my grandmother used indirection
and trickery to refuse the mammy role and to quit her job. Instead of
telling the Smiths outright that she did not want to participate in the
wedding and that she no longer wanted to work for them, she fabri-
cated the story about her brother. She even got her own daughter to
corroborate the story. Moreover, after the wedding she did not talk to

Mrs. Smith directly. She called a neighbor to tell Mrs. Smith that she was not coming back. Like the monkey who scurries back up the tree after he has duped the lion, my grandmother sat contentedly in Kings Mountain during the wedding ceremony while the Smiths thought she was visiting her brother.

The question remains as to why my grandmother has kept her leaving a secret for all of these years. I believe there are two possible reasons for her silence. Because Carol and my grandmother had a very close relationship, my grandmother might not want to hurt Carol's feelings with the truth. In addition, she might not want to tarnish the Smiths' trusting image of her by revealing that she was dishonest with them. Whatever the case, her "guileful ruse" was successful. By procuring and maintaining the lie, she simultaneously sustains a benevolent relationship with the Smiths. In addition, the lie saved her from compromising her dignity and self-respect.

My grandmother's silence is a form of covert resistance, a form of nonviolent self-preservation. Like so many domestics, she never raised her voice when dissatisfied with her conditions. She contends that if she did not like something, she "nevah did say nothin'" because "saying something" might have cost her the job or caused unnecessary tension in the home. Instead, she was silent. She firmly held her mask in place until she had the opportunity to score a victory— however fleeting. She "made do." But when the mask began to give way, when she could no longer devise tactics in the domestic space, she transformed her silence into a discourse of resistance. Silence removed her from the oppressive space of her employer. Silence saved her from being put on public display as the mammy.

As one who is illiterate and outside the "academy," my grandmother draws on the black oral tradition to theorize her life as a female domestic. In her appropriation of blackness, grandmother's performance reflects the material conditions under which she narrates her life. Whether in the Smiths' kitchen or in her home at Tate Terrace, her narrative reflects life as lived. Grandmother's performance shows that women who, in the words of D. Soyini Madison, "create sound out of silence"[55] to articulate the circumstances of their lives, enact a theory of resistance.

Although all people use the materials available to them to articulate their lives, those available to Mary and her use of them function as a discourse of agency. Indeed, Mary employs various discourses of blackness—oration, storytelling, vernacular, signifyin', food, etc.— to create a discourse that is not only "feminist" but also ambiguous—that of the "trickster." As a "trickster" narrative, Mary's performance opens up infinite possibilities for play, subversion, ambiguity, affirmation, and contradiction.[56] Given the infinite possibilities provided in the "reversals and discontinuities" of a trickster's language, grandmother fashions herself as a trickster who temporarily eludes the social constraints placed on her. The tricksterlike qualities of grandmother's discourse are like her performance of blackness: what qualifies it as unfixed is that it raises its "ugly head" where it would otherwise be absent; it is absent where it would otherwise be seen; and it resides at the center when it is expected to be located at the margins.

5

SOUNDS OF BLACKNESS DOWN UNDER

The Café of the Gate of Salvation

> I've always sung music that comes from a black
> tradition. So if it's not soul, it's funk, or reggae.
> So I think black music touches me in some way, I
> don't know why that is, a white Jewish girl from
> Sydney, what can I say, them's my roots.
> —Tracey, Café of the Gate of Salvation

> It's that once-a-week singing with other people and
> recognizing that we all have things to overcome,
> and being uplifted, and I just think music is
> universal. It conquers the language barrier.
> —Deborah, Café of the Gate of Salvation

> The distasteful truth will out: like it or not, all
> writers are "cultural impersonators."
> —Henry Louis Gates Jr.

In the previous chapters I focus on the ways in which blackness is appropriated, performed, and authenticated among black Americans. Blackness is not confined to U.S. borders, however. Indeed, like performance, to invoke Richard Schechner yet again, wherever we think blackness is going, it is not going there.[1] In the pages that follow I examine the performance of blackness in Australia, or "Down Under." Further, I shift my focus from verbal/vernacular signifiers of blackness to musical forms. As I demonstrate in earlier chapters, once signs (or, in this case, *sounds*) of blackness are disseminated, they become the site at which cultures contest and struggle over their meaning. Gospel music, as a sign/sound of "blackness," has become one of those contested sites.[2]

By focusing first on the formation and performances of the choir the Café of the Gate of Salvation, and then moving on to a general discussion of gospel performance in Australia, I examine the ways in which the medium of gospel music facilitates a dialogic performance of "blackness."[3] Given the racial, cultural, and religious composition of the Café and other Australian choirs, in this chapter I address the politics of appropriation, highlighting the ways in which Australians explain their interest in and performance of gospel music, as well as the ironies that underlie their explanations. Further, I explore the complexities of cultural usurpation by focusing on how my role as the "authentic" black American singer affected their performances and vice versa. My analysis, then, demonstrates the problematic aspects of gospel performance in terms of cross-cultural appropriation, as well as in terms of the mutual benefits garnered when self and Other performatively engage one another via gospel music. In the process, I consider some of the following questions: What is the relationship between performance and power? How does performance reproduce, enable, sustain, challenge, subvert, critique, and naturalize ideology? What are the politics involved when I, as an "outsider" to a culture, stereotype a people while simultaneously feeling dubious about their notion of the sacred?

"Couldn't Hear Nobody Pray": Discovering Gospel Down Under

An all-white, mostly atheist Australian gospel choir—at first it sounds contradictory. Yet, when situated in contested contexts of "blackness" and "performance," white Australian, atheist gospel singers are no more contradictory than black gay Republicans. Indeed, we live out the contradictions of our lives.

I learned of the Café of the Gate of Salvation through a former classmate from graduate school at the University of North Carolina at Chapel Hill, who emigrated to Australia in 1991. One of the things he and I share is a love of gospel music. Many of his letters to me included requests that I send him tapes of gospel because they were hard to find in Australia. Then in spring 1992 he wrote to tell me that he had discovered a gospel choir in Sydney. This was not just any choir. It was an a cappella, predominately non-Christian or atheist gospel choir. I refused to believe him until he sent me a recording of the choir on compact disc. Three years later I secured a grant to travel to Sydney to begin my research on the choir.

Although I had listened to the choir's recording and was amazed by the power of their voices, on my arrival in Australia I was still dubious about the effectiveness of this choir. As a black American raised in a black southern Baptist Church, I had my doubts about the ability of an all-white Australian choir to perform gospel music. My attitude began to change, however, the first time I attended one of their rehearsals. At that time they gathered at the East Side Uniting Church in Paddington, a suburb of Sydney known for its stylish shops, and which was adjacent to the city's gay scene, Darlinghurst.

I arrived at the church about a half hour before the rest of the choir. While waiting, I studied the murals hanging on the walls of the church: a picture of a beggar with his hands held as if praying; a painting of an eye; a drawing of a cross with red shapes superimposed on it; and a painting of the sun done in tie-dye fashion. Soon, the members of the choir began to drift in wrapped in their scarves and hats, greeting one another with kisses and hugs. About fifteen minutes after the start of the scheduled time, the choir members finally gathered together in a circle to start the rehearsal (I was struck by the fact that, like black gospel choirs in the United States, this choir operated on "CP" time).[4] Tony Backhouse, the choir's founder and director, greeted everyone and introduced me as a special guest. He informed the choir that I had received a grant to conduct research on them. After their looks of astonishment and surprise dissolved into curiosity and intrigue, members of the choir waved to me and welcomed me to their rehearsal. And with that, Tony took out his pitch pipe, blew a note, and the choir began to sing.

Had I closed my eyes on that occasion, I almost might have thought that I was back home at my church in western North Carolina. Not only did the choir approximate a "black" sound they created the ethos of a black devotional service as they stood, hand in hand, in a circle in the middle of the sanctuary, singing "I Woke Up This Morning with My Mind Stayed on Jesus." I was impressed. Next, the choir rehearsed a song that Tony had written, called "Save Me Some Grace," after which I was invited to sing with them. I attended two more rehearsals during this first visit. At the second rehearsal a local television station was present to film the choir for a special segment of the midday news called "Healthy, Wealthy, and Wise." Because Tony had asked me to teach the choir a song, I appeared on the television show in a short cameo of me teaching an arrangement of "There Is a Fountain."

During the three weeks of that first visit, I interviewed various choir members and, without exception, all were willing to share their experiences in the choir. Moreover, they all were curious about my impressions of their performance. Specifically, they wanted to know if I thought they were "good," if they sounded anything close to the way gospel *should* sound. My response was always encouraging but usually noncommittal. "I was *really* impressed," I often told them. Although I thought they had a great sound and, to some extent, had mastered the gospel idiom, I nevertheless felt that something was missing. I realize now what I did not then: that I was waiting to hear an "authentic" voice in their music. I was listening for the conviction, the expression of faith, that fuels much black American music in general and gospel music in particular. Because I did not hear this "authentic" sound, I did not fully appreciate the Café's music—or, I should say, I did not *allow* myself to appreciate it fully. My initial response was one of admiration, coupled with skepticism. I admitted the choir's performance as an approximation, yet I dismissed it as definitely not the "real" thing.

In retrospect, I recognize that I entered this ethnographic encounter with an "ax to grind rather than feeling for the organism."[5] Indeed, I was immersed in the essentialism that I adamantly oppose elsewhere. Compounding this, my first visit was only three weeks in length, not nearly enough time to get a sense of Australian culture, day-to-day rituals, politics, and ways of being in the world. Later in the chapter, I discuss how subsequent visits complicated my analysis of gospel performance in Australia as well as how my role as ethnographer expanded to that of teacher and then to "expert," as I conducted gospel music workshops around the country, appeared on television and radio programs, and became somewhat of a celebrity among gospel aficionados. First, however, I provide here a brief history of the Café of the Gate of Salvation and how it was formed.

"Blackness" in the Making

Tony Backhouse, a native New Zealander and former rock singer, formed the Café of the Gate of Salvation in 1986. His interest in gospel music began when he heard "You Don't Know What the Lord Had Done for Me," a track on the album *Sorrow Come Pass Me Around.* A record-shop owner whose store was located near the Badde Manners Café, which Tony managed, gave the recording to Judy Backhouse, who at the time was Tony's wife as well as co-owner of Badde Manners. When Judy played the song for Tony, both were powerfully affected:

> The voices were so strange on it and the feeling was just fantastic. To me it was weird, like it was very exotic and at the same time, kind of earthy and truthful. . . . There was one strong singer, the alto, and then there was somebody else who sounded like someone's dying grandmother, who was sort of seemingly singing a soprano part or sort of set soprano tone, but she was actually singing lower than the alto in this kind of strange voice that was not always kind of hitting the same harmonies as someone else. And then there was a sort of bass voice that you could barely hear so voices didn't blend and half of it was inaudible, and that just added a fantastic character to it and I just wanted to find out more about it.[6]

Although this song piqued Tony's interest in gospel music, he did not begin singing gospel right away; it wasn't until four years later that he "got a calling" to start a choir. The idea came to him during a ten-day Buddhist meditation retreat, and soon thereafter he put up signs in the Badde Manners Café, other cafés around Sydney, as well as in the Conservatory of Music. The signs read: "Singers Wanted for Gospel Choir. Buddhists Welcome." Forty people showed up at the first meeting, which was held in the living room of Tony and Judy's one-bedroom flat. "He had no idea what he was going to do really," Judy recalls. "He'd prepared one song, 'How I Got Over,' [Aretha Franklin's version] and that was it—the choir was born."[7] The liner notes of their first recording alludes to this initial meeting: "The idea was to see if there was a bunch of singers around ready to go down a passionate, exhilarating spiritual, but culturally specific and little known byway; i.e., to form a choir inspired by the Afro-American religious singing tradition. When we started to rehearse in Tony and Judy's lounge room we had few expectations. It was an experiment that could have lasted 20 minutes or 20 years."[8] In the months that followed, Tony continued to learn more about gospel music. He obtained gospel music recordings from Australian disc jockeys; he corresponded with white music scholars in the United States; and he read articles on gospel, as well as the liner notes of gospel recordings.

Regarding how the choir got its name, Tony recalls: "I was reading a book on coffee at the time. It's [Café of the Gate of Salvation] the name of an actual café out of Istanbul. It's been there since the thirteenth century or the sixteenth century. Just the ring of it sounds kind of nice. It's a terrible name. You can't fit it on any decent-sized poster. We should have called it "Punk" or something, a little bitty, one word [name] would have done a lot better." Nonetheless, the name stuck and now, two recordings and numerous awards later, the choir enjoys the reputation as, arguably, the best gospel choir in Australia. Today, Tony is known throughout the country for his voice and gospel music workshops. Other choirs, some of whom are spin-offs of Tony's workshops and some of whom have only performed a few gospel songs, also have just as provocative names, if not more: Flat White, Glory Bound Groove Train, Stormy Weather Choir, the Testifiers, Amazing Grace Brothers, Cleftomaniacs, the Elementals, Holy Coffee, Band of Angels, and the Honeybees.

At the time of my first visit to Australia, the Café had approximately thirty-five singers. All of the choir's members were white, except Cheryl, a black American woman from Detroit whose hospital had transferred her to Sydney, and William, a Maori from New Zealand. Cheryl sang with the choir from 1993 to 1997 before leaving the group to star in musicals and form her own female singing group. Until 1999 William sang in both the choir and Tony's quartet, the Heavenly Light Quartet. Other than Cheryl, no black American has ever been a part of the choir. The choir is, however, slightly more diverse in its religious affiliations, and includes practicing Buddhists, Jews, and "spiritualists," as well as agnostics and atheists. Based on my formal interviews and informal conversations it appears that most fall into the latter two categories. Addressing this, Tony speculates: "I suppose you could say it's serving a therapeutic purpose, not necessarily a religious purpose, but . . . there has to be a place for nonspecific spirituality, spirituality that doesn't necessarily attach itself to a label or a messiah." When I asked how one does that while singing about Jesus, Tony responded, "Well, I don't know. I mean there are Jews in the choir who have a little bit of trouble with the 'J' word, but they get around it by, I guess, making a mental flip in their mind—retranslating the word 'Jesus' to mean 'my highest welfare,' or 'my highest good,' or 'mankind's highest good,' [do you] know what I mean?" The choir—comprised of working-class and middle-class people, heterosexuals, bisexuals, homosexuals, baby boomers, generation Xers, leftists, hippies, and political activists—is the site at which multiple identities converge.

Due to its secularity, the Café rarely performs in and for churches. In fact, their first "gigs" were on street corners where they were, according to Tony, "moved on by various security guards." The most common venues in which they perform are nightclubs and outdoor arenas. Over the years the choir's audiences have become more responsive, mainly due to Australia's exposure to gospel music at a cappella music festivals that have recently begun to feature gospel choirs. In general, however, the call-and-response dynamic common to all black American musical forms, and particularly gospel, is rarely found among Australian audiences. When call-and-response does occur, a "trained" audience member who understands the gospel aesthetic sparks it, or the director of the choir or a soloist forcefully encourages it. For example, I attended a performance by the Heavenly Light Quartet, at the Basement, a jazz and blues club in downtown Sydney. The quartet was vamping the "hallelujah" line in the song, "Somewhere to Lay My Head," while the lead vocalist, Stuart Davis, ad libbed. The group was giving their all, yet no one in the audience was clapping. I was the only one in the audience standing, clapping, and urging the quartet on. As a carryover from British cultural ethos, the reserved stance by Australian audiences reflects the European division between audience and performer. Indeed, the audience thinks it rude to be demonstrative until the end of a performance. "If you're an audience listening to gospel music in Australia," says Liz Strickland, an Australian blues and gospel singer, "you sit down, you shut up and clap at the end."[9]

Because Tony has experienced gospel performance in the context of black American church services, he also notes the difference between performing for Australian audiences: "Here, there's that sort of thing about professionalism, you know, the audiences keep quiet, you close the door once all the audience is in and then you don't allow anybody in until intervals so you don't disturb the players. I don't care about that." On the other hand, he admits that without the church context the call-and-response dynamic would seem forced and phony. During my visit to Australia in 1999, however, I did notice that the audiences for which I performed were a bit more responsive, but not nearly as responsive as those in black American churches.

Generally, the gospel music aesthetic in the United States is lost in the Australian translation. In addition to the absence of the call-and-response dynamic, other traditional features of the gospel aesthetic are also lost. Clapping, rocking, discipline in rehearsals and dress—all extremely important in black gospel performance—are not the Café's strongest suits. Unlike the billowy robes and flashy "outfits" donned by black American choirs, the Café's attire is eclectic. Most of the time the choir's members wear whatever they want, and even when a dress code is enforced the singers wear all-black costumes, accented with a colored sash or scarf. And while in general the Café has competent clappers and rockers, some of them are what I call "rock-and-clap challenged." I often teased members of the Café and those attending my workshops about their lack of rhythm, and regularly found myself spending as much time teaching them how to rock and clap at the same time as I did teaching them songs. As Judy Backhouse half-jokingly noted: "We clap and rock, but we're not very good. We can't get that hard, solid clap. We can't get it. None of us have that sharp voice that cuts through, those sharp women's voices that sound like boy's voices. That's what a woman's voice should sound like in my book. There are some great solo singers in the choir, but they don't sound the same. We don't move in time, we don't clap in time. God knows what we're really doing really."

For the most part, the choir does not try to replicate the sound of American gospel music and does not necessarily try to sound "black." In fact, this was never Tony's goal. According to him, gospel was a "starting point for developing our own musical language and our own nonspecific spiritual kind of music," rather than trying to "authenti-

The Café of the Gate of Salvation performing at Geri and Houston
Spencer's wedding, Sydney, Australia, 2002.

cally" recreate the gospel experience. However, as I detail later, some
of the members' motivation for wanting to travel to the United States
was to experience the "real" thing so that they could sound better.
While one might argue that this does not necessarily translate into trying to sound "black," it does register a desire on the part of the choir
to sound more "authentic."

The Café's repertoire of songs is as eclectic as the choir itself.
They not only perform covers of traditional black American spirituals,
songs from the quartet and jubilee tradition of the 1940s and 1950s,
and traditional and contemporary gospel, but they also write and arrange their own songs. In fact, all of the songs on their debut CD are
written and arranged by Tony Backhouse and other members of the
choir. On their second CD, "A Window in Heaven," all but two of the
songs are original, the other two being a cover of Shirley Caesar's
"Holy Boldness" and an arrangement of the Negro spiritual "Mother-
less Child."

In their live performances, however, many of their songs are Tony's
arrangements of traditional quartet and black gospel songs. For instance, the choir performs versions of Aretha Franklin's "How I Got

Over"; James Cleveland's "This Too Will Pass"; Walter Hawkins's "Be Grateful"; the Caravans' "The Storm Is Passing Over"; the Harps of Melody's "Shine on Me"; and the Clark Sisters' "You Brought the Sunshine," among others. They have also added rhythm-and-blues songs to the repertoire, such as Natalie Cole's 1976 "Be Thankful." All of these songs are performed a cappella. And because many contemporary gospel songs do not have a vocal bass line (James Cleveland is given credit for removing the bass vocal from contemporary gospel and replacing it with the bass guitar in the early 1950s), Tony and other songwriters have to compose the bass part. This is one reason why they choose to write and arrange their own songs. Another reason is that many of their own songs reflect a less messiah-bound theology in favor of a more secular, spiritual ecumenical message. For example, Tony Backhouse's "In the Spirit," a track on the choir's first recording, emphasizes the power of a nonspecific "spirit" that frees the soul:

> Sometimes you don't know why you got to stand up and moan
> Sometimes you're feeling so strong you feel it in your bones
> Sometimes your spirit's running to your heavenly home
> In the spirit there is freedom
> I've heard the singing down at victory hall
> I heard the victory was given to all
> I fell down on my knees when I heard the call
> In the spirit there is freedom
> Sometimes stand up and moan when your soul
> jumpin' out of your bones[10]

In these lyrics are recognizable pieces of themes found in traditional black gospel spirituals and gospel songs. Rather than employ the motif of the Christian who is going through hard times, has lost his or her faith, and is now calling on the Holy Spirit to deliver him or her, Backhouse locates the "spirit" within, suggesting that, if unleashed, it will make you "stand up and moan." In most traditional spirituals and gospel songs, Christians usually moan when they are downtrodden, their moaning signaling that they need the Lord's help. Rarely does moaning stem from an inner joy but rather inner turmoil. Backhouse subverts the traditional function of the moan and imagines it as an expression of bottled-up joy and inner peace. Moreover, Backhouse's lyrics embrace the unconditional love and acceptance of

Christianity over its judgmental and condemning aspects. In the second stanza, for instance, the singing heard down at "victory hall" is an allusion to Judgment Day, when all God's children will be caught up to meet Him. In the Biblical story, however, only those who have been "washed by the blood of the lamb" or "saved" will make it into Heaven—all others will be banished to Hell. But we don't find the latter part of the story in "In the Spirit." On the contrary, the speaker "heard the victory was given to *all*" rather than only to a chosen few. Finally, alluding to the formulaic "just like fire shut up in my bones," which is found in black American sermons and gospel performance and refers to the Holy (Christian) Spirit (in the Book of Acts), the song emphasizes a different theological viewpoint, one more aligned with contemplative and mystical Christian traditions. Nonetheless, that spirit—self-awareness, inner peace, joy, etc.—should also not be quenched and "jumpin' out of your bones."

Songs such as "In the Spirit" reflect the choir's need to balance the hard-hitting theocracy of traditional black American gospel music, which is sometimes difficult to reconcile with its beliefs, with the words and lyrics that speak to the cultural milieu of a secular community. Tony and the choir employ certain Christian symbolism in their music, but for their own purposes. In a magazine interview, Tony stated that "Jesus is our culture's prevailing metaphor for spiritual excellence . . . and while the religion built around this metaphor has an unstable and unsound history, Jesus' contribution (nonviolent, nonsexist, nonracist, to say the least) is a wonderful thing. I feel comfortable working with the Christian metaphor."[11]

Still, other songwriters in the choir explicitly critique fundamentalist Christianity by exposing the hypocrisy of organized religion. In Scott Bennett's "Still Some Heaven Left to Find," recorded on the Café's first album, the writer contends that in spite of his disbelief in "God," he will nonetheless make it to Heaven:

> Almost every day
> There's some fool who's screaming glory
> Change your ways
> or you'll burn in hell most surely
> I don't listen to
> Salesmen like you
> No I don't. No I don't. No.

I know there's more
I know there's more
There's still some heaven left to find[12]

The narrative voice in this particular song discredits the religious witness who admonishes him to "change your ways," disparagingly referring to the fundamentalist as a "salesman." Not satisfied with commodified, guilt-ridden, and neatly packaged Christianity, the narrator deafens his ears to the religious "fool," and instead ponders a "heaven" whose entrance does not necessarily require that one repent or be "saved."

In a similar vein, Tony Backhouse's "Blessèd Is," recorded on the Café's second album, locates "Heaven" not as a fixed "place" in the hereafter, but rather as a communal process manifested in the here and now:

> Come in my friend, let's create Heaven here
> today and celebrate the fate that brought us
> here—let's lift our hearts together and
> reach that sweet forever[13]

Tony says that this song "is intended to be a song of welcome, to say 'we're here'—we're not just performing for you, we're all here today and together to be grateful for every little thing." Each of these songs, while evoking a Christian ethos, rejects fundamentalist formulations of "God," "Heaven," and "Spirit," and does not consider "Hell" to exist at all. The composers rid these terms of their dogmatic connotations in exchange for a message of peace, love, joy, and hope rather than shame, guilt, and damnation. That message is particularly evident in Tracey's "Love and Joy." By focusing on the humanitarian ideals of love and joy, Tracey's lyrics denounce established religion's focus on the "Holy Ghost" and "Trinity" and, like Backhouse and Bennett, she locates "spirit" within the self:

Now some people talk about the Holy Ghost, / some people talk about the Trinity and Host; / I think love and joy inspires me most, makes me fly. / People can tell me what to say and feel, / but I think I've found something that's real, / as long as love and joy are part of the deal I get high. / If there was no joy and love I wonder what they'd do in Heaven above.[14]

171

The last line of this song implicitly calls attention to the hypocrisy of the Christian who proselytizes that finding the Holy Ghost is the only way to get into Heaven. "God," "Jesus," and the "Holy Spirit," which comprise the Trinity, are said to embody love and joy yet, according to the song, fundamentalists rarely practice these tenets. An earlier line in the song says, "You've got to know just what turns you on, got to make sure you're not being a pawn," which would further suggest that the song is questioning blind allegiance to any organized religion. This line along with the last suggests that one should value the good within and, if one is a Christian, he or she should practice the more positive aspects of Christianity. Accordingly, the last line of the song sarcastically highlights the contradictions inherent in Christian theology versus its practice. "How can you say you love Me and not love your brother?" is the biblical reference metaphorically referenced in this line.

Even when the choir sings more traditional black gospel songs, many of the members contend that they do a mental translation when they sing words or themes that contradict their belief systems. Judy Backhouse, who is of Hungarian Jewish ancestry, explains how she has an "inner dialogue" with herself while singing gospel music. Her self-reflexivity was brought on when a singer, in another group of which she's a member, challenged her about singing music in whose lyrics she did not necessarily believe. Judy recounts her "crisis of faith":

> I always have a translation tape going in my head. For me it's very inspiring—the words are thrilling [because] they talk about coming out of fear and into love. So for me, I don't take it literally. But I had a crisis of faith at some point, because this fundamentalist friend of mine . . . said to me, "You know, Judy, we mean those words literally. When you're singing about the blood, we are singing about the blood. When I talk about Hell, it's a real place. Heaven is a place." And I thought, oh my God, maybe I'm making a big mistake, maybe I'm representing something I don't believe in, and maybe I'm being voyeuristic, or exploiting a tradition that isn't mine. Or, above all, I thought this is a tradition I don't want to represent [because] some of it teaches fear and I don't want to represent it. So, I was in a crisis [and] I stopped singing for a while. And then I kind of thought no, most of the songs the choir sings don't have those kind of words. They're songs that we've written, or Tony's written, or songs that he's chosen that actually don't quite articulate that same sort of funda-

mentalist vision. . . . As far as I know, I'm one of the few who's got this sort of inner dialogue going on about it. . . . The music works on you as well. After a while you can't help it. I think it does something to you, whether it's a classical Christian thing or not. Jesus is a fantastic example of the love person who did great works. So just to sing about that brings out a waking.

Again, Judy's sentiments underscore why the choir composes so many of its own songs while, at the same time, they buttress or justify their continual singing of gospel. Her story suggests that in spite of her resistance to the words the music "works on" and "does something" to her. What Judy does not realize is that she is not the only one performing a kind of psychological translation of the words. In addition to Judy another of the choir's Jewish members, Tracey, says that when she sings "Jesus" she thinks of "freedom": "I'm not [a] Christian, and that isn't my particular metaphor. Sometimes when I'm singing 'Jesus,' I'm thinking 'freedom.' . . . I've always been fairly political, like on the Left, and at first I felt a little compromised, [because] I was singing something that represented an institution that I didn't necessarily align myself [with]. . . . I understand the spiritual connection also touches me too. And who knows why that is, I don't know why that is, but it does. I think of myself as a spiritual person, not a religious one." [15]

Thinking of oneself as a "spiritual" rather than "religious" person seems to be the general sentiment of the choir's members and thus influences not only what they choose to sing but also their relationship to the words. In a letter written to members of the choir, Tony articulates his own reconciliation of the aspects of gospel he finds dogmatic and oppressive with those aspects he finds liberating: "I have awe, love, and respect for the black gospel tradition and its passion, love and commitment; but I also consider it my sacred duty to ridicule whatever I see as rigid or divisive concepts that are held up as cosmic truths or imperishable dogma. One side of my nature is serious about the quest for genuine spirituality. Another believes that nothing is sacred in the search for the ultimate one-liner. Singing gospel expresses my soul; taking the piss expresses my personality. The choir is an environment where I feel safe to indulge both." [16]

And indulge in both he does. I attended several parties with Tony where he and other members of the choir drank to their heart's content and sang gospel songs until the wee hours of the morning. But there seems to be something else at work here. I think the repudiation of "religion" in Australia speaks to the stodginess of the Anglican worship service as well as a general suspicion of any kind of authoritarian or totalitarian system. In the case of the former, the Anglican worship service, according to most people I interviewed, is stiff, uninspired, and uninspiring. Indeed, many of the members of the Café were former members of the Anglican Church but left because they were put off by its parochialism, conservatism, and restrained style of worship. Moreover, after experiencing a black American worship service in the United States, many singers could not imagine attending a service at the Anglican Church. Judy Backhouse remembers trying to find, to no avail, a church in Australia that captured the spiritedness of the black American worship service: "When I came back from America, from my first trip—and I'd been to those [black] churches, and I had just about cried my industrial-strength mascara off—I thought, ok, I'm going to find a church here. I couldn't find one. I went to all sorts. There was this Korean service with these horrible hymns. Probably everybody who was raised as Christian in Australia has been thirsting for a more joyful way to celebrate [his or her] religion and spirituality."

In addition to the higher level of energy found in black American worship services compared to that in the Anglican Church, some Australians who have been to the United States feel that there is more acceptance of difference in black American churches. Liz Strickland described her experience of the black church as being like "walking into a hug." She found the church members welcoming and felt a sense of community generated among them that she does not find in Australian churches. "I wish there were black churches like that in Australia," she lamented. Even more interesting was Strickland's comment about how in the black churches she attended the members did not separate religion and culture—did not see their singing as a "performance." In Australia, she argues, religion is contextualized outside the confines of everyday life. "We tend to wear a lot of masks," she says, "whereas when you go over there [the United States], your masks don't exist because they just presume that you are yourself."

In Australia, certain aspects of culture are bracketed as separate entities that inhere in "special" places. For instance, Australian culture does not share in common the blurring or interdependence of the sacred and the secular that occurs in black American culture or, as noted above, in an interdependent relationship between audience and performer. On the one hand, Liz discovered in the black church that when singing a song there is a "whole cultural, religious mix," and that "there is no separation between their culture, their religion, their being, their potato salad, it was all the same thing." On the other hand, she believes that, in Australia, "we have our religion, we have this particular job, we do this particular thing, but very few people are actually integrated." Jane MacClean, a member of the Amazing Grace Brothers quartet as well as the Café, articulated this distinction when she described what she saw as the difference between black American singers' relationship to gospel music and that of her own relationship. She explained, "You could see they had the spirit, they became the music. It wasn't just something that they did, they *were* the music, so to speak. It's part of the whole order, it's their life. . . . I've played the piano every day since I was five, practically, but it's still not central to my life. It's a different thing. I can't explain it."[17] The difference that Jane's statement registers is rooted in the function of gospel in black American culture as both aesthetic performance and a vehicle through which to survive oppression, a difference I will address later in this chapter.

There also exists in Australia a general suspicion or disdain for organized religion that influences the Café's choice of songs and some audiences' response to them. The secularity of Australian culture may be due, in part, to how it was founded. Unlike the United States, which was founded largely by white Puritans in search of religious freedom, Australia was a site for convicts exiled from the British Isles. Arguably, these "criminals" were not interested in religious institutions— particularly those sanctioned by a country that had banished them from their homeland.[18] In fact, some of the people I interviewed suggested that the rejection of the Anglican Church directly stems from a rejection of English platitudes. Consequently, in the Café's early years audiences did not know what to make of the choir because they were unclear about the choir's relationship to the music. According to Tracey, Christians in the audience would chastise them for singing music whose message they didn't believe: "We'd say we're not actually from a church and they would get really aggressive. They'd actually get angry, and [act] sort of not very Christian about it, and they would be abusing us by the end of the thing." Then there were those non-believers, who comprised most of the audience, who were put off by the music and would often ask, "Do you believe all that shit?" "You'd get the feeling that they would want you to say, 'no,' so they [could] enjoy it," Jane MacClean explains, "and if you said you did, they'd run a mile." In general, Jane believes that "Jesus and Christianity are very unfashionable and are dirty words in white, middle-class, Anglo, edu-cated, trendy . . . urban . . . culture, which is where gospel is sung in Sydney."

Although the choir members eschew religious dogma—specifically that of Christianity—they nonetheless practice the tenets of Chris-tianity within the choir. Namely, they embrace a Christian ethos through their gifts to charity of all of their performance revenue, and through their sense of social responsibility to humankind and to each other. At the first rehearsal I attended, the choir had a long discus-sion about what charity they were going to give to that year. It was a heated discussion because many members wanted to know if the charity was legitimate, if it had other major sources of funding, if the money actually reached the people it was intended to reach, and so on. The choir also gives special performances for specific charities, and those gigs are also considered very carefully. Nonetheless, none of the money they make is for profit. In fact, that's one of the reasons why Judith says she enjoys singing in the choir: "You know, one of the things I really like about being in the choir is the fact that we give a lot of money away. That, to me, is great, because it means that through my participation I'm able to give to lots of charities that I could never hope to on my income. That [is something] I really don't want us to lose sight of. That's one of our principals. One of our bases really is that we . . . share in what we have and I don't want other goals to cloud over those things, because they're really important."[19] The charities to which they donate range from mainstream foundations like the AIDS Charitable Trust of Australia to lesser-known ones such as those that assist people with alternative cures for cancer.

One of the choir's biggest expenses, however, is baby-sitting. "We all donate money to the baby-sitting . . . you know," Scot Morris con-firms. "People are always at gigs and there are a lot of babies in the choir, who are great, because they grow up around all this singing and they're going to be well-adjusted young people."[20] Although Scot is among several gay men in the choir, neither he nor any of the others are resentful of having to pay for sitters for fellow choir members' children. That Scot focuses more on the influence the singing will have on the children rather than the money issue illustrates the sense of community found within the choir. Indeed, the members' stewardship, much like that of church parishioners, helps sustain and maintain the choir. Judy Backhouse suggests that it was this way from the beginning: "Everybody's birthday was celebrated with a cake, anyone [who] needed money got money from the choir, we gave all the money away. It had a wonderful warm heart, a wonderful warm beginning." Tracey adds that the sense of family and community remains to this day: "Look, it's my community. We've all had children together. We all started [it] together. We were twenty-something then, now we're all thirty-something. It's evolved into . . . a lifestyle as much as it's a family and a community. And sometimes you hate them and sometimes you love them. And you have fallings out with some people; you adore others. We've had some incredibly ecstatic, joyful moments. Ten years. It's a part of me."

This sense of community and humanitarianism inside and outside the choir also extends across the ocean. Always grateful to the black American singers who welcome Tony each time he brings a new choir group over on his biannual tour to the United States, and grateful for the songs that they consider an honor to sing, the Café routinely sends money to black churches in the United States. During the last choir rehearsal I attended, for instance, Tony shared a thank-you letter from the pastor of the Baptist House of Prayer in Harlem, where the choir had been a special guest during its first U.S. tour. The pastor stated that with the U.S. $400 the Café sent they were able to purchase a much-needed PA system. When Tony finished reading the letter, the choir clapped and cheered.

Finally, as leader of this group, Tony Backhouse functions somewhat as a Christ figure in the Café. While the members do not necessarily worship him, they all speak of him in adoring and admiring ways—in ways that liken him to Christ. Gentle. Caring. Humble. Genius. All of these words have been used to describe Tony. "We all have Tony, Tony is the big uniting theme," says Tony's former wife, Judy. "For some reason we all love him and we just want to stay with him, whatever he suggests to us. We love his songs, whatever he suggests to us we enjoy. It's funny because he's such a low-key character. It's hard to know what he does exactly. We all trust him and love him and the choir keeps going." Even more telling is the way Judith describes him as "a real guiding light." She goes on to explain how Tony has principles that "filter down to everybody in some ways."

The way these two choir members, as well as others, characterize and explain their relationship to Tony likens him to Jesus in astonishing ways. Namely, like Jesus, Tony is a teacher and leader who has "followers" who, as Judy says, want to "stay with him." Like Jesus, Tony is humble and has a certain mysterious (holy?) aura about him ("It's hard to know what he does exactly"). The choir members put their trust in him and see him as a "guiding light" whose love and wisdom are infectious. While Tony has described himself as "avuncular and despotic"—a description that bespeaks passive aggression —members of the choir clearly do not view him in that way. They might also find my interpretation of their feelings about Tony a bit far-fetched. Nonetheless, as an outsider I made the connections they perhaps subconsciously make when they construct narratives about their choir director.

Despite their psychological and spiritual dissonance when singing gospel, members of the Café of the Gate of Salvation seem to reside in a liminal stage between the sacred and the secular, the divine and the profane. At that liminal site they enact all of the contradictions and transgressions that make these betwixt-and-between spaces sites of cultural and social reflexivity. For example, the choir disavows Christianity yet also practices Christian virtues.[21] Below, I focus on the reasons these Australians give for why they feel such a powerful connection to black American gospel music.

The Reason Why We Sing:
Blackness, Religion, and Spirituality

In 1993 gospel songwriter, composer, and singer Kirk Franklin wrote and recorded "Why We Sing," which includes the lyrics "Someone asked a question/Why do we sing?/When we lift our hands to Jesus/ What do we really mean?"[22] Although the members of the Café may sing these lyrics, they are not necessarily lifting their hands to Jesus or in praise of "God." Quite the contrary. Many sing the music simply because of the way it makes them feel: happy and joyous. Choir member after choir member expressed to me how "uplifting" and "moving" the music is to them. One member, Deborah, compared the feeling to being on drugs: "I can't tell you exactly what it is, but it [singing gospel] really just makes you feel better. I've never been on drugs, so I'm a rare person, but it's how I imagined it would be, being on drugs. It gives you the same kind of high, that sense of well-being. My husband always says he can tell when I haven't been to choir because I get a bit testy. It soothes you and calms you and puts you all back into place."[23]

Deborah's comments not only speak to how soothing and calming gospel music is, but also to how the music functions as an agent of catharsis. Similar to the way black Americans use gospel music to lay down their burdens, members of the choir use the music as a vehicle of self-expression and psychological release. Specifically, singing allows these people to express a part of themselves that they might not otherwise express. In general, Australians are self-conscious about self-display or calling attention to themselves. As Fi, a member of one of Tony's workshop choirs told me, "joy is beat out of you at an early age and this is why the music is so cathartic."[24] Fi does not necessarily mean "joy" in the literal sense but rather something closer to creative expression—like singing that might call attention to the self. Tony Backhouse registers this phenomenon in the introduction to his a cappella songbook, *A Cappella: Rehearsing for Heaven:*

> Everyone wants to sing. Singing with others in harmony is a total joy. But in our society, it seems that only a person who has been singled out early as having some special talent, and who has gone through a certain kind of musical training, is encouraged to call themselves a "singer." Singing is sometimes construed as "unmanly" or "frivolous" and as we become older we become conditioned to be seen and not heard. We stop making the spontaneous, joyful noises we creatively and unselfconsciously made as children. So we are no longer comfortable singing—because only the *real* singers are allowed to sing. This is a real shame.[25]

On the other hand, there are members like Tracey who focus less on what other people think of her singing and more on the satisfaction she receives from her performance: "I don't really give a shit what other people think. I sing this music [because] I know it brings me joy and it brings a lot of other people joy, and we can exchange the metaphors for whatever we want, and it's still uplifting."

Ultimately, I believe the music serves a kind of therapeutic function for Australian gospel singers. "It can be like a cleansing thing, and it's definitely a strengthening thing," says Judith, one of the earliest members to join the choir. "I come away feeling really strong and positive and I think that's . . . the spirit sort of giving its strength." The message notwithstanding, the medium of gospel music lifts the spirits of these singers when they are down and out and creates a sense of belongingness in the world.

When asked about what motivated them to sing gospel music, all but a few of the members cited the music's centrality in black American history. For example, Scot Morris stated: "The whole thing about gospel is the release that it gives you . . . in terms of freeing your spirit, and the joy and sharing that goes on, is universal, even though it comes from those [slave] roots. A lot of the songs are a metaphor for the freedom that people were longing for from the oppression that they found themselves in, and I think, part of the reason that we do a lot of the original sort of gospel numbers—and do them in a fairly traditional style—is out of respect [for] that tradition."

It appears that the singers revere not only the music but the history of the struggle out of which it comes. They seem to find a transcendent quality in the struggle of black American history that allows them to generalize this experience to struggles over other forms of oppression, and in this transcendence of struggle they discover a message of hope. According to Scot, "there is a common thread in terms of recognizing the spirituality and the universality of the messages that gospel music brings and the joy." Similarly, Deborah explains: "As I understand it, it [gospel] came from the slave time and was what got them through those hard times and I think a lot of people can relate to that because suddenly people go—[it] doesn't matter what race, religion, or color, whatever—everybody goes through their own constant, personal dramas and that music is like, you can overcome. Whatever. I know you can overcome adversity and you can overcome things and the strength from the unity just makes you . . . just empowers you, I guess." A common thread that seems to run through these statements is that gospel is a universal language that transcends difference in order to help others overcome their own "personal dramas" and adversity.[26]

Some choir members link their history of descent from exiled convicts to black Americans' history as descendants of slaves. For these singers, the music becomes a vehicle through which to express repressed sorrow and grief. Grant Odgers, a member of both the Café and the Honeybees states, "We do have the same history of cruelty and brutality [as black Americans], but we don't express it. I think that's why it's [gospel music] become so big, because we need the catharsis."[27] The "history of cruelty and brutality" to which Odgers refers is the settlement of the area of Australia then known as Botany Bay by the British to "contain" their "criminal" population. In *The Fatal Shore,* Australian historian Robert Hughes chronicles the exportation of British and other convicted felons to what is now Australia. Hughes notes that "in the whole period of convict transportation, the Crown shipped more than 160,000 men, women and children (due to defects in the records, the true number will never be precisely known) in bondage to Australia. This was the largest forced exile of citizens at the behest of a European government in pre-modern history. Nothing in earlier penology compares with it."[28] The fact that these criminals were excommunicated by their "own" complicates further the already ambivalent feelings the average Australian harbors toward Britain. For example, at one of the gospel music workshops I conducted, a woman who wishes to remain anonymous told me, "we know what it means to be treated like scum." "Just like black Americans, we, too, have been put down because we're not of royal stock. We're the descendents of people who the upper crust of England banished. So, in a way, we connect with black Americans and their fight to be legitimate. Singing gospel is the closest we come to making that happen."[29] While Robert Hughes maintains that this feeling of "illegitimacy" persisted until the 1960s, this the woman's statement suggests very clearly that traces of this feeling persist today.

These feelings of illegitimacy stem from at least two factors: first, the English have often reminded the Australians of their criminal ancestry; and, second, the history of criminality in Australia forged a mythology around which working-class Australians could claim a history of oppression. Thus, according to Hughes, English ridicule of Australians sent "upper-middle-class Australians into paroxysms of social embarrassment," while the working class created a stereotype of convict identity that said that "convicts were innocent victims of unjust laws, torn from their families and flung into exile on the world's periphery for offenses that would hardly earn a fine today."[30]

These two stances—denial and embarrassment and victim mythology—shape many Australians' current views of England and their relationship to British citizens, and one result has been the fomenting of Australian nationalism. In the past few years, for instance, the Australian government has engaged debates about whether to break away from the monarchy and become a self-governing republic. Another result has been a longing to reconcile the past with the present. Gospel music, some singers argue, has helped bring about that reconciliation.

Romanticization or Identification? Universal Blackness

Although I was moved by the conviction with which members of the Café and other Australian choirs express the love for humankind that gospel music brings them, I kept wondering how they were then able to justify white Australia's treatment of Aborigines. Their romanticization of black American culture and history as a justification for singing gospel exists uneasily beside the virtual obliteration of Aboriginal culture. In fact, very few of the singers I interviewed discuss the white privilege they enjoy in relation to the subjugation of the Aboriginal community. The feelings I encountered among the general public were equally remote: as one anonymous storekeeper put it, "we don't have an Aboriginal problem because we don't talk about it." This sentiment typifies the general attitude regarding the oppression of Aboriginal people, and it includes many of the singers I interviewed. On the one hand, these gospel singers identify with an oppressed group thousands of miles away, and they condemn their oppressors. On the other hand, they fail to acknowledge the ways in which they participate in the subjugation of "the blacks" of their own country. Indeed, the Aboriginals remain what Micaela di Leonardo might call "hidden in plain sight."[31] I do not wish to imply that no members of the Café or others are unconcerned about or do not actively fight for Aborigines. I only make the observation that rarely was the Aborigine plight a topic of conversation and when it was, it was brief.

The cross-identification with black Americans represents one instance of a denial of privilege. I was struck, for instance, by how many white Australians made statements such as: "I just do not understand the racism in America. Why are people so mean?" And, time and again, I saw this sentiment juxtaposed with scenes of Aboriginal homelessness and destitution around Sydney. Many Aboriginals who don't live on the streets are confined to a section of Sydney called Redfern, which is known as an Aboriginal "ghetto" where crime and alcoholism are a mainstay. I remember trying to hail a cab one evening at the Sydney train station, not too far from the Redfern area. After half an hour of watching empty taxis pass me by, an Asian driver stopped for me. When I communicated to him what had happened, he said that the other taxis did not stop because it was dark and they thought that I was a "black," meaning Aboriginal. It turns out some taxi drivers had been robbed in that area and therefore they did not stop near that particular train station or for Aborigines in general. While I understand the taxi drivers' concern for safety, I cannot overlook the unacknowledged racism underlying their actions. Unfortunately, it seems that racism, like the message of gospel music, is also "universal."

The contemporary view of Aboriginal people and culture stems from a longstanding history of denial by the first settlers of Australia. Just as criminals passed down to their descendents the narratives of the "innocent" and "oppressed" convict, so, too, did British settlers' mythology of Australia as *terra nullius* prior to the arrival of British ships filter through the generations. Even more problematic is the myth that the human inhabitants who did exist were so primitive either that they did not know how to manage the land or that they needed protecting. According to Hughes, these myths were propagated in the Australian school system until 1960. Hughes writes: "A static culture, frozen by its immemorial primitivism, unchanged in an unchanging landscape—such until quite recently was, and for many people still is, the common idea of the Australian Aborigines. It grows from several roots; myths about the Noble Savage, misreadings of aboriginal technology, traditional racism and ignorance of Australian prehistory. It is, in fact, quite false; but in the experience of white city-dwellers there is little to contradict it."[32]

Moreover, similar to the rape and destruction of Native Americans and their land by early settlers in the United States, British settlers also murdered and raped native Australians and their land. Aboriginal people, despite occasional resistance, often were thought of as less than human and more often than not were confined to specific land areas (similar to Native American reservations). Moreover, in some cases Aboriginal children were taken away from their families by "liberal" white Australian institutions known as Aboriginal Welfare Boards, and only recently have some of the victims of this program found their biological families. So widespread was this phenomenon prior to the 1960s that those taken from their families are said to be part of the "stolen generation." Many of these victims are now suing the government for the physical, mental, and sexual abuse they suffered while in the care of the institutional homes sponsored by the program. Joy Williams of the Wiradjuri people filed the first stolen-generation test case in New South Wales. She was in the custody of the Plymouth-Brethren-run Lutanda and Bomaderry homes from the age of a few weeks to eighteen years old. Not surprisingly she lost her case, the judge finding that at both homes "the women carers did so with charity, trust, devotion, care and within constraints, with appropriate discipline (measured by the standard of the day), kindness and affection."[33]

According to Peggy Brock's study of Aboriginal resistance to white colonization and dispossession, every instance of white Australian "protection" in the colonial state ultimately meant "isolation, discrimination, institutionalization and invisibility" for Aborigines.[34] More distressing, however, is the fact that much of the land taken from the Aborigines in 1788 when the first British ships arrived at Botany Bay is now "owned" by white Australians. There has been no satisfactory or acceptable resolution offered by the Federal Parliament regarding many of these land rights issues. Fearing having to pay reparations in the wake of a formal apology, which would be an acknowledgment of wrongdoing, the best Prime Minister John Howard has offered is a declaration of "deep and sincere regret" for the past injustices to Aborigines. Given this elision of white Australian complicity and participation in the continued exploitation and subjugation of Aborigines, reconciliation is not soon to come. Noel Loos and Jane Thomson interrogate white culpability in the continued oppression of Aborigines when they write:

> Until black Australians feel that they no longer have just cause to continue to resist the invaders, that is, until there is an act of reconciliation fully acceptable to black Australians, we, the invaders, can have no legitimate claim to this land. We will continue to be white squatters in black Australia and we will have to continue justifying this situation in our own eyes, and in the eyes of an increasingly skeptical world, by the most blatant and immoral application of a British law based on the lie that Aborigines and Torres Strait Islanders did not occupy and own this land before white colonization. Until white Australians can persuade black Australians to sign a just treaty with us legitimizing our place in this land, we will continue to be the inheritors of stolen property. The situation will continue to be one in which white wealth is the result of black poverty; white comfort based on black squalor; and white peace and tranquillity based on the past and continuing subjugation of black Australians.[35]

Parliament's most recent declaration notwithstanding, Loos and Thomson's observations reflect the hegemony of colonization and white privilege in Australia. It is no wonder, then, that rather than celebrating Australia Day, a national holiday that marks the "founding" of Australia, Aborigines on the same day celebrate Survival Day, thereby transgressively marking the colonization of their land and culture. On January 26 of each year, Aborigines gather at Waverly Park on Bondi Beach, whose shores were once inhabited by the Darwhool people. This celebration grew out of the 1988 political marches in protest of Australia's bicentennial celebration in which Aboriginal political activists galvanized to demand recognition of Aboriginal rights and cultural identity.

Survival Day is also a venue for celebrating Aboriginal music and dance. Like black Americans, Aborigines employ music as a strategy for social change. Walbira Watts, coordinator of the 1998 Survival Day, emphasized the importance of music in his culture when he stated that "for 60,000 years or more, my people in this country, when we've wanted something, we've sung it up. We sing our boys into men, we sing our girls into women, we sing the season's changes. And if we all sing loud enough together, black and white . . . ?"[36] While Walbira sees music as an agent of racial reconciliation for Aborigines and white Australians, white Australian gospel singers seem to be oblivious to Aboriginal musical traditions. Instead, they cross-identify with a group of people thousands of miles from their shores.

Like many white Americans, many Australians do not feel responsible for the past—at least in terms of acknowledging how they benefit, on a daily basis, from the subjugation of Australia's indigenous people. Thus, it was odd for me, as a black American, to have an Australian shake his or her head in disdain at what white Americans have "done to me." When I have addressed the problem of racism in Australia with members of the various choirs or with Australians in general, they have seemed uncertain as to what to say.[37]

Another problem associated with Australian singers universalizing the ethos of gospel music is that it does not acknowledge the specificity of black American history. Black Americans who sing gospel do so from a place of struggle *and* faith within the United States. For them, the music functions not only as a testimony of their secular struggles of living in a white supremacist society, but also of their sacred faith in a God who has delivered them and continues to sustain them through those struggles. As Ben Sidran argues, "black music [is not] escapist in nature . . . but . . . a direct reflection of the combined experiences of many individuals, all of them grounded in reality."[38] Therefore, when Australian gospel singers state that they identify with black Americans who sing gospel, the comparison seems misplaced and inappropriate. Their rationale for singing gospel fails to recognize that the "struggle" they inherit as descendents of convicts differs markedly from the struggle black Americans inherit in the move from chattel slavery to freedom. In light of the white privilege they enjoy in their own country in relation to the Aborigines, their "struggles" seem decidedly different from black Americans. This is not to suggest that white Australians do not carry the pain of their criminal heritage. Rather, I believe that that history and its long-term material effects are distinct from and do not have the same impact as the history of oppression for either black Americans or black Australians. White Australians do not experience their bodies through the same racial lens as black Australians and black Americans, and to romantically dissolve the specificity of the history of "black" bodies remains problematic.

Nevertheless, the psychological wounds of convict heritage and second-class citizenry may allow these singers to connect to the black American experience. As much as spirituals and gospel music were a survivalist strategy to physically escape oppression, they also provided and provide a psychological escape of oppression. That psychological release stems from the shared witnessing of joy and pain and the corresponding cathartic moment generated in gospel performance. The rhythm, syncopation, repetition, and call-and-response all coalesce as a generative force that facilitates a psychological release. Among black Americans that release is most often manifested physically. Whether through the waving of hands, dancing, rocking, crying, shouting, praying or laying on of hands, the catharsis comes through bodily and/or verbal expression. Further, it is a communal act of experiencing this gestalt in the presence of others in that moment of mutual affirmation of faith and witnessing.

When members of the Café and other Australian singers talk about how gospel music makes them "feel better" and "picks them up," they, too, are naming the cathartic power of gospel. I argue, however, that that catharsis is brought on not by the universality of gospel "touching" them in the same way it does black Americans, but rather from the shedding of the residual traces of British propriety. Liz Strickland commented on this propriety when she described the difference between black American audiences and Australian ones. She explained:

> I've been to a Café gig where people sort of get up and start clapping and singing along, but only . . . when a soloist really goes off and the audience thinks, "ok, we're allowed to do this. Are we? Are we? Ah she's doing it, ah, hang on, I can clap. OK. Ten people are standing up, ok, I'll stand up." That's more how it works, rather than a spontaneous "Alright now! That was good now! Yeah! Sing that girl!" You don't get that here. There are all those inhibitions and we think we're being loud, or stupid, or something or other. So it's difficult being here now after that experience because it's like I gotta hold all this stuff back. It's like every time I go to gospel gigs now, I've gotta hold back and it's annoying as hell.

It is precisely this "holding back" that speaks to the British sense of decorum and restraint that gospel music dissolves. In other words, it is the physicality, emotionality, and self-display inherent in gospel performance that does not accommodate self-consciousness, timidity, or taciturnity and that provides an opportunity for self-expression.

Because Australian culture devalues self-display and thwarts creativity in youngsters, when Australians sing gospel music they cannot help but feel a release. It is as if they are discovering for the first time a hidden part of themselves. What they are "connecting with," however, is not the oppression of black Americans, but rather a part of themselves that had been underdeveloped or lying dormant.

Not surprisingly, the release Australians experience when they sing gospel music brings about a sense of joy and happiness. All of the testimonies chronicled earlier confirm that singing gospel brings about that transformative experience. Judy Backhouse believes that it has had an impact at the individual level. "There are very few ways in which people can authenticate themselves as singers or as artists of any kind," she states. "Usually, no one would come out and say, 'I'm a singer. I'm an artist,' even in this gospel community. But if they stand in a group and sing, they can sing without having to say anything about themselves. So it's a vehicle for their creativity and it's a vehicle for belonging, for joining." The sense of community created is, I maintain, based less on a superficial connection with black Americans than on the communal feeling stimulated when a group of people come together to share previously unexpressed parts of themselves with one another.

Authenticating Blackness: Body, Place, and Space

Before 1999, one of the major goals of the Café of the Gate of Salvation was to raise enough money to travel to the United States to tour black churches, to experience the "real" thing. Tony, of course, had made several trips to the United States and various other members of the choir had as well. But the choir had never been as a group. One of the reasons that making the journey to the United States was so important to the choir members was that, according to them, experiencing the music in its "original" context would help them both better to understand and to perform the music. When I asked Deborah about why the choir wanted to travel to the United States, for instance, she stated that "there is always, to a certain extent, [the feeling that] we're mimicking [the music] rather than understanding it. Tony . . . has a rare talent, I think, of understanding the music because he's been over there several times and it's like when he sings it, he understands it." Perhaps more revealing is Liz Strickland's observation that "even watching the Café perform, they're performing, they're not being a gospel choir, they're performing a cappella gospel music. Different perspective altogether, which is, I think, why Tony wants to take the Café over there [to the United States], so [that] they get that. You don't get it till you get there, right?"

What one "gets" by experiencing gospel music in its "original" context, then, appears to be a prerequisite of its authenticity. In other words, one has to "go there to know there," for without that contextual experience one cannot truly "understand" gospel music and that lack of understanding affects one's performance. Thus, the singing is seen as mere mimicry as opposed to a "heart relationship" or an authentic expression of something more profound.

While I feel it is laudable that the choir would want to better understand the history and context of gospel music, to do so as a way to "authenticate" their own singing of gospel is misguided. Generally speaking, to assume that all black Americans who sing gospel in the church are not "performing" is to deny the aesthetic components of gospel, namely the formulaic rituals of the gospel idiom. As ethnomusicologist Joyce Jackson notes: "While gospel music is strongly entrenched in the black American 'folk church' tradition, it also attracts many who identify as much with its expression of black American values, aesthetics, and life experiences as with its expression of religion."[39] The implication here is that gospel is not only a sacred tradition but a secular one as well.

Part of gospel's secularity derives from the performer's competence as a *singer* rather than specifically as a *gospel* singer. Some gospel music performers, for instance, incorporate recognizable musical techniques when performing to showcase their vocal virtuosity, even when they offer the formulaic disclaimer that they are not performing for "show, form, or fashion."[40] In fact, there are some church members who only attend church on Sundays that feature the "good" choir or a famous soloist because they appreciate not only the content of the music but the quality of the singer(s) as well. Given this concept of secularity, the Australians' notion that the context of the church makes gospel more "real" or "authentic" fails to acknowledge the complex dynamic inherent in gospel performance. Further, and perhaps more important, while exposure to gospel within the church may lead to a better appreciation of the origin and expression of the music, it will not bring one closer to an "essence" of the music. For as much as gospel is a communal experience that reflects black American cultural values and religious practices, it is also an individual and personal expression. Therefore, gospel performance is an amalgamation of black cultural ethos, aesthetics, and values as well as individuality, virtuosity, and spontaneity.

The Australians' beliefs about the authenticating process of gospel reflect a larger global logic regarding "black" art forms and authenticity. The closer to "home," the logic goes, the more authentic the art form. In other words, the farther away from North American shores the gospel art form emerges, the more bastardized it becomes. This sentiment is expressed and perpetuated not only by black Americans but also by nonblack, non-Americans as well. Paul Gilroy describes this phenomenon in the following way:

> The problem of cultural origins and authenticity . . . has persisted and assumed an enhanced significance as mass culture has acquired new technological bases and black music has become a truly global phenomenon. It has taken on greater proportions as original, folk or local expressions of black culture were identified as authentic and positively evaluated for that reason, while subsequent hemispheric or global manifestations of the same cultural forms got dismissed as inauthentic and therefore lacking in cultural or aesthetic value precisely because of their distance (supposed or actual) from a readily identifiable point of origin.[41]

Gilroy's analysis of the consequence of the dissemination of black music into a global community implies a geopolitical struggle over origins and authenticity. Although it is not surprising that black Americans would rage such turf wars against global and local appropriation of black art forms (especially given the history of white musicians exploiting and profiting from the work of black musicians), I find it ironic that non-American nonblacks fuel such wars by linking "authentic" black music with the United States. Nonetheless, their motivations for holding such beliefs further perpetuate and collude with, in Gilroy's words, the "discourse of authenticity [that] has been a notable presence in the mass marketing of successive black folkcultural forms to white audiences" (105).

In addition to place and space, the fact of blackness is often sutured to physical characteristics as opposed to sociocultural ones. As a primary signifier of race, skin color in particular functions to legitimate claims of black authenticity. This legitimizing works both ways: black folk strategically rely on their black skin when they become arbiters of "good" and "bad" black performances by nonblacks, and nonblacks either refrain from performing "black" art forms or equate black skin with artistic ability because they see skin color as endemic to artistic skill. Whatever the case, both stances are misguided attempts to essentialize blackness by ontologically linking the body with cultural performance.

In the case of many Australian singers, black skin automatically connotes the ability (or the expectation) that one can sing. As I will discuss later, this was certainly how I was perceived, and it was also the assumption most of the members of the Café had about Cheryl, the only black American member of the choir. Ironically, although many of the choir members assumed that Cheryl not only could sing gospel but that she grew up singing it, she was actually raised Catholic and learned most about gospel music from Tony. She reflects:

> Actually, my parents were Catholic—strange enough—and I survived to tell the tale. They were Catholic, so I was brought up in the Catholic Church until I was about fourteen or fifteen . . . so I didn't grow up [listening to gospel as] a little kid but from fifteen until I left home at twenty-two. I wasn't much into the gospel singing I must say, which I'm paying for it now, far more than I could ever imagine. I wasn't quite into it. . . . You know, when you have it around, you take it so much for granted, like it was just a thing you did on Sunday, and you come over here and it's such a prized thing. . . . When I first started [singing with the Café] it was a bit strange, because it's like, you get the vibe where they think you're singing gospel and you're black, obviously you just know everything there is to know about it, you know what I mean? It's kind of like, do you know this song? Well, of course you do, you're black, you came from America, you must know every single gospel song known to man. . . . But once people found out that I was just a normal person and didn't have a vast gospel knowledge that everybody thought I did have, it kind of mellows out.[42]

Cheryl's black skin betrayed her in this context, as the fact of it did not automatically provide her with the skill and knowledge of gospel that the choir assumed she had. And although Cheryl's vocal skills were actually honed by taking several of Tony Backhouse's singing classes, Deborah assumed that Cheryl's talent was "natural" as opposed to acquired: "And when Cheryl sings, it's like, well she sang it since she was a little girl so she understands it, but the rest of us are doing our best to sort of mimic her rather than really understand [the music]." Deborah's and others' assumptions, however, have more to do with conflating black skin and the innate ability to sing gospel than with understanding the music.

Related to the notion of bodily presence as a sign of authenticity as it relates to gospel is the fact that all of the gospel choirs in Australia sing a cappella. In fact, to my knowledge there are only two choirs in Australia—one in Melbourne and one in Fremantle—that sing with accompaniment. Part of this is due to the lack of availability of musicians steeped in the gospel tradition; another part, however, has to do with the value placed on the a cappella sound. In fact, Tony and another member of the Café, Stuart, founded the Sydney A Cappella Association to perpetuate a cappella singing in Australia.

Because Tony has always been most interested in the quartet sound, which features a cappella singing as well as four-part harmony, he adopted that style for the Café, as opposed to that of the contemporary gospel choir. Tony says:

> The thing is that I was always more interested in the kind of older styles and really not that interested in choirs. I'm more interested in quartets. So my main listening has always been the Soul Stirrers, the Dixie Hummingbirds, and Spirit of Memphis Quartet, and Golden Gate Quartet and so on. . . . So a lot of the arrangements we do are actually based on quartet-kind of arrangements, because of all of the basses. Most modern choirs don't have bass singers. Like, "You Brought the Sunshine"— I invented the bass part, kind of the bass guitar, and a couple of other sort of things in there as well. That's one way where we differ a lot from modern church groups . . . I mean there aren't any a cappella choirs.

It would appear, then, that the choir's decision to sing a cappella stems from Tony's affinity toward the quartet as opposed to the choir sound. Consequently, when he wants to teach the choir contemporary gospel songs he has to write the bass part, which, according to Tracey, can be extremely difficult. In fact, it was after she experienced gospel music at the New Orleans Jazz Festival that she began to appreciate Tony's a cappella arrangements. Tracey recalls her experience at the festival: "I kept thinking, so when is the a cappella stuff coming out? . . . Everyone had a band, and I thought, oh, fascinating. And some of the arrangements were incredibly middle of the road. I mean there were a real variety of bands and choral groups over the seven days, but it was sort of like, oh my God, this is so middle of the road. I can't believe this—beautiful singing, but just the actual arrangements." For Tracey, then, the musical composition of many of the gospel choir songs left something to be desired. Moreover, implicit in her critique is a value judgment based on the privileging of the music over the voice. The "beautiful singing" is somehow compromised by the lackluster musical accompaniment; the purity of the voice is contaminated by the volume and sheer busyness of the instruments.

When Judy Backhouse discusses her preference for the a cappella sound, she, too, privileges the voice over musical instruments, but I also detected that part of the reason for her attraction to the a cappella quartet sound is that, for her, it is more authentic. She admitted:

> I have to say I'm a quartet girl, I'm not a big modern gospel girl. I really like the quartets. . . . Generally, the quartets, the ones I'm thinking of— the older ones—where they didn't have instruments, I actually like it just for the rhythm they can give, the intensity and the harmony. Big choirs are good, but big choirs tend to get a bit loud. You don't have the subtleties as much, and then to get the subtleties you have to make it more theatrical. [motions her hands as if directing the choir] You have to bring it right up or bring it right down, and it's more of a show then, rather than this sort of intimate thing. With just four people to look at, you can see the sweat on everybody's faces. It just seems to spring out of a different thing, too—the lounge room or something, living room. The quartet is a living room thing.

Judy's focus is on the tension between what is perceived as "real" and what is viewed as "performance." In Judy's eyes the musical accompaniment and technique of gospel choir performance bespeaks "theatricality" as opposed to the intimacy created by the a cappella quartet sound—an intimacy that lures the audience in, close enough to see the "sweat on everybody's faces." The implication here is that a cappella music is pure because of its simplicity, understated sound, and lack of accompaniment; the focus is solely on the voice and the body of the performer.

These Australian singers' privileging of the a cappella sound may also be yet another example of whites reifying a kind of tribalism and emotionality with blackness. While their reasons for preferring the a cappella sound may reflect a genuine affinity for that musical style, their rationales also register a return to eighteenth-century racialized discourse that equates blacks with nature and primitivism. In its current manifestation, this discourse circulates as a compliment and an appreciation but also as authentication. Tony's reflection on hearing gospel for the first time is an example: "The voices were so strange on it and the feeling was just fantastic. To me it was weird, like it was very exotic and at the same time kind of earthy and truthful." Tony's description of the voices as "earthy and truthful," as well as Judy's focus on the "sweat on everybody's faces," foregrounds the racialized authenticating process of blackness as stemming from nature and the body. According to Stuart Hall, this discourse reflects "the place prepared for black cultural expression in the hierarchy of creativity generated by the pernicious metaphysical dualism that identifies Blacks with the body and whites with the mind."[43] In the case of the Australian singers, this "metaphysical dualism" is most notable in their preference for a cappella versus accompaniment—the latter being associated with a more formalized (i.e., intellectual) musical performance and the former with raw emotionality and the body.

The Australians are not the only ones who perpetuate this authenticating discourse. Indeed, blacks around the globe cling to essentialist notions of black cultural aesthetics as a way of preserving their cultural heritage as well as, in some cases, promoting Black Nationalism. This was the case among black American immigrants in Australia. During my fourth trip to Australia, I attended a meeting of Australia's United Black Community, an organization formed "to establish a forum for fellow black people from diverse backgrounds and experiences to unite under a spirit of harmony, mutual friendship and freedom of expression."[44] I had met one of the members at the Gospel Groove concert sponsored by the Sydney A Cappella Association. This particular gentleman was the only other black American present at the concert besides myself. He introduced himself as Jesse, a native of Milwaukee, Wisconsin, gave me his card, and invited me to come to a meeting "of the black folk" of Australia. Amazed that there were enough blacks in Sydney to have a "meeting," I made plans to attend the gathering.

The meetings of Australia's United Black Community (AUBC) are held on the fourth Sunday of each month at various restaurants around town. This particular Sunday the group was gathering at an eatery in Darling Harbor. When I arrived at the restaurant, a waiter saw me and, without saying a word, pointed to the staircase in front of me (he obviously knew that I was a part of the "folk"!). I had already ascertained that I was in the right place because James Cleveland's "I Don't Feel No Ways Tired" was blaring in every direction. As I approached the bottom of the stairs, a large, dark-skinned black American woman yelled down to me, "You in the right place, baby. Come on up!" Her name was Emma, and she was a native of Columbia, South Carolina. At one point she had come to visit her son who was on a military assignment, and later she decided to emigrate. When I reached the top of the stairs, Emma officially greeted me with one of those southern hugs that black matriarchs often bestow on strangers. Her hug was followed by a series of verbal greetings and handshakes from other people, as well as from Jesse, who ushered me over to the secretary to put my name on the mailing list. The room was chockablock full of black folk, the most I had ever seen at one time in all of my visits to Australia. Although most of them were black Americans, there were other blacks, West Indians, and Samoans sprinkled throughout the crowd as well.

I made my way to a table and joined a mother and her daughter. Robbi, the mother, introduced herself and her daughter. She later disclosed that she was a native of Los Angeles, California, but had lived in Sydney for close to twenty years. When I asked her what brought her to Australia she disclosed that her husband was Australian and they decided that as an interracial and binational couple they and their children could live more comfortably in Australia: "Here, when people see you for the first time, they don't prepare to respond to you in a certain way because you're black. They just talk to you like anybody else. It's not like that in the United States." I think I understood what she meant, but I had never heard it articulated in that way. "It's hard, though," she lamented. "I really miss soul food. But, we're working on trying to get grits and yellow Cracker Barrel cheese through one of the

Mexican restaurants here who gets shipments from the United States. The food issue is one of the reasons we got this group together. You know how blacks folks are about their food." Emma chimed in, "And, chile, I got me some collard green seeds" (collard greens are not commonly grown in Australia). "How did you get collard green seeds?" I asked. "If I tell you, I'll have to kill you," she responded with a cackle. Robbi began to inquire about my visit to Australia, and I told her that I was doing research on gospel music in Australia. She responded with a giggle and asked incredulously, "*What* gospel in Australia?" I asked if she had heard of the Café of the Gate of Salvation. She replied, "Yeah, I know Tony Backhouse and that group, but I'm not a fan. If I want to hear real gospel, I listen to my records—like the ones we're listening to now." Tramaine Hawkins was hitting the high note in "He's That Kind of Friend," the composition by her husband, Walter Hawkins. Robbi closed her eyes and hummed a few bars. "See, Tony and those guys do nothing for me because they have not lived the life behind the music. It's not the same. You can tell the difference."

I have provided here some of the details of my visit to the AUBC meeting to make the point that members of diaspora groups have a tendency toward communality and racial solidarity, however politically fragile that alliance might be. And similar to many black cultural conservatives in the United States, the members of AUBC also deploy authenticating discourse based on skin color, cultural traditions (e.g., food preparation or "soul" food), and experience narratives (e.g., living the life behind the music). To a degree, this move toward black authenticity is understandable, particularly given the miniscule black population of Australia and the uprootedness many black Americans must feel in that context. Indeed, to quote Stuart Hall, their "projection of a coherent and stable culture [is] a means to establish the political legitimacy of Black nationalism and the notions of ethnic particularity on which it has come to rely."[45] In the context of Australia, the pressure to cohere under the auspices of an essentialized blackness is enormous. This pressure notwithstanding, however, these black immigrants cannot contain the proliferation of black cultural production—in the United States or elsewhere in the world. Hybrids of black cultural art forms emerge in the most unlikely places and function in those contexts in peculiar (and sometimes problematic and disturbing) ways. As I argue later in this chapter, such boundary blurring is not necessarily a bad thing. Indeed, the mutual border crossing of identities may be a productive cultural and social process that furthers a progressive politics of difference.

The tendency on both sides to naturalize gospel as a "black" thing draws the focus away from how the music may function for whomever sings it, regardless of who originated it. Moreover, as Hall suggests, "the narcissism which unites both standpoints is revealed by the way that they both forsake discussion of music and its attendant dramaturgy, performance, ritual and gesture in favor of an obsessive fascination with the bodies of the performers themselves" (107). On the other hand, once the authenticity question is put aside, another set of possibilities emerges. And yet the authenticity bug persists. In his self-reflexive essay, "In Search of What We Are Searching For," for example, Australian choir director Stephen Taberner questions the motivations behind Australians singing the Others' songs. Taberner argues that Australians place too much emphasis on the music of other cultures. In singing this music out of context, he argues, its integrity is often destroyed; it is a matter of not being able to tap into the music's "essence" because it is not one's own. Taberner writes:

Okay. I've got this far without mentioning gospel, and at the risk of offending almost everybody, let me say that maybe hundreds of people have said to me: Isn't it funny that there's all these choirs singing about Jesus who don't really believe in him? Why are these mostly white agnostics/atheists/spiritualists up there singing this song? Now there are plenty of times when I'm able to answer that question myself: because they wrote it, because it's a great song, because it's allegorical, not literal. It's when I can't answer the question that I'm in trouble: as for example when I heard Sisters singing (very beautifully) the words "Jesus is my only friend." On what level am I supposed to respond to that?

I'm looking for the essence here . . . where is it? I suspect what happens is that gospel lovers get a strong whiff of someone else's essence and would like to make it theirs. Whether or not they succeed, I think says much about whether or not they can bring their own essence to it as well. Reviewing COTGOS's [Café of the Gate of Salvation] second album a few years ago, I remember being excited by the emergence of a real Afro-American-Australian voice. But witnessing gospel groups in Sydney I've sometimes felt ambivalent, even hostile, because I don't perceive a genuine relationship with the essence of the song. It's more a stylistic love affair; I love the surface of you.[46]

Although Taberner employs the "essence" trope to argue his point, I believe the subtext of his argument is something much more equivocal. Specifically, when he suggests "whether or not they succeed, I think says much about whether or not they can bring their own essence to it as well," he is arguing for bringing self and Other together. The "Afro-American-Australian" voice he imagines is a wonderful trope to suggest the site of intercultural exchange. The blind side of Taberner's argument, of course, is that he fails to articulate the discursivity of music. This is not to say that gospel music has no relation to black bodies and the specific historical context of the Jim Crow South out of which it grew. But it is too rich a cultural form to be confined to a simplistic essentialist/antiessentialist binary. Indeed, what Taberner describes as "the essence of the song" is an intangible thing, located somewhere between the performer and her or his listening audience. Taberner assumes that because he "knows" that the members of the Sisters are not Christian or black American that their singing the line "Jesus is my only friend" reflects a superficial engagement with the song and culture from which it comes. This may be true, but it is only one way to read this performance. As I discuss later, performance, and in particular gospel performance, has the potential to alter one's epistemological frame of reference. Taberner should be less concerned with whether or not Australian singers discern the music's essence and more concerned with the complicated and political processes of intercultural exchange.

Authorizing Blackness: Singing Black into Being

On my second trip to Australia Grant Odgers asked me if I would consider conducting a workshop or two in and around Sydney, and I happily agreed. What began as something to do for "fun" materialized into something much more. I appeared on several national radio and television programs, and I was asked to perform at or to give concerts around the country. These programs positioned me as the "authentic" black gospel singer, and often people requested that I sing on command to demonstrate how gospel *should* sound. Many of the radio and television commentators, their listening audiences, and those who came to my workshops had preconceived notions about me before I sang a note: I am a black American, therefore I can sing. Or, so the stereotype goes.

The more I was interviewed and the more workshops I conducted in the city, the more the news spread about the black singer from the United States who could sing "authentic" gospel. The Sydney A Cappella Association, which sponsored and organized many of my workshops, circulated flyers stating: "E. Patrick Johnson, Direct from the U.S.A, Black Gospel Workout." The posters, featuring a picture of me that had been taken without my knowledge and used without my permission, emphasized my "authentic" talents. It also served as a palimpsest of those flyers that circulated during the slave trade that read "Direct from Africa" so as to increase the market value of the "merchandise" by emphasizing the authenticity of enslaved blacks.[47] These images became one of several ways in which my own blackness affected the ethnographic field. Indeed, my black and American identities were deployed in ways that I no longer controlled. Thus, as I moved from ethnographer to teacher and performer, I was catapulted into the center of identity politics. Because I am a singer raised in the gospel tradition, my workshops only worked to further the often racist perception of me as the authentic, black, exotic Other.

When I traveled to Adelaide to conduct a workshop, my host, Briar Eyers, a sixty-seven-year-old white Australian woman with dreadlocks, told me: "When Rhonda rang and said that you would be willing to come down, I wasn't too sure of the response because of everything going on at the moment. But I've had a great response because you're black, you see, and they've never seen you and they want the real thing."[48] At the second workshop I conducted in Adelaide, Briar introduced me in the following fashion: "We're fortunate to have Patrick Johnson with us tonight. He's the authentic thing from the United States. I'm just (grabbing and shaking her dreadlocks) you know, and came to the music through the CDs, but Patrick, he's the real thing." That same evening, a woman came up to me after the workshop and said, "If I'm listening to the radio, I can tell if it's a black singer in the first two notes. I heard it tonight in your voice—what is that?" I responded, "My mama."[49] (While my Signifyin' was totally lost on her, it nevertheless gave me a great deal of satisfaction!)

At my workshop with the Band of Angels, a community choir in Perth, the largest city in western Australia, I was also heralded as an authentic black gospel singer. In this case, however, the choir's view of me as authentic did not manifest itself verbally in comments directed toward me like those in Adelaide. On the contrary, it was their deference to *my* authority over their own choir director's that revealed how they saw me. For example, Rosie, the choir's founder and director, asked me to take charge of one of their rehearsals. The choir hung onto my every word. They obediently stopped talking when I asked; they ended their notes when I gave them the signal; they never clapped before I indicated that it was time; and, they responded when I asked them to give me more volume. These were all things that Rosie had tried to get the choir to do, but to no avail. Although the choir's response to me was in part probably due to the fact that I was a guest and they were being respectful and polite, their deference to my authority undoubtedly was also partly due to my blackness and their perceptions of me as an "authentic" black gospel singer from the United States—one whose "expertise" they respected more than that of their white Australian conductor.

During the course of my fieldwork, I became increasingly aware of my role in the dissemination of "blackness" in Australia vis-à-vis my workshops and the media. I grew self-conscious about my teaching gospel songs to nonbelievers whose only connection to the music might be a secular/romantic one. Was I not accountable to my black American community, who regards this music as sacred? At the same time, I was also aware of how I, an "outsider," was beginning to essentialize Australian culture in general and Australian singers specifically, while simultaneously feeling dubious about their notion of the sacred. By viewing Australians as fixed subjects and by juxtaposing that view against my own authenticating narratives of blackness, I began to fall prey to the same essentializing discourse I found among those who attended my workshops.

Nowhere was my complicity in this construction of my authentic blackness more at issue than in my television and radio interviews. Often I would authenticate my blackness and my authority on gospel by narrativizing my experience of growing up in the South in the black church and singing in the choir since the age of five, and by emphasizing the physicality of gospel singing. These experience narratives ontologically linked race, region, and religion as epistemological

E. Patrick Johnson performing "I Got Heaven on My Mind"
with the Café of the Gate of Salvation.

sites, foregrounding "blackness," "southernness," and "Christianity"
as authenticating features of gospel expertise.

My first radio interview was with Peter Thompson, an announcer
on the Australian Broadcast Company (ABC), which is the Australian
equivalent of National Public Radio in the United States. One of my
American friends who happened to work for the *Sydney Morning Herald* warned me that Thompson could be obnoxious, and so I prepared
myself for the worse. Indeed, not only was Thompson obnoxious but
he immediately put me on the defensive because of the way he framed
the interview:

Thompson: When the American academic and singer Patrick Johnston
[*sic*] first heard that there was a black gospel choir in Sydney full of . . .
well . . . white heathens, he was incredulous. So he came out to see
it. And [he] was so impressed by the Café of the Gate of Salvation,
as it is called, he's incorporating a chapter about it in his upcoming
book . . . *Appropriating Blackness*. Patrick Johnston himself grew up
singing nothing else but gospel. It was a true southern Baptist childhood. He sees it [gospel music] as much more than just a beautiful
sound. And he's concerned that white Australians are romanticizing

the music of oppressed black Americans when our own indigenous Aboriginal communities are still suffering. . . . Patrick, good morning to you. What do you make of the Café of the Gate of Salvation?[50]

Prior to the interview I had had no interaction with Thompson; therefore, I was surprised that he knew so much about my "true southern Baptist childhood" because he had not learned it from me. I was particularly offended by Thompson's introduction because of his use of the word "heathens" to describe the choir members. I had never referred to them that way, yet Thompson had credited the comment to me. I immediately tried to find a way to diffuse the comment by praising the choir:

> EPJ: Well I think they're wonderful. They have great voices and they've been singing for a while now, so they have a great sound and they're very committed to the music.

But Thompson was baiting me, wanting me to incite controversy by disparaging the Café as inauthentic:

> Thompson: But they obviously love the music of black American beat, particularly gospel. When you listen to them, and compare them to, say, the real thing, the authentic singers, what comparisons can you make?

Hedging a bit, my response was:

> EPJ: Well . . . actually . . . it sounds a little different. I think because of the cultural differences, but also because many Australians aren't used to singing gospel music. It's not just music sung with the voice, it's sung with the whole body.
> Thompson: What do you mean by that?
> EPJ: Well . . . you can't just stand still and sing gospel, for instance. In the United States you sing gospel and you rock, you move, you clap, and you use the whole body. It's a very physical way of singing, rather than traditional choral singing.
> Thompson: And our Café boys don't?
> EPJ: Yes. They do, but not in the same way that we do in the United States. And they don't pretend to, I should add. But they're very interested in the idiom and they're pretty good. Some of the songs they sing I wouldn't call gospel, but many others I would.
> Thompson: Also, in the sense that these lyrics have grown out of the ex-

periences of black Americans can anyone else, if you like, replicate them in the same way when performed?

EPJ: [pause] Yes. In fact, there are a few Australians I've heard since I've been here who have the idiom down. I mean, they really do a great job with what we call riffs, ad-libbing, or melismas and things like that, but it's the exceptional Australian, I find, who can really replicate that idiom. But others, I find it takes a lot of work to pull the sound out of them.

Albeit for different reasons, Thompson and I both engaged in authenticating constructions of gospel. For Thompson, the Café "boys" (the implicit sexism of his statement did not escape me) are mere imitators of the "real" thing. I discerned from the outset of the interview that his ultimate agenda was to have me affirm that view. In response, I tried to present a more diplomatic portrait of the choir by suggesting that their sound was *different,* rather than engaging a discussion on origin and essence. I nonetheless reinforced the belief that only black Americans can sing gospel the "right" way, with my statements such as "many of the songs they sing I wouldn't call gospel" and "it is the *exceptional* Australian, I find, who can really replicate that idiom."

My first radio interview set the tone for those that followed, although the other radio personalities were a bit more affable than Thompson. In each interview the announcer assumed that Australians could not sing gospel very well, and that this "fact" was my motivation for coming to teach them how to do it "right." Often, in Australian singers' defense, I would suggest that there are indeed "good" Australian gospel singers and that they can sing gospel as well as anyone else. Ultimately, however, I wound up implicitly reifying the essentialist position that framed the interview by suggesting that white Australians had to be coached in order to sing the music; by speaking as an "expert" on the history of gospel; and by singing on air. Consider, for example, the following excerpt from an interview with Philip Adams, a radio talk show host:

Adams: His name is Patrick Johnson and he sings gospel music. And he's been doing that since he was, well, five years old, in Hickory, North Carolina. Patrick is a black American. He's professor of literature and choir director at Amherst College in Massachusetts and I welcome him to the program. . . . As well as performing here, you're also teaching people how to sing gospel. Can white people sing gospel?

EPJ: Of course they can. Anybody can sing gospel.

Adams: But can they sing it *great?*

EPJ: Of course they can . . . with a little . . . help.

Adams: From you.

EPJ: [laughs] From me or from other capable hands.

Adams: Well hands are important aren't they because you've got a teaching technique that involves parts of the body. Can you briefly explain that?

EPJ: Yes. Gospel music is very physical. You can't just stand and sing. You have to use the diaphragm. You have to use your hands. You have to use the voice. And in the United States, choreography is also very important—clapping and moving and swaying and stomping.

Adams: Are you going to do all of that tonight?

EPJ: No.

Adams: [sighing disappointedly] Awwwww.

EPJ: [laughs]

Adams: I want the choreography. I want the stomping and the clapping. Oh dear oh dear.[51]

In addition to Adams's obvious exoticization and fetishization of gospel and me, what stands out in this interview is how complicitous I am in the construction of the authenticating narrative of gospel. I was invited on the show as a scholar on the topic, and, as such, I spoke with scholarly authority on a subject about which I was conducting research. However, in the context of a public interview where the assumption was that white Australians cannot sing gospel music well (or worse, that they can't sing it at all), my scholarly authority registered as cultural and social authority rooted in my blackness. No matter how I tried to undermine that authority, the fact of my blackness carried more cultural capital than the fact of my scholarship. The fact that Adams's initial inquiry was whether *white* people can sing gospel, not whether Australians can sing gospel, underscored the cultural capital of race in this context. The lack of a qualifying ethnic or national identity of whiteness is telling here, for the underlying assumption in his question is that if all white people cannot sing gospel, then all black ones can. My singing in the studio and my "lecture" on gospel, coupled with my thoughts and comments on Australian singers as novices, secured the legitimacy of not only my own (black) authority, but the discursive representation of Australian gospel singers as inauthentic.

Another interview indicates how my "stardom" around Sydney began to affect my integrity. In this instance, I began to pander to the stereotype of the theatrical preacher and black churchgoer by affirming the authenticity of the problematic representation of a church service in a scene from the film *The Blues Brothers*. Richard Glover, one of Sydney's more popular news radio personalities, conducted the interview:

Glover: He's a great singer. He can teach the history of gospel music, but he can also sing it. Now in Australia to conduct choir and lead workshops, Patrick Johnson joins us in the studio. G'day.

EPJ: G'day.

Glover: In those *Blues Brothers* films, which many Australians have seen, we got an image of the black southern church with the preachers singing and dancing. Realistic or not at all?

EPJ: Not only is it realistic, but there are some churches that are even more charismatic than those in those *Blues Brothers* films.

Glover: Including the priest, the Reverend singing the whole sermon virtually, and sort of doing high kicks and all of that?

EPJ: Yes, that's what we call a chant, when a preacher will begin speaking as I'm speaking to you, and then it will [begins chanting] go into a little hum-huh—somethin' a little like that-huh. Ohhhhhh yeeeeaaaahhh. So it's kind of a singsong, chant, and that really gets the congregation going.

Glover: Do a little bit more of that. What would they then go on to say? Would they go on to sing or to give a sermon in a sense?

EPJ: Well, it's both a song and a sermon. Most of the time these preachers will call upon formulaic expressions that the congregation is quite familiar with, things like "I was sick and I couldn't get well. The Lord healed my body, now I can tell. I went to the valley, but I didn't to stay. My soul got happy and I stayed all day."

Glover: Can you do that as they would do it? Or is it outside your range?

EPJ: Well, not on the spot I can't. But sometimes when I'm goofing off I can do it.

Glover/EPJ: [laughter][52]

In retrospect I realize how insidious the interview was. Rather than critique the racist stereotype captured in the film, I perpetuated it with the confidence of a seasoned minstrel.

Each of the radio personalities positioned me as an exotic, racial Other that they wanted to put on display for their radio audience, and I was both consciously and unconsciously complicit with that positioning. That said, my goal in this discussion is not to demonize the announcers or myself. Rather, my aim here is to point out that there are no innocents in the perpetuation of narratives of black authenticity. The reference to *The Blues Brothers* in the interview context underscores Paul Gilroy's claim that "the discourse of authenticity has been a notable presence in the mass marketing of successive black folk-cultural forms to white audiences."[53] That this marketing has been at the hands of nonblacks as well as blacks should come as no surprise. In either case, there is a premium placed on authenticity and particularly on black authenticity. In regard to gospel in Australia, it seems that the most productive way to rise above the identity politics that singing the music incurs is to look to the music not as a universalizing agent nor as an essential one but rather as an opportunity to engage in a conversation with the Other and the self so that both may be better understood.

Blackness and Dialogic Performance

There is no easy way to avoid the identity politics that arise when one group or culture appropriates another group or culture's art form and when members of the "indigenous" culture and the appropriating culture, as well as critics from both cultures, articulate conservationist or pluralistic arguments. Conservationists argue in essentialist ways that totalize and reduce black culture, most often in the name of Black Nationalism, while many pluralists explode the notion of any coherent organizing principal of blackness or black cultural production. There is, however, an alternative to either of these positions, particularly in relation to black music. Paul Gilroy summarizes it best when he writes:

> Music and its rituals can be used to create a model whereby identity can be understood neither as a fixed essence nor as a vague and utterly contingent construction to be re-invented by the will and whim of aesthetes, symbolists and language gamers. Black identity is not simply a social and political category to be used or abandoned according to the extent to which the rhetoric that supports and legitimizes it is persuasive or in-

stantly powerful. Whatever the racial constructionists may say, it is lived as a coherent (if not always stable) experiential sense of self. Though it is often felt to be natural and spontaneous, it remains the outcome of practical activity: language, gesture, bodily significations, desires. These significations are condensed in musical performance, though it does not, of course, monopolize them. In this context, they produce the imaginary effect of an internal racial core or essence by acting on the body through the specific mechanisms of identification and recognition that are produced in the intimate inter-action of performer and crowd. This reciprocal relationship serves as strategy and an ideal communicative situation even when the original makers of the music and its eventual consumers are separated in space and time.[54]

Key to Gilroy's demolition of the essentialist/antiessentialist binary is the primacy he places on the relationship between the body and discourse as a complex, dynamic, intricate web of significations and meanings that are simultaneously experienced as real and imaginatively produced. This view of "black" performance opens up new possibilities for interpreting the performance of gospel music by Australians.

One way to view the Australians' performance of gospel is as an instance of cultural performance, wherein their performances provide a space for social and cultural reflection and critique. Although they are performing an Other's culture, their engagement with the music emerges from a cultural site specific to their own history as well— namely the legacy of British propriety and the secularity of contemporary Australian culture. Because their gospel performances are in striking contrast to the socially and culturally sanctioned Australian cultural performances, they hold the potential of transgressing the strictures of white hegemonic systems that sanction behaviors, beliefs, and attitudes. It is specifically the liminal space of performance that provides this occasion for cultural reflection and critique, this space where, in the words of Victor Turner, "the past is momentarily negated, suspended, or abrogated, and the future has not yet begun, an instant of pure potentiality when everything, as it were, trembles in the balance."[55] In this liminal state, according to Dwight Conquergood, "cultural performance holds the potential for negation, as well as affirmation," but nonetheless "[induces] self-knowledge, self-awareness, [and] plural reflexivity."[56] When, for instance, the Café of the Gate of Salvation members speak of the joy, love, and sense of belonging they experience when they perform, they are naming the process of self-knowledge and self-awareness facilitated by gospel. The fact that such self-awareness is induced by a cultural discourse (gospel) that transgresses the cultural milieu of Australia highlights the political nature endemic to cultural performance. Turner suggests that cultural performances set in motion "a set of meta-languages whereby a group or community not merely expresses itself, but more actively, tries to understand itself in order to change itself."[57]

This change is also facilitated by what Conquergood calls "dialogic" performance.[58] Through dialogic performance the performer may come to know himself or herself by performing the Other. The dialogic performance paradigm foregrounds the tensions between the self and the Other such that, despite evidence to the contrary, self and Other temporally and spatially come together and converse. This productive view of performance elides narrow, essentialist views of performance, while at the same time acknowledges difference. Indeed, in the words of Conquergood, "dialogic performance celebrates the paradox of 'how the deeply different can be deeply known without becoming any less different.'"[59]

In "Performance, Personal Narratives, and the Politics of Possibility," D. Soyini Madison theorizes the politics, benefits, and limits of performance with regard to three subject positions that comprise dialogic performance: the audience, the performers, and the subjects being performed.[60] From each of these subjective positions, Madison highlights what she calls the *performance of possibilities* in order to articulate a politicized practice of dialogic performance. In what follows I relate each of these three subject positions to Australian gospel performance.

In Australia, the audiences of gospel performance usually comprise everyday folk who are vested in musical performance of any kind. During most of the gospel performances I attended, the audience most often lacked the cultural capital to respond to the performance in ways that conform to the black gospel aesthetic of call-and-response, hand clapping, standing, hand waving, and so on. However, because the singers are familiar with the cultural aesthetic of gospel in the United States, the singers would often encourage the audience to participate, sometimes to no avail and at other times with much success.

As some of the performers have revealed to me, reactions to gospel performance vary from venue to venue, ranging from a response of total disinterest to lukewarm reception, from appreciation to interrogation of the history of the music. No matter what the "goal" of gospel performance, the engagement of the audience, at whatever level, speaks to the *possibilities* that such performances create. For Madison, the audience's engagement with the performance is a critical component of political and social action (282). Regarding Australian audiences, their witnessing of gospel provides them a glimpse into the lives and history of a geographically and racially distant Other, a glimpse that may motivate them to join in the Other's struggle for humanity and equality. Although this is an idealistic and perhaps romantic view of audience, the performance of gospel in Australia nonetheless provides that "possibility" for political action.

Self-reflexivity is usually a by-product of cultural performance, and this is particularly true for the performer who performs the Other. In the meeting between self and Other in performance, the performer, according to Madison, "is transported slowly, deliberately, and incrementally, at each rehearsal and at each encounter toward knowledges and life-world of the Subject," and thus "creatively and intellectually taking it all in internalizing and receiving partial 'maps of meaning' that reflect the subjects' consciousness and context" (285). If the performer is "taking it all in," then he or she cannot help but be transformed. Madison further adds: "The process of being transported, or receiving meanings and generating meanings, is a more intimate and, potentially, a more traumatic engagement for the performers than for the audience members, because the transportation is mentally and viscerally more intense" (283). The intimacy and visceral and mental intensity inherent in cross-cultural performance implies that an internal dialogue between self and Other is inevitable. This "felt-sensing" experience energizes, inducing self-reflexivity, self-knowledge, and empowerment.[61] Judith Carson, for example, an elderly woman who sings with the Honeybees, discovered her own singing voice again after having been discouraged from singing in her younger years. Now in her seventies, Judith is rediscovering a part of herself that she thought she had lost, a rediscovery facilitated by her willingness to engage the Other. In an e-mail message to me she narrates the joy of her discovery:

Dear Patrick,
This is your most enthusiastic Sydney student. I am dotty about singing,
as you probably realise. All my life it has been my dearest interest. Tragi-
cally for me, in 1952 I started having singing lessons. The teacher said,
"Do it from the diaphragm," and "Lift your palate." Never, "Listen to that
awful noise you are making." I broke my voice and could not sing at all
for years. It was too important to me to give up, and I tried teacher after
teacher. It has been disastrous. I love the power of your sweet voice, and
the beauty of the music you made. Since you left, I have sung with your
tapes, copying the sound and lilt of the music, and my body responds to
the music I make and I am beginning to sing with my own voice. Perhaps you can imagine what this means to me? It's all a bit of a miracle. If
you come to Sydney again soon I should enjoy very much singing with
you again. . . .
Much affection,
Judith[62]

Judith's testimony exemplifies Madison's call for the performer to
be "committed—doing what must be done or going where one must
go—to 'experience the felt-sensing dynamics' of the social world of the
Other: it's tone and color—the sights, sounds, smells, tastes, textures,
rhythms—the visceral ethos of that world."[63] Although she was "copying the sound and lilt of the music," something in that process and
in the music made Judith's body respond. When Judith placed those
sights, sounds, and rhythms in her body, her body responded in ways
that empowered her to find her own voice by singing with and through
Others' voices. Her "transformation" was emotional, psychological,
and physical. It was emotional in the sense that she was deeply moved
by the music; psychological in the sense that her attitude toward singing changed from one of disquietude to that of confidence; and physical because her voice became stronger and her body responded to the
music. Her "broken" voice was "healed" through the "miracle" and
power of gospel.

Judy Backhouse reports a similar self-discovery when she was per-
suaded to perform in New Orleans. In this instance, however, she
and the black subjects mutually benefited from the performance, in
part because of the space in which the performance occurred. Bor-
rowing from Lawrence Grossberg's notion of "spatial territorializa-
tion," Madison argues that identities are "constituted by identification
with certain cultural practices and connect to certain locales that are

often ripe with struggle, conflict, and difference just as they are with creation, empowerment, and belonging" (283). In the following anecdote, Judy Backhouse underscores the importance of place in relation to identity and dialogic performance:

It was one of the most harrowing nights of my life. . . . I was in this church. I made friends with this choir called John Lee and the Heralds of Christ in New Orleans. They said come to their church, they were giving a program, and I went along and I was sitting in the audience. They were singing and everything was great: there was call-and-response, when, suddenly, John Lee said, "We have a good friend here from Australia, Ms. Judy Backhouse, and she's going to come up and sing." And I said, "Oh no! I'm not a soloist. I'm not a soloist, really." And he said, "Oh no, you're going to come up." And I said, "No, no, no." And I was very certain that I wasn't going to have to go up. I'm a strong person. No one's going to make me do what I don't want to do. However, I just couldn't not go up because it would have been an insult to everybody—everybody was wanting me to go up. And I had to go up. I was so scared, cause I thought, "I can't sing, they'll see that I can't sing. It will be the worst insult to them to sing badly in this great place where everybody is singing." Everything crossed my mind. I had to go up, I had to sing "Precious Lord." They said, "What do you want to sing?" and . . . [the song] I really love more than anything else in the world is "Precious Lord." Well, I've got a tape of this, and it just sounds like someone on their death bed, their last gasp, you know. But there they were, starting to encourage me: "Alright," "Go on," "Do it." And that encouragement and that love they directed toward me, encouraged me really, it really emboldened me. By the end of the song, I was singing it, instead of just gasping it and panting it. I was singing it and I just thought what it gives the performer, just makes you feel like you're in Heaven. And I wish we did that here in Australia. It will probably come in time.

Clearly, Judy was transformed by this experience. Her repeated emphasis on the place in which the performance occurred speaks to the fact that, in Madison's words, "identity is definable yet multiple, contested yet affirmed, contextual yet personal and a matter of difference and a matter of identification" (283). Judy's reluctance to perform was based on her own rigid notion of identity and performance, especially within the culturally prescribed space of the black church. She briefly took the stance that Dwight Conquergood calls the "Skeptic's Cop-out," in which the performer refuses to perform the Other because of empirical and biological difference.[64] Quickly swept up in the centripetal energy of the church space, however, she slowly moved to the center of dialogic performance. Once she began the performance, that liminal space where self and Other converse began to emerge, thereby generating a powerful, dynamic transformative space. The encouragement of the audience whose art and cultural history was being performed helped Judy to "travel" into their world and, thus, provided her with a sense of belonging such that "by the end of the song, [she] was singing it, instead of just gasping it and panting it."

The words of the song that Judy sang were also crucial to the transformative power of this performance. Thomas Dorsey's classic hymn "Precious Lord" exclaims: "Precious Lord, take my hand. Lead me on, let me stand. I am tired. I am weak, I am worn." Because Judy is a nonbeliever, her singing of that song takes on mythic status insofar as she calls on the trope of the anthropomorphic God to take her hand and help her through the song, to "take her hand and lead her on." With the encouragement of the black subjects in the church, and despite her non-Christianity, Judy appropriated an Other's religious myth to empower herself to sing "in this great place where everybody is singing." The performed myth aided Judy in this moment of personal crisis. Conquergood writes: "It is through the liminal and transformative act of performance that myth and reality dissolve into a molten power that charges life with meaning and purpose."[65] Indeed, the liminal state of being betwixt and between black church culture and Australian secular culture created a tension that allowed Judy, through the immediacy and intensity of performance, to become self-reflexive about her own sense of identity. Ultimately, Judy's sounding like "someone on their deathbed" was not the point. Rather, the fact that the subjects sanctioned her performance of their culture is what transformed her relationship to and with the Other, what made her "feel like [she was] in Heaven."

Witnessing this performance was meaningful to the black subjects in the church as well. Their personhood, history, culture, and spirituality were affirmed and validated. This kind of validation is key to the *performance of possibilities* because it presents and represents, according to Madison, "subjects as made and makers of meaning, symbol, and history in their fullest sensory and social dimensions."[66] It acknowledges their existence in the eyes of others. The reflection of our selves through others is elemental to understanding the performance of possibilities. As the events chronicled above attest, space, place, and time are each important in the making of the performance of possibilities. Still, for "the deeply different" to become "deeply known," per Madison, there must be a move "beyond the *acknowledgement* of voice within experience to that of actual *engagement*" (284). Performers and their audiences must engage the Others' political, social, and cultural landscape, contextually constituted subjectivities within contested spaces. Through this process of dialogic engagement, according to Madison, "subjectivity linked to performance becomes a poetic and polemic admixture of personal experience, cultural politics, social power, and resistance" (279).

In the performance of possibilities, when this sharing of two worlds occurs both the subjects and performers benefit, as was the case when as a choir the Café of the Gate of Salvation first visited the United States in April 1999. Many individuals from the Café had come to the United States with Tony on one of his many "tours," but this was the first time that most of the choir's members came together to tour U.S. black churches. Traveling from New York City to Birmingham to New Orleans, Tony arranged for the choir to give concerts, attend choir anniversary programs and rehearsals and church services, and experience the New Orleans Jazz Festival. During the choir's visit to New York, I managed to arrange a trip there in order to see one of their performances. I was curious about how the choir would be received by black American churchgoers and how, in turn, they would react to that reception. I was especially anxious to experience the choir's performance in Harlem at the Baptist House of Prayer; an unlikely place, I thought, to invite a group of nonbelieving, white Australians to sing gospel music.

Located on 125th Street, across from the famous Sylvia's Restaurant and down the road from the Apollo Theater, the Baptist House of Prayer is a typical storefront church. The performance was scheduled for Easter Sunday—the evening service—and in the church an array of fuchsia, canary, and white wide-brimmed hats decorated the sanctuary. At first the crowd was small, but the pews gradually filled as the preprogram testimonies wore on. The members of the Café were seated in various places in the sanctuary rather than sitting together as a group (at one point there seemed to be more white congregants

The Café of the Gate of Salvation performing at the Baptist House of
Prayer, Harlem, New York, April 1999. (photo by the author)

than black!). My partner and I sat in the back of the church trying to be
inconspicuous, but to no avail as members of the Café discovered my
presence and tapped others on the shoulder to point me out or sent
notes to those on the other side of the church who, on recognizing
me, smiled and waved furiously. The devotional service went on for
at least an hour and a half before the master of ceremonies then welcomed everyone to their special Easter concert, featuring their special
guests all the way from Australia: the Café of the Gate of Salvation.
The choir members rose and gathered at the altar. All were dressed in
black, but each member had added his or her own tie or scarf: a splash
of brilliant color—red, purple, blue, yellow. A nervous energy filled
the air as the motley crew stood before the church. No one, including
the choir members, knew quite what to expect.

Tony Backhouse greeted the congregation with his consummate
charm and graciousness, expressing the choir's gratitude for the invitation to sing. Their journey had not been easy, he said, as they had
to leave several fellow singers behind due to family commitments
or because they could not afford to make the trip. But one member,
Deborah, had joined the tour in spite of her own brother's death just
days before the choir left Sydney. Deborah stepped forward and ad-

dressed the congregation. "He told me to come. 'Sing your heart out,' he said. He died the next day," she said tearfully, prompting cries of "Have mercy" and "Bless her Lord" from the congregation. Then the teary–eyed choir lifted their voices to sing.

The congregation appreciated the first few numbers, but I had a sense that the choir was not really reaching them. They clapped along in affectionate tolerance (the ways parents encourage their children's bad piano concerts or dance recitals). Then something broke. The basses set an upbeat tempo, their heads bobbing in time and their faces lighting up. The tenors, altos, and sopranos joined the basses in harmony and rhythm. Soloist Tracey Greenberg stepped up to the microphone and launched into "You Brought the Sunshine," a song by the Clark Sisters of Detroit that was popular in the early 1980s. The church pianist began to play, and there was uproar as the congregants rose to their feet and began to sing along: "You made my day / You paved my way / You heard me, every, every time I prayed / You brought the sunshine (You brought the sunshine) / In my life (You are the lifeline)." The choir beamed as the congregation's enthusiasm intensified in shouts of "Hallelujah!" and "Saaaaaannnng choir," syncopated by clapping hands, rocking bodies, and stomping feet that shook the church's creaky, wooden floorboards. At that moment, as the melodious voices lifted in the air, the Baptist House of Prayer fell under the spell of the spirit that moved the foundation of the church.

During and proceeding dialogic performance, and specifically within the performance of possibilities, performer, subject, and audience are transformed. Each comes away from the performance changed. They traverse the world of the Other, glimpse its landscape, and this "sighting" leaves a lasting imprint on the consciousness of all who experience this symbolic journey. Indeed, in Madison's words, they enter "albeit symbolically and temporarily, in [the Others'] locations of voice within experience" (279). The performance of "You Brought the Sunshine" tapped into the Others' voice within experience, because this particular song registered with the congregation as a "difficult" one, and the Café's performance of it demonstrated their commitment to, investment in, and reverence for gospel music. The choir's performance competence initiated genuine dialogue in that contested space where identities and subjectivities conjoin, converse, commune, and contrast. According to Madison, "performance becomes the vehicle by which we travel to the worlds of Subjects and enter domains of intersubjectivity that problematize how we categorize who is 'us' and who is 'them,' and how we see ourselves with 'other' and different eyes" (282).

This blurring of subjectivities in the symbolic space of performance foregrounds the discursive nature of identity, such that during their performance in the Baptist House of Prayer, the Australian choir and the black listening audience participated in the coproduction of blackness. Thus, for all intents and purposes, the Café of the Gate of Salvation, in face of evidence to the contrary, "became" black. This is not to suggest that outside this symbolic space of performance and within the specific confines of the black church the choir does not enjoy white-skin privilege. On the contrary, as soon as they stepped outside the church and onto the streets of New York, they enjoyed the material fruits of their skin color's labor. Nonetheless, their performance inside the church and during this particular song foregrounded the arbitrariness of black signification as well as the possibilities created by means of performance. Indeed, the choir was engaging in what Richard Schechner calls "believed-in theater," where "at site-specific, event-specific, audience-specific performances, people gather as cocreators, participants, actors, spectators, witnesses, citizens, activists . . . doers. The occasions are frequently more social or personal or quasi-religious (ritual-like) than aesthetic. Sincerity and making an honest effort are appreciated."[67]

The transformative power of dialogic performance should never be underestimated. For the members of the Café of the Gate of Salvation, their experiences during their tour were life altering, collectively and individually. Four months after their tour, I traveled to Sydney to conduct more research and follow-up interviews. What I found was a choir "transfixed"—to borrow Judy Backhouse's term—by the power of their intercultural exchange. Their relationship to one another and to the music had changed. Members who did not go on the tour, for example, resented what they felt to be a new "religiosity" taking over the choir, which, according to them, flew in the face of the choir's past stance on fundamentalist dogma. Indeed, a few of the members became "saved" on the tour. Judith Foster, in particular, told me that her life had been changed on the tour, that she was no longer a nonbeliever. In fact, she and another member asked me to interview them again because they no longer felt the same way about issues of spirituality and God.

The emergence of rituals and practices and shifts in beliefs by members of the Café acknowledge the malleability of the human spirit as well as the mobilizing force of performance. Despite their resistance to the spiritual ethos enlivened by gospel, through performance the choir came to realize, as Judy Backhouse had done already, that the music "does something to you" or, as Tony Backhouse put it, "changes you for the better."

In their 1989 hit single, Huey Lewis and the News proclaim, "It's Hip to Be Square." In some instances, the same can be said of blackness. In recent times, blackness seems to have particular currency in popular culture, whether represented by middle-class white youths who embrace hip hop or by well-intentioned liberals who, in an attempt at interracial bonding, appropriate black vernacular (e.g., "you go, girl"). On the other side of the coin, black Americans themselves circulate blackness in as many troubling ways, often grounding it in biological essence or confining it to a particular brand of politics as an agent of social efficacy. Whatever the case, blackness has definitely become a "hip" signifier of identity and difference.

As a national and global commodity, black music has penetrated the boundaries between and among cultures around the world. As such, it becomes bound up in an intricately spun web of cultural, social, and political battles over origin, ownership, circulation, and performance. Until fairly recently, gospel music existed on the margins of this political minefield, due in part to its relatively limited circulation and popularity among mostly southern blacks. As gospel music has found currency among a younger audience—a currency made possible due to a shift in how it is marketed and, more important, how it is produced—the music, like its musical sister and brother, rhythm and blues, has become more popular intra- and intercontinentally. It has, indeed, made its way over and "Down Under." Although black American culture is widely disseminated in Australia, gospel music's particular popularity in recent years may be due to the sense of community it encourages. Singing together in choirs provides an opportunity for an otherwise internationally diverse group of people to come together as *Australians*. Indeed, Judy Backhouse believes that the emergence of gospel singing groups in Australia represents the "first full community, the tribal thing, the group thing." This sense of group identity that gospel provides for Australians is not so unlike that which it provides for black Americans, although clearly for different purposes and aims.

Like other black cultural art forms when they are let loose into the world, gospel music has become enshrouded in identity politics. The case of the Café of the Gate of Salvation is one example of how "messy" those politics may become. Like all identity politics and notions of "authenticity," the choir members' appropriation of blackness is both/and rather than either/or. Each time the choir performs gospel music they participate in what has become one of the most recognizable signifiers of black culture. In that regard, they perform blackness when they sing. On the other hand, their performance of blackness does not diminish the white-skin privilege they enjoy in their country or in the United States. Their performance of their own and the Other's identity, however, is never a static process but rather one of flux and flow—of *possibilities.*

Negotiating any identity is a dangerous adventure, particularly in a postmodern world in which we have come to recognize that identities are made, not given. We also must realize that the postmodern push to theorize identity discursively must be balanced with theories of corporeality and materiality. In other words, "blackness" may exist as a floating signifier in various cultures, but the consequences of its signification vary materially, politically, socially, and culturally depending on the body on which it settles. I, for instance, walk this precarious tightrope of identity politics each time I conduct ethnographic research on Australian gospel.

6

PERFORMANCE AND / AS PEDAGOGY

Performing Blackness in the Classroom

True understanding of diversity can come only when
we move across barriers that history and custom have
put in our way. — Trudier Harris

We understand that in performing the contested
identities of Subjects there must be caution and politics.
We are involved in an ethics guided by caution and a
strategy informed by cultural politics. We are not recklessly
speaking to and against one location, but to ourselves
and our very endeavor. — D. Soyini Madison

How can we as teachers bring to the classroom a
nonauthoritarian, open-ended, and process-oriented
approach — and, at the same time, retain the respect and
authority of the students for our positions as blacks and
women — categories themselves identified with absence,
lack, irrationality, emotion, and sexuality[?]
— Mae G. Henderson

When I began writing this book, I knew that I would "save the best
for last," as it were, in terms of the chapter I most looked forward
to writing. The following essay on pedagogy is that chapter. Since
my first experience teaching as a graduate student at the University
of North Carolina at Chapel Hill, I have grown tremendously as a

teacher/scholar. Although the path has not been at all smooth (nor was it supposed to be), teaching is something I believe I do well— something for which I have a passion. Because I seize every opportunity to perform, the classroom has become the stage on which I test out my latest "acting" skills. Anyone who says that teaching is not a performance has failed to self-reflexively take stock; has failed to feel her pulse when she "emerges" before her class to pontificate the latest theoretical musings of her discipline; has not, indeed, reconciled the fact that time and space are circumscribed in that moment when student and teacher meet discursively and corporeally under the spotlight of the knowledge-making process.

Perhaps the performance studies classroom takes such awareness for granted, privileging as it does performance as methodology for understanding human communication and cultural production. For those of us who teach performance of literature, the performances that occur in our classrooms are multiple: pedagogy as performance, learning as performance, texts as performance, critique as performance, and so on. It is not surprising, then, that the postmodernist turn in literary study did not eclipse the simultaneous epoch occurring in oral interpretation: the shift to "performance studies," that is, the view of performance as process, contingent, historically and culturally situated, itself a text-making praxis.[1] As with literary studies, performance studies has also become embattled in the crisis of representation, that slippery site in which by and through performance "we" demarcate who the Other is. In recent performance scholarship, much has been made of the problematic of this ethical conundrum: How do we negotiate representing the Other in performance in a self-reflexive, dialogical, nonracist, nonsexist, nonhomophobic, nonclassist way?[2] Yet, we have not fully excavated this political and ethical minefield; there is yet another patch of ground to be unearthed. That ground, for some of us, particularly performance scholars of color, is a familiar one because it is where we have lived all of our lives, where we have been positioned as Other. Our familiarity with the minefield, however, has lulled some of us into the belief that we are immune to its threat; we "know" where the soil gives way to danger below. Far from following the "safe" assumption, I want to pose that not only are we unsafe but, indeed, we run the risk of dismemberment each time we take for granted the foothold we think we have on such "familiar" ground.

That familiar ground is, of course, our raced, gendered, and sexual bodies, through which we experience the world. But how do we account for the multiplicity of our own experiences even within the same moment? From others who share our race, class, gender, and sexuality? Is there not an Other within that confounds our sense of self in the midst of history, place, and space? And does not the discursivity of our identity affect how teachers, students, and literary texts perform? And, more crucial to my project here, how do we come to terms with the ways in which bodies — black and otherwise — produce, authorize, and authenticate "black" readings and performance strategies of black literature? These are difficult questions — ones for which I do not offer easy answers. Rather, I wish to offer several strategies for the negotiation of this relationship among texts, teachers, and students in the performance studies classroom.

In what follows I meditate on the processes by which black literary texts and students and teachers of various backgrounds (especially myself) authorize and authenticate blackness through performance. What I hope to glean from this medi(t)ation is not the foreclosing of performed blackness. On the contrary, my desire is to open up further the possibilities of blackness in and through performance by encouraging a dialogic relationship among texts, students, teachers, the self, and the self as Other. In addition, I use this occasion to pay tribute to the teachers who have taught me (almost) everything I know about teaching, learning, and the performance of blackness in the classroom.

Searching for Blackness: Performing Black Literary Criticism

In fall 1988 I enrolled in a course titled "Performance of African American Literature," offered in the Department of Speech Communication (now Communication Studies) at the University of North Carolina at Chapel Hill. Dr. Wallace Ray Peppers, an African American professor who was at the university for only three short years, created the course. After his death in 1987, Dr. D. Soyini Madison, a recent graduate of Northwestern University's Department of Performance Studies (coincidentally the department in which I now teach), filled Dr. Pepper's position. Dr. Madison ("Soyini") taught "Performance of African American Literature" in fall 1988, her first semester at UNC, and it was in that class that she taught me (almost) everything I know about the performance of African American literature.

One of the most useful things I learned from Soyini in that class was the importance of providing a cultural context for African American literature. In that particular semester we read Zora Neale Hurston's *Their Eyes Were Watching God;* Toni Morrison's *Sula;* Jean Toomer's *Cane;* Dorothy West's *The Living Is Easy;* Gloria Naylor's *Mama Day;* and James Baldwin's *Go Tell It on the Mountain.* In each instance, Soyini guided us through these texts, reading them, as stated in the course description on the syllabus, "as both a literary text and a cultural text." The description continued: "As a literary text we will discuss narrative structure, plot construction, literal and figurative language, and closure. As a cultural text we will discuss the historical (political and social) dynamics of these novels as they reflect African American and Euro-American experience." Whether discussing the function of myth and story in African American culture in relation to *Mama Day* or folklore in *Their Eyes Were Watching God,* we always received a critical and historical context for the novels we read, and we were encouraged to use that knowledge in our performances. In fact, as the semester wore on, Soyini evaluated us less on our competence as performers and more on the kind of risks we took in performance, risks that challenged the very information her lectures imparted to us in the first place. In other words, although Soyini provided a "black" context for the literature, that context was never presented in such a way that would reduce it to a static reading of African American literature or culture. To be sure, performance was one way to worry the line between the "authentic" blackness of the text as grounded in "the black experience" and its blackness as figured in and through performance.

This is an important, yet difficult, pedagogical line to toe. On the one hand, it is important to provide students with the historical and cultural context of literature in order to discern the conditions of its

production, especially in this age when reading is no longer fundamental and MTV and "reality TV" shows all but increase the illiteracy
of American youth. The trick, however, is not to close off the text in
such a way that the blackness mapped onto it (historical, cultural, or
otherwise) becomes the only possibility of reading it. The text *performs*
its blackness as much as we perform it. Either way, the focus is on
the meaning-making process rather than on unearthing a fixed underlying meaning.

All of these issues have been hashed and rehashed among black literary scholars. Indeed, the need to "legitimate" black literature in the
face of the hegemony of the white canon led to "in-fighting" among
these scholars about the best way to proceed in such endeavors. In
their pursuit to legitimate black literature, many of these critics devised and argued for strategies of reading black literature that necessarily depended on the critic's knowledge of "black" culture. In *Understanding the New Black Poetry*, Stephen Henderson for example, he
argued that black poetry could be understood only in terms of the
categories theme, structure, and saturation. The latter of which Henderson defines as the "communication of 'Blackness' and fidelity to
the observed or intuited *truth* of the Black Experience in the United
States."[3] Henderson goes on to elaborate how poems communicate
their "blackness," but he fails to discern what constitutes *the* "truth"
of the "Black Experience." Although he offers a caveat by saying "as
Black people in the United States refine and clarify their conceptions
of themselves the poetry reflects the process," Henderson's theory of
black poetry nonetheless mires it in essentialism. We might ask, for
example, if the poetry of the Harlem Renaissance speaks lesser "truth"
of the black experience than does that of the Black Arts movement
or rap music? "Truth," like "blackness" itself, is temporally and spatially located at the crossroads between here and yon. Black poetry, for
its salt, provides only a pallet for critics, readers, and performers on
which to lay their particular blackness alongside those of others whose
grubby little "black" hands do not know the power of their strange
hold on the signifier's throat.

Henderson's theorizing of the tautology "the blacker the poem the
mo' blackness it communicates" should not be dismissed, for it is a
product of its time and as such was meant to validate black poetry and
identify its uniqueness. Other critics followed suit but pursued a dif-

ferent path of valuation. Those such as Joyce A. Joyce objected to the use of "Western" theories such as poststructuralism and deconstruction to explicate black texts, favoring instead a black literary criticism that sees a "direct relationship between Black lives—Black realities—and Black literature."[4] Unfortunately, Joyce indirectly attributes the ability to tap into "black reality" with being a part of the "folk" (as I discuss in chapter 1). She also adds gender to the mix by suggesting that not only is it the black middle-class critic who has adopted "mainstream [read 'white'] lifestyles and ideology" but middle-class black *men* in particular. She then narrows her scope to focus on two "black middle-class male critics": Henry Louis Gates Jr. and Houston A. Baker Jr.

In what would become known as the "showdown of all showdowns" in black literary history, Joyce, Gates, and Baker engage in "dubious battle" following Joyce wading in the water of racial essentialism. Gates and Baker respond in kind. By literally Signifyin(g) on Joyce's invocation of black "love" as a necessary feature of the black literary critical act, Gates titles his response "What's Love Got to Do with It?" wherein he accuses Joyce, and those of her (inferior?) critical ilk, of being "resistant to theory";[5] a resistance, I might add, that Gates suggests is endemic to Joyce's misunderstanding of the critical terms of his theorizing. Baker's response to Joyce imbues a subtle sexism that seems to suggest that it is black women critics who find his theorizing problematic. Baker states: "Within the past month . . . I have found myself in conflict with other Afro-American critics." And following that statement, in a parenthetical aside, he continues: "The fact that both [critics] were Afro-American women may be altogether fortuitous."[6] This is not a throwaway line, but more cultural signifyin'. Indeed, Baker is relentless in his critical "dozens" as he creates a numbered list of Joyce's "errors and misstatements."[7]

While Gates and Baker point to the "errors" of Joyce's essentialist ways, these two literary critics, despite their poststructuralist leanings, do not escape the essentialist trap entirely in their pursuit of a text's "blackness." In Gates's *Signifying Monkey,* for example, he posits that "the black vernacular has assumed the most singular role as the black person's ultimate sign of difference, a blackness of tongue."[8] For Gates, then, the "founding" (i.e., "ultimate") site of black subjectivity is located in language use. From there he develops a theory of black literary production and criticism that distinguishes it from its white counterpart. It is in black vernacular as manifested in black speech and as registered in black literature where signs and signifiers represent the "black critical difference" and where "the black language of black texts . . . expresses the distinctive quality of our literary tradition."[9]

Gates is unclear, however, about what constitutes "black" vernacular or who is included among the "blacks" who speak it. Although he traces the art of Signifyin(g) back to Esu Elegbara, an African trickster god who sits at the crossroads and is the high priest/priestess of indeterminacy, African inclusion in the category "black" is always forthcoming but never actualized in his theorizing. African cultural mythology is analogized to what Gates sees as its diasporan rearticulation—the Signifying Monkey—to arrive at a vernacular theory to read African *American* literature, implying that the "black vernacular" applies to African language only as an antecedent, not a contemporary, to black social linguistic and literary practices. Could it be possible that *black* language, depending on how it is defined, might exclude Yoruba, Ibo, and Xhosa? Gates fails to address these questions in his focus on vernacular theory, which makes his theorizing vulnerable to an essentialism that would foreclose the possibility of "authentic" blackness outside the contours of black American linguistic and literary production. In other words, Gates's postulating that the black person's "ultimate" sign of difference is a "blackness of tongue" performs a double essentialist logic. First, it corrals black difference under the unifying sign of language use to distinguish it from the white Western canon, a move that does not take into account the "whiteness" embedded within the production of blackness—literary or otherwise. Second, it does not account for the difference *within* black vernacular production in terms of other ethnicities of blackness, class, gender, and sexuality.

Baker, in *Long Black Song*, also finds refuge in the "blackness" of African American texts by suggesting that its distinctiveness is grounded in an "index of repudiation" of white American culture and values. In a move similar to that of Gates, Baker theorizes this distinction on the basis of some aspect of black vernacular culture—in this instance, folklore. Baker argues that "Black Folklore and the black American literary tradition that grew out of it reflect a culture that is distinctive both of white American and of African culture, and therefore neither can provide valid standards by which black American folklore and literature may be judged."[10] He locates the distinctiveness of black American literature at the level of orality, collective ethos, and repudiation of white values.

Beyond the implicit linking of "the folk" with "authentic" blackness as I discuss in chapter 1, Baker also, problematically, universalizes black orality as the ultimate mode of difference in relation to whiteness while failing to account for differences within. The notion of a "collective ethos" must also be questioned in the face of the lack of sustained discussion of what or who constitutes such a collectivity. Finally, Baker does not acknowledge the inadvertent connectedness established in the act of repudiation. Insofar as repudiation requires first an acknowledgment that the thing repudiated exists, black American folklore and literature would also register its "whiteness" even if the register is that of absorption and incorporation. If, as Toni Morrison suggests, Euro-American literature is haunted by an ever-present "Africanism," then surely that anxious racial stream of influence flows in both directions.[11] In the face of interhuman contact, subjective and cultural imbrication is inevitable.[12]

I offer these readings of various black American literary scholars' work and the critical literary "battles" the work incites not to discredit its merit, for the seriousness with which these critics undertake their theorizing demonstrates a commitment to and "love" of blackness and black people. On the contrary, I merely wish to suggest that no matter how noble the motivation behind such critical and necessary theorizing, the theorists still become susceptible to delimiting the bounds of blackness in a text. My call, then, like that of Bernard Bell, is to view African American literature not as a "solipsistic, self-referential linguistic system, but a symbolic sociocultural act."[13]

A few teachers and critics of African American literature have devised strategies of resistance to locating a text's authentic blackness. One such strategy is to offer the cultural context out of which the text emerges as well as the conditions and terms of its production. The motivation behind this particular pedagogical practice is to dissuade students from canonizing African American literature and people in a way that views it and them as monolithic. Jane Skelton, for example, who teaches African American literature in a Boston high school, emphasizes the cultural context in order to dispel the myth that "all black authors write about slavery and oppression; that we have all lived the same life" as well as to dissuade students from thinking that "reading one piece of literature by a black American is like reading any other."[14]

Other professors of African American literature deploy the strategy of throwing the whole category of "race" into disarray so as to deconstruct "whiteness" as a fixed biological category as much as "blackness." The logic of this pedagogy is undergirded by the belief that if all racial categories are revealed as "fiction," then students are more likely to read African American as well as Euro-American literature in ways that allow them to see the imbrication of "race" in each.

Studies such as Toni Morrison's *Playing in the Dark*, which examines Euro-American representations of "blackness"; representations that reveal more about "whiteness"; and Aldon Nielsen's *Reading Race in American Poetry*, which examines white poets' racist representations of blackness, as well as a whole host of critical texts that emerged with "whiteness studies," are employed by teachers to deconstruct "race" in the concept of literature.[15] What is productive about such a pedagogical strategy, of course, is that it may possibly intervene in students' thinking of race in transhistorical terms, thus providing the opportunity to discuss the ways in which humans have variously privileged aspects of their identity outside of racialized terms. Irish immigrants, who phenotypically may have looked "white" according to today's reductionist race logic, but who did not *become* "white" until a long sordid history of "ascendancy to white republic," is an example of this dismantling of biological race.[16]

The downside to this move, however, is that there are ways in which a *focus* on "whiteness" may paradoxically reify the hierarchical racial binary between "black" and "white" that currently exists. Further, there is a way in which theorizing "whiteness" and "blackness" in such terms turns on the assumption that the categories are still somehow sewn to the bodies to which they refer—not in any arbitrary way, but, according to Ann Louise Keating, "as an unchanging biological fact." To escape this reification of racial essentialism, Keating says that her approach is twofold "where [she and her students] explore the artificial, constantly changing nature of 'black,' 'white,' and other racialized identities without ignoring their concrete material effects."[17] The texts she includes in her course—those by Nella

Larsen, Zora Neale Hurston, and Langston Hughes—necessarily lend themselves to Keating's approach because these authors' texts highlight "racialized identities as transitional states," featuring as they do "black" characters who construct themselves ("pass") as "white" and "whites" who act like "blacks."

One literary scholar, however, who comes close to proposing what I believe to be a more critically nuanced way of teaching African American literature also happens to be another former teacher of mine—Trudier Harris. As a graduate student at the University of North Carolina, I enrolled in Dr. Harris's "African American Folklore" course. It was in this course where I first learned to value and appreciate the cultural context of not only black literary texts but black oral culture as well. In her course, Dr. Harris introduced students to the formulaic expressions contained within the folk sermon by playing audio tapes for us, and she encouraged us to attend a revival service at a local black church so that we could experience a sermon for ourselves. Although many of us in the course grew up in the black southern Baptist tradition and had attended many revival services, this assignment afforded us the opportunity to experience on new critical ground a tradition we claimed as our own. We were to attend a revival as critical ethnographers who, as well as being participants in the ritual process, also had to observe with an analytical eye. The familiarity of the church service had to be shelved to give way to nuance and *de*familiarity. Such experiential learning challenged our fixed notions about a tradition of which we felt a part. Moreover, it gave students for whom the folk preaching and revival services were not a part of their culture an opportunity to experience the Other.

Harris's pedagogy demands that we "get down to the nitty-gritty of our cultural diversity" so that we may "transform our perceptions of the world we live in and the people who share it with us."[18] Her pedagogical strategy for confronting diversity, particularly in relation to African American literature, is thus to entrench students in the cultural context of the literature. Importantly, Harris does not suggest that this entrenchment occur by dousing students with static representations of "authentic" blackness linked to abstract notions of language, music, or "the folk"; rather, she advocates taking students to the places and spaces where culture is experienced as a creative and organic process. When teaching Ralph Ellison's *Invisible Man*, for instance, Harris argues that the best way to help students understand the cultural context of the novel's prologue, influenced as it is by jazz, is to take them to a jazz club:

> If we really want to know what jazz experience means, perhaps we would take our students to a jazz set in a black club—or a mostly black one—to allow them the opportunity to get a feel for the music in its context. There they could rub elbows with people who are not like them, but from whom the impetus for a great novel came. There smoke is thick, the vocal interactions loud, and status is negotiated on the basis of performance, not on the basis of color. There the booze flows, and someone might look at us strangely, but ultimately no one is going to eat us alive or kiss us, and we can learn a lot about the musical traditions that gave shape to Ellison's novel. For not only is the prologue [to *Invisible Man*] saturated with jazz and blues, but the entire composition might be viewed as a blues piece. . . . Will we allow our students to get to know the blues tradition, not only from records, but from living practitioners? (213–14)

The "nitty-gritty" of what Harris describes here is the interanimation of texts—literature, culture, lived experience, bodies—that forms the corpus of the dialectic between text and readerly subject. Moving the students' own bodies out of the safe space of the classroom and into the jazz club provides an opportunity for them to experience the text in ways that situate it within the cultural context of the black jazz idiom at the same time that it allows the students to see the text as a meaning-making process. The latter is accomplished by the almost ethnographic pedagogical assignment Harris prescribes. She indexes the particulars of the jazz club herself—"There the smoke is thick, the vocal interactions loud"—and in doing so draws on the sensual and somatic nature of performance as epistemology: how one knows has everything to do with "rubbing elbows" with the Other. Unlike other strategies of reading the "blackness" of texts, Harris's does not take for granted the stasis of cultural forms or identity; rather, she suggests that "status is negotiated on the basis of performance, not on the basis of color," prioritizing performance as a trope that mediates the blackness of texts and the identity claims of people.

Moreover, the pedagogical praxis Harris envisions is not unselfreflexive about how such field trips or, trips into the "field," might make for an uncomfortable border crossing for the students as well as for the jazz musicians and patrons. Nonetheless, the initial discomfort becomes the site where issues of difference and sameness come to the fore, removed from the abstract and supplanted in that space where self and Other meet toe to toe. The importance of these meetings, of course, is that they provide a more nuanced reading of African American literature and culture. Beyond debunking or reifying stereotypes and myths, such experiences encourage students to understand that while black cultural forms such as blues and jazz are crucial to reading texts, these forms have no more authenticating power than other tropes. A musical idiom is but one of an infinite number of culturally sanctioned signifiers of blackness.

While Professor Harris's pedagogical strategy encourages implicating the students' bodies by moving them out of the context of the classroom and into the space of black cultural production, I want to go one step further to encourage embodiment as a way of knowing. Celebrated among oral interpretation and performance studies as an invaluable way to "know" literature, the performance of literature offers an important way to disrupt the notion of authentic blackness in texts.

I would argue that performance scholars, teachers, and practitioners, drawing on the rich histories and methodological strategies of literary theory, have cultivated ways to complicate the production of blackness in literary texts and in culture more generally. Indeed, students and directors of performance studies have long since employed Toni Morrison's call for an interrogation of the "whiteness" imbricated in the production of representation of black peoples and vice versa. Many of these students—including those in my own "Performance of African American Literature" course—and directors have done so without reifying "race" in essentialist terms.

Intertextuality is one literary critical method used by students and directors of performance studies to effect this deconstructive process. Intertextuality focuses on the dialogue of one text with another; it refers to the interpretation of texts in relation to other texts. Insofar as cultural "texts" implicitly respond to one another, their meanings are linked to that implied interaction. Yet, intertextual relations, their emergent meanings and values, are dependent on the discursive practices and interpretive frameworks of a given culture. As Jonathan Culler explains: "Intertextuality . . . becomes less a name for a work's relation to particular prior texts than a designation of its participation in the discursive space of culture: the relationship between a text and the various languages or signifying practices of a culture and its relation to those texts which articulate for it the possibilities of that culture."[19] Thus, when used in performance, intertextuality has two implications for the field of African American literature: first, it may point to the relationship between African American texts and the various signifying practices of African American culture such that we see the formation of a literary "tradition"; second, in performance it is a way of revising, reinventing, and refiguring African American texts, as Henry Louis Gates's theory on signification suggests. An example of this kind of intertextual play occurred in my class one semester when a group of black male students constructed a performance that refigured as lovers James Baldwin's incarcerated character, Fonny, in *If Beale Street Could Talk* and Richard Wright's Bigger Thomas in *Native Son*, by connecting two masturbation scenes from each of the novels. In addition, to comment on Baldwin's critique of religion, the students framed the performance with passages from the Bible that focus on male friendship and intimacy.

Beyond revisioning texts, the use of intertextuality in performance may also underscore what Aldon Nielsen believes to be "the radical mobility of subjectivities and agencies in American culture."[20] Thus, through the critical practice of intertextuality we might read "black" texts (literary and otherwise) in relation to all English writing, such that, according to Nielsen, "we must read Melville within the text of Ralph Ellison's *Invisible Man*, but we must also read Melville differently because of Ellison's text." He continues: "A historicized reading today must take account of the innumerable ways in which America differs from itself. Critics have begun the work of theorizing and tabulating the polysemous signifying forms elaborated by black Americans. Such work must be carried forward along with equally insistent readings of the blackness of white writing" (24).

Performance is one way of engaging such a reading. I use the example of a 1990 performance titled *Rapping the Odyssey*, which was directed by Paul Ferguson, a faculty member at the University of North Carolina at Chapel Hill, and of which I was a cast member. For this performance Ferguson scripted and revised Homer's canonical epic *The Odyssey*. We know that in the original text Homer tells the story of Odysseus, the oversexed, testosterone-driven, chauvinist adventurer who leaves his sad and pitiful wife, Penelope, at home spinning on her loom in anticipation of his return (she would wait twenty years!). During his "adventures" he island hops, adding notches to his belt along the way for each fair maiden he beds. Even Circe, the powerful sorceress who turns Odysseus's crew into pigs, succumbs to the hero's charm, sleeps with him, takes the spell off his crew, lets them stay on her island for a year feasting on her food, and then gives them directions to tarry on their way out. When Odysseus finally returns home, disguised as a beggar, he finds his palace overtaken with suitors for Penelope. He then challenges the suitors to a bending-of-the-bow contest: he who is able to bend the bow will win Penelope, the archetypal female object. Of course, Odysseus bends the bow and kills all of the suitors, and Penelope takes him back—no questions asked—and they all live happily ever after.

Ferguson's 1990 version, however, implores the intertextual practice of reading race and gender in *The Odyssey* by using the African American cultural text of hip hop and the theoretical texts of feminism and deconstruction. In *Rapping the Odyssey*, which signifies on the original title, the crew is cast in cross-gendered roles such that women are cast in the roles of the men who accompany Odysseus in the original story. The first-person narrator, Odysseus, is bifurcated. An older, reflector narrator (played by me) narrates all description, commenting at times on the foolish bravado of his former, younger self, while a younger, in-the-moment narrator performs all of the dialogue. The two are transfigured as the rap artists Kid-N-Play—high flattops and hip-hop garb to boot. In addition, the invocation of the Muse takes the form of a black folk preacher's sermon, also cross-gender cast, and embellished with call-and-response from members of the crew. Other revisions abound. For instance, the Cyclops is refigured as Republican senator Jesse Helms, whose "sheep," by the way, are actually boom boxes with recorded "baa's" on them. The Sirens become the rhythm and blues female singing group En Vogue; and Charybdis, the treacherous, evil whirlpool, dons rubber facemasks of political conservatives such as George Bush Sr., Tipper Gore, and Nancy and Ronald Reagan.

Most striking about Ferguson's *Odyssey*, however, is his refiguring of feminine sexual agency. Although Ferguson's Circe still turns the crew back into humans and sleeps with Odysseus, she only does so begrudgingly and on her on accord. With regard to lovemaking, it is she who initiates it and determines the positions and the length of time. Moreover, instead of a bow-bending contest, the suitors engage in a dance contest. The suitor who wins the dance contest is able to bend the bow and win Penelope's hand. Ferguson rewrites the ending such that it is Penelope who is the best dancer and it is she who strings the bow, kills the suitors, and then turns the arrow toward Odysseus, who proceeds to try to win over her affection by singing the Luther Vandross love ballad "Superstar/Until You Come Back to Me." Penelope maintains her aim after his crooning and breaks out into a song of her own: Aretha Franklin's "I Never Loved a Man the Way I Love You," the first line of which proclaims, "You're a no-good heartbreaker/You're a liar and you're a cheat." After she finishes the song, she continues to aim the arrow at Odysseus. The final image of the performance is that of Penelope (with bow and arrow still in tow) standing center stage and slightly elevated on a platform, with the younger Odysseus still extending his hand and looking up at his wife.

Racialized and gendered intertextual performances such as these do the work that Nielson calls for. That is, that we "read the texts that black writers inscribed between the lines of America's master texts, and [that] we . . . read the echoes of those palimpsestic black texts in the writings of white readers." [21]

Students of performance also apply literary theory to texts in performance. For example, one group of students in my "Performance of African American Literature" course used Michel Foucault to explicate Gayl Jones's *Eva's Man*. In *Discipline and Punish*, Foucault argues that society has historically desired to control the body. This desire, according to Foucault, was institutionalized through the creation of penal and mental institutions, as well as through the creation of laws that prohibited certain sexual behaviors. [22] For Foucault, the body is a battleground, a place where differing factions in various societies through time have competed for dominance over how the body would be enclosed, treated, rewarded, and pleased. In Jones's *Eva's Man*, Eva Medina Canada's body is the site of such a struggle. The victim of sexual abuse all her life, Eva is imprisoned for biting off the penis of one of her lovers, and she is judged mad by her white male psychiatrist because she refuses to speak in her own defense. Thus, the students used Foucault's notion that "a judgment of madness is an act of domination" to demonstrate how the hegemonic discourses of racism, patriarchy, and paternalism compete for control over Eva's body.

While literary critics of African American literature have devised innovative strategies to unpack the production of blackness in African American literature, I suggest that their methods sometimes reify racial essentialism. Performance might be the rejoinder needed to enhance our critical analyses of raced texts in order to understand more fully the complexity of literary blackness.

Embodying Blackness: Students as "Black" Texts

As a graduate student, two years after my introduction to the course under the tutelage of Soyini Madison, I began to teach my own section of "Performance of African American Literature." Relying heavily on what I had learned in Soyini's course, as well as on those courses in oral interpretation I had taken as an undergraduate, I eventually cultivated a pedagogy that I felt allowed me to become open to learning as much as my students did. That my own pedagogy privileged performance, then, should come as no surprise. Indeed, this course occasioned what Bryant Alexander refers to as "teachable moments," whereby the presence of raced, gendered, sexualized, and classed bodies in the classroom evinces a space where knowledge of the Other is produced and exchanged.[23] For me, those teachable moments arose precisely when students indulged in the "nitty-gritty" of performance, when their multiple identities and subjectivities engaged a dialogue with those of the text. What erupted as troubling and disturbing discussions regarding particular performances, especially those by non-identified "black" students, paradoxically provided the most productive ground on which to disentangle the knotty web of blackness and identity. To illustrate this point, I offer an anecdote about an event that occurred when I taught the performance course at Amherst College.

Located in rural western Massachusetts, Amherst College traditionally has educated the children of the nation's elite (read middle- and upper-class whites). Yet, proportionately, it is the most racially diverse campus of the schools that comprise the five-college consortium in the area: the University of Massachusetts, Hampshire College, Mt. Holyoke College, and Smith College.[24] Therefore, the courses I taught, due in no small part to the topics, almost always comprised an array of students from various backgrounds, including race, class, gender, and sexual orientation. In fall 1994, my "Performance of African American Literature" course was unusually diverse, with fewer than half of the students self-identifying as Euro-American. Even more interesting was that the diversity in the class did not inhere the typical black/white binary, for many of the students were East Indian, Latino/a, Asian, and biracial.

I almost always teach fiction in this course, and I almost always focus on twentieth-century texts. To introduce the students to performance of literature I normally make the first assignment a solo performance of no more than two minutes in order to get the students on their feet, to work on performance techniques, and to begin to build a culture of trust among them. In this particular course, the students' first reading assignment was Alice Walker's collection of short stories, *In Love and Trouble*. In this collection are some of my favorite stories, including "To Hell with Dying," the story of the female narrator's love for an avuncular neighborhood "drunk" who throughout her childhood pretends he's dying but who finally succumbs only to old age. Walker likens "Mr. Sweet" to "a rare and delicate piece of china which was always being saved from breaking, and which finally fell."[25] Typically, I would perform an excerpt from this story not only to provide an example of literature in performance but also to "put my own body on the line," as it were, to undermine the assumption of performance as "product" rather than process and to assure the students that no performance is "perfect."

When the students began their round of workshop performances of the Walker stories, many of them chose stories and excerpts that did not require them to move too far from their own experience of themselves. Many of them, for example, chose to perform narration, whereby they simply described scenes or the thoughts of certain characters, and even still fewer students selected narration that contained free indirect discourse (i.e., narration that reports a character's thoughts outside quotation but as if the narrator and character are one and the same, as in Hurston's narrator in *Their Eyes Were Watching God* who reports Janie's thoughts: "If only the doctor would come! If only anybody at all would come!").

The one exception to the students' limited choices was the selection

235

made by a white female student named "Sally."[26] A sophomore English major, Sally came from a working-class single-parent home in eastern Massachusetts. She had acquired a reputation among the black students, particularly the black women, as being a "ho," apparently because she dated black male students whom the black female students thought of as either "dogs" or "sell outs." Sally, as well as some of the black students, offered me this background information both before and after the course. I share it here only to contextualize the response to Sally's choice to perform Walker's "Everyday Use," a short story that has been anthologized widely because it poignantly relays the avowal and disavowal of black culture, the commodification of black identity through folk artifacts, and the values of sisterly and motherly love. The story centers on the Johnson family: an unnamed mother and her two daughters, Maggie and Dee. Maggie, the daughter described as "homely" and whose walk is likened to that of a "lame animal," resides at home with her mother. Dee, the "lighter-complexioned" daughter, has gone off to school where she takes on an "African" name, "Wangero," because she "couldn't bear it any longer, being named after the people who oppress [her]."[27] The tension of the story involves the ownership of some quilts that the mother has promised to give to Maggie, but that Dee/Wangero desires because they are "priceless" trinkets of the (black) culture she now simplistically romanticizes. Indeed, when her mother asks her what she will do with the quilts, Dee responds that she will "hang them" as opposed to putting them to "everyday use."

The story is a wonderful example of the ways in which identity and material culture are imbricated in the formation of blackness. Given that the mother offers Dee a quilt before she goes off to college, which at the time she refuses because she believes quilts to be "old-fashioned, out of style," it becomes clear when she returns home as "Wangero" that her relation to "blackness" has been altered. She accords African nomenclature and "folk" art with authenticity over and against the names and materials of the oppressor.

Sally chose to perform the section of this story where the mother/narrator describes her physical features and physical stamina, boasting of her abilities in the folk tradition of toast telling. The mother tells the reader and Sally performs:

In real life I am a large, big-boned woman with rough, man-working hands. In the winter I wear flannel nightgowns to bed and overalls during the day. I can kill and clean a hog as mercilessly as a man. My fat keeps me hot in zero weather. I can work outside all day, breaking ice to get water for washing; I can eat pork liver cooked over the open fire minutes after it comes streaming from the hog. One winter I knocked a bull calf straight in the brain between the eyes with a sledge hammer and had the meat hung up to chill before the nightfall. (48)

The hyperbolic language the mother/narrator employs to describe herself in such "butch" terms presented a challenge for Sally in her performance. How could she, a lanky, five-foot-nine, dirty-blonde white woman, affect the physicality of a fat, fifty-year-old black southern woman? In the performance, Sally drew on her long limbs to take up space, gesturing in broad but slow movements to mime the various chores the mother describes. She characterized the mother's speech by affecting what she believed to be a black southern dialect, speaking slowly, deliberately.

During the performance I could feel the tension rise in the class, especially among the black students. Afterward, when I asked the students to comment on Sally's performance, there was dead silence. After a few more moments I called on a black student, whom I noticed smirking throughout the performance, to talk about Sally's performance. Both stunned and angry at my singling her out, she turned to Sally, who was still seated before the class in the chair she used for the performance, and said, "I thought your performance was OK, but I didn't like the way you portrayed the mother." "What specifically in her portrayal of the mother did you not like?" I inquired further. "I don't know," she stated. "I just didn't like it." At that moment another black student, a male, spoke up: "I think the problem was a combination of the exaggerated movement and the heavy accent. It seemed to be more of a stereotype than a real portrayal of the mother." Soon, other (black) students chimed in, criticizing everything from Sally's choice of costume (she wore overalls for the performance) to her decision to choose that particular section of the story in the first place. Sally was crushed by these comments, and I became incensed by the disingenuousness of these students, because I knew that their critique stemmed from their personal feelings about Sally, and also

because their comments toed the conservative line of black authenticity: You're not black, so how could you possibly play a black woman
in a realistic way? Needless to say, my teachable moment had arrived.
To buttress the severity of the students' critique, my first response
was to praise Sally not on the competence of her performance but the
risks she took in the choices she made. I then asked her to talk about
why she made certain choices and how she saw the choices as helping
her portray the mother as well as to communicate the tension between
the mother's self-image as opposed to the image she imagines Dee has
of her. Sally responded that she struggled with the decision to physi-
calize the mother and affect the "black" southern dialect because she
was afraid of the very response she received. She decided in the end,
however, that not portraying the mother that way would flatten the
character and diminish the ethos of the story. "But I still think you fell
into stereotyping," the first black woman critic responded. "All black
people don't talk like that," she added. Realizing that this student was
determined to undermine the performance at all costs, I turned to her
and asked, "How would *you* have performed this piece differently?"
The student sat in silence. "Well?" I pushed. More silence. "I have an
idea," I said. "Why don't you direct Sally in how she should perform
this piece. In fact, why don't all of you who feel that Sally's performance was steeped in stereotype direct her now in this workshop performance." In response, Sally began until a student stopped her with
a suggestion. She then continued until the next student stopped her,
and so on. This went on for at least fifteen minutes until finally Sally
performed the entire piece seemingly to the satisfaction of all those
who worried over her "stereotypical" and "inauthentic" performance
of blackness.

I remember this moment so vividly because it was the first time in
teaching this course that issues had arisen over black authenticity. At
the University of North Carolina most of the black and white students
shared if not a common socioeconomic status then at least a common regional history. In that context, "white" southern dialects and
"black" southern dialects, while distinct in some instances, overlap in
interesting and curious ways. Thus, at UNC a white student affecting
a "black" dialect, particularly in the context of performing this story,
never created hostility. At Amherst, however, where most of the students come from the Northeast, Southwest, or West, such dialectical

imbrication was uncommon. Therefore, Sally's affectation of a "southern" black dialect was particularly offensive to the black students because it conjured up racist images of white representations of "black" speech in minstrel shows or characters such as Buckwheat from *The Little Rascals*. Although I wish to acknowledge and validate the black students' concerns, I want to work through the complexity of their responses as well.

The students' accusations of racist stereotyping, while legitimate, also obscured the more circuitous avenues they took to secure their own black authenticity. In other words, many of the students who criticized Sally's performance on the grounds of inauthenticity had no clearer frame of reference for the mother character than did Sally. As products of middle- to upper-class homes, it is most likely that these kids had never experienced killing hogs, working outside all day, or, for that matter, speaking with a southern accent, given that none of these students were raised in the South. Nonetheless, these behaviors, at least in some of their minds, are linked to authentic blackness. Sally's performance, then, drew attention to their own "distance" from the very black authenticity they accused her of not having. Following Diana Fuss, I challenged what counted as "experience" and chose not to "defer to it in [this particular] pedagogical [situation]."[28] My decision to have the students direct Sally served to make this point clear: blackness is produced and authenticated depending on the context and the authorizing subjects. That a white woman whom they held in disdain could affect such "black authenticity" struck a nerve in their essentialist bodies. Indeed, their authorizing of authentic blackness was undermined.

The other aspect of these students' response to Sally's performance that I wish to address here is my belief that many of the black students in the class could identify with Dee/Wangero. Although many of these students come from middle-class homes, they, like Dee, came to college to "discover" their blackness. Because I entertained these students in my home and interacted with them outside the classroom, particularly in my capacity as gospel choir director, I was able to learn much about their personal and family histories. While none had taken on an African name, they worked hard to downplay their middle- and upper-class status by wearing poor-fitting or well-worn clothes, dreading their hair or wearing it in "natural" hairstyles, and espousing the rhetoric of militants such as Malcolm X and Louis Farrakhan.[29] Further, they had bought into the rhetoric espoused by Langston Hughes and other middle-class blacks whose angst about their own status encouraged them to associate authentic blackness with the working class. In these contemporary times, however, "folk" culture on the black authenticity front seems to be synonymous with hip-hop culture. These students' journey to blackness, then, is both the reverse and the same as Dee's. Leaving behind the "backward" life that her mother and sister represent, Dee *learns* to value the very thing that she so desperately tried to escape—black folk culture. Along with adopting an African name she finds it fashionable to display her blackness by hanging her mother's quilts on the wall. The black students in my class, on the other hand, having no frame of reference of what it means to be black and *poor*, used their time in college to get in touch with their blackness by performing a faux nationalism vis-à-vis the hip-hop culture that they equate with black authenticity.[30] Ironically, it is Sally whose class status is most closely aligned with that of the Johnson family—one more possible reason why the black students in class felt threatened by her performance.

My characterization of Sally and her performance is not meant to position her as a saint or victim. Indeed, she was conscious of the racist overtones that her performance would register, yet she made the decision to perform her choices in spite of these risks. I also do not wish to mark the black students as pariahs or dismiss their concerns about Sally's performance, for they may have genuinely been offended by it. The point I wish to make here is that both Sally and the students were implicated in complex ways in the process of making meaning of the blackness in "Everyday Use." Both the performance and the responses to it demonstrate that authenticity is overdetermined, and that it is contingent on political and social contexts and agendas.

By the end of the course, Sally's first performance was a distant memory because she had worked in groups with most of the students who had been her harshest critics. What that initial performance initiated, then, was a dialogue between the students that moved them past their preconceived notions about their own identity claims and those they imbibe in the texts they read. Performance provided to them a space to get down to the "nitty-gritty" of diversity and provided me with several "teachable moments." My ability to take advantage of those teachable moments culminated at the end of the semester during our reflection on the course when, at one point, we returned to a discussion of Sally's first performance. I asked the class if they thought they had become more self-reflexive critics since that first round of performances. They all nodded furiously. At that moment, Sally spoke up and said she appreciated her classmates' honesty about that performance. She added that she understood why they responded the way they did, and that it made her think even more carefully about the choices she made in her subsequent performances. "But," she said, "if I had it to do all over again, I would make the same choices because for the first time at Amherst, I felt like people really had an honest conversation about race."

In that instance, Sally took advantage of a teachable moment, signifying on her black classmates by indirectly communicating to them her knowledge about how they really felt about her and how it influenced their critique of her performance. Her emphasis in that comment, however, was her appreciation of the honest dialogues that performance provoked. "The aim of dialogic performance," according to Dwight Conquergood, "is to bring self and Other together so that they can question, debate, and challenge one another."[31] Sally's performance brought her in dialogue with the mother/narrator of Walker's story as well as with the black students in the course. Perhaps more important, however, the performance also created a space for Sally and the students to engage a dialogue with the self—in ways that opened up the possibilities of performing blackness.

There were also occasions when I had this class give a public performance, both to showcase their work and to use the opportunity to open the classroom to my colleagues, many of whom did not understand performance as a methodology to "read" literature. These performances were almost always controversial because I did not require the students to censor their performances. Because a number of the books we read in class—from Gayl Jones's *Eva's Man* to Toni Morrison's *Sula*—contained provocative and explicit themes and language, it follows that their performances did as well. Thus, students and faculty alike often flocked to these public performances more out of curiosity about the sensationalist aspects of the students' work than to engage it critically. Cognizant of this risk, I was still invested in allowing the students to present their work outside the space of the classroom.

During the fall 1994 showcase, one student performance demonstrated most clearly the dialogic dynamic between self and Other in
the text and self and audience. This performance also demonstrated
that blackness is co-constructed across identity markers such as race,
class, gender, and sexuality. The performance was given by one of my
South Asian students, "Andy."[32]

Although seemingly a rather shy student, Andy came alive in/
through performance, transforming into whatever character or part
he took on with total commitment. In this particular instance, he had
chosen to perform "The Judgment Day" from James Weldon Johnson's collection of folk sermons, *God's Trombones*. Of all the sermons
in this collection, "The Judgment Day" tries to capture the cadences,
crescendos, and moans, and the half-song, half-chant speech of black
folk preaching. A challenging piece for even the most seasoned of
"black" performers, in my experience "The Judgment Day" rarely
piques the interest of non-African American student performers.

Imagine then, the look on the faces in the audience when Andy,
a nineteen-year-old, unassuming student of South Asian descent announced in his introduction that he would be performing "The Judgment Day" from Johnson's *God's Trombones*. I could not help but note
the dismissive and skeptical looks on the faces of the audience, especially on those of the blacks in the audience.

And then Andy began. In a calm, almost matter-of-fact tone, he said:
"In that great day, / People, in that great day, / God's a-going to rain
down fire. / God's a-going to sit in the middle of the air / To judge
the quick and the dead." Needless to say, the looks of skepticism dissolved into looks of amazement. Andy had commanded the attention
of the entire room in just the first line of the poem. People shifted
in their seats, sitting up straight and leaning in to focus on this "folk
preacher." Following the four phases of the black folk sermon that he
had researched for the performance—plot ("taking the text"), complication, climax (chant/song mode), and resolution—Andy moved
the audience to rapture.[33] Several older black women in the audience
began to rock and sway and wave their hands, as well as encourage
him on every now and then with a "Well," "You better speak on it?"
and "Um hum." Soon there was a chorus of antiphonal bliss as Andy
fervently preached the repetitious "Too late, sinner! Too late! / Good-
bye, sinner! Good-bye! / In hell, sinner! / In hell!" By the end of his

performance, the audience was on its feet, spent from the emotional roller coaster of the performance as well as stupefied by the competence and commitment of Andy's performance.

Performances such as Andy's bring into clear focus the slippage between "race" and biology and the dialectic between performance and performativity, unlocking as it does the wedged door to the closet of essentialist binarisms. The fact of Andy's South Asian heritage is highly visible in the performance, and yet he implicates his identity in the construction of another: blackness. Those two racial identity tropes collide in the moment of performance when self and Other call attention to the dissonance registered in their copresence as well as the communion exalted in the face of real difference. Andy was transformed by his engagement with the Other because he, according to Dwight Conquergood, respected the "Difference of the Other enough to question and make vulnerable [his] own a priori assumptions."[34] On the other hand, the black folk in the audience were also transformed by his performance because it derailed their plans to dismiss it on the basis of skin color and authentic blackness. In that moment of performance, Andy's preaching was authentic in his experience of black folk preaching. Thus, the black audience came to realize that, in the words of Conquergood, "when we have true respect for the Difference of other cultures, then we grant them the potential for challenging our own culture" (9). Andy's performance did challenge blackness as associated with folk preaching by infusing it with Asian spices and thereby providing new possibilities for the recipe that is black identity.

These students bear witness not only to the intellectual rigor of dialogic performance as critical methodology, but also to the sensual, transformative, political process of dismantling fixed notions of self, Other, and identity in general, while at the same time remaining cognizant of the impact of racism, sexism, classism, and homophobia in our lives. They know, too, that performance is not magic: there are "pitfalls" to performance that may result in tragic misreadings by colonizing the Other, exoticizing or fetishizing the Other, trivializing the Other, or by not engaging the Other at all.[35] Like any critical methodology, performance is vulnerable to being blinded by its own terms and methods. As some of my literary-scholar colleagues have pointed out, performance cannot always unearth the nuances, themes, and narrative strategies that literary criticism can. And yet the goal of performance is not necessarily the same as that of literary criticism. Performative exegesis emphasizes the performer as critic, implicating the performer/critic's body in the process of meaning making. Embodiment, then, turns precisely on the notion that the meaning of a text is coproduced in the critical act of reading.

This concept is nothing new to literary theory, but performance scholars take it a step further by insisting that the performance of literature has political and social implications for transforming the world. Thus, when non–African American as well as African American students perform "black" texts, the boundaries of race, class, gender, and sexual identities become blurred. Because of the immediacy of performance, not only is the literature exposed as an ideological construction of racial boundaries (both those seen as constructed and those experienced as real) but the body also becomes a site of discursive signifying practices that simultaneously dismantles hegemonic notions of race, class, gender, and sexual identity and exposes the constructed nature of such demarcations.

Indeed, these boundaries are exposed and blurred as the audience suspends disbelief with regard to white students performing black characters, black male students performing black female characters, middle-class, white males performing poor southern black women, Asian American males performing black lesbian characters, or South Asian students performing black folk preachers, and so on. Like the act of writing, performance can open itself up to what Homi Bhabha, rereading Lévi-Strauss, calls "the uncanny structure of cultural difference"; that structure that, rather than revealing the stability of our innermost self, allows us "to coincide with forms of activity which are both at once ours and other."[36] When the words, thoughts, and culture of the Other are placed inside the body in the process of performance, the performer as critic is transformed as she/he enters what Joni Jones argues is "a borderland in which they must challenge the construction of the self along with the construction of the Other."[37] Insofar as the performer is transformed by the "sense of the Other"[38] procured in/through performance, she has the potential to effect social change. The *experiential* process of performance facilitated the students' cross-cultural engagement—their "border crossing"—in ways that altered the manner of their understanding of themselves and African American culture. Mary Strine writes:

Performance and/as Pedagogy

In the broad scheme of current methods available for literary study, performance-centered scholarship remains ideally positioned for exploring the dynamic features of literature as the complex interworkings of understanding, pleasure and power having far-reaching social consequences. As we near the twenty-first century faced with increasing cultural diversification and fragmentation, coupled with growing demands for public accountability from higher education, the disciplinary tasks of performance studies should include a vigorous recommitment to the study of literature through performance, a uniquely productive way of understanding and appreciating culture as unity within the simultaneity, interanimation and negotiation of differences.[39]

The performance of literature, then, may complement the work of more traditional literary study, drawing on its methods while bringing students to literature and the cultural differences registered in it through their own bodies. Privileging this mode of intellectual inquiry with regard to African American literature provides a way to complicate the ways in which blackness is narrativized, experienced, and produced in the ongoing process of culture.

Teacher as Text: Authorizing Blackness in the Classroom

Student bodies in performance are not the only ones implicated in the production of blackness in the classroom. Indeed, in this venue my own performance of blackness becomes a text to read in conjunction with all of the other texts in that space. Because of the inherent hierarchy always already in place between student and teacher, my blackness carries an authority that alters and shifts the meaning-making process. Therefore, in this last section of the chapter I want to focus on the ways in which the black teacher's body's multiple significations, transcribed by students to read and perform "black" texts, may be put in the service of what I see as a productive pedagogical intervention in the performance studies classroom. Toward that aim, I wish to raise a question regarding performance and the Other in the classroom—one that Mae Henderson asks regarding black women in the black women's literature classroom: "What does it mean to teach the Other when the Other is the Self?"[40] Specifically, how does my black body's agency as a teacher of performance of African American literature authorize and authenticate my critical readings of African American literature? Simultaneously, how do the involuntary signifiers that my black body signs in the classroom space authorize and authenticate a *particular* "black" reading and performance strategy?

I begin by examining the ways in which my blackness authorizes a problematic "authentic" reading and performance of blackness of texts. This occurs because my position as authority figure in the classroom coupled with my corporeality forecloses, to an extent, alternative readings of blackness within the texts under study. Although my exegeses of African American texts are no more valid or "correct" than other readings, my agency as a teacher, a *black* teacher, legitimizes for my students an "authentic" reading of African American texts. Within this discursive terrain both the students and I are implicated in black authorial production. My authority as teacher, for example, is established well before I walk into the classroom space and long before I give any lecture on the literature taught in the course. My black skin always already signifies in ways that ontologically link black bodily experience as evidence of racial epistemological authority. More simply put, because I am black I "know" black literature because, presumably, I have lived the life of the texts I teach. Academic institutions also accord scholars of color this authorial power (however fragile and tenuous that "power" might be) by hiring them on grounds not solely based on assumptions about and documentation of their pedigree, intellectual acumen, research interests, pedagogical skills, etc., but also on the assumption that these scholars' blackness brings with it some sort of "authentic" relationship to the subject they are asked to teach. Although professors sometimes excel and at other times plunge far beneath these expectations, none of the assumptions are completely in step with the reality of who "we" are in the world. Nonetheless, these credentializing rituals function to create the illusion—on behalf of the students and sometimes the professor—of unmitigated authorial "black" power.

More often than not students are close readers. And they are particularly close readers of teachers. Mae Henderson reminds us that our intentions notwithstanding, professors "will indeed be 'read' by the students (either consciously or unconsciously)—and in spite of her 'authorial intention,' so to speak."[41] As with any text, my black teacher's body signifies in ways over which I do not necessarily have

246

control, but for the performative reiteration of "blackness" my body compels by its mere presence. Here, I refer to blackness in discursive terms, as my body signifies in various and multiple ways that may be deployed in the service of reading it as text and, in turn, reading and performing other "black" texts, particularly those taught in the course.

My students bring with them to the classroom strategies of reading race, class, gender, and sexuality. Their own reading strategies have been influenced by the discourses that circulate in popular culture, among their families and friends, and in history. They read my blackness alongside those constructions and my performed black identity in the classroom. Although unintentional, I reinforce my authorial power by explicating texts based on the authority of my own "black" experience. Indira Karamcheti remarks on this authorizing process when she writes: "If the minority teacher has traditionally been allowed into the groves of academe as a native informant, on the basis of the authority of experience, then the impersonation of the personal allows him or her the experience of authority."[42] For example, when I draw on my experience as a "black southerner" to read black cultural tropes in Zora Neale Hurston's *Their Eyes Were Watching God*, my students are more likely to trust that reading than if I drew on those same experiences to read black cultural tropes in T. S. Eliot's "The Love Song of J. Alfred Prufrock." Because of the association of the object of inquiry to the critic, certain readings become more "legitimate" than others. This is why many African American students resent having white professors teach them "black" books, for in their minds these texts necessarily reflect a worldview and experience of blackness to which their white professors have no access. In these instances, black corporeality problematically becomes a prerequisite for reading black cultural production. According to Judith Butler, this delimitation of reading is necessarily a feature of any reiterative behavior. "This delimitation," she writes, "marks a boundary that includes and excludes, that decides, as it were, what will and will not be the stuff of the object to which we then refer. This marking off will have had some normative force and, indeed, some violence, for it can construct only through erasing; it can bound a thing only through enforcing a certain criterion, a principle of selectivity."[43] While one could argue that this delimiting of interpretation would be true of any reading of a text by an authorial figure, delimitation and authorization would necessarily vary depending on the racial, gender, class, and sexual identifications and significations of the professor and her or his students.

The difficulty, of course, lies in the negotiation of when and where "I" enter, to borrow the title of Paula Giddings's work on black women's history.[44] For, on the one hand, the black body, and in my case, a black *gay* body, is always already decentered within the context of a white supremacist and homophobic academy. On the other hand, how does one reposition that same body from margin to center without indulging in a narcissistic and solipsistic pedagogical praxis? This, perhaps, is the conundrum facing the minority teacher in the classroom. One's "visibility" simultaneously authorizes readings of the "raced" texts under study and deauthorizes the black teacherly subject because of institutional racism. Indira Karamcheti reinforces this notion when she writes: "The minority teacher does not necessarily have the choice of deliberately engaging the machinery of the personal in order to problematize authority. Authority has already been problematized by the fact of visible difference. The insistence of the personal preexists the decision to engage in the practice of self-inclusion, the politics of the personal."[45]

Drawing specifically on her own position as a black woman teacher in relation to teaching black women's literature, Mae Henderson offers insight into working through the difficult task of teaching the Other when the Other is the self. One theoretical move she suggests is "to locate oneself in the body—that is for the teacher to represent herself as embodied text—produced by certain personal and historical experiences."[46] For Henderson, achieving embodiment requires more than "re-figuring the traditional and stereotypical" or "privileging the personal at the risk of the socio-political as a primary category of analysis"; rather, she suggests that the teacher must "listen to the otherness within—that otherness which is defined not in its relation to the Self as Same, but in its relation to Self as Other" (436). This dialogic, self-reflexive pedagogy is not new to performance theory, but rarely has there been a focus on reading/performing the Other when the Other is the self. If we make this performative turn in our scholarship on performance pedagogy, we might discover yet more productive ways to invigorate our sometimes overdetermined pedagogical strategies of teaching/performing the Other.

When, for example, the professor foregrounds himself or herself as an embodied text, according to Henderson, "we can learn and teach from positions of authoritative knowledge as well as from positions that challenge authoritative knowledge. It is in sites of ambivalence and exchange frequently where real learning (and teaching) takes place" (437). In order to engage Henderson's call for professors to represent themselves as embodied text, I must simultaneously locate the (black) Other within—that Other that is always in the process of becoming. This task is most often accomplished by historicizing one's racial subjectivity. Ironically, in my instance I locate the formation of my racial subjectivity in my first-grade classroom. I say, "ironic" because my racial knowledge of self occurred in the space where one's first impressions of self and Other are acquired. I find it only fitting that I employ the performative now to narrativize how I came into my "blackness."

I was barely a year old when James Brown recorded his manifesto urging black folks to affirm their "blackness." But my mother tells the story of my dancing to the rhythm of Brown's song, holding onto my diaper with one hand and my bottle with the other, coo-cooing after each and every, "Good Gawd!" Like so many other black babies who are exposed to rhythm and blues (one woman in my community claims that she played Al Green up until the time she went to the hospital to give birth to her firstborn!) I was already being culturally saturated by one of the most powerful signifiers of blackness: soul music.

In 1973, the first year of desegregation in my small hometown in western North Carolina, I was among the first generation of black children bussed across town to attend school. In my first-grade class there were only three other black children besides myself. One day, another black classmate and I accidentally broke a record (probably James Brown!) while fighting over who would get to put the record on the player. Mrs. White,[47] my first-grade teacher, ran over to us, snatched the record out of our hands, and yelled, "You two little *colored* boys!" My classmate began to cry while I stood there looking up into the angry white face wondering what "colored" was.

I didn't have to search long for the answer. When I asked my mother why Mrs. White had called me "colored," she said, "Because you are." "And to some people," she added, "that means you're dumb, that you

249

don't know nothing, that you're lazy and dirty and don't deserve to be treated like everybody else." She paused. Then she lifted my chin with her index finger so that I looked directly into her eyes: "I don't care what nobody says to you, you goin' be somebody. You may be black, but you ain't dumb. You may be poor, but the Father has many riches in store for you. People gonna call you names and say ugly things about you. You just remember what I told you and hold your head up. Don't ever be ashamed of being black. That's how God made you." Then she took me into her arms and prayed.

These two childhood incidents began my journey into "blackness," and they point to the ways in which racial identity is and is not a matter of bodily experience. In the instance of my baby body enjoying James Brown, it was the rhythm and syncopation of language rather than language itself that propelled my little body into motion. Moreover, the fact of my black skin had little if anything to do with my *ability* to move to the beat of the music. For that matter, the baby who found himself moving to James Brown's song could just as easily have been Asian or white. On the other hand, one might ask whether James Brown or soul music would be played on a continual basis, if at all, in the home of whites or Asians. The difference, I would suspect, lies in the valuing (or not) of soul music in the first place. Nonetheless, what did happen in that moment is that I had my mother's eyes watching, encouraging, valuing, and appreciating my enjoyment of the music, and then I had her recollection of it later. Although it was my baby body enjoying the music, "felt-sensing" it, as it were, it was not until my mother retold the story to me that body and identity conjoined—and that fusion was through words/discourse—performativity—and not bodily experience.

The second incident, with the record and Mrs. White, was a part of typical childish play. In fact, I still have no guilt about breaking the record, nor do I find delight in retelling the story, except now I can rerun the scene and insert James Brown. The point I wish to make, however, is that the accident with the record set in motion a series of events that facilitated my coming into racial identity. After the incident, for example, my mother's explanation of "colored" was the moment in which she named the identity I did not know I had. That racial knowledge came to me through an accident, followed by anger (Mrs. White's) and then by my mother's loving embrace. In this case both my body (in my mother's arms) and language (Mrs. White's epithet) became the "origin" of my racial knowledge. Racial knowledge followed by a (classroom) "sin" was the epistemological moment. This incident exemplifies the play between performativity and performance, between discourse and life as lived. Although I was on the other end of a racist remark because I embodied blackness (performance), I was not conscious of the ways in which my blackness signified in the eyes of Mrs. White or my mother (performativity). We might assume, for instance, that Mrs. White would never have said "You two little *white* boys!"—because of the ways in which "whiteness," as opposed to being "colored," goes unmarked.

Generally, the rhetoric of James Brown's song reflects the politicized battle over blackness during the 1960s. Like my mother's response to my first-grade experience, Brown's anthem counters the construction of black as "dirty" and inherently inferior and even boasts the superiority of blackness: "Say It Loud (I'm Black and I'm Proud!)" But my journey into blackness reveals that the interplay between bodily knowledge and discourse is the site at which the status of blackness becomes embattled—James Brown and my mother's definitions notwithstanding.

As my anecdote about Mrs. White demonstrates, European Americans also construct blackness. Although Mrs. White went on to become my patron (she paid for my first piano lessons, bought my first musical instrument, and sent me money when I graduated from high school and college), her epithet is what comes to mind when I think of her. "You two little *colored* boys!" is forever imprinted on my psyche as the moment when I became "black." More to the point, like others who come into their blackness through trauma, it was a painful knowledge of identity (as opposed to learning it from my mother or James Brown) because it came to me as a reprimand. Mrs. White's benevolent racism, however, speaks to the multiple ways in which blackness is grounded in ambivalence and ambiguity, how blackness is both loved and averted, pitied and ridiculed, embraced and repulsed. As do black people themselves, in her actions as my teacher Mrs. White constructs blackness from multiple sites. And yet, her white privilege blinded her from reading her own "whiteness" and the authority it signified in and outside the classroom. Indeed, she was unselfconscious about the ways in which her whiteness authorized the reading of my body—a body that up until that moment had yet to discover its "colored" potential. The irony of her name notwithstanding, Mrs. White assumed the invisibility of her whiteness while hailing me into existence: "Hey you! Colored Boy." What she failed to realize in her misrecognition, however, was that she, too, became all too visible to me at that moment—a visibility that would influence how I currently inhabit and perform blackness, as well as highlight how blacks and whites simultaneously construct racial knowledge.

My memory of Mrs. White, James Brown, and my mother is one that I most often share with my students. As a narrative performance, it allows me to provide an example of the ways in which racism and racial identity cohere. It also provides a space of self-reflexivity that keeps me cognizant that my (black) subjectivity is a site of social, political, and cultural negotiations. I am a product of the texts I teach as much as they are a part of me. Yet, these texts and my subjectivity are not static but rather change over time; indeed, they and I have an Other of ourselves. By foregrounding this process for the students, I try to privilege meaning making and knowledge as process rather than as product or commodity.

In addition to performing the personal narratives that facilitate de-essentializing and othering the self, while simultaneously calling attention to the material consequences of inhabiting blackness, there are other strategies that performance scholars activate in the service of deauthorizing authentic identity. In fall 1997, for example, I team taught "Performance of African American Literature" with Judy Frank, a Jewish lesbian colleague. I mention here her ethnicity and sexuality to make the point that I was skeptical about how her presence in the classroom would change the rapport I typically have with students, particularly the African Americans. In other words, I was worried about her presence undermining my authority not necessarily in relation to "blackness" as much as my "experience" of queerness. The angst I felt was intensified by the fact that Judy was tenured and I was not. And yet it was this teaching experience that solidified for me the slipperiness of race, gender, and sexual authority. This revelation came by means of performance.

Judy and I decided to change slightly the focus of the course and teach a seminar on race and sexuality, using only the texts of James Baldwin and Toni Morrison. We also decided to perform for the class.

This presented another challenge given that Judy had never performed in her life—especially not for an audience and most notably
not before a class of her own students. Nonetheless, we chose to script
a performance of Baldwin's *Another Country*. I performed the role of
Rufus, the black protagonist whose inability to come to terms with his
sexuality leads him to commit suicide, and Judy played Vivaldo, his
white friend and sometime lover who, along with other friends and
family, is left to deal with the aftermath of Rufus's death. We spliced
the scene in which Rufus jumps off a bridge with that of Vivaldo re-
membering a night when he failed to take Rufus into his arms, la-
menting that if Rufus had felt that he loved him, he, Rufus, would not
have committed suicide.

We framed the performance with a sensual dance that I choreo-
graphed to Billie Holiday's "Gloomy Sunday." The narrator of the song
believes that her lover is dead, only to discover that she was only
dreaming: "I wake and I find you asleep in the deep of my heart, dear."
The dance to this song ended with Judy and I pressed together front to
back, spoonlike, on the floor. The first lines of the performance accen-
tuate the intimacy shared between Rufus and Vivaldo implicit in the
dance. Bifurcating the narrator's description of Rufus and Vivaldo's
relationship, we performed:

Judy and Patrick: "They were friends"
Judy: "Far beyond the reach of anything so banal and corny as color. They
    had slept together,"
Patrick: "Got drunk together,"
Judy and Patrick: "balled chicks together,"
Patrick: "Cursed each other out"
Judy: "And loaned each other money."

In these lines we find Baldwin's call for a transcendence of interracial friendship and homosexual sex taboos. Given the fact of our
bodies, Judy and I discursively echoed Baldwin's call in our performance: we were not only "friends" who, on occasion, got "drunk together," but we were also colleagues who had broken unspoken academic decorum by explicitly and exclusively focusing on issues of
race and sexuality in a piece of literature and foregrounding that
focus with our own bodily performance. The provocative dance that
preceded these lines was meant to capture the sensuousness of the

novel as well as to disrupt any one reading of our race and sexuality. Given that both Judy and I were "out" in the classroom, our sexy dance before the class (the sexual tension as believable as Patrick Swayze and Jennifer Grey in *Dirty Dancing*) deconstructed essentialist notions about (homo)sexuality, black/Jewish relations, and blackness and whiteness.

Baldwin's novel refuses to delineate sexual or racial categories: characters have sex with members of the same and opposite sex and the same and opposite race. Accordingly, our performance attempted to highlight the fluidity of sexual and racial identity not only by choosing excerpts that draw attention to that fluidity but also by appropriating the discursivity of our bodies and our identities as black gay man and Jewish lesbian. Thus, during our dance and throughout the performance we could be "read" simultaneously as heterosexual and homosexual, black and white, male and female, Jew and gentile. In effect, we deauthorized our own "experience" narratives of blackness, Jewishness, and queerness in the classroom as well as authentic notions of racial, sexual, and gender identity in Baldwin's novel.

Due to the nature of the course, focusing as it did on race and sexuality, Judy and I could have easily fallen into the pedagogical and epistemological trap that Diana Fuss describes as follows: "Who we are becomes what we know; ontology shades into epistemology."[48] As members of oppressed groups—black, queer, Jewish—we were cognizant that our experience narratives held sway in a classroom predicated on those very terms of difference. Indeed, we were faced with how to teach the Other when the Other was the self. We made a conscious decision, however, to other ourselves in performance to highlight the ways in which texts evince racial, gender, and sexual identity in equivocal terms. At the same time, we did not want to undercut the very real material consequences of inhabiting a raced, gendered, and homosexual body. Rufus's suicide in *Another Country* calls attention to this fact. Therefore, our performance tried to capture the sentiment registered in the character Eric's comment to Vivaldo: "It's very hard to live with that [the fact that people are unpredictable]. . . . I mean, with the sense that one is never what one seems—never—and yet, what one seems to be is probably, in some sense, almost exactly what one *is*."[49] Here, Eric's statement captures well the tense relationship between performance and performativity, between being and seeming. As difficult and politically fraught as negotiating this dialectic is, it is imperative nonetheless that we take the risks necessary to prepare students to read critically and self-reflexively.

In the performance studies classroom these issues are writ large, especially when the course's subject matter and the subjectivity of the teacher are closely aligned. One must forever thwart the lure of becoming the sovereign subject whose positionality hegemonically hovers on high from the safe nest of solipsism. On the other hand, when critical performance pedagogy is animated the teacherly subject, as embodied text, becomes part of an ongoing dialogic enterprise whereby, according to Henderson, "difference is affirmed and the reduction of experience, reading, and interpretation is contested."[50] And in the instance of the "colored" performance classroom, such an engagement shifts the focus from questions of authority and authenticity to that of heterogeneity and multiplicity while, at the same time, it repositions the "colored" body from margin to center in the ongoing processes of performance pedagogical praxis.

APPENDIX A

Mary Rhyne's Narrative

As stated in chapter 4, I have chosen to include Mary's narrative in its entirety to contextualize my analysis and to allow Mary to "speak" for herself. The narrative is divided into episodes and each is titled thematically throughout the longer narrative. The narrative transcription also highlights Mary's body movements from which I infer meaning in relation to what she narrates. The translation of the poetic transcription symbols is as follows:

The end of a poetic line represents a half-second pause. A period (.) represents at least a two-second pause. A solidus (/) between words with no space represents words spoken so rapidly together that they are all pronounced as one word. Capital letters represent an increase in volume. A dash (—) represents an abrupt shift or change in theme. Spacing between letters in a word represents a deliberate slowing down to emphasize each sound in the word for effect (example: He needs p l e n t y help). *An arrowhead pointing up (∧) represents a rise in voice pitch after each word; two arrows or more represent a further increase in pitch. A line at the bottom of a word (so what_) represents a lowering in voice pitch; two lines or more represent a further decrease in pitch (so what__). Angle brackets (<>) between words, phrases, and lines represent the voice whispering; double (or more) brackets represent a quieter whisper (example:* on the road it was <<dark>>). *A word in italics represents an emotional emphasis, an intensity in breath and sound, not volume (example:* I sacrificed *all my life). Three periods (. . .) represent a pause while thinking or while contemplating what has just been said. A hyphen between words, phrases, and lines represents mumbling (example:* I-don't-know-what-they-do).

The interview took place on Tuesday, May 18, 1993. We had just finished supper and had moved to the living room with our bowls of ice cream. After we ate the ice cream, I got out my pad and pencil and tested the tape recorder. Mary did not look at me. Instead, she looked out of the window to her right over which a shade was half pulled. She sat on a green faux-leather couch with floral-print pillows surrounding her. The armrest had a rust-colored crocheted arm cover over it. On the back of the couch was a multicolored crocheted quilt. My grandmother was dressed in her customary polyester cut-off shorts, lime-and-white striped, and a pink polyester blouse. She did not wear a bra or shoes. Loosely tied around her head was a sheer scarf with an apricot flower design on it. After I tested the tape, I sat it on the end table next to her and asked the first question.

Nevah Had uh Cross Word

HOW LONG DID YOU WORK FOR THE SMITHS?

Ah stayed at the Smiths' 'bout
twenty/*nineteen* yeahs.

(10 sec. pause)

When Ah first went there
Ca'uh [Carol] wasn't/born
Jimmy.
was *eight*months ol'.
Eddie was eight *yeah* ol'
and.
Patty was *six* yeah ol'

(looks at me)

and.

(10 sec. pause)

and
Ah stayed deah an
kep' 'em/kept de house/Mrs. Smith 'nem went to
uh
Shelby
an' bought uh
mo'/uh/hotel
down in *Shelby*
bought uh hotel down in Shelby
an' Ah/dey stayed down neah/an' Ah stayed in de house
an' looked at dem *chil'ren*
an Ah sent 'em tuh school

Appendix A

Ah sent Eddie/Eddie
an Patty went tuh *Appalachian*
tuh *college*
an Ah kep' Jimmy and Ca'uh deah at de house
an' sent dem tuh school
at Oakwood school__

(There is a one-minute pause here. She crosses her right leg over her left,
   jiggling it while staring out the window)

Ah raised
Ah *raised* dem kids—
did/ever'thang

(30 sec. pause)

WHAT WERE SOME OF THE THINGS YOU DID?

(abruptly)
Oh Ah cleaned *house*.
did all de *wash*in'/an' Mrs. Smith didn't know nothin' 'bout
what de chil'ren *need*
they clothes/an' when dey git out uh clothes/when dey needed somthin'
AH had tuh
tell/'uh
what the chil'ren need—
dresses.
panties/whatever/dey/need/Ah/had/tuh/tell/'uh
she didn't know dat stuff 'cause see
she/wa'n't/*deah.*
wit' de chil'ren.

(15 sec. pause)

HOW OLD WERE THE KIDS?

OK.
Like Ah was tellin' yuh
Ah thought Ah tol' yuh Ca'uh wasn't born__
Jimmy was *eight* months old
an'
Eddie was de ol'est one/he was eight *yeah* old
an' Patty was *six* yeah old
dat's when Ah first went ovah deah—
an' den Ca'uh was born
uh.—

an' when Ah lef' deah
Ca'uh was
ol' enough/Ca'uh was
sixteen or seventeen/Lord/Ah/done/forgot

(30 sec. pause)

YOU WORKED FOR THE FRIERS TOO?

Yeah
went ovah at Mrs. *Frier's*
Ah worked at Mrs. *Frier's* house
worked for Mrs. Frier
Mr. Frier got *sick*
an' Ah'd leave the Smiths
an' got ovah deah an'
clean/up/an'
rake the y a r d
go out deah an' rake de y a r d
an' Ah w a s h an' *ahrn*
an'
cook
an' clean de house___

THEN YOU WOULD GO BACK OVER TO THE SMITHS?

(cuts me off)
go back ovah to de Smiths—
Mrs. Smith is ol' Mrs. Frier's *daughter*

OH?

uh huh
dat's Mrs. Frier's daughter
dat's/how/come/Ah/did/that
Mrs. Frier's daughter__
so dat's what Ah'd communicate
to de board
but Ah stayed with the Smiths
an' worked fuh huh motha

SO YOU LIVED WITH THEM ALL THE TIME?

(cuts me off again)
ALL THE TIME.
Ah lived wit' the *Smiths* all de time__

Appendix A

Ah lived with them all de time
Ah didn't go home till sometime middle of de weekend
ovah tuh *my* house __
som'time/an'/den
de weekend
Ah'd start baking *cakes*
on
Friday
started baking cakes on Friday
four or five or six
cakes
that Ah'd *bake*
on
Friday __
an' den Mrs. Smith would come up aftah me and de
chil'ren
on uh
Saturday
mornin'
or maybe it was
FRIDAY
night __
ovah deah/we/have/tuh/go/back
but Ah'd take de chil'ren
an' all dem
cakes
an' we go back down neah
an' stay till Sunday *evenin'*

AT THE HOTEL?

At the *mo*tel
Ah meant the *ho*tel
an' den dey'd bring me back home.
an' have tuh send the youngin's tuh school—
Ca'uh say
Ca'uh will tell yuh right now/say
"Ah ain't got but two mamas
Ah got one *white* mama and one *black* mama"
she tickle me

(giggles)

black mama and uh white mama_

261

Appendix A

(10 sec. pause)

an' she'd d a n c e

Y'all Ain't Havin' No Party

<small>WERE THE KIDS BAD?</small>

N O∧
Ca'uh was de sweetest lil' thang you ever seen/evah time she's go out—
she wouldn't go out uh dat y a r d∧
but she'd come an' tell me about that *Jimmy*
Lord Jesus
that *Jimmy*

(shakes her head)

that Jimmy was some'in'
that lil' fellah
when he was about.
two yeah old Ah reckon
Ah looked for 'im one day
an' he goin' on up through deah wit' nothin' on but his *diaper*
goin' up through deah/*in snow*

(points out the window with her finger)

Ah had tuh run out get 'im
den.
Mrs. Smith nem used tuh live in Shelby
so
dey had uh motorbike up deah
give him uh motorbike
so
de *police*—
Jimmy had went on de highway
wit' dis motorbike/an' dey wouldn't 'low den
so
de police brought Jimmy in
an' heah come Jimmy
an' he started cryin'__

(closes her eyes and shakes her head)

he s t a r t e d c r y i n'__

Appendix A

Ah said
"Jimmy∧"
Ah said
"Now Ah tol' you not to go out uh dis yard."
Ah said
"Now you been WAY OVAH YONDAH ON DE *HIGH*WAY WIT DAT
MOTORBIKE."
Ah said
"Now you know bettah than t h a t."
he was just uh *cryin'*__/he just cried__
so
de police brought 'im on
an' Ah said,
"Your/mothah/an'/fathah/gwoin/git/you/boy"__
dat was tuh scare 'im up
so

WELL
dey wanted tuh have uh
party
dis night
Saturday night__—
mother/nem/wa'n't/neah—
dey git so mad at me til dey didn't know what tuh do/wanted tuh have
uh p a r t y
Ah said
"Y'all ain't havin' no party h e a h."
Ah said
"Your mother an' daddy tol' me tuh stay heah an' take ca'uh uh y'all
an' take care of dis house"/an'
Ah said
"I'm gonna *do* it."

(switches to a whiny voice)

"You can go tuhnight."
Ah said
"Ah ain't goin' *no*where!"__

(shakes her head)

Ah said
"Ah ain't goin' nowhere."
Oh dey'd get so mad at me dey didn't know what tuh do/Ah said
"Ah ain't goin' nowhere"/an' Ah said

Appendix A

"An' y'all ain't havin' no *party* in heah *either.*"

(emphatically)

Ah said
"Y'all ain't *havin'* no party."
Dey'd get so mad at me dey'd didn't know what tuh do __.

(15 sec. pause)

(abruptly, in whiny voice)

"Daisy [Mary] won't let us do *nuthin'* "
"Don't want us tuh do *nuthin'* "
Ah said
"YOU AIN'T GONNA DO IT WHILE *AH'M* HEAH.
wait till your mama an' daddy come home." —

THEY WERE IN HIGH SCHOOL THEN?

LORD, YEAH IN HIGH SCHOOL
Patty had uh b o y f r i e n d

(laughs and shakes her head)

YEAH∧∧
Patty had huh boyfriend/an'/Jimmy
he
big ol' thang/he didn't have no
date or nuthin' for uh
big boy
an'
an' uh
Ca'uh wa'n't no
no trouble/but that
that *Eddie*
an' *Patty*/see dey was growin'
an' dey wanted tuh
have dey p a r t y wit' dey *friends*
want dey *friends* tuh come in
an' have uh party on Saturday night
"They ain't havin' none heah."
Oh
dey could've killed me.

DID THEY LISTEN TO YOU PRETTY WELL?

(nods her head)

Appendix A

<<yeah>>
dey listened tuh me good 'cause
dey mutha' an' dey fatha' *'allowed* 'em to
dey-'llowed-'em-to
uh-numbah-uh-yeahs
only dem times when dey wanted tuh have uh lil' *party*
an' couldn't *have* any
dey'd git mad
but/Ah/didn'/care/nuthin'/'bout/dat
but other than dat
they'd listen to meh

Dey Didn't Pay Nuthin'

WHAT WAS YOUR WORKDAY LIKE? WOULD YOU GET UP IN THE MORNING?

(looks at me)

Me?
OK
first thang Ah'd do was get up in the morning__
at dat time dey didn't have no dishwasher
at dat time
Ah'd go
an' fix
breakfast__
Ah'd fix breakfas' in de mornin'
an'

(puts her hands together as if praying)

first thing Ah'd do/Ah'd go an' git everybody outtah bed
Ah'd get up in de mornin'
gwoin in de kitchen
an' fix *breakfas'*
an' dey'd come an' eat
Ah'd clean up de kitchen
an' den
Ah'd *wash*
Ah'd do the washin'
an' git my lil' washin' done

(spreads both hands and makes prancing motion as if playing a piano)

an' den Ah'd fix *dinnah*
get mah dinner fixed
an' den Ah'd fix *suppah*.
den aftah Ah fixed suppah
den of course Ah cleaned de house/Ah/had/tuh/clean/de/house/up

(10 sec. pause)

oh Ah just did *e*verythang__
Ah did everythang around that house__
had *eight* rooms/dat house had eight rooms
an' Ah did everythang around dat house
everythang__
plus be dem chaps' [children's] nanny

DID THEY PAY WELL?

nah
dey didn't pay nuthin'
didn't pay
Ah don't think

(crosses her legs)

back *den*
you know
wa'n't
wa'n't gittin' too much *p a y*
Ah thank Ah got twenty-five dollahs uh week

(10 sec. pause)

have stayed day and night

(opens her hands)

stayin' there
you know
on de
on de lot
stayin' there
all de time

SO YOU GOT TO EAT?

oh yeah/oh yeah
Ah got tuh eat whatevah Ah wanted
whatevah they got

an' dey'd
buy me c l o t h e s __—
an' Ah
one/thang/about/it/Ah/got/sick/deah/one/time
Ah got sick∧
an'
Ah b'lieve it was three of us in de bed at de s a m e time__
three-of-us-in-de-bed-at-de-same-time
sick
all of us/me/an'/dem/youngin's/in/de/bed
an' dey looked aftah me just like dey did de rest of 'em
an' Ah got sick one day an' had tuh go to de hospital_
dey/put/me/in/de/hospital
dey took ca'uh of d a t
an'
dem s c a r s deah

(points to her left hand and makes a circling motion)

Ah got all dat burned off
a l l dat deah
all dat was cooked/all dat just cooked
so
it took me uh l o n g time tuh get up
so
dey had tuh take ca'uh of all uh dat

HOW DID IT HAPPEN?

WELL
hit was a frying pan
on de stove__
an' it caught—
this had grease or some'in' or anothah on de *stove*
an' Ah ran to it

(pulls her hand up, imagining the fire)

it blazed up
an' Ah ran to it
tuh
put it out/but/Ah/couldn't/so/Ah/couldn't/put/it/out/so
SCARED me so
Ah just
grabbed it up

just grabbed the handle∧∧
an' dat grease just *cooked*
just *cooked* dat hand
all dat skin was just like
tar
so
Ah had tuh
keep de bandage on it
fuh Ah don't know how long
everyday/e v e r y d a y—
thought one time they was gonna have tuh take the skin off my *hip*

(puts her hand on her hip)

an' draft it on
but dey didn't have to do that
Dr. Fry
that was mah doctah

YOU WERE COOKING SOMETHING FOR THEM?

yeah
Ah was cookin' dey *suppah*
yeah Ah was cookin' suppah
porkchops
Ah b'lieve it was porkchops
wa'n't nobody deah at dat time an' Mrs. Smith had went aftah de *chil'ren*
fuh school de next day

(30 sec. pause)

We All Just One Family

YOU GOT ALONG WITH MR. SMITH?

Mr. Smith?
yeah
he-was-nice.
we a l l just one family __
one big family __
it was nevah uh cross word
we all just/everybody/went/along

THERE WAS NEVER A TIME WHEN YOU AND MRS. SMITH OR ANY OF THE
OTHERS HAD A DISAGREEMENT OR ANYTHING?

Appendix A

(10 sec. pause)

(she tilts her head back and puts her right index finger under her chin)

Mr. Smith use tuh drank
sometime/an'
he came in deah drankin' one time an' said he was gwoin *leave*
he went in neah an' got de
suitcases

(points to the floor)

an' he was gonna leave/dem little youngins just uh hoopin' an' uh
    hollerin'
an' uh screamin' an' uh holdin' de do'
got on mah nerves so bad/Ah went in neah/Ah tol' 'em
Ah said
"Now
what in de w o r l d do you mean?"
Ah said
"Dese lil' chil'ren is jus' hollerin' an'
an' goin' on heah"
Ah said
"PUT DEM SUITCASES DOWN!
SET DEM SUITCASES BACK DOWN"
an' de chil'ren/a l l
fo' of 'em
just whoopin' an' hollerin'
"*d a d d y* don't leave/*d a d d y* don't leave/*d a d d y* don't leave"
Ah didn' wanna git in to it/but Ah had tuh git in to it *dat* time

WHAT DID MRS. SMITH SAY?

(emphatically, jerking her head to the right)

NOTHIN'
just

(begins to giggle)

NOTHIN'
'cause see him an' huh had been into it
she wa'n't doing nu'in' but just *stan'in'* neah

(stiffens her body)

Ah went in neah/Oh Lord Ah was jus'/dis/upset me so bad
Ah didn't know what tuh do_ _

Ah jus' got all ovah Mr. Smith
he come brought the suitcase in neah an' sat it down
an' dem chil'ren

(makes pulling motion)

dey just *pullin'*
dey was pullin' de suitcase
some at de do'
holdin' de do'
so he couldn't go out de do'

(we both get tickled)

LORD∧∧
dat was de biggest mess you evah see.

SO HE STAYED?

oh yeah
he stayed

(she giggles)

(10 sec. pause)

YOU USED TO GO ON TRIPS WITH THEM, DIDN'T YOU?

L o r d/yeah/Ah went
u h
where is
where was it that
uh
where/'bout/is/it/that/uh
that part of Florida that/uh
Ray Charles went tuh school?
blind school down neah/some part of Florida down neah
where he went

TALLAHASSEE?

n o
hit was de
o l' part
dey say hit was de *o l'* part uh Florida
de *o l'* part of Florida__
Ah can't think of dat name

JACKSONVILLE?

n o
hit wasn't Jacksonville
Patty live in Jacksonville
Florida
dat's where dese chil'ren was—
'course
Patty
didn't have no child till lil' aftah she
m a r r i e d—
WE HAD TO GO CROSS DAT *WATAH*
Lord/hammercy/Jesus
Ah'm just so upset Ah didn't know what in dis world tuh/Ah thought we
nevah was gonna get across dat *watah*
w a y on

(waves her hands)

w a y cross
de ocean
way cross
miles/an'/*miles*/an'/*miles*
an' we went down neah
at *dat* place__
an'
Ah went tuh JACKSONVILLE
stayed down neah about two weeks
an' Ah went tuh—
since uh
Eddie
Ah mean
Jimmy
an' *his* wife

(mumbles to herself trying to remember where Jimmy lives)

is-it-Miami?
you know where
Flossie live?

ATLANTA?

Atlanta__
Ah went down neah

Ah went down neah about two weeks
yeah
Ah/was/all/de/time/goin'/somewhere/wid/'em
wherevah dey'd go Ah'd go
Ah misses dat *too*—
dey went tuh
Mrs. Smith nem took me to
she took me tuh—
took de two *oldes'*
Patty an'
Eddie/Ah thank
an' left the two
little ones there wid *me*
dey went off an' stayed uh week
an' Ah had tuh stay home an' keep dem two lil'
*chil'ren*__

(10 sec. pause)

EVEN AFTER YOU STOPPED WORKING FOR THEM AT THE HOUSE, YOU STILL
WENT OVER THERE TO WORK FOR THEM?

AND STILL TUH NOW!
STILL

(waving her hands)

STILL TUH DE *DAY*!/STILL TUH DE *DAY*!
she called me *las'* week
wanted tuh know when Ah was comin' up
an' Ah was up tuh yuh mama's house las' week/but
Ah thought she wanted me tuh come ovah deah
an' spend de day or spend de night wid' 'uh
so she wanted me tuh come ovah deah an'
talk wid 'uh
yeah Ah go ovah deah
you know
an' if Ah see some'in'—
WHATEVAH
you know
Ah'll do it—
yeah
s t i l l—
aftah Ah

Aftah Ah
quit *work*
well
still
Ah'd g o
Ah'd still go ovah an' do thangs
tuh *he'p*/'em
tuh/he'p/'em/out

AND THE KIDS STILL KEEP IN TOUCH WITH YOU?

L o r d hammercy/yeah
Ah didn't show yuh Ca'uh's lil' ol'
lil' ol'
youngin'?
Ah showed yuh one of 'em didn't Ah?—
yeah Ca'uh
Ca'uh live
in Fort
Fort Myers?

(thinking to herself)

Fort Myers
Florida
an' uh
she
she write me
an' when she has huh babies she

(switches to a whiny voice)

"Well Daisy you got another GRAND
Got another GRAND"
an' uh
an'
Jimmy
send me/he/ain't/been/long/sunt[sent]/me/*dis*/picture
dis

(shows me the picture)

family/whole family
dis is his *wife* an'
two girls
an'

Eddie
Ah don't heah
from Eddie any much regular as Ah used to
he sends his—
he got three boys
he sends me dey pictures—
DEY ALL STAY IN *TOUCH*
all of 'em
send me uh card or some'in'—
Patty
she live in
Jacksonville
dey-always-think-'bout-me
AN' E V E R Y CHRIS'MAS THAT CA'UH
every Chris'mas dat Ca'uh send me uh

(pats the sofa with her hand)

fruit basket
every Chris'mas
so many oranges
so many othah grapes/e v e r y Chris'mas
she'll do that
every Chris'mas—
an' Mrs. Smith'll send me uh
uh case of
pickles

WHEN YOU WERE WORKING FOR THEM, DID THEY GIVE YOU THINGS?
CLOTHES?

oh-yeah/oh-yeah
when Ah was stayin' wid' e'm
Mrs. Smith bought me most of my clothes
she'd buy my clothes
they bought me clothes
Mr. Frier
would go up in de mountains

(spreads her hands apart)

an' go git one of dem great big ol' hams
an' bring 'em back
an' so
he'd spice 'em an' Ah had tuh trim 'em

had/tuh/trim/'em

(long pause)

Oh Dey Nice People

WHAT KIND OF WORK DID YOU DO BEFORE YOU WENT TO WORK FOR THE
SMITHS?

Let's see
Ah moved
let me see
me and Coleman

(points out the window)

lived ovah yondah on [unintelligible] highway
when Ah lived
when Ah moved ovah *heah*
Ah worked ovah heah at de
school house
an' uh
right underneath dat bridge right out yondah
School
worked up deah at E. School
fuh *lunch*
an' den Ah didn't work up deah long before Ah went up deah
til Ah found out about Mrs. Smith

HOW DID YOU FIND OUT ABOUT IT?

Mrs. Smith's?

UH HUH.

Ca'uhlyn Rinehart/now/*you*/know/Mrs. Ca'uhlyn
Ca'uhlyn useta work fuh 'em
Ca'uhlyn was gonna have uh c h i l e/Ca'uhlyn was pregnant
an' she was gonna have uh baby
an'
she knowed Ah had moved up deah an' knew Ah wanted uh
job
Ca'uhlyn did
so/she called me
an' as' me

would Ah go
an' work fuh de Smiths
Ca'uhlyn recommended dem

(smooths out her pants)

said/"Oh dey n i c e people"
say
"Ah been workin' fuh 'em" —
how long had she been workin' fuh 'em
let's see
Ah-don't-know
but she was pregnant
so dat's how
dat's how Ah got tuh get on wit Mrs. Smith

WOULD MRS. SMITH COME PICK YOU UP?

Yeah
she/come/an'/picked/me/up/'fo/Ah/started/*stayin'*/wit'/'em
she come an' pick me up an' bring me back home
an' den
Ah just started *stayin'* ovah deah —
an' den Ah moved in one —
see Ah was up deah in de Smiths'
apartment

(puts her hands together as if praying)

Ah moved in one of de
'partments
Ah moved in one —
no
when Ah first moved
Ah stayed wit' yuh *mama*
an' daddy
till Ah
till Ah got uh 'partment
next *door*

(motions to the left with right hand)

an' d e n
an' d e n
Ah got
Ah tol' dat Ah had tuh have uh *house* —

Appendix A

DAT'S/HOW/COME/MY/LEGS/LIKE/DEY/IS
my arthritis
dis is all from de *mill* houses
dese ain't nuthin' but mill floors
dese ol' cement floors
my legs
an' so
Ah told Mrs. Smith
Ah tol' 'em
ef Ah couldn't get uh *house* somewhere
den Ah was gonna
move back tuh Kings Mountain__
so.
dey got me dat lil' fo' room
white house
down neah
an' Ah let
Boot an' Jake live wit' me down neah
in de
white house
down below de
Zerdens nem
where ya'll useta stay right deah at the Zerdens'∧
so dat's how come Ah was down *neah*
Ah was *still.*
at dey *house*
but Ah didn't have tuh pay no *rent*
didn't have tuh do nuthin' but buy mah gas
so

HOW LONG DID YOU LIVE IN YOUR APARTMENT BEFORE YOU MOVED IN
WITH THEM?

OH
befo' Ah just stayed wit' dem
an' stayed wit' dem?
Ah don't know how long Ah stayed up deah
when Ah started workin' fuh dem
when Ah was up deah in de
'partment
you know back den we called it de
Em'assy [Embassy]
Em'assy 'partments

277

Appendix A

(points at me)

stayed up deah
'bout uh yeah
Ah reckon it was uh yeah
den Ah moved down neah—
dey let me have *dat* house down neah
an' Ah moved down *neah*
an' den Ah come back an' forth fuh uh *w h i l e*
back/an'/forth
an' den aftah
aftah
Ca'uh
aftah Ca'uh was born
den Ah jus' started *stayin'*
ovah deah at *night*
course Ah'd come home sometime de week*end*
you know 'cause
Boot an' *Jake* was deah
an' so Ah'd come home
de weekend
you/know
Ah'd *c a l l*
Ah'd call evah now an' then
an' Ah'd go ovah deah an' see yuh *mothah*

(30 sec. pause)

Better dan Makin' Nuthin'

YOU STILL DO HOUSEWORK NOW?

Um hum
still/yeah
dat's what Ah do at home

DO YOU DO THE SAME THING?

WELL
Ah jus' clean house/Ah run de *v a c u u m*
now let's see
Ah got fo' *r o o m s*
an'
two bathrooms tuh clean tomah [tomorrow]

278

Ah run de vacuum an' dust—
de man's wife DEAD
Henderson Pike
Henderson Pike
Ah don't *go* ovah deah
but
some time in de *day*

HE'S AN OLDER MAN?

(matter of factly)

he's seventy-fo'__
yeah
'bout seventy-fo'

WERE YOU WORKING FOR HIM BEFORE HIS WIFE DIED?

yeah
'fore his wife died
Ah'd go ovah deah an'
he'p/'im
fuh his wife died
she had altimey [Alzheimer's]

(10 sec. pause)

WHAT DO YOU THINK ABOUT PEOPLE WHO SAY HOUSEWORK AIN'T A
DECENT JOB?

AH don't say nuthin'

(jiggles her leg)

'cause/Ah/feel/it
did de job fuh *me*
BETTAH DAN MAKIN' *NUTHIN'*
make *good* money housekeepin'
doing housework__
Ah done ol' an' broke down
Ah can't
Ah can't
Ah jus' go an' do—
dey know
dat Ah can't do like Ah used to
so Ah jus' tell him

(10 sec. pause)

Ah can't do uh w h o l e lot of *hard* work
like Ah have when Ah was
younger
Ah go ovah tuh Mrs. Pfifer's—
now when Ah'm *feelin'* good
when my hip don't hurt meh so bad__
Ah go ovah tuh Mrs. Pfifer's
an' stay.
dat's on Friday__
Ah go ovah deah tuh *huh* house__
an' Ah jus'
Ah jus' c l e a n
jus' clean—
Ah have two bathrooms at *huh* house

(prancing motion with her hands)

an' Ah run de vacuum
in de
bedroom an'
git de
living room
an' de
dining room
fo'
fo' rooms
Ah run de *vacuum*
an' *dus'*
an' do de
two baths__
Ah go at eight o'clock
an' stay deah till 'bout twelve

DO YOU THINK IT'S HONEST WORK?

(annoyed at the question)

YEAH HITS GOOD HONES' HARD WORK
well
hit's *work*
Ah admit it's hard—
dey nice/dey nice tuh meh
dey v e r y nice people
very nice people
real-nice

Appendix A

As Long as Ah Stay Black

WELL
you know
aftah Ah moved back hyeah__
Ah moved back tuh Kings *Mountain*
you know Ah worked at uh
oh what's de name of it
dey sol' out tuh—

(pauses to think)

down de road there
down heah
Ah can't remembah dat name right now
de *cloth* place
maybe hit'll come tuh meh
but Ah worked on *production*

(puts her hands together as if praying)

an' Ah had to uh
stack *shirts*
DOZEN SHIRTS
DAT'S T H I R T Y DOZEN SHIRTS
Ah b'lieve uh day/we/were/on/*production*/thirty dozen
uh day
Ah say
you know

(closes her eyes)

as long as Ah stay black
Ah'll nevah have another *production* job
workin' on production
Lord hammercy—
dat's how come Ah can't [unintelligible]
but Ah worked deah
worked deah three yeahs
dat's where Ah reti'ed deah__
at dat job

281

(holds her hands out)

Ah was sixty-two
Ah was gwoin be sixty-two
an' so.
aftah dey sold out
aftah dey sold out tuh
Piedmont
dey didn't want
dey didn't want nobody
sixty-two
dey didn't wanna hire anybody sixty-two
an' Ah was sixty-two

(10 sec. pause)

MOST OF THE WOMEN DOWN HERE, DID THEY DO HOUSEWORK? THE
BLACK FOLK?

n o
nevah/did/do/housework/chile
didn't nobody do housework
can't nobody do housework
most of 'em worked in de *mills*
most of the peoples now work in de mill
can't hardly get nobody tuh do housework
no
didn't wanna do housework
black
but dey didn't wanna do it—

(points to me)

OXFORD
dat's de name of where Ah worked at
where dey sold it
de name of it is
Oxford
down neah
sol' out

(15 sec. pause)

(remembers the previous subject)

(makes a nasty face)

Appendix A

n o
you'd hear

(switches to whiny voice)

"Ah don't wanna do no ol' housework."
Ah don't mind doin' it
if it ain't
lot uh dat ol'
w a s h i n' an' ahrnin'
got tuh keep dat ol' ahrn hot

(interrupts to check on a pot of stewed beef on the stove)

IS THAT WHAT YOU HATED THE MOST? WASHING AND STUFF LIKE THAT?

AW IT DIDN'T MATTER
hit didn't matter tuh me
Ah was jus' sayin'—
hit didn't really matter

(opens her arms)

Ah didn't pay it no attention
wash
Ah jus' went ahead an' did it
an' a l l
dat long Ah worked
Ah nevah did have tuh argue
nevah did have any w o r d s wid 'em
always got along wid 'em

(5 sec. pause)

som'in' Ah didn't lak
well
Ah nevah did *say* nothin'

(10 sec. pause)

Every Chris'mas

DID YOU HAVE TO GO OVER THERE ON THE HOLIDAYS LIKE CHRISTMAS?

where?
ovah tuh Mrs. Smith's?
oh yes

oh yes
yeah Ah went ovah deah
EVERY *Chris'mas*
every Chris'mas
dey had
salt fish

(sits up as if she has found new energy)

EVERY Chris'mas
salt fish
an' uh
Dr. Niles
worked
ovah deah
y'know
at uh
Lenoir *Rhyne*
E V E R Y Chris'mas
here come Dr. Niles
he'd come an' dey'd have salt fish
an' dey'd have—
he'd come in
de first thang he call

(switches to whiny voice)

"Eh Gene yah got any Wild Turkey?"
den
everybody had tuh come in the dining room

(spreads her arms to show the size of the table)

round de big family table
everybody be sittin' deah
'round dat table
so
Dr. Niles

(points to each place each person would be around the table)

he'd be right heah at *dis* end
an' Ah'd be right *heah*
Mrs. Smith would be right *deah*
Mr. Smith would be right *deah*
an' de othah chil'ren 'round

everybody sittin' 'round dat table
an' Dr. Niles would
would as'

(closes her eyes)

de blessin'
he would as' one of de sweetes' blessin's __
so
everybody would eat
Chris'mas
an' Ah'd he'p tuh *cook*
we'd make all kinds of
shrimp
salad
pickled *shrimp*
all dat stuff—
done so *much*

(puts her hand on her heart)

when Ah use tuh/Ah/done/done/dat/sorta/cookin'/
Ah/can't/do/now
it jus' done
it jus' done
left meh
Ah done done mah part of it—
an Jimmy used tuh like
hamburger
uh
casserole
he have me make 'im one

(switches to excited child's voice)

"Daisy make me uh hamburger casserole"
an' Ah'd go in deah an make 'im uh
hamburger casserole __

SO AFTER YOU WOULD GO OVER TO THEIR HOUSE, YOU'D GO HOME?

oh yeah/oh yeah
see aftah Ah'd go ovah deah an' fix breakfas'
an'
dinnah
an' den dey'd take meh home/Ah would go home

Appendix A

(points at me)

Ah'd go tuh *my* house
Ah'd go home
or to yuh *mama's*
OH AND MY HOME
see
Ah lived right below yuh mama nem
Ah'd go down neah
yeah
Ah'd go home

(15 sec. pause)

Dey Nevah Was Too Much Trouble

DO YOU HAVE ANY MORE STORIES ABOUT THE KIDS?

'bout *dem* chil'ren?
'bout Eddie nem?
uh
let me see
Eddie
Eddie nem
dey was pretty good
dey nevah was too much trouble__
sometime dey didn't wanna listen
but aftah Eddie an' Patti went off tuh school
see Ah didn't have nothin' but those two other ones
Jimmy
an' *Ca'uh*
an' Jimmy
like Ah said
Jimmy was de worse one
Jimmy didn't wanna listen tuh *anybody*
Jimmy
Ca'uh was uh different story/she was *so* sweet

(closes her eyes)

Ah jus'
L o r d Ah jus' love dat lil' ol' youngin' tuh death
Ah hated tuh leave—

Appendix A

Ah had tuh cry one day
Ah/jus'/hated/tuh/leave/Ca'uh
Ah jus' had got attached tuh Ca'uh 'cause she was jus' uh sweet lil' ol'
youngin'
she wa'n't like *Jimmy*
DAT *Jimmy* was som'in' else
Jimmy'll tell yuh

(gets tickled)

he'll laugh an' tell yuh now
how Ah used tuh/"Yeah Daisy
can you 'member how you useta
run meh 'round de house with de broom?"

(laughs harder at the recollection)

yeah
he'll tell yuh
tell anybody
how Ah used tuh
run/'im/around/de/house/wid/de/broom__
he was de BOOGIE MAN
dat Jimmy
he was uh MESS

(10 sec. pause)

all/every kind of mischievous
wouldn't
wouldn't *listen* tuh yuh
wouldn't listen tuh nuthin'
jus' in tuh som'in' a l l d e t i m e

(10 sec. pause)

he was uh Jimmy an' uh half

DID THEY EVER TALK ABOUT THEIR PARENTS BEING GONE SO MUCH?

WELL
Jimmy
Jimmy
when dey was down in
Shelby
stayin' down neah
Ah nevah will forget

287

Appendix A

Jimmy would tell me
say

(switches to whiny voice)

"Ah wish my mama an' daddy would stay home like
other parents"
dat's what he'd say
"Ah wish my mama an' daddy would stay home like
other parents
jus' stay down neah in dat
Shelby
in dat ol'
Shelby
all de t i m e"
Ca'uh
Ca'uh nevah did have nothin' tuh say

DO YOU THINK JIMMY WAS BEING BAD BECAUSE OF THAT?

he could have
um hum
could have 'sented his parents fuh not being 'round
Ah imagine it was
but he'd say dat so many times
kicking rocks

(kicks her foot out and giggles)

KICKIN' ROCKS
"Ah wish my mama/my parents
would stay home like *other*
parents
stay gone all de time down yondah
in
Shelby"

(serious)

an' Ah know he did miss/'em—

(closes her eyes)

Ah'd git up e v e r y Sunday mornin'
an' git him an'
Ca'uh off tuh *church*
e v e r y Sunday mornin'

288

everybody 'round neah/dey say
"Ah 'clare Daisy"
say
"You d o e s such uh good job"
say
"You git dem chil'ren up an' gettin' 'em ready tuh send 'em tuh c h u r c h
every Sunday mornin' "/Ah said
"Ah know"
Ca'uh
Ca'uh had uh lil' ol' hat

(mimes the hat)

wit' one of dem lil' ol' ribbons in it—
huh an' Jimmy
Ah'd dress 'em
an'
dey'd go
tuh church
an' come on back

DID SOMEBODY COME PICK THEM UP?

no
ovah deah where Holy Trinity
you know where Holy Trinity?

RIGHT DOWN THE STREET?

um hum
so hit wa'n't far
dey'd walk
dey'd walk up to de church
an' Mrs. Frier
Mrs. Frier at dat time
lived right across de street
from de church
Mrs. Frier was right beside it
so

(15 sec. pause)

WHAT WAS SOME OF THE STUFF YOU'D FIX FOR THEM?

de regular everyday stuff?
WELL

sometime
I'd fix uh
kraut dumplin's
dey l o v e d kraut dumplin's

KRAUT DUMPLINGS?

KRAUT DUMPLIN'S∧∧
you know
KRAUT

LIKE SAUERKRAUT?

SAUERKRAUT
Ah'd fix sauerkraut dumplin's
Ah'd fix
Ah'd put mah—
Ah'd open mah kraut

(makes mixing motion with her right hand)

mix mah kraut
an' then
Ah would put
jus' uh taste
you take you uh
cup uh *flour*
self-rising flour
put/jus'/uh/lil'/touch/of/baking/powder/in/dat
an'
an' uh
egg
an' beat it up
an' let yuh
kraut cook
let yuh kraut cook—
an' Bell
she tol' meh de othah day when she called meh/she say
"Ah thought you was gonna come up heah"
say
"An' Ah was gonna make us some kraut dumplin's"—
an' so
ef yuh want som'in' *good*
have uh lil' bit uh
uh

pork
lil' bit uh pork∧∧
an' cook/it
put dat pork in deah
de pork in deah
an' den put yuh kraut in deah
an' cook it in de pork grease
an' den put yuh
fix yuh *dumplin's*

(spoons out dumplings)

spoon/'em
spoon/'em
an' den put de led [lid] on dat
right ovah dat
an' when hit gits done/you know/it jus'
get tuh where it
you can jus' take you uh spoon an' jus'
dip dat up
an' put you uh lil' of dat kraut juice in it
an' dat stuff is d e l i c i o u s

(shakes her head emphatically)

UMPH! it's delicious
yeah Ah'd fix dat
an' den Ah'd
sometimes she'd want meh tuh fix
macaroni p i e
an'
butter beans an'
white potatoes
an'
pinto beans an'
stuff like dat

DID THEY LIKE YOUR COOKING?

(cuts me off)

L O R D yes
dey liked mah cookin'
"Daisy fix meh"—
AH DON'T KNOW MAHSE'F HOW AH GOT TUH—

Ah fix
Ah make
slaw
an' Ah wouldn't grate it
Ah jus'—
dey had big sharp knives an' Ah jus'
Ah jus'

(mimes cutting the cabbage)

t h i n
dey'd be right thin
an' Ah'd fix dat
an' dey'd say
"Daisy make me some more of dat good slaw like you made"
say
"Ah don't know how you did it"
Ah didn't know either how Ah made it
but Ah made it
an' Ah'd make slaw
an' den Ah'd make uh

(slaps her thigh)

uh
casserole
squash casserole
dey l o v e d squash casserole
Ah'd fix dat
Ah/was/all/de/time/makin'/som'in'
yeah dey liked what Ah cooked
dey loved mah *cookin'*—
fo' dey got uh dishwasher
Ah washed dishes everyday_ _ —
dey looked
Mrs. uh
Mrs.
Grandmama say

(switches to old, decrepit voice)

"Ah 'clare"
say
"one of dese days yuh jus' look out ovah deah"
say

"jus' look in dat windah
she'll be standin' in dat windah
washin' dishes"__

(smiles)

Ah thought
not ef dey had uh *dish*washer

(15 sec. pause)

SO THE KIDS STILL KEEP IN TOUCH WITH YOU NOW? THEY CALL YOU?

ALL of 'em
every *one* of 'em
keep in touch wit' meh
dey eithah send meh uh c a r d
or cakes or dey c a l l__ —
Ca'uh's de baby
dat Ca'uh's gwoin talk tuh meh
Ca'uh's de baby
Ca'uh's gwoin call
dey all send me
dey'll send meh uh
card
or send meh uh family picture
wit' dey
chil'ren
Mrs. Smith wants meh tuh go down tuh Eddie's wid/'uh
you know
pretty soon
an'
Eddie lives down heah at

(points to the right)

Belmont now
an Ca'uh's comin' up
dis month *comin'*
an' so Mrs. Smith wants me tuh come up deah
Ca'uh an' huh two kids comin' up

YOU'VE SEEN SOME OF THOSE GRANDKIDS HAVEN'T YOU?

oh yeah
Ah've seen a l l de grandkids 'cept
Ca'uh's got two now

Ah ain't seen dis *las'* one
Ah've seen dat othah lil' ol' round head boy

(she frowns)

dey say he's playing *golf*
he three yeah ol'
say

(gets tickled)

say dey had it in de paper
say he de first three year old tuh evah play golf

(looks at me)

(emphatically)

GOLF—
PATTY GOT TWO
Madeline
an'
what is his name?
Lord how come Ah can't 'call dat othah lil' boy's name
she got two
Eddie got
Eddie got t h r e e
lil' boys＿＿
an' Jimmy got
t w o
lil' girls＿＿
Ah showed yuh de pictures of dem lil' girls
Dey had de name of some of 'em on heah

(shows me the pictures)

heah dey are
see
all of 'em's Gene

Dey's More in Managin' dan Dey Is in Money

IF YOU HADN'T BEEN STAYING WITH THEM DO YOU THINK YOU COULD
HAVE LIVED OFF OF WHAT THEY PAID YOU? IF YOU WEREN'T STAYING IN
THE HOUSE WITH THEM?

now ef Ah coulda stayed an' ate—
now see Ah stayed in dey house an' didn't pay no *rent*
you know/Ah/had/tuh/pay/mah/bills/Ah/had/tuh/pay/mah
light bill still
but Ah didn't have tuh pay no *rent*
den course
as time went o n
Ah even had tuh pay
watah
you know yuh had tuh pay watah
'cause back den
you know wa'n't nobody gonna pay fuh yuh watah—
when Ah first worked at Oxford
when Ah went down neah
tuh work fuh Oxford
Ah didn't make but 'bout
two dollah an' som'in' an hour
dat's all
Ah thank Ah got some—
when yuh get through
Ah got some ol'
stubs
in deah
Ah'm gonna let yuh see 'em
Ah kep' 'em fuh souvenirs
jus' let people *know*
HOW PEOPLES HAD TUH *LIVE*
what you had tuh live *off* of
an' den now peoples makin' good an' dey still say dey can't
dey can't do it__
Ah jus' don't understand it
Ah cannot understand it

HAVE YOU HEARD ABOUT WOMEN'S LIB AND ABOUT THE WOMEN NOT
MAKING AS MUCH AS THE MEN?

yeah
Ah heard 'em talkin' 'bout it

DO YOU THINK IT'S TRUE?

yeah
some of 'em do make more
but women make *good* though

Appendix A

some of these women make more than de *men*
some of 'em do
some make more
dey jus' don't know how tuh spend
don't know how tuh spend dey money
don't know how tuh
MANAGE

(points at me)

dey's more in *managin'* dan dey is in *money*
ef yuh don't know how tuh manage den yuh in bad shape__
jus' buy everythang yuh *see*

(10 sec. pause)

Dat's de Exact Reason I Could Always Get uh Job

LOOKING BACK, DO YOU STILL THINK YOU WOULD HAVE WORKED FOR
THEM AS LONG AS YOU DID?

what?
worked fuh de Smiths?

UH HUH.

oh yeah
yeah
if Ah had tuh do it all ovah again Ah'd work
Ah'd he'p 'em
Ah *still* he'p 'em
like Ah said
Ah *have* worked for 'em since Ah *left* deah
an' *work*/an'/*work*/an'/*work*/an'
so
you know
now Ah stayed
as long as Ah s t a y e d at dey
at dat house__
long as Ah stayed deah
Ah nevah
rambled
in dey *stuff*

(opens imaginary drawers)

in dey d r a w s
in dey stuff
Ah didn't know bit mo' dan some of de thangs on de—only
foldin' de chil'ren's *clothes*
but like RAMBLIN' IN EVERYTHANG/SEE
Ah didn't *do* that
Ah didn't do that
Ah nevah did—
when dey come back everythang was jus' like dey *left*/it
Ah didn't *ramble* in dey stuff
Ah'd fol' de chil'ren's c l o t h e s
Ah'd fol' 'em
de chil'ren's clothes

DID SOME PEOPLE DO THAT?

yeah
some people stayin' de house
dey ramble thu' thangs
you know
ramble an'
tamper

(10 sec. pause)

SOME MAIDS TALK ABOUT HOW THEY USED TO STEAL STUFF AND TAKE
THINGS.

(cuts me off)

n o
DAT'S DE EXACT REASON AH COULD A L W A Y S GET UH JOB/'CAUSE
peoples k n o w

(spreads her hands)

when Ah went tuh dey house
Ah didn't bother *nuthin'*
everythang was jus' like dey *left* it
Ah didn't bother dey stuff—
an' people s t e a l—/dey/can't/git/no/job
yuh *heah* me∧∧
dey/can't/git/no/job
an' peoples ain't wantin' nobody in dey house dat *steal*

(emphatically)

297

an' Ah don't *blame* 'em

(15 sec. pause)

THEY'D TAKE STUFF?

UH HUH
dey *take* it
Ah jus' nevah did do that
Ah nevah did do that
Ah was always
a l w a y s honest
Ah didn't want nuthin' Ah didn't work fuh
if dey give me some'in' Ah'd take it
if she didn't
if she didn't *give* it Ah didn't *git* it_ _
Ah nevah *did*
an' Ah nevah *would*
take de chile's stuff—
an' dat's de reason NOW
people's uh
uh *suffer*
wantin' help
but
you know
you can't trust peoples in yuh house like you—
dey'll steal
dey'll steal
shortenin' out uh *biscuit* now
an' people jus' rather
jus' do de bes' dey *can*
dan tuh have somebody in de house *workin'*

(5 sec. pause)

Dey Nevah Did Say Nuthin' 'bout It in Front uh Me

NOW, YOU WERE WORKING FOR THEM DURING THE TIME WHEN THE CIVIL
RIGHTS MOVEMENT AND MARTIN LUTHER KING AND ALL THAT STUFF WAS
GOING ON?

(overlaps my question)

WELL LORD YES

Appendix A

LORD/YES/YES/Y E Sʌ

DID YOU EVER HEAR THE SMITHS TALK ABOUT IT?

no
well
if dey did dey nevah did say nuthin' 'bout it in front uh me
yeah Ah was ovah deah
time all dat was
goin' on—
no
dey nevah did
nevah did say nuthin' tuh me 'bout it
quite natural Ah know dey talk tuh dey selves
Ah know dey say some'in' 'bout it tuh each other

DID IT MAKE THINGS TENSE AROUND THERE WITH ALL THAT STUFF
GOING ON?

no
it didn't tense up bad
if it did Ah didn't have sense enough tuh pay attention tuh it

(giggles)

didn't bother *me*

WHAT ABOUT THE OTHER PEOPLE WHO WORKED AROUND THERE?

oh
dey didn't pay it no attention—
L A W D Ah nevah will forget when
President Kennedy got shot＿＿
Mrs. Smith took it real hard
Mr. Smith say
"SHE AIN'T GOT NO SENSE"
say
"AH DONE TOL' 'UH"
say
"SHE JUS' ACT LIKE SHE DON'T HEAR ME"
an' did po' thang/she was jus' whoopin' an' hollerin' an' havin' uh *fit*

THAT WAS IN THE EARLY SIXTIES WHEN KENNEDY GOT SHOT? '63 OR '64?

SOME'IN' LIKE DAT
WHEN *WAS* DAT?ʌʌ
Ah wish Ah had uh kep' up wid dat＿＿

299

HE GOT SHOT BEFORE MARTIN LUTHER KING GOT SHOT, RIGHT?

oh y e a h
yeah he got shot 'fo Martin Luther King

(10 sec. pause)

DID YOU SEE IT ON TV ALL THIS STUFF ABOUT PRESIDENT KENNEDY?

y e s
hit was uh shame
LAWD
dat was uh s a d time
Ah'm tellin' you de truth
dat was uh sad time
s a d time__—
yeah
way back den
see
de Smiths was workin' down neah at
at Shelby__
at de *motel*
down neah__
an' so
dey'd be down neah/so one de cooks
in de kitchen
Ah forget his name
he didn't like *black* peoples
an' one of de othah cooks she was talkin' 'bout
'bout uh
[unintelligible]
so
dis guy didn't *like*/it
you know

A WHITE GUY?

oh yeah hit was uh white guy
he didn't like it
an' dis woman

(rubs her leg)

she was talkin' *good* about it
an' Ah said tuh mahse'f
Ah said "Why don't dis woman shut huh mouth/'cause

Appendix A

ain't no use in *arg'in'* wit' dese p e o p l e s
dey don't like somebody/jus' shut yuh *mouth*
jus' don't say *nuthin"*
dat's what *Ah* say

WERE THERE A LOT OF BLACK PEOPLE WHO SEEMED TO, TO TRY TO
HELP KING?

if/if
K i n g hadn't uh lead us
if G o d hadn't uh been here we wouldn't did—
we still be r i d i n' on de back of de bus__
tuh de day
but you know
he knowed he was gwoin
die
he knowed
'cause he said "Ah have
been tuh de top of de mountain/Ah've seen"—
oh Ah heared dat thang
he said
"Ah've s e e n
de top of de mountain"
"Ah've been tuh de top of de mountain"/he *tol'* 'em
he's seen
let de people know dat whatevah happen jus' happen—
WELL
did you see de othah night/dat uh
his wife wants dat
what was it she wants
wants some'in'
some kind of history he had
she said he had lef'—
everybody—
some
some of 'em up yondah
as'ed
somewhere
dat she wantin' 'em back down *neah*
an' dey say—
an' she say he had changed his *mind*
Ah/wouldn't/let/them/*have*/it—/dey/say/he/*hadn't*
say he tol' 'em dat

dat *dey* could have it —
whatevah/hit/was
Ah know you heard 'em talk about it
no longer dan l a s' week
musta been las' week
dey showed huh up deah
up on de court house
up on de court house
an' so
say she say she was so disappointed
say she
she

WHO WAS THAT, CORETTA KING?

yeah
Coretta__
whatevah dis w a s
of Martin Luther King's
she wanted it —
DEY SAY he had donated it
whatevah dis w a s
tuh dat
tuh dat
Ah forget de name of de town__

SOMEWHERE UP NORTH?

um hum
but uh
Lorretta [Corretta]
she wanted it tuh stay down *neah*
in *dat* town__

IN ATLANTA?

um hum
in Atlanta

SO YOU'VE SEEN A LOT OF CHANGES FROM THEN TO NOW?

(she puts her right hand under her chin and looks away)

(5 sec. pause)

DO YOU THINK IT HAS GOTTEN A WHOLE LOT BETTER?

it's got uh

it's got bettah
but it's still bad
still bad
DEM DEAH KLAN
Ah'm uh lil' fearful of dem
still
jus'-be-careful

(10 sec. pause)

Ain't Nuthin' but uh Sick Group

ALL THESE PEOPLE THAT LIVE DOWN HERE, Y'ALL ABOUT THE SAME AGE.
NOW, BACK IN THE SIXTIES, DO YOU THINK Y'ALL WOULD HAVE BEEN THE
SAME KIND OF FRIENDS THAT YOU ARE NOW IF YOU HAD KNOWN THEM
BACK THEN? OR DO YOU THINK BECAUSE THEY ARE ELDERLY AND LIVE IN
THE SAME PLACE THAT THAT'S WHY YOU'RE FRIENDS?

Ah make uh
friend de same everywhere Ah go
an' Ah'm n i c e—
an' way back in de sixties dey—
you know
Ah went aroun' most of de
whites
dey didn't
make me no difference/dey didn't
Ah didn't see uh whole lot uh

(opens her hands)

HATE
you know
an' 'sentment/Ah didn't
Ah didn't pay 'em no 'tention
'cause Ah was tryin' tuh be *nice* tuh everybody/you know
dey didn't have no—
course now
when we went
an' got on de *bus*
Ah/we did have tuh git in de *back*
had tuh git in de *back*
now Ah know *that*

but
othah den dat
Ah didn't have no trouble

(10 sec. pause)

<small>I KNOW CLAUDINE LETS THE WHITE MAN DOWN THERE DO HER
HOUSEWORK.</small>
p o lil' fellah
everybody down heah ain't able tuh pull one anothah out de *FIRE*
dey ain't able tuh do nuthin'__
<small>NANNA</small>
see
she's about dead__
an' Mrs. *Johnson*
she ain't able tuh do nuthin'__
Madeline ain't able tuh do nuthin'__
Mr. *Bullock* ain't able tuh do nuthin'__
Mr. *Littlejohn* ain't able tuh do nuthin'__
an' *Ah'm* not able tuh do nuthin'__

(wrinkles up her nose)

Claudine ain't able tuh do nuthin'__
dat ol' *man* is seventy-fo'
he ain't able tuh do nuthin'__
an'
Glenn an' his wife ain't able tuh do nuthin'__
an' Pauline is sick__
an' *Ruby's* sick__
an' dat othah one on de othah end/she ain't able tuh do nuthin'__

(giggle)

dis heah's uh
uh *sick* group down *heah*
ain't nuthin' but uh
sick group

<small>BUT YOU'RE FRIENDS WITH ALL OF THEM?</small>

a l l of 'em

(closes her eyes)

e v e r y *one* of 'em
yes Lord

Appendix A

yeah
yeah
Ah check 'em—
not all of 'em but
Ah check on 'em—
Claudine
she call me e v e r y mornin'__
she done already tol' me

(switches to a whiny voice)

"Yeah
yo' grandson'll be up deah/Ah won't check on yuh
every mornin'/'cause see he's deah"
an' she call me an' she makes me sick/every mornin' 'bout
seven o'clock/ain't no *sense* in dat tho'__
every mornin' seven o'clock__
don't care about what Ah wanna do/Ah wanna sleep—

(switches to a whiny voice)

"MA'UH [MARY]
how you doin'?"
makes me sick
an'
GUSSIE
she'll wait 'til 'bout 'leven o'clock fo' *she* call__
an' dat burns me up—

Ah'd Cut de Grass

(15 sec. pause)

(refers back to working for the Smiths)

AH CUT DE GRASS

YOU CUT THE GRASS?

Ah'd go out deah an' take dat lawn mower an' cut dat *grass*
yes Ah would
Ah'd go out deah an' cut de grass

Appendix A

not today
Ah'd never try tuh cut no grass today chile__

WHAT WOULD THEY HAVE DONE IF YOU HADN'T BEEN THERE?

n o
they wouldn't have *done*
dat's what everybody say__
good Lord
L O R D/Ah say
dey ought tuh have paid me uh thousand dollahs uh week
'cause see Ah stayed—
YOU/HEAH/ME/SAY/AH/STAYED/DEAH/AN'/TOOK/CARE
UH/DEM/CHAPS
an'
an' dey was down yondah in
in SHELBY
an' wouldn't nobody else
nobody else

(folds her arms)

wouldn't nobody else stay deah an—
day an' night an' take care uh dem chil'ren like *Ah'd* do it
course if de Smiths had uh been *rich*
den maybe Ah woulda
maybe Ah woulda did some'in'

(10 sec. pause)

yessah
Ah'd go out deah an' cut dat grass
cut dat grass
take de lawn mower an' cut dat grass out deah
in de *back*
on around out deah
sho' would—
Ah did uh w h o l e lot of work fuh dem
dey oughten nevah forget me

(shakes her head)

DEY OUGHTEN *NEVAH*
'cause Ah s h o' saved dem uh many time
many uh time

(10 sec. pause)

Appendix A

(looks at me and begins to giggle)

Ah don't know chile
dey had tuh make it Ah guess

yeah dey got somebody
dey got somebody tuh work fuh 'em
an' dey didn't
take out de woman's
social security
social security or some'in' or another
an'
Mrs. Smith had tuh pay back uh lot uh dat social security

yeah
Ah thank dey did
but
dey didn't take none out on dat woman
so
Ah thank she went tuh go draw huh lil' social security
say

(giggles)

dey hadn't took none out on 'uh
an' see dey got on tuh Mrs. Smith nem

(crosses her legs)

an' dey had tuh pay all dat *back*
had tuh pay dat
had tuh pay it
you know dey s'ppose tuh take out social security on yuh
everywhere you *work*
dey-didn't-take-it-out-on-'uh

dey paid me wit' uh *check*
sometime dey pay wit' cash/but
most of de time dey pay me wit' uh check

307

Appendix A

DID THEY EVER GIVE YOU A BONUS AT CHRISTMAS OR ANYTHING LIKE
THAT?

(abruptly)

naw

(looks at me and sneers and begins to laugh)

what?∧∧

(more laughing)

what kind uh *BONUS*?

(turns her head away from me)

no
no bonus
Ah didn't git no bonus—
dis lady up heah
my friend *Lonnie*
she been workin' fuh dese peoples uh l o n g/long/time＿＿
now she work—
she go one day
she go half uh day on Monday
an' she go half uh day on Friday＿＿
an' dat's uh whole day an' dey gives huh fifty dollahs
yeah
an' she don't do nuthin' only git ovah deah an'—
if dey *gone*
she'll go ovah deah an' look around de house
an'
git de paper
an' take de paper in
an' mess around
an' stay ovah deah uh lil' bit
an' dey—
she'll tell dem tuh leave huh money
an' dey leave huh money
she have tuh do like dat if you wanna work
Ah tol' Lonnie
Ah say
"Ah don't blame yuh Lonnie"
Ah say
"As long as you can c r a w l"/Ah/said

308

Appendix A

"You go on tuh *work*"

(smiles)

Ah said/"You crawl on"
she earn fifty dollars fuh dat one day
she ain't drawin' enough money
she said she don't be able tuh —

(begins to laugh)

but she say she jus' crawl on an' do it
jus' c r a w l on∧
an'
c r a w l on_ _
an' den deah at Chris'mas time dey gives huh uh big *bonus*∧
yeah dey's give huh uh bonus
he'p/'uh/out

Ain't Worth It

HOW MUCH IS THIS MAN PAYING YOU THAT YOU WORK FOR ONCE A WEEK?

dat man ovah deah?

(she looks at me and bursts out in laughter)

twelve dollars

(we both laugh for about ten seconds)

AIN'T WORTH
AIN'T WORTH GOIN'/BUT AH SAY AH'LL GO AN' GIT ME SOME
BREAD AN' *MILK*

(we laugh again)

(5 sec. pause)

if it was uh whole lot uh hard work Ah wouldn't go
now if hit was hard work Ah couldn't/Ah *wouldn't*
Ah wouldn't uh had
but
he'll come an' git me an' take me
Ah go deah an' do two or three lil' thangs
an' rake
rake —

Appendix A

(breaks out into laughter then gets serious again)

now you know dey could pay yuh 'bout sixteen or seventeen dollars
or fifteen dollars
yeah dey could
Ah'll go when Ah want to
ef Ah don't Ah don't do it
Ah said de other day
Ah said Ah'm too ti'ed
but Ah'll go ovah deah an' do uh lil' some'in'—
when his wife was deah
Ah'd go two or three HOURS
get home 'fo *dark*
an' uh
when she come out de hospital
Ah went ovah deah an' stayed
three *days*
yeah
de lady came out de hospital
an' wa'n't nobody ovah deah wit'/'uh
an she gave me uh *hunerd* dollars __—
s e e
back then Ah reckon dey didn't have no money much
an' see she knowed what work—
what
she knowed what work—
all of 'em know what work w a s
how high everythang is/you can't
git nuthin'
git nuthin' fuh nuthin'__—
now some of dese peoples 'round heah git ten dollars worth of food
    stamps
now what can yuh git wit' ten dollars^^
now what can yuh *git?*^^

APPENDIX B

Interview with Mrs. Smith

The following interview took place on August 5, 1994, at the home of Mrs. Smith (a pseudonym), my grandmother's former employer. Present were Mrs. Smith, my grandmother (Mary), and myself. The interview lasted about thirty minutes.

EPJ: Did you have other domestics to work for you before grandmama?

Mrs. Smith: Yeah. Had Shirley. She worked a couple days a week. And then I had Carolyn Rinehart work for me till your grandmother came. See, every time I got pregnant *she* got pregnant. Now I said, "Carolyn. Now, here you are expecting and you're not gonna be able to come over and take care of two kids. I want you to find me a *good* mammy. I wants me a *real* mammy." Well, she said, "I'll find you one." Well, I never will forget the day when your grandmother called. She just called and she talked so dignified. She talked so big and everything and she'd *love* to come and work for me. Didn't know that she'd be working next door. My mother had Charlie [unintelligible] house. She said, oh she would love to come. She could take care of children. So she started out working each day and we'd take her home—about five in the afternoon. Then in 1966 my father and my husband, they went to Shelby to see about this hotel down there and it was for sale at auction. And my daddy just lucked up and told him what he'd give for it. And they went down and got it. And first thing he did, he got a call from Shelby that the sons wanted to sell it. They were gonna sell it at auction. So, they went on and had the sale and everything and this, uh, I forget this guy's name from Shelby, but he bidded it off at the sale but did not make [unintelligible] and he died of a heart attack that Saturday night. So he came back to my father and said, "Well. We're just gonna take you up on what you said you'd give."

So we split it up. Daddy says, "I get a—they get a third. Mama a third. And I'll take a third." So that was it. We had went up there and [unintelligible] the hotel. They just started fussing, so Gene and I had to go up there. So that meant that your grandmother and my family would come down every weekend. She would come down on Friday. I'd have to come to Hickory to get her. They'd come down and then my family would come down on Sunday and they'd take her back. So Gene and I was staying over there at the house. She got to where she was scared over there by herself and every-thing. And we had gotten her a house. And she just decided she couldn't stay over there. She was having problems with the house. So, she just got in there and she did the cooking and taking care of the kids and I think run-ning day, morning to night. She'd tell Jimmy if he didn't stay in that house she was gonna whip his butt.

And then. Carol, Patti, she was gettin' married. And your mother—Jimmy said Sarah had been here. And I had to work at the sale that day. Said that your grandmother was going to Washington to see her brother—real bad off. And of course I told her all the time that she would have to come down the aisle right after me when Carol and Patti got married and sit down there with me. Cause she *raised* those kids. So Daisy went up there to her brother that was so bad off. She went up there and she didn't come home.

Mary: Didn't I come back?

Mrs. Smith: NOOOOOOOO. You finally got up the nerve to call Tanya H. Told Tanya to tell me that you was gonna stay up there, cause he was real sick and you weren't coming back.

She was with us eighteen years. You were with me. . . . She even been down to Jacksonville, Florida, to Atlanta. You always went down with me to see Carol. Remember that we was going down there to Florida and the police stopped me? [laughs] Daisy just sat there like this [stiffens her body], you know.

Mary: [laughs] I never will forget that.

Mrs. Smith: I had my red suit on and I said, "Oh I'm just so sorry. We on our way to see my daughter and her little baby but I just had to stop at the uni-versity to see my youngest daughter and she's gonna have to go to class and I didn't mean to be speeding." And he was so nice. He said, "I'll just give you a warning ticket." Oh Daisy just said, "Shew." [turns to Mary] And I guess after they all left home, that's when you went back to Kings Mountain.

EPJ: Did you have anybody to come work for you after that?

Mrs. Smith: No, cause I couldn't ever trust nobody. That's why I make her come up here now. I told somebody the other day. I said I wouldn't have one of those girls down there at the college or one of those guys come over here and work for me cause they might break in . . .

Mary: [interrupting] Ah tell de chil'ren now, Ah say well Lord de reason why peoples can't get jobs anymore is because dey do nothin' but steal, steal, steal. And take things that don't belong tuh 'em.

Mrs. Smith: That's right. Yeah, we were talking about it day before yesterday. See Roxy Rich, her husband died about a year ago and she got arthritis in her legs and her hands, and elbows. Well, her elbows, that bone stick way out like that. [demonstrates] And she went about her feet and they had to operate on her. That one and they were gonna do the other one in six months. And it was something to do with that bone. Took the bone off or something and she had to stay in a cast for six months.

Mary: Oh my God.

Mrs. Smith: And it was this lady over here—over there—who works at the library at the college. She was over there helping her. She was getting ready to leave and Roxy said, "I just tell you, you never know with people. Trust 'em and everything." Said this lady worked for [unintelligible] and she asked me if I needed some help. She was gonna help me out twice a week. I said, "That's the way I am about Daisy." I said, "I'm not gonna get no one I don't know to come in." And it's just me and I just wait till Daisy comes up here. Everybody says, "Oh we won't have another Daisy. You won't find another Daisy."

NOTES

Introduction: "Blackness" and Authenticity
What's Performance Got to Do with It?

1 Richard Schechner, "What Is Performance Studies Anyway?" in *The Ends of Performance*, ed. Peggy Phelan and Jill Lane (New York: New York University Press, 1998), 357.

2 See Regina Bendix, *In Search of Authenticity: The Formation of Folklore Studies* (Madison: University of Wisconsin Press, 1997), 7.

3 With few exceptions, throughout this book I use the term "black" as opposed to "African American" and "white" as opposed to "European American" to suggest a more equivocal relationship between bodies and racial and cultural identity and to mark these terms as signs constantly under contestation. In those places in the text where I deploy the term "African American," it is done so to designate a specific function, such as in the name of courses I have taught.

4 Bendix, *In Search of Authenticity*, 9.

5 Henry Louis Gates Jr., "'Authenticity,' or the Lesson of Little Tree," *New York Times Book Review*, November 24, 1991, 26.

6 For an extended discussion on the exclusion of black gays and lesbians from the circle of blacks who are authorized to speak on the black community's behalf, see Dwight A. McBride, "Can the Queen Speak? Racial Essentialism, Sexuality, and the Problem of Authority," *Callaloo* 22 (1998): 432–60.

7 Wahneema Lubiano, "'But Compared to What?' Reading Realism, Representation, and Essentialism in *School Daze*, *Do the Right Thing*, and Spike Lee Discourse," in *Representing Black Men*, ed. Marcellus Blount and George P. Cunningham (New York: Routledge, 1996), 189.

8 See Eric Lott, *Love and Theft: Blackface Minstrelsy and the American Work-*

ing Class (New York: Oxford University Press, 1993); and Michael Rogin, *Blackface, White Noise: Jewish Immigrants in the Hollywood Melting Pot* (Berkeley: University of California Press, 1996).

9 See George Lipsitz, *The Possessive Investment in Whiteness: How White People Profit from Identity Politics* (Philadelphia: Temple University Press, 1998).

10 bell hooks, *Black Looks: Race and Representation* (Boston: South End Press, 1992), 21–40.

11 I do not mean to suggest that cultural imbrication only occurs between black and white youth. Indeed, given the multicultural composition of the United States, I am well aware that other cross-cultural exchanges, appropriations, and racial performances exist among and between blacks and many other races. I only use this example to specify a particular dynamic that I have observed between white and black youth.

12 Several scholars have traced the history of racial mimicry on the part of whites, namely studies on the history of minstrelsy. See Lott, *Love and Theft*, and Rogin, *Blackface, White Noise.*

13 Bendix, *In Search of Authenticity*, 8.

14 Mary Strine, Beverly Whitaker Long, and Mary Frances HopKins, "Research in Interpretation and Performance Studies: Trends, Issues, Priorities," in *Speech Communication: Essays to Commemorate the Seventy-Fifth Anniversary of the Speech Communication Association*, ed. Gerald Phillips and Julia Woods (Carbondale: Southern Illinois University Press, 1990) 183.

15 The 1990s saw an explosion of books, anthologies, and essays deploying "performance" as a critical analytic, especially in philosophical, literary, cultural, and theater studies. See Judith Butler, *Gender Trouble* (New York: Routledge, 1990); Janelle G. Reinelt and Joseph R. Roach, eds., *Critical Theory and Performance* (Ann Arbor: University of Michigan Press, 1992); Eve Kosofsky Sedgwick, "Queer Performativity: Henry James's *The Art of the Novel*," *GLQ* 1.1 (fall 1993): 13–28; Peggy Phelan, *Unmarked: The Politics of Performance* (New York: Routledge, 1993); Eve Kosofsky Sedgwick, *Tendencies* (Duke University Press, 1993); Andrew Parker and Eve Kosofsky Sedgwick, eds., *Performance and Performativity* (New York: Routledge, 1996); Marvin Carlson, *Performance: An Introduction* (New York: Routledge, 1996); and Peggy Phelan and Jill Lane, eds., *The Ends of Performance* (New York: New York University Press, 1998).

16 Dwight Conquergood, "Performance Theory, Hmong Shamans, and Cultural Politics," in *Critical Theory and Performance*, ed. Janelle G. Reinelt and Joseph R. Roach (Ann Arbor: University of Michigan Press, 1992), 57.

17 Jonah Barrish, *The Antitheatrical Tradition* (Berkeley: University of California Press, 1981).

18 Conquergood, "Performance Theory," 58.
19 Patricia Williams, "The Pantomime of Race," in *Seeing a Color-Blind Future: The Parodox of Race* (New York: Noonday Press, 1997), 17.
20 Williams "Pantomime of Race," 27.
21 See, for example, Zora Neale Hurston's oft-quoted lines from *Mules and Men* (New York: Harper Collins, 1990): "And the Negro, in spite of his open faced laughter, his seeming acquiescence, is particularly evasive. You see we are a polite people and we do not say to our questioner, 'Get out of here!' We smile and tell him or her something that satisfies the white person because, knowing so little about us, he doesn't know what he is missing. The Indian resists curiosity by a stony silence. The Negro offers a feather bed resistance, that is, we let the probe enter, but it never comes out. It gets smothered under a lot of laughter and pleasantries" (1).
22 Susan Manning, "Modern Dance, Negro Dance, and Katherine Dunham," *Textual Practice* 15.3 (2001): 489; and Manning, *Modern Dance, Negro Dance, and Queer Culture* (Minneapolis: University of Minnesota Press, forthcoming), 22.
23 Rinaldo Walcott, *Black like Who?* (Toronto: Insomniac Press, 1997), xi.
24 For more on blackness and performance, see Kimberly W. Benston, *Performing Blackness: Enactments of African-American Modernism* (New York: Routledge, 2000); Walcott, *Black Like Who?*; and Jennifer Brody, *Impossible Purity: Blackness and Victorian Culture* (Durham: Duke University Press, 1998).
25 Johannes Fabian, *Power and Performance: Ethnographic Explorations through Proverbial Wisdom and Theater in Shaba, Zaire* (Madison: University of Wisconsin Press, 1990), xiv–xv.
26 Clifford Geertz, "Thinking as a Moral Act: Ethical Dimensions of Anthropological Fieldwork in the New States," *Antioch Review* 28 (1968): 142.
27 Dwight Conquergood, "Performing Cultures: Ethnography, Epistemology, and Ethics," in *Miteinander Sprechen Und Handelm: Festschrift Fur Hellmut Geissner*, ed. Edith Sembek (Frankfurt: Scriptor, 1986), 61. Mikhail Bakhtin's comments concerning the novelistic form are also useful in regard to how I legitimize my fieldwork research as a dialogic practice. As a dialogic construct, Bakhtin claims that the novel "shift[s] . . . the temporal center of artistic orientation" (Bakhtin, *The Dialogic Imagination*, ed. Michael Holquist, trans. Caryl Emerson and Michael Holquist [Austin: University of Texas Press, 1984], 27). Whereas in the monologic epic the author exists on a separate temporal plane than that of the fictional world and its heroes, the novel "permits the author, in all his masks and faces, to move freely onto the field of his represented world, a field that in the epic had been absolutely inaccessible and

closed" (27). This aspect of Bakhtin's theory serves as an apt analogy for the kind of ethnographic research I practiced—as it was essential that I not exist on a separate plane, that I move into the "field" that constitutes the Other's world, and that I, like them, wear the different "masks and faces" required of and permitted to me. As a result, our subject positions were constantly shifting, evolving, and transforming what are, otherwise, relatively stable and familiar roles and positions.

28   See Richard Bauman, *Verbal Art as Performance* (Prospect Heights, Ill.: Waveland Press, 1977); Elizabeth Fine, *The Folklore Text* (Bloomington: Indiana University Press, 1984); Geneva Smitherman, *Talkin' and Testifyin': The Language of Black America* (Detroit: Wayne State University Press, 1977); and Claudia Mitchell-Kernan, "Signifying," in *Mother Wit from the Laughing Barrel: Readings in the Interpretation of Afro-American Folklore*, ed. Alan Dundes (New York: Garland Press, 1973), 310–28.

29   See Jill Taft-Kaufman, "Oral Interpretation: Twentieth-Century Theory and Practice," in *Speech Communication in the Twentieth Century*, ed. Thomas W. Benson (Carbondale: Southern Illinois University Press, 1985), 158–65.

30   The discipline now known as "performance studies" has a rich and contested history. In Carlson's *Performance: A Critical Introduction*, for example, there is no mention of the oral interpretation roots of performance studies. Instead, Carlson aligns the history of performance studies with anthropology, sociology, linguistics, and other social science disciplines. Ironically, however, Carlson begins the book with a quote from an essay written by three progenitors of the field of oral interpretation: Mary Strine, Beverly Whitaker Long, and Mary Francis Hopkins. For a counternarrative to Carlson's, see Paul Edwards, "Unstoried: Teaching Literature in the Age of Performance Studies," *Theatre Annual* 53 (1999): 1–147.

31   The narrative event constitutes the present-tense telling situation, while the narrated event constitutes the past-tense "told" situations and events. In performance, the narrated events are contextualized by the present telling.

32   See Kimberly William Crenshaw, "Mapping the Margins: Intersectionality, Identity Politics, and Violence against Women of Color," *Stanford Law Review* 43 (1991): 1241–99; Patricia Hill Collins, *Black Feminist Thought* (New York: Routledge, 1990); Cathy Cohen, "Punks, Bulldaggers, and Welfare Queens: The Radical Potential of Queer Politics?" *GLQ* 3 (1997): 437–65; Dwight A. McBride, "Can the Queen Speak?"; and E. Patrick Johnson, "'Quare' Studies or (Almost) Everything I Know about Queer Studies I Learned from My Grandmother," *Text and Performance Quarterly* 21.1 (2001): 1–25.

1 The Pot Is Brewing:
Marlon Riggs's *Black Is . . . Black Ain't*

1   Essex Hemphill, "Now We Think," in *Ceremonies* (San Francisco: Cleis Press, 1992), 169, cited in the film *Tongues Untied,* dir. Marlon Riggs, Frameline, 1989. All quotes from the film are my transcriptions.

2   *Black Is . . . Black Ain't,* dir. Marlon Riggs, Independent Film Series, 1995. All quotes from the film are my transcriptions.

3   Martin Favor, *Authentic Blackness: The Folk in the New Negro Renaissance* (Durham: Duke University Press, 1999), 2.

4   McBride, "Can the Queen Speak?, 377.

5   I would like to thank Tess Chakkalakal for pointing out this possible reading of the film.

6   In addition to the failure of governmental responses to HIV/AIDS infection, Cathy Cohen has meticulously chronicled the consequences of the blind eye that black leadership has turned toward the HIV/AIDS pandemic in the black community. See Cathy Cohen, *The Boundaries of Blackness: AIDS and the Breakdown of Black Politics* (Chicago: University of Chicago Press, 1999).

7   Given the history of PBS's programs on HIV/AIDS, such a motive would not be surprising. The first feature program on HIV/AIDS that aired on PBS on the *Frontline* series in 1985, for instance, focused on Fabian Bridges, a black man inflicted with AIDS. According to Martha Gever, the program "portrayed [the] unemployed black, gay protagonist as a dangerous criminal irresponsibly roaming the country and engaging in sex with unsuspecting victims. The *Frontline* producers tracked the man down, pretended to befriend him in order to elicit personal information, then turned him in to the health authorities after they got their footage" (Gever, "Pictures of Sickness: Stuart Marshall's *Bright Eyes,*" in *AIDS: Cultural Analysis, Cultural Activism,* ed. Douglas Crimp [Cambridge: MIT Press, 1996], 111; see 109–26 for a history of PBS's problematic representation of HIV/AIDS).

8   David Román, *Acts of Intervention: Performance, Gay Culture, and AIDS* (Bloomington: Indiana University Press, 1998), xxvi.

9   Teresa de Lauretis, *Technologies of Gender: Essays on Theory, Film, and Fiction* (Bloomington: Indiana University Press, 1987), 139.

10   Román, *Acts of Intervention,* xxii.

11   Stuart Hall, "Signification, Representation, Ideology: Althusser and the Post-Structuralist Debates," *Critical Studies in Mass Communication* 2.2 (1985): 112.

12   Favor, *Authentic Blackness,* 4.

13   Houston A. Baker's *Blues, Ideology, and Afro-American Literature: A Ver-nacular Theory* (Chicago: University of Chicago Press, 1984) is an ex-ample of this equation of the blues with folk culture and the working class. Baker writes that the blues is "the performance that sings of abys-mal poverty and deprivation" (9). Hazel Carby, in "The Sexual Politics of Women's Blues," in *Cultures of Babylon* (New York: Verso, 1999), 7–21, makes a similar connection between the blues and the folk, but in a slightly different manner. In her attempt to valorize the contribution of black women blues singers to a black theory of sexuality, Carby suggests that scholars should look to black women blues singers for a fuller ex-pression of black female sexuality rather than at black women writers, especially given the "limitations of their middle-class responses to black women's sexuality" (10). Black women blues singers, on the other hand, transcended such limitations due to the "urban" context out of which the genre known as "city blues" arose. While Carby recasts the context of the blues from the rural south to the urban north, the urban place that provides a space for these women blues singers' sexual liberation is still tied to a working-class sensibility.

14   Valerie Smith, *Not Just Race, Not Just Gender: Black Feminist Readings* (New York: Routledge, 1998), 67.

15   Langston Hughes, "The Negro Artist and the Racial Mountain," *The Na-tion*, June 23, 1926, 692 (my emphasis).

16   Favor, *Authentic Blackness*, 13.

17   Imamu Amiri Baraka [LeRoi Jones], "Black Bourgeoisie," in *The Black Poets*, ed. Dudley Randall (New York: Bantam, 1971), 223.

18   Note that black women's contributions to the Civil Rights movement were thought to be so insignificant that they rarely became the subject of black male poets of this era, except as objects of his gaze or scorn. See Baraka's "Beautiful Black Women" in Randall, ed., *The Black Poets*.

19   Imamu Amiri Baraka [LeRoi Jones], "Poem for Some Half White College Students," in Randall, ed., *The Black Poets*, 225.

20   For an in-depth discussion of the antiwhite poetry of the Black Arts movement and the poetry that serves to "solidify the meaning of the Black Aesthetic," see Phillip Brian Harper, *Are We Not Men? Masculine Anxiety and the Problem of African-American Identity* (New York: Oxford University Press, 1996), 44–49.

21   Adolph Reed Jr., "The 'Black Revolution' and the Reconstitution of Domination," in *Race, Politics, and Culture: Critical Essays on the Radical-ism of the 1960s*, ed. Adolph Reed Jr. (New York: Greenwood, 1986), 74.

22   Cornel West, "The Paradox of the Afro-American Rebellion," in *The Sixties without Apology*, ed. Sohnya Sayres, Anders Stephanson, Stanley Aronowitz, and Fredric Jameson (Minneapolis: University of Minnesota Press, 1984), 44–58.

23 Cornel West, *Race Matters* (Boston: Beacon, 1993), 14.

24 I am not so naive as to think that a poor person's aspiration to middle-class or even wealthy status is not what maintains capitalist hegemony. Indeed, the imperialism of capitalism depends on and is secured by the entrenchment of the proletariat in the psychological discourse of upward mobility. Nonetheless, I would argue that in a capitalist society the working class is not always happy with the status quo, as Hughes's essay implies. But more to the point, the articulation of the desire not to be "in the ghetto" or to be "rich" implies that the working class is also susceptible to the baits of white materialism and political capitulation—that of which the black middle class is accused. As Sandra Richards suggests regarding the "folk," "no one escapes the reaches of global commodification. Therefore, issues of folk authenticity or purity become untenable in today's culture, if indeed they were valid concerns in the 1920s" (Richards, "Writing the Absent Potential: Drama, Performance, and the Canon of African American Culture," in *Performativity and Performance,* ed. Andrew Parker and Eve Kosofsky Sedgwick [New York: Routledge, 1995], 69–70). Urban black-on-black crime, especially that motivated by the acquiring of material goods, is an example of the cultural practices that undermine a "progressive" politics of blackness.

25 Favor, *Authentic Blackness,* 22.

26 Stuart Hall, "What Is This 'Black' in Black Popular Culture?" in *Black Popular Culture,* ed. Gina Dent (Seattle: Bay Press, 1992), 30.

27 Ice Cube, "True to the Game," *Death Certificate,* Priority Records, 1991.

28 Lubiano, "But Compared to What?," 186.

29 Again, I do not wish to imply that class, in the marxist sense, is merely a product of ideology. What I am suggesting, however, is that the representation of class does not exist outside ideology and thus cannot be linked to notions of authentic racial identity. More to the point, class status is relative in relation to race, gender, and in some instances, sexuality, thus marking class as a social phenomenon as much as an economic one.

30 Harper, *Are We Not Men?,* x.

31 For an extended discussion on Jackson and Cleaver and the contradictions found within their rhetoric, homosocial bonds, misogyny, and homophobia, see Robert F. Reid-Pharr, *Black Gay Man* (New York: New York University Press, 2001), 62–82, 99–134.

32 George Jackson, *Soledad Brother: The Prison Letters of George Jackson* (New York: Bantam, 1970), 45.

33 Reid-Pharr, *Black Gay Man,* 69.

34 Judith Halberstam, *Female Masculinity* (Durham: Duke University Press, 1999), 1–42.

35 Reid-Pharr, *Black Gay Man,* 103.

36 For more on the policing of gay sexuality in the black church and the

binary emphasized between the spirit and the flesh, see E. Patrick Johnson, "Feeling the Spirit in the Dark: Expanding Notions of the Sacred in the African American Gay Community," *Callaloo* 21.1 (1998): 399–416.

37 For an extended discussion of the ironies of black gay and lesbian participation in the black church to their own detriment, see Michael Dyson, *Race Rules: Navigating the Color Line* (Reading, Mass.: Addison-Wesley, 1996), 105.

38 See José Esteban Muñoz, *Disidentifications: Queers of Color and the Performance of Politics* (Minneapolis: University of Minnesota Press, 1999), 11–12.

39 Paul Gilroy's construction of the "Diaspora" functions similarly to what I mean here in that he proposes that the "Diaspora" "allows for a complex conception of sameness and an idea of solidarity that does not repress the differences within in order to maximize the differences between one 'essential' community and others" (Gilroy, " '. . . To Be Real': The Dissident Forms of Black Expressive Culture," in *Let's Get it On: The Politics of Black Performance*, ed. Catherine Ugwu [Seattle: Bay Press, 1995], 24).

40 Elizabeth Alexander, " 'Can You Be Black and Watch This?' Reading the Rodney King Video(s)," in *Black Male: Representations of Black Masculinity in Contemporary Art*, ed. Thelma Golden (New York: Whitney Museum of Contemporary Art, 1994), 94.

41 Joan W. Scott, "The Evidence of Experience," in *The Lesbian and Gay Studies Reader*, ed. Henry Abelove, Michèle A. Barale, and David Halperin (New York: Routledge, 1993), 397–415.

42 Dwight McBride, "Speaking the Unspeakable: On Toni Morrison, African American Intellectuals, and the Uses of Essentialist Rhetoric," in *Toni Morrison: Critical and Theoretical Approaches*, ed. Nancy J. Peterson (Baltimore: Johns Hopkins University Press, 1997), 149.

43 Scott, "The Evidence of Experience," 399.

44 Gilroy, " '. . . To Be Real,' " 24.

45 This motif is immortalized in Ralph Ellison's *Invisible Man* (New York: Random House, 1994), 26, when the nameless protagonist/narrator dreams of a letter in his briefcase with this salutation. See also Andy Razaf, "African American Folk Song: Run, Nigger, Run," in *Cultural Contexts for Ralph Ellison's "Invisible Man,"* ed. Eric Sundquist (Boston: Bedford, 1995), 117–19.

46 Alexander, "Can You Be Black and Watch This?," 92–93.

47 For more on the dominant culture's linkage of AIDS and homosexuals, see Douglas Crimp, "How to Have Promiscuity in an Epidemic" (237–71); Simon Watney, "The Spectacle of AIDS" (71–86); and Paula Treichler, "AIDS, Homophobia, and Biomedical Discourse: An Epidemic of Signification" (31–70), all in *AIDS: Cultural Analysis, Cultural Activism,*

ed. Douglas Crimp (Cambridge: MIT Press, 1996), and Cindy Patton, *Inventing AIDS* (New York: Routledge, 1990).

48 Toni Morrison, *Sula* (New York: Plume, 1973) 149.

2 Manifest Faggotry:
Queering Masculinity in African American Culture

1 Sigmund Freud, "Mourning and Melancholia," in *General Psychological Theories* (New York: Touchstone, 1997), 164.

2 Judith Butler, *Bodies That Matter: On the Discursive Limits of "Sex"* (New York: Routledge, 1993), 235.

3 See Butler, "Melancholy Gender/Refused Identification," in *Constructing Masculinity*, ed. Maurice Berger, Brian Wallis, and Simon Watson (New York: Routledge, 1995), 35.

4 Freud, "Mourning and Melancholia," 173 (my emphasis).

5 Anne Anlin Cheng, *The Melancholy of Race: Psychoanalysis, Assimilation, and Hidden Grief* (New York: Oxford University Press, 2001), 9.

6 Phillip Brian Harper, *Are We Not Men?*, iv.

7 In his essay "Tearing the Goat's Flesh," in *Black Gay Man* (99–134), Robert Reid-Pharr provides a reading of Eldridge Cleaver's attack on James Baldwin that is similar to the one I offer. For his part, Reid-Pharr argues that the black gay "stands in for the border crossing and boundarylessness that has so preoccupied contemporary Black American intellectuals" (103). Baldwin, according to Reid-Pharr, is emblematic of that "boundarylessness" for Cleaver. Although I employ a different theoretical frame, both Reid-Pharr and I come to the same conclusion regarding the fact that black heterosexuality as evinced by racial purists always already remains owing to the black homosexual he repudiates. My reading here remains indebted to Reid-Pharr's, which precedes it.

8 Marlon Riggs, "Black Macho Revisited: Reflections of a SNAP! Queen," in *Brother to Brother: New Writings by Black Gay Men*, ed. Essex Hemphill (Boston: Alyson Press, 1991), 253–57.

9 Butler, "Melancholy Gender," 31.

10 Although I begin my analysis with black male figures of the 1960s, I do not wish to suggest that homophobic rhetoric among self-identified heterosexual black male writers, performers, and scholars was nonexistent prior to that era. I merely focus on the 1960s because of the rise of a Black Nationalist movement that partially predicated its effectiveness in combating the "ills" of racism on the repudiation of all things associated with whiteness, including homosexuality.

11 Cheng, *The Melancholy Race*, 10.

12 Eldridge Cleaver, *Soul on Ice* (New York: Laurel, 1968), 30.
13 For more on this process, see Rhonda M. Williams, "Living at the Cross-roads: Explorations in Race, Nationality, Sexuality, and Gender," in *The House That Race Built: Black Americans, U.S. Terrain,* ed. Wahneema Lubiano (New York: Pantheon Books, 1997), 147.
14 Darieck Scott, for instance, suggests through a reading of the character Paul D's experience on the chain gang in Toni Morrison's *Beloved* that black male emasculation might be traced to white male sexual domination as opposed to physical and psychological domination. Consequently, Scott argues, "The emasculation trope's account of black male subjectivity tends toward a denial or erasure of part of the history of slavery: the sexual exploitation of enslaved black men by white men, the horror of male rape and of homosexuality—all these memories are bundled together, each made equal to and synonymous with one another, and all are hidden behind the more abstract notion of lost or stolen manhood, and most readily figured by the castration which was so much a part of the practice of lynching" (Scott, "More Man than You'll Ever Be: Antonio Fargas, Eldridge Cleaver, and Toni Morrison's *Beloved,*" in *Dangerous Liaisons: Blacks, Gays, and the Struggle for Equality,* ed. Eric Brandt [New York: New Press, 1999], 236).
15 Riggs, speaking in *Tongues Untied,* 1990.
16 Cleaver, *Soul on Ice,* 96 (my emphasis).
17 Huey P. Newton, "Playboy Interview: Huey Newton," *Playboy Magazine,* May 1973, 84.
18 Ironically, Newton's tale-telling participates in the same homosexual disavowal as Cleaver's disavowal of Baldwin. Indeed, Newton's revelation that Cleaver was possibly a repressed homosexual functions to secure Newton's own heterosexuality and blackness in that his breach of the secret pact he made with Cleaver distances him from any suspicions of homosexual identification. Newton's seeming openness to accepting homosexuals panders to the popular belief that if a man is "secure" in his masculinity then he is not threatened by homosexuality and vice versa. But, as Darieck Scott suggests, "the very claim of being secure in one's heterosexuality is no more than that: a claim—and claims can be contested" ("More Man Than You'll Ever Be," 221).
19 Newton, "Playboy Interview," 84.
20 Butler, "Melancholy Gender," 28.
21 Darieck Scott makes a similar argument with regard to Cleaver in relation to the drag character Lindy in the film *Car Wash* when he writes: "Cleaver and his cohort fear and hate the queer that lurks in the figure of the strong black male, that 'more woman than you'll ever get' that Lindy embraces with a mocking smile" ("More Man Than You'll Ever Be," 221).
22 Harper, *Are We Not Men?,* 41.

23 Imamu Amiri Baraka [LeRoi Jones], "American Sexual Reference: Black Male," in *Home: Social Essays* (New York: William Morrow, 1966), 216

24 It is interesting to note that both Cleaver and Baraka dated, and in Baraka's case married, white women.

25 Harper, *Are We Not Men?*, 49.

26 Imamu Amiri Baraka, *Selected Poetry of Amiri Baraka/LeRoi Jones* (New York: William Morrow, 1979), 115.

27 Harper, *Are We Not Men?*, 51.

28 Ron Simmons, "Some Thoughts on the Challenges Facing Black Gay Intellectuals," in *Brother to Brother: New Writings by Black Gay Men*, ed. Essex Hemphill (Boston: Alyson, 1991), 218.

29 Imamu Amiri Baraka [LeRoi Jones], *The System of Dante's Hell* (London: MacGibbon and Kee, 1966), 57–58 (my emphasis).

30 See, for example, Barbara Smith, ed., *Home Girls: A Black Feminist Anthology* (New York: Kitchen Table—Women of Color Press, 1983); and Gloria T. Hull, Patricia Bell Scott, and Barbara Smith, eds., *All the Women Are White, All the Blacks Are Men, But Some of Us Are Brave: Black Women's Studies* (New York: Feminist Press, 1982).

31 Susan Faludi, *Backlash: The Undeclared War against American Women* (New York: Anchor, 1991), xi.

32 Harper, *Are We Not Men?*, 3.

33 See, for example, Crimp, ed., *AIDS: Cultural Analysis, Cultural Criticism*. For coverage in black presses, see Cohen, *The Boundaries of Blackness* 231–47.

34 For more on the proliferation of heteronormative images in the media, see Larry Gross and James D. Woods, eds., *The Columbia Reader on Lesbians and Gay Men in Media, Society, and Politics* (New York: Columbia University Press, 1999).

35 *Delirious*, dir. Bruce Gowers, Paramount, 1983.

36 Granted, in 1983 there was not as much information available as there is today about how HIV/AIDS is spread and contracted; nonetheless, as a public figure this lack of information should have made Murphy even more sensitive regarding the reality of such a fatal yet mysterious disease.

37 See, for example, Nathan Hare and Julia Hare, *The Endangered Black Family: Coping with the Unisexualization and Coming Extinction of the Black Race* (San Francisco: Black Think Tank, 1984); Molefi Asante, *Afrocentricity: The Theory of Social Change* (Buffalo: Amulefi, 1980); and Haki Madhubuti, *Black Men: Obsolete, Single, Dangerous? The Afrikan American in Transition: Essays in Discovery, Solution, and Hope* (Chicago: Third World Press, 1990).

38 Marianne Ruuth, *Eddie: Eddie Murphy from A to Z* (Los Angeles: Holloway House Publishing, 1985), 41.

39   Murphy is signifying on the gay vernacular term "gaydar," which is used by gays to "detect" other gay people.

40   *Eddie Murphy: Raw*, dir. Robert Townsend, Paramount, 1987.

41   *Delirious*, 1983.

42   Ruuth, *Eddie*, 41.

43   See "Eddie Murphy, One Sorry Comic Actor," *Weekly News*, May 11, 1996, and May 12, 2002, online at www.canoe.ca/JamMoviesArtistsM/murphy_eddie.html.

44   "Transsexual Prostitute Arrested in Eddie Murphy's Car," May 2, 1997, online at www.cnn.com/SHOWBIZ/9705/02/murphy.html.

45   See Louis Althusser, "Ideology and Ideological State Apparatuses," in *Lenin and Philosophy and Other Essays* (New York: Monthly Review Press, 1971).

46   See, for example, West, *Race Matters*, ix–xi.

47   For another queer reading of Murphy's films in relation to his life, see Mark Anthony Neal, *Soul Babies: Black Popular Culture and the Post-Soul Aesthetic*, (New York: Routledge, 2002) 126–28.

48   Butler, *Gender Trouble*, 128.

49   In the context of discussing drag as a site of parodic gender performance, Judith Butler suggests that parodic performances always already maintain an ambivalent site with regard to subversion or reiteration of cultural hegemony. She writes: "Parody by itself is not subversive, and there must be a way to understand what makes certain kinds of parodic repetitions effectively disruptive, truly troubling, and which repetitions become domesticated and recirculated as instruments of cultural hegemony. A typology of actions would clearly not suffice, for parodic displacements, indeed parodic laughter, depends on the context and reception in which subversive confusions can be fostered" (*Gender Trouble*, 139).

50   Butler, *Bodies That Matter*, 94–119.

51   Herman Gray, *Watching Race: Television and the Struggle for "Blackness"* (Minneapolis: University of Minnesota Press, 1995), 130.

52   For more on the SNAP!, see Thomas Becquer, "SNAP!thology and Other Discursive Practices in *Tongues Untied*," *Wide Angle* 13.2 (1991): 7–17; and E. Patrick Johnson, "SNAP! Culture: A Different Kind of Reading," *Text and Performance Quarterly* 15.2 (1995): 122–42.

53   "The Best of Men On," written by Franklyn Ajaye et al., on *In Living Color*, created by Keenan Ivory Wayans, dir. Terri McCoy. FOX WGMB, Baton Rouge, February 28, 1993. Transcription by the author.

54   Quoted in Essex Hemphill, " 'In Living Color': Toms, Coons, Mammies, Faggots, and Bucks," in *Out in Culture: Gay, Lesbian, and Queer Essays on Popular Culture*, ed. Corey K. Creekmur and Alexander Doty (Durham: Duke University Press, 1995), 392.

55 Gray, *Watching Race*, 142.

56 See Asante, *Afrocentricity*, 65; and Joseph Eure and Richard Jerome, eds., *Back Where We Belong: Selected Speeches by Minister Louis Farrakhan* (Philadelphia: PC International Press, 1989), 138.

57 I do not wish to diminish the humor of this skit. Certainly, many gay men find "Men On . . ." extremely funny and do not take offense. My argument, however, is that the humor is based on a particular kind of cultural logic that sustains heteronormative constructions of maleness and blackness—constructions that exclude black gay men in particular from the boundaries of "authentic" blackness and maleness.

58 hooks, *Black Looks*, 147.

59 Carole Anne Tyler, "Boys Will Be Girls: The Politics of Gay Drag," in *Inside Out: Lesbian Theories/Gay Theories*, ed. Diana Fuss (New York: Routledge, 1997), 52.

60 West, *Race Matters*, 89.

61 Gray, *Watching Race*, 142.

62 Riggs, quoted in Hemphill, "'In Living Color'," 392.

63 Gray, *Watching Race*, 140.

64 Butler, "Melancholy Gender," 33.

65 Gray, *Watching Race*, 140.

66 See Johnson, "SNAP! Culture."

67 Butler, "Melancholy Gender," 35.

3 Mother Knows Best:
Blackness and Transgressive Domestic Space

1 Butler, "Melancholy Gender/Refused Identification," 35.

2 Lubiano, "But Compared to What?," 183.

3 This research includes interviews of self-identified black gay men between the ages of twenty-five and forty-five who reside in the United States (including Atlanta; Greenville, S.C.; Durham, N.C.; Washington, D.C.; New York City; Springfield, Mass.; Chicago; and San Francisco). Pseudonyms are used to protect the identity of the informants. Moreover, while the informants in this study live in various parts of the United States, the majority of them live in the South and Northeast. Therefore, while many of the terms and phrases discussed herein are found in various black gay communities, their usage and function may differ according to region. Finally, because of the limitations of this study, I do not examine the vernacular traditions of black lesbians. I might add, however, that there is both overlap and major divergence in the ways in which black gay men and women deploy language, mostly due to gendered ways of speaking.

4 "A House Is Not a Home," written by Hal David. Rec. in 1981 by Luther Vandross, *Always and Forever: The Classics*, Epic, 1998.

5 In the black gay community, rumors about Luther Vandross's homosexuality have circulated for years. Indeed, the rumors are so embedded in black gay culture that references to his gayness have been incorporated into plays and cited in scholarly essays. Although Vandross has never publicly outed himself, he has often spoken of his significant other in the third person (e.g., "When I find *that* special someone *they* will have to . . ."). On his CD titled *Songs*, in which he remade love ballads, he does not change the gender of the song's subject in the remake of Roberta Flack's "Killing Me Softly" (e.g., "*He* was strumming my pain with *his* fingers"), which led many to speculate that Vandross is indeed singing to another man. For a "queer" reading of Luther Vandross as cultural icon, and especially of his remake of "A House Is Not a Home," see Jason King, "Any Love: Silence, Theft, and Rumor in the Work of Luther Vandross," *Callaloo* 23.1 (2000): 422–47.

6 According to Steven Mintz and Susan Kellogg, by the mid-1980s less than 15 percent of American households reflected the traditional family. More women were working and postponing marriage for their careers, divorce rates were up, birthrates were down, and single-parent homes were becoming a "normal" concept. It is no wonder, then, that we witnessed the feminist "backlash" that Susan Faludi suggests was brought on by the Reagan presidency. See Steven Mintz and Susan Kellogg, *Domestic Revolutions: A Social History of American Family Life* (New York: Free Press, 1988); and Faludi, *Backlash*.

7 Chandan Reddy, "Home, House, and Nonidentity: *Paris Is Burning*," in *Burning Down the House: Recycling Domesticity*, ed. Rosemary George (Boulder: Westview Press, 1997), 367.

8 See Johnson, "Feeling the Spirit in the Dark."

9 Anthony Thomas, "The House the Kids Built: The Gay Black Imprint on American Dance Music," in *Out in Culture: Gay, Lesbian, and Queer Essays on Popular Culture*, ed. Corey K. Creekmur and Alexander Doty (Durham: Duke University Press, 1990), 438. For other readings of the function of house music, see Brian Currid, "We Are Family: House Music and Queer Performativity," in *Cruising the Performative: Interventions into the Representations of Ethnicity, Nationality, and Sexuality*, ed. Sue Ellen Case, Phillip Brett, and Susan Foster (Bloomington: Indiana University Press, 1995), 165–96.

10 *Living with Pride: Ruth Ellis @ 100*, dir. Yvonne Welbon, Our Film Works Productions, 1999. All quotes from the film are my transcriptions.

11 For a detailed analysis of the function of "house" and "home" in *Paris Is Burning* as these terms relate to the exclusion of gays by heterosexuals, see Reddy, "Home, Houses, Nonidentity." See also Peggy Phelan, "The

Golden Apple: Jennie Livingston's *Paris Is Burning*," in her *Unmarked: The Politics of Performance*, 93–111; and Phillip Brian Harper, *"Paris Is Burning*, Social Critique and the Limits of Subjective Agency," in his *Private Affairs: Critical Ventures in the Culture of Social Relations* (New York: New York University Press, 1999), 33–59.

12 In the film, "legendary" refers to someone who has won a number of drag/vogue ball contests.

13 *Paris Is Burning*, dir. Jennie Livingston, Off-White Productions, 1990. All quotes from the film are my transcriptions.

14 Phil Hubbard, "Sex Zones: Intimacy, Citizenship, and Public Space," *Sexualities* 4.1 (2001): 56.

15 Ibid., 57. For further discussion of the drag/vogue performers in *Paris Is Burning* and citizenship, see Harper, "The Subversive Edge," in his *Private Affairs*, 33–59.

16 Essex Hemphill, "To Be Real," in *Ceremonies* (San Francisco: Cleis Press, 1992), 126.

17 Victor Turner, *From Ritual to Theatre: The Human Seriousness of Play* (New York: PAJ Publications, 1982), 44.

18 Muñoz, *Disidentifications*.

19 Kath Weston, *Families We Choose: Lesbians, Gays, Kinship* (New York: Columbia University Press, 1991) 22.

20 William G. Hawkeswood, *One of the Children: Gay Black Men in Harlem* (Berkeley: University of California Press, 1996), 62.

21 "Rob," interview with the author, June 20, 2000. Subsequent quotations are from this interview.

22 Thomas, "The House the Kids Built," 438.

23 In Lacanian psychoanalytic terms, the "Law of the Father" refers to the symbolic law that governs kinship systems in which one is forbidden sexual access to those the father has named as family. The concept has less to do with biology and more to do with a discursive system that maintains patriarchal control, including social laws. See Elizabeth Grosz, *Jacques Lacan: A Feminist Introduction* (New York: Routledge, 1990), 67–74.

24 Deborah Gray White, *Ar'n't I a Woman? Female Slaves in the Plantation South* (New York: Norton, 1985), 145.

25 See Susan Tucker, *Telling Memories among Southern Women: Domestic Workers and Their Employers in the Segregated South* (Baton Rouge: Louisiana State University Press, 1988); Jacqueline Jones, *Labor of Love, Labor of Sorrow: Black Women, Work and the Family from Slavery to the Present* (New York: Vintage, 1985), 110–51; and Paula Giddings, *When and Where I Enter: The Impact of Black Women on Race and Sex in America* (New York: William Morrow, 1984).

26 Daniel Patrick Moynihan, *The Negro Family: The Case for National Action*

(Washington, D.C.: GPO, 1965). For a critique of the Moynihan report as well as a well-theorized history of the role of black women in the black family, see Hortense Spillers, "Mama's Baby, Papa's Maybe: An American Grammar Book," *Diacritics* 17.2 (1987): 61–87.

27 Essex Hemphill, "The Father, Son and Unholy Ghosts," in *Tongues Untied*, Dirg Aaab-Richards, Craig G. Harris, Essex Hemphill, Isaac Jackson, Assotto Sainte (London: GMP, 1987), 50–54.

28 Leo Bersani, "Is the Rectum a Grave?" in *AIDS: Cultural Analysis, Cultural Criticism*, ed. Douglas Crimp (Cambridge: MIT Press, 1988), 197–222.

29 I should quickly note that I do not wish to paint the black community as necessarily more homophobic than white communities. My discussion here is offered to explain the complexity of the origin and varying degrees of black heterosexual homophobia. Insofar as black heterosexual men's homophobia is merely a reflection of that found in the white heterosexual supremacist society in which we live, black gay men's disavowal of stereotypical masculine tropes and performances reflects a general disdain of hegemonic masculinity. Given the oppression enacted in the name of the father it is not surprising that black gay men would be hesitant to emulate the father figure in black gay culture.

30 I should also note that just as black gay men embrace tropes of black femininity, black lesbians embrace tropes of black masculinity. For example, Judith Halberstam, in her book *Female Masculinity* (Durham: Duke University Press, 1998), notes "whereas a white drag king might parody a macho guy from Brooklyn . . . a black drag king tends to lip-synch to a rap song or perform as a macdaddy or playboy or pimp character . . . not to parody, but to appropriate black masculine style for dyke performance" (257). The disavowal of masculine tropes by black gay men and feminine tropes by black lesbians suggests not only the performativity of gender but also that men and women are, as Eve Sedgwick suggests, simultaneously consumers, producers, and performers of masculinity and femininity (Sedgwick, "Gosh, Boy George, You Must Be Awfully Secure in Your Masculinity!" in *Constructing Masculinity*, ed. Maurice Berger, Brian Wallis, and Simon Watson [New York: Routledge, 1995], 11–20).

31 See for example, Hazel Carby, *Race Men* (Cambridge: Harvard University Press, 1998), 1–6.

32 See Johnson, "SNAP! Culture."

33 "Gil," interview with the author, April 4, 1999. Subsequent quotations are from this interview.

34 I discuss the term "children" later in this chapter.

35 Jackie Goldsby, "Queens of Language: *Paris Is Burning*," in *Queer Looks:*

Perspectives on Lesbian and Gay Film and Video, ed. Martha Gever, John Greyson, and Pratibha Parmar (New York: Routledge, 1995), 109.

36 "Kirby," interview with the author, January 8, 1999.

37 "Vancouver," interview with the author, October 6, 2000.

38 Eddie Murphy's stand-up routine in *Delirious* is a prime example of this depiction of black mothers.

39 Personal conversation, June 1998.

40 "Brett," interview with the author, October 7, 1999.

41 "BJ," interview with the author, April 20, 1999.

42 In Marlon Riggs's 1990 documentary *Tongues Untied*, there is a scene between two black gay men walking down the street, one of whom relates to the camera the way "houses" function on the vogue ball scene. The other man, who apparently lives in Washington, D.C., reveals that he has never heard of such practices, to which the other responds, "Well, that's what they do here in New York. Each state, each gay community, does different things. Like your community in D.C. speak 'aga.'" I make this point here to demonstrate that the uses of "mother" may also vary from region to region.

43 Personal conversation, May 2000.

44 "CB," interview with the author, November 28, 1999.

45 This is not to suggest that an actual black female churchgoer does not have middle-class status or that such status wouldn't contribute to her conservatism. I am suggesting instead that the trope of such a persona registers as someone whose religious convictions and not her class status positions her as pious.

46 "Dee," interview with the author, April 11, 1999.

47 Hubbard, "Sex Zones," 53.

48 I realize that I am treading on thin ice here. I neither want to diminish the prevalence of black gay male misogyny nor the fact of black female oppression. What I wish to do is discuss the complexities of how identity formations and subject positions may allow for the inhabitance of more than one social location. An example is the ways in which white women are the objects of gender oppression but at the same time enact racial oppression.

49 Hubbard, "Sex Zones," 57.

50 Hemphill, *Ceremonies*, 133.

51 During the days of slavery, black Christians often likened themselves to the Hebrew "children" who were oppressed under the rule of Pharaoh. Thus, being called "children of God" or a "child of God" is part of the black church vernacular.

52 Black feminists have also located "home" as a contested and ambivalent space. For example, see bell hooks, "Homeplace: A Site of Resistance,"

in *Yearning: Race, Gender, and Cultural Politics* (Boston: South End Press, 1990), 41–49; Jewell Gomez and Barbara Smith, "Taking the Home Out of Homophobia: Black Lesbians Look in Their Own Backyards," *Outlook* 8 (1990): 32–37; and Smith, *Home Girls*.

53 Joseph Beam, "Brother to Brother: Words from the Heart," in *In the Life: A Black Gay Anthology*, ed. Joseph Beam (Boston: Alyson Press, 1986), 231.

54 Reddy, "Home, House, and Nonidentity," 373.

55 Goldsby, "Queens of Language," 114.

56 Butler, *Bodies That Matter*, 240–41.

4 "Nevah Had uh Cross Word": Mammy and the Trope of Black Womanhood

1 Jones, *Labor of Love, Labor of Sorrow;* and Elizabeth Fox-Genovese, *Within the Plantation Household: Black and White Women of the Old South* (Chapel Hill: University of North Carolina Press, 1988).

2 Trudier Harris, *From Mammies to Militants: Domestics in Black American Literature* (Philadelphia: Temple University Press, 1982).

3 Judith Rollins, *Between Women: Domestics and Their Employers* (Philadelphia: Temple University Press, 1985).

4 Patricia Turner, *Ceramic Uncles and Celluloid Mammies: Black Images and Their Influence on Culture* (New York: Anchor, 1994).

5 Frantz Fanon, *Black Skin, White Mask* (New York: Grove Weidenfeld Press, 1967).

6 Turner, *Ceramic Uncles*, 25.

7 Rollins, *Between Women*, 169.

8 Harris, *From Mammies to Militants*, 16.

9 Fanon, *Black Skin*, 17.

10 Michel de Certeau, *The Practice of Everyday Life* (Berkeley: University of California Press, 1984), 37.

11 Collins, *Black Feminist Thought*, 11.

12 de Certeau, *Practice of Everyday Life*, 37.

13 See Gates, *The Signifying Monkey: A Theory of African-American Literary Criticism* (Oxford: Oxford University Press, 1988); and Bruce Jackson, *"Get Your Ass in the Water and Swim Like Me": Narrative Poetry from the Black Oral Tradition* (Cambridge: Harvard University Press, 1974).

14 Gates, *Signifying Monkey*, 9–20.

15 John Langston Gwaltney, *Drylongso: A Self-Portrait of Black America* (New York: Random House, 1980), 240.

16 "Mary Rhyne" is a pseudonym to protect both my grandmother's identity and those whom she mentions in her narrative.

17 In "On the Writing of Ethnography," Vincent Crapanzano discusses the duality of "self-constitution" when he writes: "The ethnographer wants to reconstitute his old self—or his new professional self—through an act of writing that is addressed to the significant others within his own world. He wants, too, to address, and must inevitably address, those illiterate others of his fieldwork—not simply out of good faith, professional responsibility, obligation, but also out of a necessity to declare them worthy of having been and continuing to be that silent audience by which he identifies himself as an ethnographer and obtains his sense of self" (Crapanzano, "On the Writing of Ethnography," *Dialectical Anthropology* 2 (1977): 72.

18 The symbols I use to transcribe the narrative are the same as those used by D. Soyini Madison. Madison believes that "by placing words on a page in a way that resembles the human voice and the speaker as a social-historical being who colors each word based on that existential fact, the text comes closer to capturing the depth inherent in the indigenous performance speech" (Madison, " 'That Was My Occupation': Oral Narrative, Performance, and Black Feminist Thought," in *Exceptional Spaces: Essays in Performance and History*, ed. Della Pollock [Chapel Hill: University of North Carolina Press, 1998], 323). Note that Madison's transcription method is a hybrid of those developed by Elizabeth Fine and Dennis Tedlock. For more on the performance-centered transcription method, see Fine, *The Folklore Text;* and Dennis Tedlock, *The Spoken Word and the Work of Interpretation* (Philadelphia: University of Pennsylvania Press, 1983).

19 My grandmother's work schedule was not atypical for domestics in the South. In fact, hers was a more humane situation compared to workloads chronicled in other studies about southern domestic workers. See Elizabeth Clark-Lewis, *Living In, Living Out: African American Domestics and the Great Migration* (New York: Kodansha Globe, 1996), 9–49.

20 Six years after my interview with Mrs. Smith, she was diagnosed with Alzheimer's and currently resides in a nursing home.

21 Ruby and Claudine, as well as many of the other residents of Tate Terrace who lived there at the time of my interview with Mary, are now deceased.

22 Since the writing of this chapter, due to her declining health my grandmother spends most of her days in Hickory with her granddaughter, who lives next door to my mother. Still adamant about retaining her independence, however, Mary still maintains her apartment in Kings Mountain.

23 See E. Patrick Johnson, "An Ethnography of Performance: Interpreting the Personal Narrative of Mary Rhyne," Master's thesis, University of North Carolina, 1991.

24 This quote from Mrs. Smith, as well as all others in this chapter, are

from my interview with her on August 5, 1994. The complete text of this interview appears in appendix B.

25 Rollins, *Between Women*, 64.

26 A mill house is a house made of cinder blocks that is usually white-washed on the outside. The name mill house comes from the use of these buildings as residences for people who worked in cotton and furniture mills. There were usually whole communities of mill workers who lived in these kinds of houses.

27 Rollins, *Between Women*, 63.

28 In recent history there have been a number of public figures, especially presidential nominees for important cabinet positions, who have been denied appointment by Congress because it was discovered that they had illegally employed domestics.

29 See Paul Eckman and Wallace Friesen, "The Repertoire of Nonverbal Behavior: Categories, Origins, Usage and Coding," *Semiotica* 1 (1969): 70.

30 Carol Simpson Stern and Bruce Henderson, *Performance: Texts and Contexts* (New York: Longman, 1993), 321.

31 For more on women laborers' "choreography of labor" and identity, see Sally Ann Ness, *Body, Movement, and Culture: Kinesthetic and Visual Symbolism in a Philippine Community* (Philadelphia: University of Pennsylvania Press, 1992).

32 Mikhail Bakhtin, *Rabelais and His World*, trans. Hélène Iswolsky (Bloomington: Indiana University Press, 1984), 19.

33 Peter Stallybrass and Allon White, *The Politics and Poetics of Transgression* (Ithaca: Cornell University Press, 1986), 23.

34 Bakhtin, *Rabelais*, 317.

35 See Harris, *From Mammies to Militants*, 15.

36 David Katzman, *Seven Days a Week: Women and Domestic Service in Industrializing America* (New York: Oxford University Press, 1978), 108.

37 See ibid., 188–89.

38 Toni Morrison, *The Bluest Eye* (New York: Washington Square Press, 1970), 100–1.

39 Harris, *From Mammies to Militants*, 62.

40 Rollins, *Between Women*, 193.

41 de Certeau, *Practice of Everyday Life*, 18.

42 Ervin Goffman, "The Nature of Deference and Demeanor," *American Anthropologist* 58 (1956): 473.

43 See Goffman, "The Nature of Defence," 477, 481.

44 Alice Childress, *Like One of the Family: Conversations from a Domestic's Life* (Boston: Beacon, 1986), 2.

45 Victor Turner, *The Anthropology of Performance* (New York: Performing Arts Journal Publications, 1986), 168.

46 Richard Schechner, *Performance Theory* (New York: Routledge, 1988), 171.
47 See Kristin Langellier, "Personal Narratives: Perspectives on Theory and Research," *Text and Performance Quarterly* 9 (1989): 243–76.
48 Lawrence Levine, *Black Culture and Black Consciousness: Afro-American Thought from Slavery to Freedom* (Oxford: Oxford University Press, 1977), 123.
49 Katzman, *Seven Days a Week,* 193.
50 Up until December 1993, Mary and Mrs. Smith maintained a "visit"-to-work relationship. Apparently, when Mary came to Hickory to see her children, Mrs. Smith would ask Mary to "visit." The "visit" was actually a euphemism for "work." Although on many occasions Mary obliged Mrs. Smith's request, at other times she avoided contact with her. Grandmother details her later relationship with Mrs. Smith in the episode "We All Just One Family."
51 Hortense Spillers, "Fabrics of History: Essays on the Black Sermon," Ph.D. diss., Brandeis University, 1974, 4.
52 Turner, *The Anthropology of Performance,* 169.
53 Collins, *Black Feminist Thought,* 72.
54 Harris, *From Mammies to Militants,* 21.
55 D. Soyini Madison, ed., *The Woman That I Am: The Literature and Culture of Contemporary Women of Color* (New York: St. Martin's Press, 1994), 1.
56 See, Anne Doueihi, "Inhabiting the Space between Discourse and Story in Trickster Narratives," in *Mythical Trickster Figures: Contours, Contexts, and Criticisms,* ed. William J. Hynes and William G. Doty (Tuscaloosa: University of Alabama Press, 1993), 199.

5 Sounds of Blackness Down Under:
The Café of the Gate of Salvation

1 Richard Schechner, "Believed-in Theatre," *Performance Research* 2.2 (1997): 89–90.
2 Little attention has been given to the social, cultural, and political significance of black gospel music. Indeed, most of the scholarship on gospel music focuses on the music's history. Two exceptions are Michael W. Harris, *The Rise of Gospel Blues: The Music of Thomas Dorsey in the Urban Church* (New York: Oxford University Press, 1992); and Joyce Jackson, "The Changing Nature of Gospel Music: A Southern Case Study," *Black American Review* 29 (1995): 2. See also Mellonee Burnim, "The Black Gospel Music Tradition: Symbol of Ethnicity," Ph.D. diss., Indiana University, 1980.

I also want to emphasize that I construe gospel as a *signifier* of black-ness, rather than equate the two. Inasmuch as gospel music arose from black culture, it is most often associated with black people. Nonetheless, there are countless black people who do not sing, perform, or value gospel music and who do not register it as a part of their experience of race. For more on the history of gospel music, see Horace Boyer, *How Sweet the Sound: The Golden Age of Gospel* (Washington, D.C.: Elliott and Clark, 1995); and Tony Heilbut, *The Gospel Sound: Good News and Bad Times* (New York: Simon and Schuster, 1971).

3 My research for this study occurred over the six-year period from 1996 to 2002 and included six trips to Australia, with each trip lasting from three to six weeks. During these trips I formally interviewed fifteen members of an Australian gospel choir called the Café of the Gate of Salvation and informally interviewed thirty-five Australian gospel singers at workshops I conducted in Sydney, Canberra, Wollongong, Newcastle, Melbourne, Adelaide, and Perth. Not all of the interviews are referenced in this chapter. Except where indicated by omission, the subjects interviewed all consented to using their full, real names.

4 In black American culture, being "fashionably" late is often referred to as CPT or "colored people's time."

5 I credit Emith Toth with this phrase.

6 Tony Backhouse, interview with the author, June 8, 1996. Subsequent quotations are from this interview. What Tony is actually describing here is called heterophony, a musical term used to describe singing that is not in harmony but rather a mixture of voices singing in unison with one or two voices harmonizing in between. This style of singing is common in standard black American worship services, particularly in rural southern churches.

7 Judy Backhouse, interview with the author, January 10, 1998. Subsequent quotations are from this interview.

8 Tony Backhouse et al., liner notes, *Café of the Gate of Salvation*, Polygram, 1991.

9 Liz Strickland, interview with the author, June 9, 1996. Subsequent quotations are from this interview.

10 Tony Backhouse, "In the Spirit," *Café of the Gate of Salvation*, Polygram, 1991.

11 "Praise the Lord and Pass the Lipstick," *HQ* (January/February 1995): 107–8.

12 Scott Bennett, "Still Some Heaven Left to Find," *Café of the Gate of Salvation*, Polygram, 1991.

13 Tony Backhouse, "Blessèd Is," *A Window in Heaven*, Polygram, 1993.

14 Tracey Greenberg, "Love and Joy," *A Window in Heaven*, Polygram, 1995.

15 Tracey Greenberg, interview with the author, June 14, 1996. Subsequent quotations are from this interview.

16 "Praise the Lord and Pass the Lipstick," 106.

17 Jane MacClean, interview with the author, January 20, 1998. Subsequent quotations are from this interview.

18 One might argue that Christianity is also not the indigenous religion of enslaved blacks, yet many adopted it. While this is true, enslaved blacks also employed Christianity as a survival mechanism.

19 Judith, interview with the author, June 12, 1996. Subsequent quotations are from this interview.

20 Scot Morris, interview with the author, June 8, 1996. Subsequent quotations are from this interview.

21 Not all members of the choir disavow Christianity. In fact, there are a few members who call themselves "Christian" but who are not "saved" in the black American religious sense. Rather, they are "walking by faith."

22 Kirk Franklin, "Why We Sing," *Kirk Franklin and the Family,* Gospo Centric, 1993.

23 Deborah, interview with the author, June 12, 1996. Subsequent quotations are from this interview.

24 Fi, personal conversation with the author, August 24, 1999.

25 Tony Backhouse, "Introduction," *A Cappella: RehearSING for Heaven* (Chatswood, N.S.W.: Redback Press, 1995), 1.

26 In fact, this focus on the history of gospel and the "empowerment" gleaned from that history was one of the motivations for the choir organizing a trip to the United States. They felt that by experiencing this music in the context in which it is performed they would better understand what makes it so uplifting. According to Judy Backhouse, she and Tony wanted the choir to "see what they're representing and which tradition they're relating to. I don't think they really realize. We think they'd be really inspired and it would make a huge difference in their singing, to their heart relationship to it." Eventually, the choir did travel to the United States, visiting churches in New York, Alabama, and New Orleans. As I discuss later in the chapter, the trip to the United States did "change" them in various ways—in ways that complicated their earlier tendency to universalize gospel music.

27 Quoted in Lauren Martin, "A Black and White Gospel," *Sydney Morning Herald,* September 13, 1999, 12.

28 Robert Hughes, *The Fatal Shore,* (New York: Knopf, 1987), 2.

29 Anonymous, personal conversation with the author, August 24, 1999.

30 Hughes, *The Fatal Shore,* 158–59.

31 Micaela di Leonardo, *Exotics at Home: Anthropologies, Others, American Modernity* (Chicago: University of Chicago Press, 1998), 1–24.

32 Hughes, *The Fatal Shore*, 7.

33 Debra Jopson, "Stolen Generation Test Case Crashes," *Sydney Morning Herald*, August 27, 1999, 5.

34 Peggy Brock, *Outback Ghettos: Aborigines, Institutionalization, and Survival* (Cambridge: Cambridge University Press, 1990), 2.

35 Noel Loos and Jane Thomson, "Black Resistance Past and Present: An Overview," in *Black Australians: The Prospects For Change*, ed. Erik Olbrei (Townsville: James Cook University of North Queensland, 1982), 10.

36 "Music Fills Minds, Minds Make a Difference," *Revolver*, January 21, 1998, 17.

37 In an e-mail he wrote to me after reading a draft of this chapter, Tony Backhouse offered reasons why he and other singers are more attracted to black American gospel music over Aboriginal or Maori music. Tony states: "The Aboriginal question: that's partly situational, in that aside from a part-Aboriginal I shared a house with in New Zealand once, I've had very little contact with Aboriginals. Similarly, where I grew up in NZ, there were virtually no Maoris. If we'd heard Aboriginal (or Maori) music on the radio growing up, we would no doubt have a different idea of the culture. As it is, I heard American music. So did all the other whites—and it's easier to identify with someone singing in your language. As an adult I've worked in a Maori performing arts college, played in a Maori band and had a Maori girlfriend, but we all listened to black [American] music. (I support the Aboriginal cause through processes like Australians for Native Title and Reconciliation, but I don't feel drawn to explore the Aboriginal culture in the way I feel drawn to others—African American, East European, Renaissance European, etc. Can't speak for anyone else, of course.) One of the reasons we feel more at ease with African American culture is its accessibility and its high level of visibility (or audibility)—not only is it available and influential via the radio, but in the case of gospel, its very message encourages an openness (outreach) and African Americans seem to take pride in their gifts to the world: gospel, spirituals, and more. In the case of the Aboriginals or the Maori, they are far more protective of their cultures (understandably unwilling to see them diluted or misunderstood) thus keep a distance from the white culture (understandably)." Tony's statements speak to the imperialism of U.S. capitalism and the commodification and dissemination of black art forms, as well as to the complexity and politics of cultural imbrication within domestic spaces. For example, what accounts for one marginal group being "far more protective of their cultures" and the other offering its traditions as "gifts to the world"?

38 Ben Sidran, *Black Talk* (1971; New York: Da Capo, 1981), 17.

39 Jackson, "The Changing Nature of Gospel Music," 185.

40 This is a common statement made by choir directors or soloists just be-

fore they are about to begin singing. This expression not only demonstrates their deference to God as the one on whom the church should focus, but it also indirectly focuses more attention on the performer, especially if he or she sings exceptionally well.

41 Paul Gilroy, "Sounds Authentic: Black Music, Ethnicity, and the Challenge of a Changing Same" in *Imagining Home: Class, Culture, and Nationalism in the Black Diaspora*, ed. Sidney Lemelle and Robin D. G. Kelley (New York: Verso, 1994), 103.

42 Cheryl, interview with the author, June 12, 1996.

43 Gilroy, "Sounds Authentic," 104.

44 *AUBC Newsletter*, vol. 1, August 1999, 1. The quotations in this section are from the author's field notes of August 29, 1999.

45 Gilroy, "Sounds Authentic," 104.

46 Stephen Taberner, "In Search of What We Are Searching For," *Oral Majority* 52 (October 1999): 10.

47 I do not mean to suggest that the circulation of these flyers announcing my gospel music workshops is the same as those flyers that reduced enslaved blacks to objects. Rather, I merely make the point that the two flyers are discursively interconnected in that they authenticate, by way of fetishizing and commodifying, black bodies.

48 Briar Eyers, personal conversation with the author, September 8, 1999.

49 Anonymous, personal conversation with the author, September 9, 1999.

50 E. Patrick Johnson, interview with Peter Thompson, ABC Radio National, March 19, 1998.

51 E. Patrick Johnson, interview with Philip Adams, *Late Night Live*, ABC Radio National, August 17, 1999.

52 E. Patrick Johnson, interview with Richard Glover, 2BL ABC, Sydney, August 19, 1999.

53 Gilroy, "Sounds Authentic," 105.

54 Ibid., 108–9.

55 Turner, *From Ritual to Theater*, 44.

56 Conquergood, "Performing Cultures," 59.

57 Victor Turner, "A Review of 'Ethnopoetics,'" in *Symposium of the Whole: A Range of Discourse Toward an Ethnopoetics*, ed. Jerome Rothenberg and Diane Rothenberg (Berkeley: University of California Press, 1983), 338.

58 Dwight Conquergood, "Between Experience and Meaning: Performance as a Paradigm for Meaningful Action," in *Renewal and Revision: The Future of Interpretation*, ed. Ted Colson (Denton, Tex.: Omega, 1986), 47–48.

59 Dwight Conquergood, "Performing as a Moral Act: Ethical Dimensions of the Ethnography of Performance," *Literature in Performance* 5.2 (1985): 10.

60 D. Soyini Madison, "Performance, Personal Narratives, and the Politics

of Possibility," in *The Future of Performance Studies: The Next Millennium,*
ed. Sheron J. Dailey (Annandale, VA: National Communication Association, 1998).

61 On "felt-sensing," see Wallace Bacon, *The Art of Interpretation* (New York:
Holt, Rinehart and Winston, 1979).

62 Judith Carson, e-mail to the author, April 20, 1998.

63 Madison, "Performance, Personal Narratives," 284.

64 Conquergood, "Performing as a Moral Act," 8.

65 Dwight Conquergood, "Between Experience and Expression: The Performed Myth," in *Essays on the Theory, Practice, and Criticism of Performance: Festchrift for Isabel Crouch,* ed. Wallace A. Bacon (Las Cruces, New
Mexico: New Mexico State University, 1988) 34.

66 Madison, "Performance, Personal Narrative," 278.

67 Schechner, "Believed-in Theatre," 89–90.

6 Performance and/as Pedagogy:
Performing Blackness in the Classroom

1 Poststructuralism also created quite a stir in the field of what was then
called Oral Interpretation. So influential were these poststructuralist
theories that a whole issue of *Literature in Performance* (now *Text and
Performance Quarterly*) was devoted to the topic in 1983. See Eric E.
Peterson, "Representation and the Limits of Interpretation"; John Hollo-
witz, "The Performance Psychology of Jacques Lacan"; Kay Ellen Capo,
"Performance of Literature as Social Dialect"; Jacqueline Taylor, "Performance Centered Research: Post-Structuralist Implications"; Carol
Simpson Stern, "Deconstruction and the Phenomenological Alterna-
tive"; Kristin Minister, "Doing Deconstruction: The Extra-Institutional
Performance of Literature"; Jill Taft-Kaufman, "Deconstructing the
Text: Performance Implications"; and Stanley Deetz, "Response: The
Politics of the Oral Interpretation of Literature," all in *Literature in Per-
formance* 4.1 (1983): 21–64. For more recent articulations of postmod-
ernism and performance studies, see Ron Pelias and James Van Oosting,
"A Paradigm for Performance Studies," *Quarterly Journal of Speech* 73
(1987): 219–31; Conquergood, "Between Experience and Meaning"; and
Mary Strine, "Articulating Performance: Disciplinary Tasks and the Con-
tingencies of Practice," paper presented at the Speech Communication
Association Convention, San Diego, California, November 1996.

2 See Conquergood, "Performing as a Moral Act."

3 Stephen Henderson, *Understanding the New Black Poetry: Black Music
and Black Speech as Poetic References* (New York: William Morrow, 1973),

excerpted in *African American Literary Criticism, 1773–2000*, ed. Hazel Ervin (New York: Twayne, 1999), 141 (my emphasis).

4   Joyce A. Joyce, "The Black Canon: Reconstructing Black American Literary Criticism," in *African American Literary Criticism: A Reader*, ed. Winston Napier (New York: New York University Press, 2000), 293.

5   Henry Louis Gates Jr., "What's Love Got to Do with It? Critical Theory, Integrity, and the Black Idiom," in Napier, ed., *African American Literary Criticism: A Reader*, 301.

6   Houston A. Baker Jr., "In Dubious Battle," in Napier, ed., *African American Literary Criticism: A Reader*, 313.

7   Ironically, in an essay published just six years earlier, Baker, like Joyce, equates the black middle-class critic's socioeconomic status with the disavowal of "authentic" black literary criticism. Indeed, Baker suggests that the 1970s saw the "emergence of Afro-American spokesmen whose class status (new, black middle-class) and privileges are, in fact, contingent upon their adherence to accepted (i.e., white) standards of their profession" (Baker, "Generational Shifts and the Recent Criticism of Afro-American Literature," in Napier, ed., *African American Literary Criticism: A Reader*, 196).

8   Henry Louis Gates Jr., *The Signifying Monkey: A Theory of Afro-American Literary Criticism* (New York: Oxford University Press, 1988), xix.

9   Gates, "What's Love Got to Do with It?" 304.

10 Houston A. Baker Jr., *Long Black Song* (Charlottesville: University of Virginia Press, 1970).

11 See Toni Morrison, *Playing in the Dark: Whiteness and the Literary Imagination* (New York: Vintage, 1992).

12 Both Gates and Baker eschew such delimitations in their subsequent work. See, for example, Gates's *Loose Canons: Notes on the Culture War* (New York: Oxford University Press, 1993); and Baker's "Belief, Theory, and Blues: Notes for a Post-Structuralist Criticism of Afro-American Literature," in Napier, ed., *African American Literary Criticism: A Reader*, 224–41.

13 Bernard Bell, "Voices of Double Consciousness in African American Fiction: Charles W. Chestnutt, Zora Neale Hurston, Dorothy West, and Richard Wright," in *Teaching African American Literature: Theory and Practice*, ed. Maryemma Graham, Sharon Pineault-Burke, and Marianna White Davis (New York: Routledge, 1998), 132.

14 Jane Skelton, "Multiple Voices, Multiple Identities: Teaching African American Literature," in Graham et al., eds., *Teaching African American Literature*, 54.

15 See Aldon Nielsen, *Reading Race in American Poetry: An Area of Act* (Champaign: University of Illinois Press, 2000); Ruth Frankenburg, ed.,

Displacing Whiteness: Essays in Social and Cultural Criticism (Durham: Duke University Press, 1997); Mike Hill, ed., *Whiteness: A Critical Reader* (New York: New York University Press, 1997); Lipsitz, *The Possessive Investment in Whiteness;* and David Roediger, *The Wages of Whiteness: Race and the Making of the American Working Class* (New York: Verso, 1990).

16 See Noel Ignatiev, *How the Irish Became White* (New York: Routledge, 1995).

17 Ann Louise Keating, "Interrogating 'Whiteness,' (De)Constructing 'Race,'" in Graham et al., eds., *Teaching African American Literature*, 205.

18 Trudier Harris, "Lying through Our Teeth? The Quagmire of Cultural Diversity," in Graham et al., eds., *Teaching African American Literature*, 213–14.

19 Jonathan Culler, *The Pursuit of Signs: Semiotics, Literature, Deconstruction* (Ithaca: Cornell University Press, 1981), 103.

20 Aldon Nielsen, *Writing between the Lines: Race and Intertextuality* (Athens: University of Georgia Press, 1994).

21 Ibid., 24.

22 Michel Foucault, *Discipline and Punish: The Birth of the Prison*, trans. Alan Sheridan (New York: Vintage, 1995).

23 See Bryant Keith Alexander, "Embracing the Teachable Moment: The Black Gay Body in the Classroom as Embodied Text," in *Black Queer Studies: A Critical Anthology*, ed. E. Patrick Johnson and Mae G. Henderson (Durham: Duke University Press, forthcoming).

24 According to "Points of View: Ethnicity at Amherst," a publication produced by the Amherst College Admissions Office and Office of Public Affairs, the class of 1998 "was made up of a record 32.7 percent minority students. This percentage is more than double that of minority students enrolling in 1987" (23).

25 Alice Walker, "To Hell with Dying," in *In Love and Trouble* (San Diego: Harcourt Brace Jovanovich, 1973), 137.

26 I have used a pseudonym here to protect the identity of the student.

27 Alice Walker, "Everyday Use," in *In Love and Trouble*, 53.

28 Diana Fuss, *Essentially Speaking: Feminism, Nature, and Difference* (New York: Routledge, 1989), 113.

29 I'm not at all suggesting that any of these behaviors are necessarily or exclusively the domain of working-class African Americans. On the contrary, many middle- and upper-class African Americans dress and adorn themselves in the ways I describe, and this has nothing to do with their trying to perform black authenticity. In the instance of these students, however, by their own admission they were trying to avoid what they saw as assimilationist ways of being in the world, particularly in the context of Amherst College, where "whiteness" still provided a slightly more comfortable cachet than even class status. These students' performances

of black counterculture thus were meant to disavow an association with white hegemony.

30 Although I have generalized about the class status of the black students at Amherst, I wish to note that many of the students in my courses, of all racial backgrounds, were not from middle- and upper-class homes. In fact, many of my working-class students would lament the pressures of attending college with so many wealthy classmates. The fact that Amherst has any working-class students at all is due in part to its policy of need-blind admission. Nonetheless, more than 65 percent of its students receive no financial assistance—a telling statistic given that the tuition at Amherst is well over thirty thousand dollars a year.

31 Dwight Conquergood, "Performing as a Moral Act," 9.

32 I have used a pseudonym here to protect the identity of the student.

33 For further discussion of these phases, see Spillers, "Fabrics of History," 4.

34 Conquergood, "Performing as a Moral Act," 9.

35 For more on these pitfalls, see Conquergood, "Performing as a Moral Act."

36 Homi Bhabha, ed., *Nation and Narration* (New York: Routledge, 1990), 313.

37 Joni Jones, "Teaching in the Borderlands," in *Teaching Performance Studies*, ed. Nathan Stucky and Cynthia Wimmer (Carbondale: Southern Illinois University Press, 2002), 175.

38 Bacon, *The Art of Interpretation*.

39 Mary Strine, "Articulating Performance/Performativity," 10–11.

40 Mae Henderson, "What It Means to Teach the Other When the Other Is the Self," *Callaloo* 17.2 (1994): 432–38.

41 Ibid., 437.

42 Indira Karamcheti, "Caliban in the Classroom," in *Pedagogy*, ed. Jane Gallop (Bloomington: Indiana University Press, 1995), 146.

43 Butler, *Bodies That Matter*, 11.

44 Giddings, *When and Where I Enter*.

45 Karamcheti, "Caliban in the Classroom," 138.

46 Henderson, "What It Means to Teach the Other," 436.

47 No pun is intended here; "White" really is her last name.

48 Fuss, *Essentially Speaking*, 113.

49 Baldwin, *Another Country*.

50 Henderson, "What It Means to Teach the Other," 437.

BIBLIOGRAPHY

Alexander, Bryant. "Embracing the Teachable Moment: The Black Gay Body in the Classroom as Embodied Text." In *Black Queer Studies: A Critical Anthology,* ed. E. Patrick Johnson and Mae G. Henderson. Durham: Duke University Press, forthcoming.

Alexander, Elizabeth. " 'Can You Be Black and Watch This?' Reading the Rodney King Video(s)." In *Black Male: Representations of Black Masculinity in Contemporary Art,* ed. Thelma Golden. New York: Whitney Museum of Contemporary Art, 1994. 91–110.

Althusser, Louis. "Ideology and Ideological State Apparatuses." In *Lenin and Philosophy and Other Essays.* New York: Monthly Review Press, 1971.

Asante, Molefi. *Afrocentricity: The Theory of Social Change.* Buffalo: Amulefi, 1980.

Austin, J. L. *How to Do Things with Words.* Cambridge: Harvard University Press, 1975.

Backhouse, Tony. "Introduction." In *A Cappella: RehearSING for Heaven.* Chatswood, N. S. W.: Redback Press, 1995.

Bacon, Wallace. *The Art of Interpretation.* 3rd ed. New York: Holt, Rinehart and Winston, 1979.

Bakhtin, Mikhail. *The Dialogic Imagination.* Ed. Michael Holquist. Trans. Caryl Emerson and Michael Holquist. Austin: University of Texas Press, 1981.

————. "Discourse Typology in Prose." In *Readings in Russian Poetics: Formalist and Structuralist Views,* ed. Ladislav Matejka and Krystyna Pomorska. Cambridge: Harvard University Press, 1971. 17–196.

————. *Rabelais and His World.* Trans. Hélène Iswolsky. Bloomington: Indiana University Press, 1984.

Baker, Houston A. Jr. "Belief, Theory, and Blues: Notes for a Post-Structuralist Criticism of Afro-American Literature." In *African American*

Bibliography

Literary Criticism: A Reader, ed. Winston Napier. New York: New York University Press, 2000. 224–41.

——. "In Dubious Battle." In *African American Literary Criticism: A Reader*, ed. Winston Napier. New York: New York University Press, 2000. 313–18.

——. "Generational Shifts and the Recent Criticism of Afro-American Literature." In *African American Literary Criticism: A Reader*, ed. Winston Napier. New York: New York University Press, 2000. 179–217.

——. *Long Black Song*. Charlottesville: University of Virginia Press, 1970.

Baldwin, James. *Another Country*. New York: Knopf, 1994.

——. "Color." In *Baldwin: Collected Essays*. New York: Penguin Putnam, 1998. 673–77.

Baraka, Imamu Amiri [LeRoi Jones]. "Black Bourgeoisie." In *The Black Poets*, ed. Dudley Randall. New York: Bantam Books, 1971. 223.

——. "1965: American Sexual Reference." In *Home: Social Essays*. New York: William Morrow, 1966.

——. "Poem for Some Half White College Students." In *The Black Poets*, ed. Dudley Randall. New York: Bantam Books, 1971. 225.

——. *Selected Poetry of Amiri Baraka/LeRoi Jones*. New York: William Morrow, 1979.

——. *The System of Dante's Hell*. London: MacGibbon and Kee, 1966.

Bauman, Richard. *Story, Performance, and Event: Contextual Studies in Oral Narrative*. Cambridge: Cambridge University Press, 1986.

——. *Verbal Art as Performance*. Prospect Heights, Ill: Waveland Press, 1977.

Beam, Joseph. "Brother to Brother: Words from the Heart." In *In the Life: A Black Gay Anthology*, ed. Joseph Beam. Boston: Alyson Press, 1986. 231.

Becquer, Thomas. "SNAP!thology and Other Discursive Practices in *Tongues Untied*." *Wide Angle* 13.2 (1991): 7–17.

Bell, Bernard. "Voices of Double Consciousness in African American Fiction: Charles W. Chestnutt, Zora Neale Hurston, Dorothy West, and Richard Wright." In *Teaching African American Literature: Theory and Practice*, ed. Maryemma Graham, Sharon Pineault-Burke, and Marianna White Davis. New York: Routledge, 1998. 132–40.

Bendix, Regina. *In Search of Authenticity: The Formation of Folklore Studies*. Madison: University of Wisconsin Press, 1997.

Bennett, Scott. "Still Some Heaven Left for Me to Find." *Café of the Gate of Salvation*. Polygram, 1991.

Benston, Kimberly. *Performing Blackness: Enactments of African-American Modernism*. New York: Routledge, 2000.

Bersani, Leo. "Is the Rectum a Grave?" In *AIDS: Cultural Analysis, Cultural Criticism*, ed. Douglas Crimp. Cambridge: MIT Press, 1988. 197–222.

Bhabha, Homi, ed. *Nation and Narration*. New York: Routledge, 1990.

Bibliography

Black Is . . . Black Ain't. Dir. Marlon Riggs. Independent Film Series, 1995.

Boyer, Horace. *How Sweet the Sound: The Golden Age of Gospel.* Washington, D.C.: Elliott and Clark Publishing, 1995.

Brock, Peggy. *Outback Ghettos: Aborigines, Institutionalization, and Survival.* Cambridge: Cambridge University Press, 1990.

Brody, Jennifer. *Impossible Purities: Blackness, Femininity, and Victorian Culture.* Durham: Duke University Press, 1998.

Burnim, Mellonee. "The Black Gospel Music Tradition: Symbol of Ethnicity." Ph.D. diss, Indiana University, 1980.

Butler, Judith. *Bodies That Matter: On the Discursive Limits of "Sex."* New York: Routledge, 1993.

———. *Gender Trouble: Feminism and the Subversion of Identity.* New York: Routledge, 1990.

———. "Melancholy Gender/Refused Identification." In *Constructing Masculinity,* ed. Maurice Berger, Brian Wallis, and Simon Watson. New York: Routledge, 1995. 21–36.

Capo, Kay Ellen. "Performance of Literature as Social Dialect." *Literature in Performance* 4.1 (1983): 31–36.

Carby, Hazel. *Race Men.* Cambridge: Harvard University Press, 1998.

———. "The Sexual Politics of Women's Blues." In *Cultures of Babylon.* New York: Verso, 1999. 7–21.

Carlson, Marvin. *Performance: A Critical Introduction.* New York: Routledge, 1996.

Cheng, Anne Anlin. *The Melancholy of Race: Psychoanalysis, Assimilation, and Hidden Grief.* New York: Oxford University Press, 2001.

Childress, Alice. *Like One of the Family: Conversations from a Domestic's Life.* Boston: Beacon, 1986.

Christian, Barbara. *Black Feminist Criticism: Perspectives on Black Women Writers.* New York: Pergamon, 1985.

———. "The Race for Theory." *Feminist Studies* 14 (1988): 67–80.

Clark-Lewis, Elizabeth. *Living In, Living Out: African American Domestics and the Great Migration.* New York: Kodansha Globe, 1996.

Cleaver, Eldridge. *Soul on Ice.* New York: Laurel, 1968.

Cohen, Cathy J. *The Boundaries of Blackness: AIDS and the Breakdown of Black Politics.* Chicago: University of Chicago Press, 1999.

———. "Punks, Bulldaggers, and Welfare Queens: The Radical Potential of Queer Politics?" *GLQ* 3.4 (1997): 437–65.

Collins, Patricia Hill. *Black Feminist Thought: Knowledge, Consciousness, and the Politics of Empowerment.* New York: Routledge, 1990.

Conquergood, Dwight. "Between Experience and Expression: The Performed Myth." In *Essays on the Theory, Practice, and Criticism of Performance: Festchrift for Isabel Crouch.* ed. Wallace A. Bacon. Las Cruces, New Mexico: New Mexico State University, 1988. 33–57.

347

Bibliography

———. "Between Experience and Meaning: Performance as Paradigm for Meaningful Action." In *Renewal and Revision: The Future of Interpretation,* ed. Ted Colson. Denton, Tex.: Omega, 1986. 26–59.

———. "Performance Theory, Hmong Shamans, and Cultural Politics." In *Critical Theory and Performance,* ed. Janelle G. Reinelt and Joseph R. Roach. Ann Arbor: University of Michigan Press, 1992. 41–64.

———. "Performing as a Moral Act: Ethical Dimensions of the Ethnography of Performance." *Literature in Performance* 5.2 (1985): 1–13.

———. "Performing Cultures: Ethnography, Epistemology, and Ethics." In *Miteinander Sprechen Und Handeln: Festschrift Fur Hellmut Geissner,* ed. Edith Sembek. Frankfurt: Scriptor, 1986. 55–66.

———. "Rethinking Ethnography: Cultural Politics and Rhetorical Strategies." *Communication Monographs* 58 (1991): 179–94.

Crapanzano, Vincent. "On the Writing of Ethnography." *Dialectical Anthropology* 2 (1977): 69–73.

Crenshaw, Kimberly Williams. "Mapping the Margins: Intersectionality, Identity Politics, and Violence against Women of Color." *Stanford Law Review* 43 (1991): 1241–99.

Crimp, Douglas. "How to Have Promiscuity in an Epidemic." In *AIDS: Cultural Analysis, Cultural Criticism,* ed. Douglas Crimp. Cambridge: MIT Press, 1988.

Culler, Jonathan. *The Pursuit of Signs: Semiotics, Literature, Deconstruction.* Ithaca: Cornell University Press, 1981.

Currid, Brian. "We Are Family: House Music and Queer Performativity." In *Cruising the Performative: Interventions into the Representations of Ethnicity, Nationality, and Sexuality,* ed. Sue Ellen Case, Phillip Brett, and Susan Foster. Bloomington: Indiana University Press, 1995. 165–96.

Davis, Gerald L. *I Got the Word in Me and I Can Sing It, You Know: A Study of the Performed African-American Sermon.* Philadelphia: University of Pennsylvania Press, 1985.

de Certeau, Michel. *The Practice of Everyday Life.* Berkeley: University of California Press, 1984.

Deetz, Stanley. "Response: The Politics of Oral Interpretation of Literature." *Literature in Performance* 4.1 (1983): 60–64.

de Lauretis, Teresa. *Technologies of Gender: Essays on Theory, Film, and Fiction.* Bloomington: Indiana University Press, 1987.

Derrida, Jacques. "Signature, Event, Context." In *Margins of Philosophy.* Trans. Alan Bass. Chicago: University of Chicago Press, 1982.

Diamond, Elin, ed. *Performance and Cultural Politics.* New York: Routledge, 1996.

di Leonardo, Micaela. *Exotics at Home: Anthropologies, Others, American Modernity.* Chicago: University of Chicago Press, 1998.

Bibliography

Doueihi, Anne. "Inhabiting the Space Between Discourse and Story in Trickster Narratives." In *Mythical Trickster Figures: Contours, Contexts, and Criticisms*, ed. William J. Hynes and William G. Doty. Tuscaloosa: University of Alabama Press, 1993. 193–201.

Dyson, Michael. *Race Rules: Navigating the Color Line*. Reading, Mass.: Addison-Wesley, 1996.

Eckman, Paul, and Wallace Friesen. "The Repertoire of Nonverbal Behavior: Categories, Origins, Usage, and Coding." *Semiotica* 1 (1969): 49–98.

Eddie Murphy: Raw. Dir. Robert Townsend, Paramount, 1987.

Edwards, Paul. "Unstoried: Teaching Literature in the Age of Performance Studies." *Theatre Annual* 53 (1999): 1–147.

Ellison, Ralph. *Invisible Man*. New York: Random House, 1994.

Eure, Joseph, and Richard Jerome, eds. *Back Where We Belong: Selected Speeches by Minister Louis Farrakhan*. Philadelphia: PC International Press, 1989.

Fabian, Johannes. *Power and Performance: Ethnographic Explorations through Proverbial Wisdom and Theater in Shaba, Zaire*. Madison: University of Wisconsin Press, 1990.

Faludi, Susan. *Backlash: The Undeclared War against American Women*. New York: Crown, 1991.

Fanon, Frantz. *Black Skin, White Masks*. New York: Grove Weidenfeld Press, 1967.

Favor, Martin. *Authentic Blackness: The Folk in the New Negro Renaissance*. Durham: Duke University Press, 1999.

Fine, Elizabeth. *The Folklore Text: From Performance to Print*. Bloomington: Indiana University Press, 1984.

Foucault, Michel. *Discipline and Punish: The Birth of the Prison*. Trans. Alan Sheridan. New York: Vintage, 1977.

Fox-Genevese, Elizabeth. *Within the Plantation Household: Black and White Women of the Old South*. Chapel Hill: University of North Carolina Press, 1988.

Freud, Sigmund. "Mourning and Melancholia." In *General Psychological Theory*. New York: Touchstone, 1997.

Fuss, Diana. *Essentially Speaking: Feminism, Nature, and Difference*. New York: Routledge, 1989.

———. *Inside Out: Lesbian Theories/Gay Theories*. New York: Routledge, 1991.

Frankenburg, Ruth, ed. *Displacing Whiteness: Essays in Social and Cultural Criticism*. Durham: Duke University Press, 1997.

Gates, Henry Louis Jr. " 'Authenticity,' or The Lesson of Little Tree." *New York Times Book Review*, November 24, 1990. 1, 26–30.

———. *Loose Canons: Notes on the Culture War*. New York: Oxford University Press, 1993.

Bibliography

———. *The Signifying Monkey: A Theory of Afro-American Literary Criticism*. Oxford: Oxford University Press, 1988.

———. "What's Love Got to Do with It? Critical Theory, Integrity, and the Black Idiom." In *African American Literary Criticism: A Reader*, ed. Winston Napier. New York: New York University Press, 2000. 298–312.

Geertz, Clifford. "Blurred Genres: The Refiguration of Social Thought." In *Local Knowledge: Further Essays in Interpretive Anthropology*. New York: Basic Books, 1983. 19–35.

———. *The Interpretation of Cultures: Selected Essays*. New York: Basic Books, 1973.

———. "Thinking as a Moral Act: Ethical Dimensions of Anthropological Fieldwork in the New States." *Antioch Review* 28 (1968): 139–58.

Giddings, Paula. *When and Where I Enter: The Impact of Black Women on Race and Sex in America*. New York: William Morrow, 1984.

Gilroy, Paul. "Sounds Authentic: Black Music, Ethnicity, and the Challenge of a Changing Same." In *Imagining Home: Class, Culture, and Nationalism in the African Diaspora*, ed. Sidney Lemelle and Robin D. G. Kelley. New York: Verso, 1994. 93–117.

———. " '. . . To Be Real': The Dissident Forms of Black Expressive Culture." In *Let's Get It On: The Politics of Black Performance*, ed. Catherine Ugwu. Seattle: Bay Press, 1995. 12–33.

Goffman, Erving. "The Nature of Deference and Demeanor." *American Anthropologist* 58 (1956): 473–502.

———. *The Presentation of Self in Everyday Life*. Garden City, N.Y.: Doubleday, 1959.

Goldsby, Jackie. "Queens of Language: *Paris Is Burning*." In *Queer Looks: Perspectives on Lesbian and Gay Film and Video*, ed. Martha Gever, John Greyson, and Pratibha Parmar. New York: Routledge, 1995. 108–15.

Gomez, Jewel, and Barbara Smith. "Taking the Home Out of Homophobia: Black Lesbians Look in Their Own Backyards," *Outlook* 8 (1990): 32–37.

Gray, Herman. *Watching Race: Television and the Struggle for "Blackness."* Minneapolis: University of Minnesota Press, 1995.

Greenberg, Tracey. "Love and Joy." *A Window in Heaven*. Polygram, 1995.

Gross, Larry, and James D. Woods. *The Columbia Reader on Lesbians and Gay Men in Media, Society, and Politics*. New York: Columbia University Press, 1999.

Grossberg, Lawrence. "Bringing It All Back Home—Pedagogy and Cultural Studies." In *Between Borders: Pedagogy and the Politics of Cultural Studies*. Ed. Henry Giroux and Peter McClaren (New York: Routledge, 1994).

Grosz, Elizabeth. *Jacques Lacan: A Feminist Introduction*. New York: Routledge, 1990.

Gwaltney, John Langston. *Drylongso: A Self-Portrait of Black America*. New York: Random House, 1980.

Bibliography

Halberstam, Judith. *Female Masculinity*. Durham: Duke University Press, 1998.

Hall, Stuart. "Signification, Representation, Ideology: Althusser and the Post-Structuralist Debates." *Critical Studies in Mass Communication* 2.2 (1985): 91–114.

———. "What Is This 'Black' in Black Popular Culture?" In *Black Popular Culture*, ed. Gina Dent. Seattle: Bay Press, 1992. 21–33.

Hare, Nathan, and Julia Hare. *The Endangered Black Family: Coping with the Unisexualization and Coming Extinction of the Black Race*. San Francisco: Black Think Tank, 1984.

Harper, Phillip Brian. *Are We Not Men? Masculine Anxiety and the Problem of African-American Identity*. New York: Oxford, 1996.

———. *Private Affairs: Critical Ventures in the Culture of Social Relations*. New York: New York University Press, 1999. 33–59.

Harris, Michael W. *The Rise of Gospel Blues: The Music of Thomas Dorsey in the Urban Church*. New York: Oxford University Press, 1992.

Harris, Trudier. *From Mammies to Militants: Domestics in Black American Literature*. Philadelphia: Temple University Press, 1982.

———. "Lying through Our Teeth? The Quagmire of Cultural Diversity." In *Teaching African American Literature: Theory and Practice*, ed. Maryemma Graham, Sharon Pineault-Burke, and Marianna White Davis. New York: Routledge, 1998. 210–22.

Hawkeswood, William G. *One of the Children: Gay Black Men in Harlem*. Berkeley: University of California Press, 1996.

Heilbut, Tony. *The Gospel Sound: Good News and Bad Times*. New York: Simon and Schuster, 1971.

Hemphill, Essex. *Ceremonies*. San Francisco: Cleis Press, 1992.

———. "The Father, Son and Unholy Ghosts." In *Tongues Untied*, ed. Dirg Aaab-Richards, Craig G. Harris, Essex Hemphill, Isaac Jackson, and Assotto Sainte. London: GMP, 1987. 50–52.

———. " 'In Living Color': Toms, Coons, Mammies, Faggots, and Bucks." In *Out in Culture: Gay, Lesbian, and Queer Essays on Popular Culture*, ed. Corey K. Creekmur and Alexander Doty. Durham: Duke University Press, 1995. 387–401.

Henderson, Mae. "What It Means to Teach the Other When the Other Is the Self." *Callaloo* 17.2 (1994): 432–38.

Henderson, Stephen. *Understanding the New Black Poetry: Black Music and Black Speech as Poetic References* (New York: William Morrow, 1973). Excerpted in *African American Literary Criticism, 1773–2000*, ed. Hazel Ervin (New York: Twayne, 1999). 141–52.

Hill, Mike, ed. *Whiteness: A Critical Reader*. New York: New York University Press, 1997.

Bibliography

Hollowitz, John. "The Performance Psychology of Jacques Lacan." *Literature in Performance* 4.1 (1983): 27–30.

hooks, bell. *Ain't I a Woman: Black Women and Feminism.* Boston: South End Press, 1981.

———. *Black Looks: Race and Representation.* Boston: South End Press, 1992. 21–40.

———. "Homeplace: A Site of Resistance." In *Yearning: Race, Gender, and Cultural Politics.* Boston: South End Press, 1990.

Hubbard, Phil. "Sex Zones: Intimacy, Citizenship, and Public Space." *Sexualities* 4.1 (2001): 51–71.

Hughes, Langston. "The Negro Artist and the Racial Mountain." *The Nation,* June 23, 1926.

Hughes, Robert. *The Fatal Shore.* New York: Knopf, 1987.

Hull, Gloria T., Patricia Bell Scott, and Barbara Smith, eds. *All the Women Are White, All the Blacks Are Men, but Some of Us Are Brave: Black Women's Studies.* New York: The Feminist Press, 1982.

Hurston, Zora Neale. *Mules and Men.* New York: Harper Collins, 1990.

Ignatiev, Noel. *How the Irish Became White.* New York: Routledge, 1995.

Jackson, Bruce. *"Get Your Ass in the Water and Swim Like Me": Narrative Poetry from the Black Oral Tradition.* Cambridge: Harvard University Press, 1974.

Jackson, George. *Soledad Brother: The Prison Letters of George Jackson.* New York: Bantam, 1970.

Jackson, Joyce. "The Changing Nature of Gospel Music: A Southern Case Study." *African American Review* 29.2 (1995): 185.

Jewell, K. Sue. *From Mammy to Miss America and Beyond: Cultural Images and the Shaping of U.S. Social Policy.* New York: Routledge, 1993.

Johnson, E. Patrick. "An Ethnography of Performance: Interpreting the Personal Narrative of Mary Rhyne." Master's thesis. University of North Carolina, 1991.

———. "Feeling the Spirit in the Dark: Expanding Notions of the Sacred in the African American Gay Community." *Callaloo* 21.1 (1998): 399–416.

———. "'Quare' Studies OR (Almost) Everything I Know about Queer Studies I Learned from My Grandmother." *Text and Performance Quarterly* 21.1 (2001): 1–25.

———. "SNAP! Culture: A Different Kind of Reading." *Text and Performance Quarterly* 15 (1995): 122–42.

Jones, Jacqueline. *Labor of Love, Labor of Sorrow: Black Women, Work, and the Family from Slavery to the Present.* New York: Vintage, 1985.

Jones, Joni L. "Teaching in the Borderlands." In *Teaching Performance Studies,* ed. Nathan Stucky and Cynthia Wimmer. Carbondale: Southern Illinois University Press, 2002.

Jones, LeRoi. See Baraka, Imamu Amiri.

Bibliography

Jopson, Debra. "Stolen Generation Test Case Crashes." *Sydney Morning Herald*, August 27, 1999.

Joyce, Joyce A. "The Black Canon: Reconstructing Black American Literary Criticism." In *African American Literary Criticism: A Reader*, ed. Winston Napier. New York: New York University Press, 2000. 290–97.

Karamcheti, Indira. "Caliban in the Classroom." In *Pedagogy*, ed. Jane Gallop. Bloomington: Indiana University Press, 1995. 138–46.

Katzman, David. *Seven Days a Week: Women and Domestic Service in Industrializing America*. New York: Oxford University Press, 1978.

Keating, Ann Louise. "Interrogating 'Whiteness,' (De)Constructing 'Race'." In *Teaching African American Literature: Theory and Practice*, ed. Maryemma Graham, Sharon Pineault-Burke, and Marianna White Davis. New York: Routledge, 1998. 186–209.

Kenan, Randall. *Walking on Water: Black American Lives at the Turn of the Century*. New York: Knopf, 1999.

King, Jason. "Any Love: Silence, Theft, and Rumor in the Work of Luther Vandross." *Callaloo* 23.1 (2000): 422–47.

Labov, William, and Joshua Waletzky. "Narrative Analysis: Oral Versions of Personal Experience." In *Essays on the Verbal and Visual Arts: Proceedings of the Annual Spring Meeting of the American Ethnological Society, 1966*, ed. June Helm. Seattle: University of Washington Press, 1966. 12–44.

Langellier, Kristin. "Doing Deconstruction: The Extra-Institutional Performance of Literature." *Literature in Performance* 4.1 (1983): 45–50.

———. "Personal Narratives: Perspectives on Theory and Research." *Text and Performance Quarterly* 9 (1989): 243–76.

Levine, Lawrence. *Black Culture and Black Consciousness: Afro-American Thought from Slavery to Freedom*. Oxford: Oxford University Press, 1977.

Lipsitz, George. *The Possessive Investment in Whiteness: How White People Profit from Identity Politics*. Philadelphia: Temple University Press, 1998.

Living with Pride: Ruth Ellis @ 100. Dir. Yvonne Welbon, Our Film Works, 1999.

Loos, Noel, and Jane Thomson. "Black Resistance Past and Present: An Overview." In *Black Australians: The Prospects for Change*, ed. Erik Olbrei. Townsville, Queensland: James Cook University of North Queensland, 1982.

Lorde, Audre. "Poetry Is Not a Luxury." *Sister Outsider: Essays and Speeches*. New York: Crossing Press, 1984. 36–39.

Lott, Eric. *Love and Theft: Blackface Minstrelsy and the American Working Class*. New York: Oxford University Press, 1993.

Lubiano, Wahneema. "'But Compared to What?' Reading Realism, Representation, and Essentialism in *School Daze*, *Do the Right Thing*, and Spike Lee Discourse." In *Representing Black Men*, ed. Marcellus Blount and George P. Cunningham. New York: Routledge, 1996. 173–204.

Bibliography

Madhubuti, Haki. *Black Men: Obsolete, Single, Dangerous? The Afrikan American in Transition: Essays in Discovery, Solution, and Hope*. Chicago: Third World Press, 1990.

Madison, D. Soyini. "Performance, Personal Narratives, and the Politics of Possibility." In *The Future of Performance Studies: The Next Millennium*, ed. Sheron J. Dailey. Annandale, VA: National Communication Association, 1998. 276–86.

———. "'That Was My Occupation': Oral Narrative, Performance, and Black Feminist Thought." In *Exceptional Spaces: Essays in Performance and History*, ed. Della Pollock. Chapel Hill: University of North Carolina Press, 1998. 319–42.

———, ed. *The Woman That I Am: The Literature and Culture of Contemporary Women of Color*. New York: St. Martin's Press, 1994.

Manning, Susan. "Modern Dance, Negro Dance, and Katherine Dunham." *Textual Practice* 15.3 (2001): 487–506.

———. *Modern Dance, Negro Dance, and Queer Culture*. Minneapolis: University of Minnesota Press, forthcoming.

Martin, Lauren. "A Black and White Gospel." *Sydney Morning Herald*, September 13, 1999: 12.

McBride, Dwight A. "Can the Queen Speak? Racial Essentialism, Sexuality, and the Problem of Authority." *Callaloo* 21.2 (1998): 377.

———. "Speaking the Unspeakable: On Toni Morrison, African American Intellectuals, and the Uses of Essentialist Rhetoric." In *Toni Morrison: Critical and Theoretical Approaches*. ed. Nancy J. Peterson. Baltimore: Johns Hopkins University Press, 1997. 131–54.

Minister, Kristina. "Doing Deconstruction: The Extra-Institutional Performance of Literature." *Literature in Performance* 4.1 (1983): 51–54.

Mintz, Steven, and Susan Kellogg. *Domestic Revolutions: A Social History of American Family Life*. New York: Free Press, 1988.

Moraga, Cherríe, and Gloria Anzaldúa, eds. *This Bridge Called My Back: Writings by Radical Women of Color*. New York: Kitchen Table—Women of Color Press, 1983.

Morrison, Toni. *The Bluest Eye*. New York: Washington Square Press, 1970.

———. *Playing in the Dark: Whiteness and the Literary Imagination*. New York: Vintage, 1993.

———. *Sula*. New York: Plume, 1973.

Moynihan, Daniel Patrick. *The Negro Family: The Case for National Action*. Washington, D.C.: GPO, 1965.

Muñoz, José Esteban. *Disidentifications: Queers of Color and the Performance of Politics*. Minneapolis: University of Minnesota Press, 1999.

"Music Fills Minds, Minds Make a Difference." *Revolver*, January 21, 1998, 17.

Bibliography

Neal, Mark Anthony. *Soul Babies: Black Popular Culture and the Post-Soul Aesthetic.* New York: Routledge, 2002.

Ness, Sally Ann. *Body, Movement, and Culture: Kinesthetic and Visual Symbolism in a Philippine Community.* Philadelphia: University of Pennsylvania Press, 1992.

Nielsen, Aldon. *Reading Race in American Poetry: An Area Act.* Champaign: University of Illinois Press, 2000.

————. *Writing between the Lines: Race and Intertextuality.* Athens: University of Georgia Press, 1994.

Newton, Huey P. "Playboy Interview: Huey Newton." *Playboy Magazine,* May 1973, 73–90.

Paris Is Burning. Dir. Jennie Livingston. Off-White Productions, 1991.

Parker, Andrew, and Eve Kosofsky Sedgwick, eds. *Performance and Performativity.* New York: Routledge, 1996.

Patton, Cindy. *Inventing AIDS.* New York: Routledge, 1990.

Pelias, Ron, and James Van Oosting. "A Paradigm for Performance Studies." *Quarterly Journal of Speech* 73 (1987): 219–31.

Phelan, Peggy. *Unmarked: The Politics of Performance.* New York: Routledge, 1993.

Phelan, Peggy, and Jill Lane, eds. *The Ends of Performance.* New York: New York University Press, 1998.

Pollock, Della, ed. *Exceptional Spaces: Essays in Performance and History.* Chapel Hill: University of North Carolina Press, 1998.

"Praise the Lord and Pass the Lipstick." *HQ* (January/February 1995): 105–09.

Randall, Dudley. *The Black Poets.* New York: Bantam, 1971.

Razaf, Andy. "African American Folk Song: Run, Nigger, Run." In *Cultural Contexts for Ralph Ellison's Invisible Man,* ed. Eric Sundquist. Boston: Bedford Books, 1995. 117–19.

Reddy, Chandan. "Home, House, and Nonidentity: *Paris Is Burning.*" In *Burning Down the House: Recycling Domesticity,* ed. Rosemary George. Boulder: Westview Press, 1997. 355–79.

Reed, Aldolph Jr. "The 'Black Revolution' and the Reconstitution of Domination." In *Race, Politics, and Culture: Critical Essays on the Radicalism of the 1960s,* ed. Adolph Reed Jr. New York: Greenwood Press, 1986.

Reid-Pharr, Robert. *Black Gay Man.* New York: New York University Press, 2001.

Reinelt, Jenelle, and Joseph R. Roach, eds. *Critical Theory and Performance.* Ann Arbor: University of Michigan Press, 1992.

Reisner, Robert G. *The Legend of Charlie Parker.* New York: Bonanza, 1966.

Richards, Sandra L. "Writing the Absent Potential: Drama, Performance, and the Canon of African-American Culture." In *Performativity and Per-*

formance, ed. Andrew Parker and Eve Kosofsky Sedgwick. New York: Routledge, 1995. 64–88.

Riggs, Marlon. "Black Macho Revisited: Reflections of a SNAP! Queen." In *Brother To Brother: New Writings by Black Gay Men*, ed. Essex Hemphill. Boston: Alyson Press, 1991. 253–57.

Roediger, David. *The Wages of Whiteness: Race and the Making of the American Working Class*. New York: Verso, 1990.

Rogin, Michael. *Blackface, White Noise: Jewish Immigrants in the Hollywood Melting Pot*. Berkeley: University of California Press, 1996.

Rollins, Judith. *Between Women: Domestics and Their Employers*. Philadelphia: Temple University Press, 1985.

Román, David. *Acts of Intervention: Performance, Gay Culture, and AIDS*. Bloomington: Indiana University Press, 1998.

Ruuth, Marianne. *Eddie: Eddie Murphy From A to Z*. Los Angeles: Holloway House Publishing, 1985.

Schechner, Richard. "Believed-in Theatre." *Performance Research* 2.2 (1997): 89–90.

———. *Performance Theory*. Rev. ed. New York: Routledge, 1988.

———. "What Is Performance Studies Anyway?" In *The Ends of Performance*, ed. Peggy Phelan and Jill Lane. New York: New York University Press, 1998. 357–62.

Scott, Darieck. "More Man than You'll Ever Be: Antonio Fargas, Eldridge Cleaver, and Toni Morrison's *Beloved*." In *Dangerous Liaisons: Blacks, Gays, and the Struggle for Equality*, ed. Eric Brandt. New York: New Press, 1999.

Scott, Joan W. "The Evidence of Experience." In *The Lesbian and Gay Studies Reader*, ed. Henry Abelove, Michèle A. Barale, and David Halperin. New York: Routledge, 1993. 397–415.

Sedgwick, Eve. "Gosh, Boy George, You Must Be Awfully Secure in Your Masculinity!" In *Constructing Masculinity*, ed. Maurice Berger, Brian Wallis, and Simon Watson. New York: Routledge, 1995. 11–20.

———. "Queer Performativity: Henry James's *The Art of the Novel*." *GLQ* 1.1 (fall 1993): 13–28.

———. *Tendencies*. Durham: Duke University Press, 1993.

Sidran, Ben. *Black Talk*. 1971. New York: Da Capo, 1981.

Simmons, Ron. "Some Thoughts on the Challenges Facing Black Gay Intellectuals." In *Brother to Brother: New Writings by Black Gay Men*, ed. Essex Hemphill. Boston: Alyson Press, 1991. 212–28.

Skelton, Jane. "Multiple Voices, Multiple Identities: Teaching African American Literature." In *Teaching African American Literature: Theory and Practice*, ed. Maryemma Graham, Sharon Pineault-Burke, and Marianna White Davis. New York: Routledge, 1998. 52–64.

Smith, Barbara, ed. *Home Girls: A Black Feminist Anthology*. New York: Kitchen Table—Women of Color Press, 1983.

Bibliography

Smith, Valerie. *Not Just Race, Not Just Gender: Black Feminist Readings*. New York: Routledge, 1998.

Smitherman, Geneva. *Talkin and Testifyin: The Language of Black America*. Detroit: Wayne State University Press, 1977.

Spillers, Hortense. "Fabrics of History: Essays on the Black Sermon." Ph.D. diss., Brandeis University, 1974.

———. "Mama's Baby, Papa's Maybe: An American Grammar Book." *Diacritics* 17.2 (1987): 61–87.

Stallybrass, Peter, and Allon White. *The Politics and Poetics of Transgression*. Ithaca: Cornell University Press, 1986.

Stern, Carol Simpson. "Deconstruction and the Phenomenological Alternative." *Literature in Performance* 4.1 (1983): 41–43.

Stern, Carol Simpson, and Bruce Henderson. *Performance: Texts and Contexts*. New York: Longman, 1993.

Strine, Mary. "Articulating Performance/Performativity: Disciplinary Tasks and the Contingencies of Practice." Paper presented at the Speech Communication Association convention, San Diego, California, November 1996.

Strine, Mary, Beverly Whitaker Long, and Mary Frances HopKins. "Research in Interpretation and Performance Studies: Trends, Issues, Priorities." In *Speech Communication: Essays to Commemorate the Seventy-Fifth Anniversary of the Speech Communication Association*, ed. Gerald Phillips and Julia Woods. Carbondale: Southern Illinois University, 1990.

Taberner, Stephen. "In Search of What We Are Searching For." *Oral Majority* 52 (October 1999): 10–12.

Taft-Kaufman, Jill. "Deconstructing the Text: Performance Implications." *Literature in Performance* 4.1 (1983): 55–59.

———. "Oral Interpretation: Twentieth-Century Theory and Practice." In *Speech Communication in the Twentieth Century*, ed. Thomas W. Benson. Carbondale: Southern Illinois University Press, 1985. 158–65.

Tannen, Deborah. *Talking Voices: Repetition, Dialogue, and Imagery in Conversational Discourse*. Cambridge: Cambridge University Press, 1989.

Taylor, Jacqueline. "Performance Centered Research: Post-Structuralist Implications." *Literature in Performance* 4.1 (1983): 37–40.

Tedlock, Dennis. *The Spoken Word and the Work of Interpretation*. Philadelphia: University of Pennsylvania Press, 1983.

———. "Toward an Oral Poetics." *New Literary History* 8 (1977): 507–19.

Thomas, Anthony. "The House the Kids Built: The Gay Black Imprint on American Dance Music." In *Out in Culture: Gay, Lesbian, and Queer Essays on Popular Culture*, ed. Corey K. Creekmur and Alexander Doty. Durham: Duke University Press, 1990. 437–45.

Todorov, Tzvetan. "A Dialogic Criticism." *Raritan* 4 (1984): 64–76.

Tongues Untied. Dir. Marlon Riggs. Frameline, 1989.

Bibliography

Treichler, Paula. "AIDS, Homophobia, and Biomedical Discourse: An Epidemic of Signification." In *AIDS: Cultural Analysis, Cultural Activism*, ed. Douglas Crimp. Cambridge: MIT Press, 1996. 31–70.

Tucker, Susan. *Telling Memories among Southern Women: Domestic Workers and Their Employers in the Segregated South*. Baton Rouge: Louisiana State University Press, 1988.

Turner, Patricia. *Ceramic Uncles and Celluloid Mammies: Black Images and Their Influence on Culture*. New York: Anchor Books, 1994.

Turner, Victor. *The Anthropology of Performance*. New York: Performing Arts Journal Publications, 1986.

———. *Dramas, Fields, and Metaphors: Symbolic Action in Human Society*. Ithaca: Cornell University Press, 1974.

———. *From Ritual to Theatre: The Human Seriousness of Play*. New York: Performing Arts Journal Publications, 1982.

———. *On the Edge of the Bush: Anthropology as Experience*. Ed. Edith Turner. Tuscon: University of Arizona Press, 1985.

———. "A Review of 'Ethnopoetics'." In *Symposium of the Whole: A Range of Discourse toward an Ethnopoetics*, ed. Jerome Rothenberg and Diane Rothenberg. Berkeley: University of California Press, 1983. 338–42.

———. *The Ritual Process: Structure and Anti-Structure*. Chicago: Aldine Publishing, 1969.

Tyler, Carole Anne. "Boys Will Be Girls: The Politics of Gay Drag." In *Inside Out: Lesbian Theories/Gay Theories*, ed. Diana Fuss. New York: Routledge, 1997. 32–70.

Ugwu, Catherine. *Let's Get It On: The Politics of Black Performance*. Seattle: Bay Press, 1995.

Vandross, Luther. "A House Is Not a Home." 1981. *Always and Forever: The Classics*, Epic, 1998.

Venable, Michael. "Homosexual Hip Hop." *Images: A Journal of the Gay and Lesbian Alliance against Defamation* (summer 2001): 19–21.

———. "A Question of Identity." *Vibe* (July 2001): 98–106.

Walcott, Rinaldo. *Black like Who?* Toronto: Insomniac Press, 1997.

Walker, Alice. "Everyday Use." In *In Love and Trouble*. San Diego: Harcourt Brace Jovanovich, 1973.

———. *In Search of Our Mother's Garden: Womanist Prose*. San Diego: Harcourt Brace Jovanovich, 1983.

———. "To Hell with Dying." In *In Love and Trouble*. San Diego: Harcourt Brace Jovanovich, 1973.

Watney, Simon. "The Spectacle of AIDS." In *AIDS: Cultural Analysis, Cultural Activism*, ed. Douglas Crimp. Cambridge: MIT Press, 1996. 71–86.

West, Cornel. "The Paradox of the Afro-American Rebellion." In *The Sixties without Apology*, ed. Sohnya Sayres, Anders Stephanson, Stanley Aronowitz, and Fredric Jameson. Minneapolis: University of Minnesota Press, 1984. 44–58.

———. *Race Matters*. Boston: Beacon, 1993.

Weston, Kath. *Families We Choose: Lesbians, Gays, Kinship*. New York: Columbia University Press, 1991.

White, Deborah Gray. *Ar'n't I a Woman? Female Slaves in the Plantation South*. New York: Norton, 1985.

White, Marvin K. "for colored boys who have considered s-curls when the hot comb was enuf." In *Last Rights*. Boston: Alyson Press, 1999. 65–69.

———. "kevin the faggot." In *Last Rights*. Boston: Alyson Press, 1999. 23–26.

Williams, Patricia J. *Seeing through a Color-Blind Future: The Paradox of Race*. New York: Noonday Press, 1997.

Williams, Rhonda M. "Living at the Crossroads: Explorations in Race, Nationality, Sexuality, and Gender." In *The House That Race Built: Black Americans, U. S. Terrain*, ed. Wahneema Lubiano. New York: Pantheon, 1997. 136–56.

INDEX

A Cappella: Rehearsing for Heaven
(Tony Backhouse), 179
Aborigines, 183–86; and Survival
Day, 185
Africa, 26
African American literature, 12;
black poetry, 223; performance
of, 15, 223–28, 235–56, 252
Afrocentricism, 62, 69
AIDS, 17, 20, 46, 61–62; in *Black Is
. . . Black Ain't*, 18, 21; and black-
ness, 21 n.7; as gay disease, 61,
325 n.33, 89; in *Tongues Untied*, 18
Alexander, Elizabeth, 40, 44
Amherst College, 234
Anglican Church, 174
Another Country (James Baldwin),
253; performance of, 253–55
Antitheatrical prejudice, 7
Appropriation, 3, 13; and blackness,
4, 8, 14, 15; politics of, 9
Asante, Molefi, 69
Australia, 16; and British propriety,
187, 207; history of criminality
in, 181–82; as secular culture, 175;
settlement of, 175; and treatment
of Aborigines, 182
Australia's United Black Commu-
nity (AUBC), 194–96
Authenticity, 2, 16; and blackness,

2, 3, 11, 16, 25; and folk identity,
27; and gospel music, 190–206;
and heterosexuality, 58; and identity, 19; and masculinity, 74; and
race, 23; rhetoric of, 25

Backhouse, Judy, 164, 167, 172, 174,
188, 210
Backhouse, Tony, 162, 164, 173,
177–78
Baker, Houston, Jr., 224–25,
320 n.13
Bakhtin, Mikhail: and the grotesque
body, 127–28; and dialogism,
317 n.27
Baldwin, James, 1, 52–53, 55, 57; and
homosexuality, 4
Baraka, Imamu Amiri [LeRoi Jones],
13, 51, 57; and homosexuality,
58–60; and queerness, 13
Beam, Joseph, 101–2
Becoming, 42, 44, 46
Being, 42, 44, 46
Bendix, Regina, 5
Between Women (Judith Rollins),
105
Black Arts Movement, 24–25, 57,
59, 61
"Black Bourgeoisie" (Imamu Amiri
Baraka [LeRoi Jones]), 24

Index

E. Patrick Johnson is

Associate Professor of Performance Studies

at Northwestern University.

Library of Congress Cataloging-in-Publication Data

Johnson, E. Patrick.

Appropriating blackness : performance and the
politics of authenticity / E. Patrick Johnson.

p. cm.

Includes bibliographical references and index.

ISBN 0-8223-3154-3 (cloth : alk. paper) —

ISBN 0-8223-3191-8 (pbk. : alk. paper)

1. African Americans—Race identity.   2. African
Americans—Intellectual life.   3. African Americans
in popular culture.   4. Authenticity (Philosophy)—
Political aspects—United States.   5. Performing
arts—Social aspects—United States.   6. Performing
arts—Political aspects—United States.   7. United
States—Race relations.   I. Title.

E185.625J64   2003

305.896′073—dc21   2003005956